HISTORY

OF THE

ORIGIN, FORMATION, AND ADOPTION

OF THE

CONSTITUTION OF THE UNITED STATES;

WITH

NOTICES OF ITS PRINCIPAL FRAMERS.

BY

GEORGE TICKNOR CURTIS.

IN TWO VOLUMES.

VOLUME I.

NEW YORK:
HARPER AND BROTHERS,
FRANKLIN SQUARE.
1854.

TO

GEORGE TICKNOR, Esq.,

THE HISTORIAN OF SPANISH LITERATURE,

BY WHOSE ACCURATE SCHOLARSHIP AND CAREFUL CRITICISM
THESE PAGES HAVE LARGELY PROFITED,

I DEDICATE THIS WORK,

IN AFFECTIONATE ACKNOWLEDGMENT OF TIES,

WHICH HAVE BEEN TO ME CONSTANT SOURCES OF HAPPINESS
THROUGH MY WHOLE LIFE.

PREFACE.

A SPECIAL history of the origin and establishment of the Constitution of the United States has not yet found a place in our national literature.

Many years ago, I formed the design of writing such a work, for the purpose of exhibiting the deep causes which at once rendered the Convention of 1787 inevitable, and controlled or directed its course and decisions; the mode in which its great work was accomplished; and the foundations on which our national liberty and prosperity were then deliberately settled by the statesmen to whom the American Revolution gave birth, and on which they have rested ever since.

In the prosecution of this purpose I had, until death terminated his earthly interests, the encouragement and countenance of that illustrious person, whose relation to the Constitution of the United States, during the last forty years, has been not inferior in importance to that of any of its founders during the preceding period.

Mr. Webster had for a long time the intention of writing a work which should display the remarkable state of affairs under whose influence the Constitution was first brought into practical application; and this design he relinquished only when all the remaining plans of his life were surrendered with the solemn and religious resignation that marked its close. It was known to him that I had begun to labor upon another branch of the same subject. In the spring of 1852 I wrote to him to explain the plan of my work, and to ask him for a copy of some remarks made by his father in the Convention of New Hampshire when the Constitution was ratified by that State. I received from him the following answer.

"Washington, March 7th, [1852].

"My dear Sir, —

"I will try to find for you my father's speech, as it was collected from tradition and published some years ago. If I live to see warm weather in Marshfield, I shall be glad to see you beneath its shades, and to talk of your book.

"You are probably aware that I have meditated the writing of something upon the History of the Constitution and the Administration of Washington. I have the plan of such a work pretty definitely arranged, but whether I shall ever be able to execute it I cannot say:—'the wills above be done.'

"Yours most truly,

"DANL. WEBSTER."

Regarding this kind and gracious intimation as a wish not to be anticipated in any part of the field which he had marked out for himself, I replied, that if, when I should have the pleasure of seeing him, my work should seem to involve any material part of the subject which he had comprehended within his own plan, I should of course relinquish it at once. When, however, the period of that summer's leisure arrived, and brought with it, to his watchful observation, so many tokens that "the night cometh," he seemed anxious to impress upon me the importance of the task I had undertaken, and to remove any obstacle to its fulfilment that he might have suggested. Being with him alone, on an occasion when his physician, after a long consultation, had just left him, he said to me, with an earnestness and solemnity that can never be described or forgotten: "*You* have a future; *I* have none. You are writing a History of the Constitution. *You* will write that work; *I* shall not

Go on, by all means, and you shall have every aid that I can give you."

The event of which these words were ominous was then only four weeks distant. Many times, during those short remaining weeks, I sought "the shades of Marshfield"; but now it was for the offices and duties, not for the advantages, of friendship; — and no part of my work was ever submitted to him to whose approbation, sympathy, and aid I had so long looked forward, as to its most important stimulus and its most appropriate reward.

But the solemn injunction which I had received became to me an ever-present admonition, and gave me — if I may make such a profession — the needful fidelity to my great subject. Whatever may be thought of the manner in which it has been treated, a consciousness that the impartial spirit of History has guided me will remain, after every ordeal of criticism shall have been passed.

And here, while memories of the earlier as well as of the later lost crowd upon me with my theme, I cannot but think of him, jurist and magistrate, friend of my younger as well as riper years, who was called from all human sympathies before I had conceived the undertaking which I have now completed. Fortunate shall I be, if to those in whom his blood flows united with mine I can transmit a work that may be permitted to stand near that noble Commentary, which is known and honored wherever the Constitution of the United States bears sway.

The plan of this work is easily explained. The first volume embraces the Constitutional History of the United States from the commencement of the Revolution to the assembling of the Convention of 1787, together with some notices of the principal members of that body. The second volume is devoted to the description of the process of forming the Constitution, in which I have mainly followed, of course, the ample Record of the Debates preserved by Mr. Madison, and the official Journal of the proceedings.[1]

[1] In citing the "Madison Papers," I have constantly referred to the edition contained in the fifth (supplementary) volume of Mr. Jonathan Elliot's "Debates," &c., because it is more accessible to general readers. The accuracy of that publication, and its full and admirable Index, make it a very important volume to be consulted in connection with the subject of this work. In this relation, I may suggest the desirableness of a new and carefully revised edition of the Journals of the old Congress; — an enterprise that should be the care of the national government. A great magazine of materials for our national history, from the first Continental Congress to the adoption of the Constitution, exists in those Journals.

The period of our history from the commencement of the Revolution to the beginning of Washington's administration is the period when our State and national institutions were formed. With the events of the Revolution, its causes, its progress, its military history, and its results, the people of this country have long been familiar. But the constitutional history of the United States has not been written, and few persons have made themselves accurately acquainted with its details. How the Constitution of the United States came to be formed; from what circumstances it arose; what its relations were to institutions previously existing in the country; what necessities it satisfied; and what was its adaptation to the situation of these States, — are all points of the gravest importance to the American people, and all of them require to be distinctly stated for their permanent welfare.

For the history of this Constitution is not like the history of a monarchy, in which some things are obsolete, while some are of present importance. The Constitution of the United States is a living code, for the perpetuation of a system of free government, which the people of each succeeding generation must administer for themselves. Every line of it is as operative and as binding to-day as it was when the government was first set in motion by its provisions, and no part of it can fall into neglect or decay while that government continues to exist.

The Constitution of the United States was the means by which republican liberty was saved from the consequences of impending anarchy; it secured that liberty to posterity, and it left it to depend on their fidelity to the Union. It is morally certain that the formation of some general government, stronger and more efficient than any which had existed since the independence of the States had been declared, had become necessary to the continued existence of the Confederacy. It is equally certain, that, without the preservation of the Union, a condition of things must at once have ensued, out of which wars between the various provinces of America must have grown. The alternatives, therefore, that presented themselves to the generation by whom the Constitution was established, were either to devise a system of republican government that would answer the great purposes of a lasting union, or to resort to something in the nature of monarchy. With the latter, the institutions of the States must have been sooner or later crushed; — for they must either have crumbled away in the new combinations and fearful convulsions that would have preceded the establishment of such a power, or else they must have fallen speedily after its triumph had been settled. With the former alternative, the preservation of the States, and of all the needful institutions which marked their separate existence, though a difficult, was yet a possible result.

To this preservation of the separate States we owe that power of minute local administration, which is so prominent and important a feature of our American liberty. To this we are indebted for those principles of self-government which place their own interests in the hands of the people of every distinct community, and which enable them, by means of their own laws, to defend their own particular institutions against encroachments from without.

Finally, the Constitution of the United States made the people of these several provinces one nation, and gave them a standing among the nations of the world. Let any man compare the condition of this country at the peace of 1783, and during the four years which followed that event, with its present position, and he will see that he must look to some other cause than its merely natural and material resources to account for the proud elevation which it has now reached.

He will see a people ascending, in the comparatively short period of seventy years, from an attitude in which scarcely any nation thought it worth while to treat with them, to a place among the four principal powers of the globe. He will see a nation, once of so little account and so little strength that the corsairs of the Mediterranean could prey unchecked upon its defenceless merchantmen, now opening to their commerce, by its overawing diplomacy and influence, an ancient empire, on the opposite side of the earth we inhabit, which has for countless ages been firmly closed against the whole world. He will first see a collection of thirteen feeble republics on the eastern coast of North America, inflicting upon each other the manifold injuries of rival and hostile legislation; and then again he will behold them grown to be a powerful confederacy of more than thirty States, stretching from the Atlantic to the Pacific, with all their commercial interests blended and harmonized by one superintending legislature, and protected by one central and preponderating power. He will see a people who had at first achieved nothing but independence, and had contributed nothing to the cause of free government but the example of their determination to enjoy it, founding institutions to which mankind may look for hope, for encouragement and light. He will see the arts of peace — commerce, agriculture, manufactures, jurisprudence, letters — now languishing beneath a civil polity inadequate and incompetent, and now expanding through a continent with an energy and force unexampled in the history of our race, — subduing the farthest recesses of nature, and filling the wilderness with the beneficent fruits of civilization and Christianity.

Surveying all this, — looking back to the period which is removed from him only by the span of one mortal life, and looking around and before him, he will see, that among the causes of this unequalled growth stands prominent and decisive, far over all other human agencies, the great code of civil government which the fathers of our republic wrought out from the very perils by which they were surrounded.

It is for the purpose of tracing the history of the period in which those perils were encountered and overcome, that I have written this work. But in doing it, I have sought to write as an American. For it is, I trust, impossible to study the history of the Constitution which has made us what we are, by making us one nation, without feeling how unworthy of the subject — how unworthy of the dignity of History — would be any attempt to claim more than their just share of merit and renown for names or places endeared to us by local feeling or traditionary attachment. Historical writing that is not just, that is not impartial, that is not fearless, — looking beyond the interests of neighborhood, the claims of party, or the solicitations of pride, — is worse than useless to mankind.

BOSTON, July, 1854.

CONTETNS

OF

VOLUME FIRST.

BOOK I.

THE CONSTITUTIONAL HISTORY OF THE UNITED STATES, FROM THE COMMENCEMENT OF THE REVOLUTION TO THE ADOPTION OF THE ARTICLES OF CONFEDERATION.

CHAPTER I.

1774 - 1775.

ORGANIZATION OF THE FIRST CONTINENTAL CONGRESS. — ORIGIN OF THE UNION. — SITUATION OF THE COLONIES BEFORE THE REVOLUTION.

CHAPTER II.

1775 – 1776.

The Second Continental Congress. — Formation and Character of the Revolutionary Government. — Appointment of a Commander-in-chief. — First Army of the Revolution.

CHAPTER III.

1776 – 1777.

Continuance of the Revolutionary Government. — Declaration of Independence. — Preparations for a New Government. — Formation of the Continental Army.

CHAPTER IV.

JULY, 1776 – NOVEMBER, 1777.

CONSEQUENCES OF THE DECLARATION OF INDEPENDENCE. — REORGANIZATION OF THE CONTINENTAL ARMY. — FLIGHT OF THE CONGRESS FROM PHILADELPHIA. — PLAN OF THE CONFEDERATION PROPOSED.

CHAPTER V.

NOVEMBER, 1777 – MARCH, 1781.

ADOPTION OF THE ARTICLES OF CONFEDERATION. — CESSIONS OF WESTERN TERRITORY. — FIRST POLITICAL UNION OF THE STATES.

CHAPTER VI.

Nature and Powers of the Confederation.

BOOK II.

THE CONSTITUTIONAL HISTORY OF THE UNITED STATES, FROM THE ADOPTION OF THE ARTICLES OF CONFEDERATION, IN 1781, TO THE PEACE OF 1783.

CHAPTER I.

1781 - 1783.

REQUISITIONS. — CLAIMS OF THE ARMY. — NEWBURGH ADDRESSES. — PEACE PROCLAIMED. — THE ARMY DISBANDED.

CHAPTER II.

1781-1783.

FINANCIAL DIFFICULTIES OF THE CONFEDERATION. — REVOLUTIONARY DEBT. — REVENUE SYSTEM OF 1783.

CHAPTER III.

1781-1783.

OPINIONS AND EFFORTS OF WASHINGTON, AND OF HAMILTON. — DECLINE OF THE CONFEDERATION.

BOOK III.

THE CONSTITUTIONAL HISTORY OF THE UNITED STATES, FROM THE PEACE OF 1783 TO THE FEDERAL CONVENTION OF 1787.

CHAPTER I.

JANUARY, 1784 – MAY, 1787.

DUTIES AND NECESSITIES OF CONGRESS. — REQUISITIONS ON THE STATES. — REVENUE SYSTEM OF 1783.

CHAPTER II.

1784 – 1787.

INFRACTIONS OF THE TREATY OF PEACE.

CHAPTER III.

1786 - 1787.

NO SECURITY AFFORDED BY THE CONFEDERATION TO THE STATE GOVERNMENTS. — SHAYS'S REBELLION IN MASSACHUSETTS, AND ITS KINDRED DISTURBANCES.

CHAPTER IV.

ORIGIN AND NECESSITY OF THE POWER TO REGULATE COMMERCE.

CHAPTER V.

1783–1787.

THE PUBLIC LANDS. — GOVERNMENT OF THE NORTHWESTERN TERRITORY. — THREATENED LOSS OF THE WESTERN SETTLEMENTS.

CHAPTER VI.

1783 – 1787.

DECAY AND FAILURE OF THE CONFEDERATION. — PROGRESS OF OPINION. — STEPS WHICH LED TO THE CONVENTION OF 1787. — INFLUENCE AND EXERTIONS OF HAMILTON. — MEETING OF THE CONVENTION.

CHAPTER VII.

THE FRAMERS OF THE CONSTITUTION. — WASHINGTON, PRESIDENT OF THE CONVENTION.

CHAPTER VIII.

Hamilton.

CHAPTER IX.

Madison.

CHAPTER X.

Franklin.

CHAPTER XI.

Gouverneur Morris.

CHAPTER XII.

King.

CHAPTER XIII.

Charles Cotesworth Pinckney

CHAPTER XIV.

Wilson.

CHAPTER XV.

Randolph.

CHAPTER XVI.

Conclusion of the Present Volume.

APPENDIX.

BOOK I.

THE CONSTITUTIONAL HISTORY OF THE UNITED STATES, FROM THE COMMENCEMENT OF THE REVOLUTION TO THE ADOPTION OF THE ARTICLES OF CONFEDERATION.

CHAPTER I.

1774–1775.

ORGANIZATION OF THE FIRST CONTINENTAL CONGRESS. — ORIGIN OF THE UNION.

THE thirteen British colonies in North America, by whose inhabitants the American Revolution was achieved, were, at the commencement of that struggle, so many separate communities, having, to a considerable extent, different political organizations and different municipal laws: but their various populations spoke almost universally the English language. These colonies were Virginia, Massachusetts, New Hampshire, Connecticut, Rhode Island, Maryland, New York, New Jersey, Pennsylvania, Delaware, North Carolina, South Carolina, and Georgia. From the times when they were respectively settled, until the union formed under the necessities of a common cause at the breaking out of the Revolution, they had no political connection; but each possessed a domestic government peculiar to itself, derived directly from the crown of England, and more or less under the direct control of the mother country.

The political organizations of the colonies have been classed by jurists and historians under the three heads of Provincial, Proprietary, and Charter governments.

To the class of Provincial governments belonged the Provinces of New Hampshire, New Jersey, Virginia, the two Carolinas, and Georgia. These had no other written constitutions, or fundamental laws, than the commissions issued to the Governors appointed by the crown, explained by the instructions which accompanied them. The Governor, by his commission, was made the representative or deputy of the King, and was obliged to act in conformity with the royal instructions. He was assisted by a Council, the members of which, besides participating with him, to a certain extent, in the executive functions of the government, constituted the upper house of the provincial legislature; and he was also authorized to summon a general assembly of representatives of the freeholders of the Province. The three branches thus convened, consisting of the Governor, the Council, and the Representatives, constituted the provincial Assemblies, having the power of local legislation, subject to the ratification and disapproval of the crown. The direct control of the crown over these provincial governments may also be traced in the features, common to them all, by which the Governor had power to suspend the members of the Council from office, and, whenever vacancies occurred, to appoint to those vacancies, until the pleasure of the crown should be known; to negative all the proceedings of the assembly; and to prorogue or dissolve it at his pleasure.

The Proprietary governments, consisting of Maryland, Pennsylvania, and Delaware, were those in which the subordinate powers of legislation and government had been granted to certain individuals called the proprietaries, who appointed the Governor and authorized him to summon legislative assemblies. The authority of the proprietaries, or of the legislative bodies assembled by the Governor, was restrained by the condition, that the ends for which the grant was made to them by the crown should be substantially pursued in their legislation, and that nothing should be done, or attempted, which might derogate from the sovereignty of the mother country. In Maryland, the laws enacted by the proprietary government were not subject to the direct control of the crown; but in Pennsylvania and Delaware they were.[1]

The Charter governments, consisting, at the period of the Revolution, of Massachusetts, Rhode Island, and Connecticut, may be said, in a stricter sense, to have possessed written constitutions for their general political government. The charters, granted by the crown, established an organization of the different departments of government similar to that in the provincial governments. In Massachusetts, after the charter of William and Mary granted in 1691, the Governor was appointed by the crown; the Council were chosen annually by the General Assembly, and the House of Representatives by the people. In

[1] 1 Story's Commentaries on the Constitution, § 160.

Connecticut and Rhode Island, the Governor, Council, and Representatives were chosen annually by the freemen of the colony. In the charter, as well as the provincial governments, the general power of legislation was restrained by the condition, that the laws enacted should be, as nearly as possible, agreeable to the laws and statutes of England.

One of the principal causes which precipitated the war of the Revolution was the blow struck by Parliament at these charter governments, commencing with that of Massachusetts, by an act intended to alter the constitution of that Province as it stood upon the charter of William and Mary; a precedent which justly alarmed the entire continent, and in its principle affected all the colonies, since it assumed that none of them possessed constitutional rights which could not be altered or taken away by an act of Parliament. The "Act for the better regulating the government of the Province of Massachusetts Bay," passed in 1774, was designed to create an executive power of a totally different character from that created by the charter, and also to remodel the judiciary, in order that the laws of the imperial government might be more certainly enforced.

The charter had reserved to the King the appointment of the Governor, Lieutenant-Governor, and Secretary of the Province. It vested in the General Assembly the choice of twenty-eight councillors, subject to rejection by the Governor; it gave to the Governor, with the advice and consent of the Council, the appointment of all military and judicial officers, and to the two houses of the legislature the appointment of all other civil officers, with a right of negative by the Governor. The new law vested the appointment of councillors, judges, and magistrates of all kinds, in the crown, and in some cases in the Governor, and made them all removable at the pleasure of the crown. A change so radical as this, in the constitution of a people long accustomed to regard their charter as a compact between themselves and the crown, could not but lead to the most serious consequences.

The statements which have now been made are sufficient to remind the reader of the important fact, that, at the commencement of the Revolution, there existed, and had long existed, in all the colonies, local legislatures, one branch of which was composed of representatives chosen directly by the people, accustomed to the transaction of public business, and being in fact the real organs of the popular will. These bodies, by virtue of their relation to the people, were, in many instances, the bodies which took the initiatory steps for the organization of the first national or Continental Congress, when it became necessary for the colonies to unite in the common purpose of resistance to the mother country. But it should be again stated, before we attend to the steps thus taken, that the colonies had no direct political connection with each other before the Revolution commenced, but that each was a distinct community, with its own separate political organization, and without any power of legislation for any but its own inhabitants; that, as political communities, and upon the principles of their organizations, they possessed no power of forming any union among themselves, for any purpose whatever, without the sanction of the Crown or Parliament of England.[1] But the free and independent power of forming a union among themselves, for objects and purposes common to them all, which was denied to their colonial condition by the principles of the English Constitution, was one of the chief powers asserted and developed by the Revolution; and they were enabled to effect this union, as a revolutionary right and measure, by the fortu-

[1] That a union of the colonies into one general government, for any purpose, could not take place without the sanction of Parliament, was always assumed in both countries. The sole instance in which a plan of union was publicly proposed and acted upon, before the Revolution, was in 1753-4, when the Board of Trade sent instructions to the Governor of New York to make a treaty with the Six Nations of Indians; and the other colonies were also instructed to send commissioners to be present at the meeting, so that all the provinces might be comprised in one general treaty, to be made in the King's name. It was also recommended by the home government, that the commissioners at this meeting should form a plan of union among the colonies for their mutual protection and defence against the French. Twenty-five commissioners assembled at Albany in May, 1754, from New Hampshire, Massachusetts, Rhode Island, Connecticut, New York, Pennsylvania, and Maryland. In this body, a plan of union was digested and adopted, which was chiefly the work of Dr. Franklin. It was agreed that an act of Parliament was necessary to authorize it to be carried into effect. It was rejected by all the colonial Assemblies before which it was brought, and in England it was not thought proper by the Board of Trade to recommend it to the King. In America it was considered to have too much of *prerogative* in it, and in England to be too *democratic*. It

nate circumstances of their origin, which made the people of the different colonies, in several important senses, one people. They were, in the first place, chiefly the descendants of Englishmen, governed by the laws, inheriting the blood, and speaking the language of the people of England. As British subjects, they had enjoyed the right of dwelling in any of the colonies, without restraint, and of carrying on trade from one colony to another, under the regulation of the general laws of the empire, without restriction by colonial legislation. They had, moreover, common grievances to be redressed, and a common independence to establish, if redress could not be obtained: for although the precise grounds of dispute with the Crown or the Parliament of England

was a comprehensive scheme of government, to consist of a Governor-General, or President-General, who was to be appointed and supported by the crown, and a Grand Council, which was to consist of one member chosen by each of the smaller colonies, and two or more by each of the larger. Its duties and powers related chiefly to defence against external attacks. It was to have a general treasury, to be supplied by an excise on certain articles of consumption. See the history and details of the scheme, in Sparks's Life and Works of Franklin, I. 176, III. 22-55; Hutchinson's History of Massachusetts, III. 23; Trumbull's History of Connecticut, II. 355; Pitkin's History of the United States, I. 140-146. In 1788, Franklin said of it: "The different and contradictory reasons of dislike to my plan make me suspect that it was really the true medium; and I am still of opinion it would have been happy for both sides, if it had been adopted. The colonies so united would have been sufficiently strong to have defended themselves: there would have been no need of troops from England: of course the subsequent pretext for taxing America, and the bloody contest it occasioned, would have been avoided. But such mistakes are not new: history is full of the errors of states and princes." (Life, by Sparks, I. 178.) We may not join in his regrets now.

had not always been the same in all the colonies, yet when the Revolution actually broke out, they all stood in the same attitude of resistance to the same oppressor, making common cause with each other, and resting upon certain great principles of liberty, which had been violated with regard to many of them, and with the further violation of which all were threatened.

It was while the controversies between the mother country and the colonies were drawing towards a crisis, that Dr. Franklin, then in England as the political agent of Pennsylvania, of Massachusetts, and of Georgia, in an official letter to the Massachusetts Assembly, dated July 7th, 1773, recommended the assembling of a general congress of all the colonies. "As the strength of an empire," said he, "depends not only on the *union* of its parts, but on their readiness for united exertion of their common force; and as the discussion of rights may seem unseasonable in the commencement of actual war, and the delay it might occasion be prejudicial to the common welfare; as likewise the refusal of one or a few colonies would not be so much regarded, if the others granted liberally, which perhaps by various artifices and motives they might be prevailed on to do; and as this want of concert would defeat the expectation of general redress, that might otherwise be justly formed; perhaps it would be best and fairest for the colonies, in a general congress now in peace to be assembled, or by means of the correspondence lately proposed, after a full and solemn assertion and declaration of their rights, to engage firmly with each other, that they will never grant aids to the crown in any general war, till those rights are recognized by the King and both houses of Parliament; communicating at the same time to the crown this their resolution. Such a step I imagine will bring the dispute to a crisis."[1]

The first actual step towards this measure was taken in Virginia. A new House of Burgesses had been summoned by the royal Governor to meet in May, 1774. Soon after the members had assembled at Williamsburg, they received the news that, by an act of Parliament, the port of Boston was to be closed on the first day of the succeeding June, and that other disabilities were to be inflicted on the town. They immediately passed an order, setting apart the first day of June as a day of fasting, humiliation, and prayer, "to implore the Divine interposition for averting the heavy calamity which threatened destruction to their

[1] It is not certain by whom the first suggestion of a Continental Congress was made. Thomas Cushing, Speaker of the Massachusetts Assembly, and a correspondent of Dr. Franklin, appears to have expressed to him the opinion, previously to the date of Franklin's official letter quoted in the text, that a congress would grow out of the committees of correspondence which had been recommended by the Virginia House of Burgesses. But Mr. Sparks thinks that no other direct and public recommendation of the measure can be found before the date of Franklin's letter to the Massachusetts Assembly. Sparks's Life of Franklin, I. 350, note. In the early part of the year 1774, the necessity of such a congress began to be popularly felt throughout all the colonies. Sparks's Washington, II. 326.

civil rights, and the evils of civil war, and to give them one heart and one mind firmly to oppose, by all just and proper means, every injury to American rights." Thereupon, the Governor dissolved the House. But the members immediately assembled at another place of meeting, and, having organized themselves as a committee, drew up and subscribed an Association, in which they declared that the interests of all the colonies were equally concerned in the late doings of Parliament, and advised the local Committee of Correspondence to consult with the committees of the other colonies on the expediency of holding a general Continental Congress. Pursuant to these recommendations, a popular convention was holden at Williamsburg, on the 1st of August, which appointed seven persons as delegates to represent the people of Virginia in a general Congress to be held at Philadelphia in the September following.[1]

The Massachusetts Assembly met on the last of May, and, after negativing thirteen of the Councillors, Governor Gage adjourned the Assembly to meet at Salem on the 7th of June. When they came together at that place, the House of Representatives passed a resolve, declaring a meeting of committees from the several colonies on the continent to be highly expedient and necessary, to deliberate and determine upon proper measures to be recommended

[1] These delegates were Peyton Randolph, Richard Henry Lee, George Washington, Patrick Henry, Richard Bland, Benjamin Harrison, and Edmund Pendleton.

to all the colonies for the recovery and establishment of their just rights and liberties, civil and religious, and for the restoration of union and harmony with Great Britain. They then appointed five delegates[1] to meet the representatives of the other colonies in congress at Philadelphia, in the succeeding September.

These examples were at once followed by the other colonies. In some of them, the delegates to the Continental Congress were appointed by the popular branch of the legislature, acting for and in behalf of the people; in others, they were appointed by conventions of the people called for the express purpose, or by committees duly authorized to make the appointment.[2] The Congress, styling themselves "the delegates appointed by the good people of these colonies," assembled at Philadelphia on the 5th of September, 1774, and organized themselves as a deliberative body by the choice of officers and the adoption of rules of proceeding. Peyton Ran-

[1] Thomas Cushing, Samuel Adams, Robert Treat Paine, James Bowdoin, and John Adams.

[2] The delegates in the Congress of 1774 from New Hampshire were appointed by a Convention of Deputies chosen by the towns, and received their credentials from that Convention. In Rhode Island, they were appointed by the General Assembly, and commissioned by the Governor. In Connecticut, they were appointed and instructed by the Committee of Correspondence for the Colony, acting under authority conferred by the House of Representatives. In New York, the mode of appointment was various. In the city and county of New York, the delegates were elected by popular vote taken in seven wards. The same persons were also appointed to act for the counties of West Chester, Albany, and Duchess, by the respective committees of those counties; and another person was appointed in the same manner for the county of

dolph of Virginia was elected President, and Charles Thompson of Pennsylvania Secretary of the Congress.

No precedent existed for the mode of action to be adopted by this assembly. There was, therefore, at the outset, no established principle which might determine the nature of the union; but that union was to be shaped by the new circumstances and relations in which the Congress found itself placed. There had been no general concert among the different colonies as to the numbers of delegates, or, as they were called in many of the proceedings, "committees" of the colonies, to be sent to the meeting at Philadelphia. On the first day of their assembling, Pennsylvania and Virginia had each six delegates in attendance; New York had five; Massachusetts, New Jersey, and South Carolina had four each; Connecticut had three; New Hampshire, Rhode Island, Delaware, and Maryland had two each. The delegates from North Carolina did not arrive until the 14th.[1]

Suffolk. The New York delegates received no other instructions than those implied in the certificates, "to attend the Congress and to represent" the county designated. In New Jersey, the delegates were appointed by the committees of counties, and were simply instructed "to represent" the Colony. In Pennsylvania, they were appointed and instructed by the House of Assembly. In the counties of New Castle, Kent, and Sussex on Delaware, delegates were elected by a convention of the freemen assembled in pursuance of circular letters from the Speaker of the House of Assembly. In Maryland, the appointment was by committees of the counties. In Virginia, it was by a popular convention of the whole Colony. In South Carolina, it was by the House of Commons. Georgia was not represented in this Congress.

[1] Journals, I. 1, 12.

As soon as the choice of officers had taken place,[1] the method of voting presented itself as the first thing to be determined; and the difficulties arising from the inequalities between the colonies in respect to actual representation, population, and wealth, had to be encountered upon the threshold. Insuperable obstacles stood in the way of the adoption of interests as the basis of votes. The weight of a colony could not be ascertained by the numbers of its inhabitants, the amount of their wealth, the extent of their trade, or by any ratio to be compounded of all these elements, for no authentic evidence existed from which data could be taken.[2] As it was apparent, however, that some colonies had a larger proportion of members present than others, relatively to their size and importance, it was thought to be equally objectionable to adopt the method of voting by polls. In these circumstances, the opinion was advanced, that the colonial governments were at an end; that all America was thrown into one mass, and was in a state of nature; and consequently, that the people ought to be considered as represented in the Congress according to their numbers, by the delegations actually present.[3] Upon this principle, the voting should have been by polls.

But neither the circumstances under which they were assembled, nor the dispositions of the members,

1 The President and Secretary appear to have been chosen *viva voce*, or by a hand vote. John Adams's Works, II. 365.

2 Adams, II. 366.

3 This opinion, we are told by Mr. Adams, was advanced by Patrick Henry. See notes of the debate, in Adams, II. 366, 368.

permitted an adoption of the theory that all government was at an end, or that the boundaries of the colonies were effaced. The Congress had not assembled as the representatives of a people in a state of nature, but as the committees of different colonies, which had not yet severed themselves from the parent state. They had been clothed with no legislative or coercive authority, even of a revolutionary nature; compliance with their resolves would follow only on conviction of the utility of their measures; and all their resolves and all their measures were, by the express terms of many of their credentials, limited to the restoration of union and harmony with Great Britain, which would of course leave the colonies in their colonial state. The people of the continent, therefore, as a people in the state of nature, or even in a national existence as one people standing in a revolutionary attitude, had not then come into being.

The nature of the questions, too, which they were to discuss, and of the measures which they were to adopt, were to be considered in determining by what method of voting those questions and measures should be decided. The Congress had been called to secure the *rights* of the colonies. What were those rights? By what standard were they to be ascertained? By the law of nature, or by the principles of the English Constitution, or by the charters and fundamental laws of the colonies, regarded as compacts between the crown and the people, or by all of these combined? If the law of nature alone was to determine their rights, then all allegiance to the British crown was to be regarded as at an end. If the principles of the English Constitution, or the charters, were to be the standard, the law of nature must be excluded from consideration. This exclusion would of necessity narrow the ground, and deprive them of a resource to which Parliament might at last compel them to look.[1] In order, therefore, to leave the whole field open for consideration, and at the same time to avoid committing themselves to principles irreconcilable with the preservation of allegiance and their colonial relation to Great Britain, it was necessary to consider themselves as an assembly of committees from the different colonies, in which each colony should have one voice, through the delegates whom it had sent to represent and act for it. But, as if foreseeing the time when population would become of necessity the basis of congressional power, when the authority of Parliament should have given place to a system of American continental legislation, they inserted, in the resolve determining that each colony should have one vote, a caution that would prevent its being drawn into precedent. They declared, as the reason for the course which they adopted, that the Congress were not possessed of, or able to procure, the proper materials for ascertaining the importance of each colony.[2]

It appears, therefore, very clear, that an examina-

[1] See the very interesting notes of their debates in Adams's Works, II. 366, 370–377.

[2] Journals, I. 10.

tion of the relations of the first Congress to the colonies which instituted it will not enable us to assign to it the character of a government. Its members were not elected for the express purpose of making a revolution. It was an assembly convened from separate colonies, each of which had causes of complaint against the imperial government to which it acknowledged its allegiance to be due, and each of which regarded it as essential to its own interests to make common cause with the others, for the purpose of obtaining redress of its own grievances. The idea of separating themselves from the mother country had not been generally entertained by the people of any of the colonies. All their public proceedings, from the commencement of the disputes down to the election of delegates to the first Congress, including the instructions given to those delegates, prove, as we have seen, that they looked for redress and relief to means which they regarded as entirely consistent with the principles of the British Constitution.[1]

[1] The instructions embraced in the credentials of the delegates to the first Congress were as follows: — New Hampshire, — "to devise, consult, and adopt such measures as may have the most likely tendency to extricate the colonies from their present difficulties; to secure and perpetuate their rights, liberties, and privileges; and to restore that peace, harmony, and mutual confidence which once happily subsisted between the parent country and her colonies." Massachusetts,—"to deliberate and determine upon wise and proper measures, to be by them recommended to all the colonies, for the recovery and establishment of their just rights and liberties, civil and religious, and the restoration of union and harmony between Great Britain and the colonies, most ardently desired by all good men." Rhode Island, — "to meet and join with the other com-

Still, although this Congress did not take upon themselves the functions of a government, or propose revolution as a remedy for the wrongs of their constituents, they regarded and styled themselves as "the guardians of the rights and liberties of the colonies";[1] and in that capacity they proceeded to declare the causes of complaint, and to take the necessary steps to obtain redress, in what they believed to be a constitutional mode. These steps,

missioners or delegates from the other colonies in consulting upon proper measures to obtain a repeal of the several acts of the British Parliament for levying taxes upon his Majesty's subjects in America without their consent, and particularly the commercial connection of the colonies with the mother country, for the relief of Boston and the preservation of American liberty." VIRGINIA, — "to consider of the most proper and effectual manner of so operating on the commercial connection of the colonies with the mother country, as to procure redress for the much injured Province of Massachusetts Bay, to secure British America from the ravage and ruin of arbitrary taxes, and speedily to procure the return of that harmony and union so beneficial to the whole empire, and so ardently desired by all British America." SOUTH CAROLINA, — "to consider the acts lately passed and bills depending in Parliament with regard to the port of Boston and Colony of Massachusetts Bay, which acts and bills, in the precedent and consequences, affect the whole continent of America; — also the grievances under which America labors by reason of the several acts of Parliament that impose taxes or duties for raising a revenue, and lay unnecessary restraints and burdens on trade; — and of the statutes, parliamentary acts, and royal instructions, which make an invidious distinction between his Majesty's subjects in Great Britain and America; with full power and authority to concert, agree to, and effectually prosecute such legal measures as, in the opinion of the said deputies and of the deputies so to be assembled, shall be most likely to obtain a repeal of the said acts and a redress of these grievances." The delegates from New York and New Jersey were simply instructed "to represent" those colonies in the Congress. Journals, I. 2-9.

[1] Letter of the Congress to Governor Gage, October 10, 1774. Journals, I. 25, 26.

however, although not directly revolutionary, had a revolutionary tendency.

On the 6th of September, 1774, a resolve was passed, that a committee be appointed to state the rights of the colonies in general, the several instances in which those rights had been violated or infringed, and the means most proper to be pursued for obtaining a restoration of them. Another committee was ordered on the same day, to examine and report the several statutes affecting the trade and manufactures of the colonies. On the following day, it was ordered that the first committee should consist of two members, and the second of one member, from each of the colonies.[1] Two questions presented themselves to the first of these committees, and created a good deal of embarrassment. The first was, whether, in stating the rights of the colonies, they should recur to the law of nature, as well as to the British Constitution and the American charters and grants. The second question related to the authority which they should allow to be in Parliament; — whether they should deny it wholly, or deny it only as to internal affairs, admitting it as to external trade; and if the latter, to what extent and with what restrictions. It was soon felt that this question of the authority of Parliament was the essence of the whole controversy. Some denied it altogether. Others denied it as to every species of taxation; while others admitted it to extend to the regulation

[1] Additions were made to it.

of external trade, but denied it as to all internal affairs. The discussions had not proceeded far, before it was perceived that this subject of the regulation of trade might lead directly to the question of the continuance of the colonial relations with the mother country. For this they were not prepared. It was apparent that the right of regulating the trade of the whole country, from the local circumstances of the colonies and their disconnection with each other, could not be exercised by the colonies themselves: it was thought that the aid, assistance, and protection of the mother country were necessary to them; and therefore, as a proper equivalent, that the colonies must admit the right of regulating the trade, to some extent and in some mode, to be in Parliament. The alternatives were, either to set up an American legislature, that could control and regulate the trade of the whole country, or else to give the power to Parliament. The Congress determined to do the latter; supposing that they could limit the admission, by denying that the power extended to taxation, but ceding at the same time the right to regulate the external trade of the colonies for the common benefit of the whole empire.[1] They grounded this concession upon "the necessities of the case," and "the mutual interests of both countries";[2] meaning by these expressions to assert that all legislative control over the external and internal trade of the colonies belonged of right to the colonies themselves, but,

[1] Works of John Adams.

[2] See the origin of these expressions explained, in Adams's Works, II. 373–375.

as they were part of an empire for which Parliament legislated, it was necessary that the common legislature of the whole empire should retain the regulation of the external trade, excluding all power of taxation for purposes of revenue, in order to secure the benefits of the trade of the whole empire to the mother country.

The Congress, therefore, after having determined to confine their statement to such rights as had been infringed by acts of Parliament since the year 1763, unanimously adopted a Declaration of Rights, in which they summed up the grievances and asserted the rights of the colonies. This document placed the rights of the colonies upon the laws of nature, the principles of the English Constitution, and the several charters or compacts. It declared, that, as the colonies were not, and from their local situation could not be, represented in the English Parliament, they were entitled to a free and exclusive power of legislation in their several provincial legislatures, where their right of representation could alone be preserved, in all cases of taxation and internal polity, subject only to the negative of their sovereign, in such manner as had been before accustomed. At the same time, from the necessity of the case and from a regard to the mutual interests of both countries, they cheerfully consented to the operation of such acts of Parliament as were in good faith limited to the regulation of their external commerce, for the purpose of securing the commercial advantages of the whole to the mother country, and the commercial benefit of its respective members; excluding every idea of taxation, internal and external, for raising a revenue on the subjects in America, without their consent.[1]

In addition to this, they asserted, as great constitutional rights inherent in the people of all these colonies, that they were entitled to all the rights, liberties, and immunities of free and natural-born subjects within the realm of England; to the common law of England, and especially to trial by a jury of the vicinage; to the immunities and privileges granted and confirmed to them by royal charters, or secured by their several codes of provincial laws; and to the right of peaceably assembling to consider grievances and to petition the King.[2]

In order to enforce their complaints upon the attention of the government and people of Great Britain, and as the sole means which were open to them, short of actual revolution, of coercing the ministry into a change of measures, they resolved that after the 10th of September, 1775, the exportation of all merchandise, and every commodity whatsoever, to Great Britain, Ireland, and the West Indies, ought to cease, unless the grievances of America should be redressed before that time; and that after the first day of December, 1774, there should be no importation into British America, from Great Britain

[1] Journals, I. 29.

[2] Ibid. They adopted also an Address to the People of Great Britain, and a Petition to the King, embodying similar principles with those asserted in the Declaration of Rights. Ibid. 38, 67.

or Ireland, of any goods, wares, or merchandise whatever, or from any other place, of any such goods, wares, or merchandise as had been exported from Great Britain or Ireland, and that no such goods, wares, or merchandise be used or purchased.[1] They then prepared an association, or agreement, of non-importation, non-exportation, and non-consumption, in order, as far as lay in their power, to cause a general compliance with their resolves. This association was subscribed by every member of the Congress, and was by them recommended for adoption to the people of the colonies, and was very generally adopted and acted upon.[2] They resorted to this as the most speedy, effectual, and peaceable measure to obtain a redress of the grievances of which the colonies complained; and they entered into the agreement on behalf of the inhabitants of the several colonies for which they acted.

This Congress, which sat from the 5th of September to the 26th of October, 1774, had thus made the restoration of commercial intercourse between the colonies and the other parts of the British empire to depend upon the repeal by Parliament of the

1 Journals, I. 21.

2 This association, signed by the delegates of Maryland, Virginia, North Carolina, and South Carolina, as well as of the other colonies, contained, among other things, the following agreement: — "We will neither import nor purchase any slaves imported after the first day of December next; after which time we will wholly discontinue the slave-trade, and will neither be concerned in it ourselves, nor will we hire our vessels, nor sell our commodities or manufactures, to those who are concerned in it." Journals, I. 33.

obnoxious measures of which they complained, and upon the recognition of the rights which they asserted; for although their acts had not the foundation of laws, the general adoption of their recommendations throughout the colonies gave them a power that laws rarely possess. Before they adjourned, they recommended that another Congress of all the colonies should be held at Philadelphia on the 10th of the following May, unless their grievances were redressed before that time, and that the deputies to such new Congress should be chosen immediately.[1]

But while the Continental Congress were engaged in the adoption of these measures of constitutional resistance, and still acknowledged their colonial relations to the imperial government, the course of events in Massachusetts had put an end to the forms of law and government in that colony, as established or upheld by imperial authority. The last Assembly held in the Province upon the principles of its charter had been dissolved by the Governor's proclamation, at Salem, on the 17th of June, 1774. The new law for the alteration of the government had taken effect; and in August the Governor received from England a list of thirty-six councillors, who were to be called into office by the King's writ of *mandamus*, instead of being elected, as under the charter, by the House of Representatives. Two thirds of the number accepted their appointment; but popular

[1] Journals, I. 56. Oct. 22, 1774.

indignation, treating them as enemies of their country, compelled the greater part of them to renounce their offices. The new judges were prevented everywhere from proceeding with the business of the courts, which were obstructed by assemblies of the people, who would permit no judge to exercise his functions, save in accordance with the ancient laws and usages of the Colony.

Writs had been issued for a new General Assembly, which was to meet at Salem in October; but it was found, that, while the old constitution had been taken away by act of Parliament, the new one had been rejected by the people. The compulsory resignation of so many of the councillors left that body without power, and the Governor deemed it expedient to countermand the writs by proclamation, and to defer the holding of the Assembly until the popular temper should have had time to cool. But the legality of the proclamation was denied; the elections were everywhere held, and the members elect assembled at Salem, pursuant to the precepts. There they waited a day for the Governor to attend, administer the oaths, and open the session; but as he did not appear, they resolved themselves into a Provincial Congress, to be joined by others who had been or might be elected for that purpose, and adjourned to the town of Cambridge, to take into consideration the affairs of the Colony, in which the regular and established government was now at an end. Their acts were at first couched in the form of recommendations to the people, whose ready compliance gave to them the weight and efficacy of laws, and there was thus formed something like a new and independent government. Under the form of recommendation and advice, they settled the militia, regulated the public revenue, provided arms, and prepared to resist the British troops. In December, 1774, they elected five persons to represent the Colony in the Continental Congress that was to assemble at Philadelphia in the ensuing May. They were met by a proclamation, issued by the Governor, in which their assembly was declared unlawful, and the people were prohibited, in the King's name, from complying with their recommendations, requisitions, or resolves. Through the winter, the Governor held the town of Boston, with a considerable body of royal troops, but the rest of the Province generally yielded obedience to the Provincial Congress. In this posture of affairs, the encounter between a detachment of the King's forces and a body of militia, commonly called the battle of Lexington, occurred, on the 19th of April, 1775.

CHAPTER II.

1775–1776.

THE SECOND CONTINENTAL CONGRESS. — FORMATION AND CHARACTER OF THE REVOLUTIONARY GOVERNMENT. — APPOINTMENT OF A COMMANDER-IN-CHIEF. — FIRST ARMY OF THE REVOLUTION.

A NEW Continental Congress assembled at Philadelphia on the 10th of May, 1775; and in order to observe the growth of the Union, it is necessary to trace the organization of this body, and to describe briefly the kind of sovereignty which it exercised, from the time of its assembling until the adoption and promulgation of the Declaration of Independence.[1]

[1] Peyton Randolph, President of the first and reëlected President of the second Congress, died very suddenly at Philadelphia on the 22d of October, 1775, and was succeeded in that office by John Hancock. Mr. Randolph was one of the most eminent of the Virginia patriots, and an intimate friend of Washington. Richard Henry Lee wrote to Washington, on the day after his death, that "in him American liberty lost a powerful advocate, and human nature a sincere friend." He was formerly Attorney-General of Virginia, and in 1753 went to England as agent of the House of Burgesses, to procure the abolition of a fee, known as the pistole fee, which it had been the custom of the Governors of Virginia to charge for signing land patents, as a perquisite of their office. He succeeded in getting the fee abolished in cases where the quantity of land exceeded one hundred acres. He was commander of a company of mounted volunteers called the Gentlemen Associators, who served in the

The delegates to this Congress were chosen partly by the popular branch of such of the colonial legislatures as were in session at the time, the choice being afterwards ratified by conventions of the people; but they were principally appointed by conventions of the people held in the various colonies. All these appointments, except those made in New York, took place before the battle of Lexington, and most of them had been made in the course of the previous winter.[1] The credentials of the delegates, therefore, while they conferred authority to adopt measures to recover and establish American rights, still expressed, in many instances, a desire for the restoration of harmony between Great Britain and her colonies. In some cases, however, this desire was not expressed, but a naked authority was granted, to consent and agree to all such measures as the Congress should deem necessary and effectual to obtain a redress of American grievances.

When this Congress assembled, it seems to have been tacitly assumed that each colony should continue to have one vote through its delegation actually present. All the thirteen colonies were represented at the opening of the session, except Georgia

French war. He was President of the Virginia Convention, as well as a Delegate in Congress, at the time of his death. Sparks's Washington, II. 58, 161; III. 139, 140; XII. 420.

[1] In Massachusetts, Pennsylvania, and Maryland, they were made in December; in Connecticut, in November; in New Jersey, in January; in South Carolina, in February; in the Lower Counties on Delaware and in Virginia, in March; in North Carolina, on the 5th of April; and in New York, on the 22d of April.

and Rhode Island. Three days after the session commenced, a delegate appeared from the Parish of St. Johns in Georgia, who was admitted to a seat, but did not claim the right of voting for the colony. On the 15th of May, a delegation from Rhode Island appeared and took their seats.

The credentials of the delegates contained no limitation of their powers with respect to time, with the exception of those from Massachusetts and South Carolina, whose authority was not to extend beyond the end of the year. The Congress continued in session until the 1st of August, and then adjourned for a recess to the 5th of September. When they were again assembled, the delegations of several of the colonies were renewed, with different limitations as to their time of service. Georgia sent a full delegation, who took their seats on the 13th of September. Still later, the delegations of several other colonies were renewed from time to time, and this practice was pursued both before and after the Declaration of Independence, thus rendering the Congress a permanent body.[1]

Notwithstanding the absence of any express authority in their instructions to enter upon revolu-

[1] Virginia renewed her delegation for one year from the 11th of August, 1775, and Maryland hers with powers to act until the 25th of March, 1776. These new delegations, as well as that of Georgia, appeared on the 13th of September, 1775. On the 16th of September, a renewed delegation appeared from New Hampshire, without limitation of time; Connecticut sent a new delegation on the 16th of January, 1776, and Massachusetts did the same on the 31st of January, for the year 1776. The persons of the delegates were not often changed.

tionary measures, the circumstances under which the Congress assembled placed it in the position and cast upon it the powers of a revolutionary government. Civil war had actually commenced, and blood had been shed. Whether this war was to be carried on for independence, or was only to be waged until the British ministry could be compelled to acknowledge the rights which the colonies had asserted, the Congress necessarily became, at once, the organ of the common resistance of the colonies against the parent state. The first thing which evinces its new relation to the country was the application made to it by the Provincial Congress of Massachusetts, immediately after the battle of Lexington, for direction and assistance. While they informed the Continental Congress that they had proceeded, at once, to raise a force of thirteen thousand six hundred men, and had made proposals to the other New England colonies to furnish men in the same proportions, stating that the sudden exigency of their affairs precluded the possibility of waiting for direction, they suggested that an American army ought forthwith to be raised for the common cause.[1] In the same manner, the city and county of New York applied for the advice of Congress, how to conduct themselves with regard to the British troops expected in that quarter. These applications caused the Congress at once to resolve itself into a committee of the whole, to take into consideration the state of America.[2]

[1] Journals, I. 81, 82. [2] May 15, 1775. Journals, I. 162.

These proceedings were soon followed by another application on the part of the Provincial Convention of Massachusetts, setting forth the difficulties under which they were laboring for want of a regular form of government; requesting explicit advice respecting the formation of a new government; and offering to submit to such a general plan as the Congress might direct for the colonies, or to endeavor to form such a government for themselves as should not only promote their own advantage, but the union and interest of the whole country.[1]

Placed in this manner at the head of American affairs, the Continental Congress proceeded, at once, to put the country into a state of defence, and virtually assumed a control over the military operations of all the colonies. They appointed committees to prepare reports on military measures: first, to recommend what posts should be occupied in the city of New York; secondly, to devise ways and means for procuring ammunition and military stores; thirdly, to make an estimate of the moneys necessary to be raised; and fourthly, to prepare rules and regulations for the government of the army.

They then proceeded to create a continental, or national army. To the battle of Lexington had succeeded the investment of Boston, by an army composed of regiments raised by the New England provinces, under the command of General Ward of Massachusetts. This army was adopted by the Con-

[1] Journals, I. 112.

gress; and, with other forces raised for the common defence, became known and designated as the American Continental Army.[1] Six companies of riflemen were ordered to be immediately raised in Pennsylvania, two in Maryland, and two in Virginia, and directed to join the army near Boston, and to be paid by the continent.[2]

On the 15th of June, 1775, Colonel George Washington, one of the delegates in Congress from Virginia, was unanimously chosen to be commander-in-chief of the continental forces.[3] Having accepted the appointment, he received from the Congress a commission, together with a resolution by which they pledged their lives and fortunes to maintain, assist, and adhere to him in his great office, and a letter of instructions, in which they charged him to make it his special care, "that the liberties of America receive no detriment."[4] In the commission given to the general, the style of "the United Colonies" was for the first time adopted, and the defence of American Liberty was assumed as the great object of their union.[5] On the 21st of June, Washington left Philadelphia to take command of the army, and arrived at Cambridge in Massachusetts on the 2d of July. Four major-generals and eight brigadier-generals were also appointed by the Congress for the continental army; rules and regulations for its government were adopted

[1] Form of enlistment, Journals, I. 118.

[2] Ibid.

[3] See note at end of the chapter.

[4] Secret Journals of Congress, I. 18; Pitkin's History of the United States, I. 334, 335.

[5] Journals, I. 122.

and proclaimed, and the pay of the officers and privates was fixed.[1]

The Congress also proceeded, as the legislative authority of the United Colonies, to create a continental currency, in order to defray the expenses of the war. This was done by issuing two millions of dollars, in bills of credit, for the redemption of which the faith of the confederated colonies was pledged. A quota of this sum was apportioned to each colony, and each colony was made liable to discharge its proportion of the whole, but the United Colonies were obligated to pay any part which either of the colonies should fail to discharge.[2] The first of these quotas was made payable in four, the second in five, the third in six, and the fourth in seven years from the last day of November, 1775, and the provincial assemblies or conventions were required, by the resolves of the Congress, to provide taxes in their respective provinces or colonies, to discharge their several quotas.[3] The Congress also directed reprisals to be made, both by public and private armed vessels, against the ships and goods of the inhabitants of Great Britain found on the high seas, or between high and low water-mark; this being a measure of retaliation against an act of Parliament, which had authorized the capture and condemnation of American vessels, and which was considered equivalent to a declaration of war. They also threw open the ports

[1] June 16 - July 4, 1775. Journals, I. 112 - 133.

[2] Journals, I. 125, June 23, 1775. Ibid., I. 185, July 29, 1775.

[3] Ibid.

of the United Colonies to all the world, except the dominions and dependencies of Great Britain.

Further, they established a general Treasury Department, by the appointment of two joint Treasurers of the United Colonies, who were required to give bonds for the faithful performance of the duties of their office,[1] and they organized a general Post-Office, by the appointment of a Postmaster-General for the United Colonies, to hold his office at Philadelphia, to appoint deputies, and to establish a line of posts from Falmouth in Massachusetts to Savannah in Georgia, with such cross posts as he should judge proper.[2]

The proceedings of the Congress on the subject of the Militia were, of course, in the nature of recommendations only. They advised the arming and training of the militia of New York, in May, 1775,[3] and in July they recommended to all the colonies to enroll all the able-bodied, effective men among their inhabitants, between sixteen and fifty years of age, and to form them into proper regiments.[4] The powers of the Congress to call into the field the militia thus embodied were considered to be subject to the consent of those exercising the executive powers of government in the colony, for the time being.[5]

The relations of the country with the Indian tribes

[1] Journals, I. 186, July 29, 1775. Michael Hillegas and George Clymer, Esquires, were elected Treasurers.

[2] Journals, I. 177, 178, July 26, 1775. Dr. Franklin was elected Postmaster-General for one year, and until another should be appointed by a future Congress.

[3] Journals, I. 106.

[4] Journals, I. 170.

[5] Journals, I. 285.

and nations were deemed to be properly within the exclusive jurisdiction of the Congress. Three departments of Indian Affairs, Northern, Southern, and Middle, with separate commissioners for each, were therefore established in July, having power to treat with the Indians in the name and on behalf of the United Colonies.[1] Negotiations and treaties were entered into by these departments, and all affairs with the Indians were conducted by them, under the direction and authority of the Congress.[2]

With regard to those inhabitants of the country who adhered to the royalist side of the controversy, the Congress of 1775 – 6 did not assume and exercise directly the powers of arrest or restraint, but left the exercise of such powers to the provincial assemblies, or conventions, and committees of safety, in the respective colonies, with recommendations from time to time as to the mode in which such powers ought to be exercised.[3]

Besides all this, the different applications made to the Congress by the people of Massachusetts,[4] of New Hampshire,[5] of Virginia,[6] and of South Carolina, concerning the proper exercise of the powers of government in those colonies, and the answers to those applications, furnish very important illustrations of the position in which the Congress were placed. To the people of Massachusetts, they de-

[1] Journals, I. 161, 162.

[2] Journals, II. 112, 141, 163, 201, 255, 302, 304.

[3] Journals, I. 213; II. 5.

[4] June 9, 1775.

[5] November 3, 1775.

[6] December 4, 1775.

clared that no obedience was due to the act of Parliament for altering their charter, and that, as the Governor and Lieutenant-Governor would not observe the directions of that instrument, but had endeavored to subvert it, their offices ought to be considered vacant; and, as the Council was actually vacant, in order to conform as near as might be to the spirit and substance of the charter, they recommended to the Provincial Convention to write letters to the inhabitants of the several towns entitled to representation in the Assembly, requesting them to choose representatives, and requesting the Assembly when chosen to elect councillors; adding their wish, that these bodies should exercise the powers of government until a Governor of the King's appointment would consent to govern the colony according to its charter.[1] The Provincial Conventions of New Hampshire, Virginia, and South Carolina were advised to call a full and free representation of the people, in order to establish such a form of government as, in their judgment, would best promote the happiness of the people and most effectually secure peace and good order in their Provinces, during the continuance of the dispute with Great Britain.[2] This advice manifestly contemplated the establishment of provisional governments only.

But between the date of these last proceedings and the following spring a marked change took place, both in the expectations and wishes of the people of

[1] Journals, I. 115. [2] Journals, I. 231, 235, 279.

most of the colonies, with regard to an accommodation of the great controversy. The last petition of the Congress to the King was refused a hearing in Parliament, as emanating from an unlawful assembly, in arms against their sovereign. In November, the town of Falmouth in Massachusetts was bombarded and destroyed by the King's cruisers. In the latter part of December, an act was passed in Parliament, prohibiting all trade and commerce with the colonies; warranting the capture and condemnation of all American vessels, with their cargoes, and authorizing the commanders of the King's ships to compel the masters, crews, and other persons found in such vessels, to enter the King's service. The act also empowered the King to appoint commissioners, with authority to grant pardon, on submission, to individuals and to colonies, and after such submission to exempt them from its operation.[1] Great preparations were made to reduce the colonies to the submission required by this act, and a part of the troops that were to be employed were foreign mercenaries.

The necessity of a complete separation from the mother country, and the establishment of independent governments, had, therefore, in the winter of 1775 – 6, become apparent to the people of America. Accordingly, the Congress, asserting it to be irreconcilable to reason and good conscience for the people of the colonies any longer to take the oaths and affirmations necessary for the support of any govern-

[1] Annual Register.

ment under the crown of Great Britain, and declaring that the exercise of every kind of authority under that crown ought to be suppressed, and a government of the people of the colonies substituted in its place, recommended to the respective assemblies and conventions of the colonies, where no government sufficient for the exigencies of their affairs had been already established, to adopt such a government as in the opinion of the representatives of the people would best conduce to the happiness and safety of their constituents and of America in general.[1]

It is apparent, therefore, that, previously to the Declaration of Independence, the people of the several colonies had established a national government of a revolutionary character, which undertook to act, and did act, in the name and with the general consent of the inhabitants of the country. This government was established by the union, in one body, of delegates representing the people of each colony; who, after they had thus united for national purposes, proceeded, in their respective jurisdictions, by means of conventions and other temporary arrangements, to provide for their domestic concerns by the establishment of local governments, which should be the successors of that authority of the British crown which they had "everywhere suppressed." The fact that these local or state governments were not formed until a union of the people of the differ-

[1] May 10, 1776. Journals, II. 166, 174.

ent colonies for national purposes had already taken place, and until the national power had authorized and recommended their establishment, is of great importance in the constitutional history of this country; for it shows that no colony, acting separately for itself, dissolved its own allegiance to the British crown, but that this allegiance was dissolved by the supreme authority of the people of all the colonies, acting through their general agent, the Congress, and not only declaring that the authority of Great Britain ought to be suppressed, but recommending that each colony should supplant that authority by a local government, to be framed by and for the people of the colony itself.

The powers exercised by the Congress, before the Declaration of Independence, show, therefore, that its functions were those of a revolutionary government. It is a maxim of political science, that, when such a government has been instituted for the accomplishment of great purposes of public safety, its powers are limited only by the necessities of the case out of which they have arisen, and of the objects for which they were to be exercised. When the acts of such a government are acquiesced in by the people, they are presumed to have been ratified by the people. To the case of our Revolution, these principles are strictly applicable, throughout. The Congress assumed, at once, the exercise of all the powers demanded by the public exigency, and their exercise of those powers was fully acquiesced in and confirmed by the people. It does not at all detract from the authoritative character of their acts, nor diminish the real powers of the Revolutionary Congress, that it was obliged to rely on local bodies for the execution of most of its orders, or that it couched many of those orders in the form of recommendations. They were complied with and executed, in point of fact, by the provincial congresses, conventions, and local committees, to such an extent as fully to confirm the revolutionary powers of the Congress, as the guardians of the rights and liberties of the country. But we shall see, in the further progress of the history of the Congress, that while its powers remained entirely revolutionary, and were consequently coextensive with the great national objects to be accomplished, the want of the proper machinery of civil government and of independent agents of its own rendered it wholly incapable of wielding those powers successfully.

NOTE TO PAGE 33.

ON WASHINGTON'S APPOINTMENT AS COMMANDER-IN-CHIEF.

THE circumstances which attended the appointment of Washington to this great command are now quite well known. He had been a member of the Congress of 1774, and his military experience and accomplishments, and the great resources of his character, had caused his appointment on all the committees charged with making preparations for the defence of the colonies. Returned as a delegate from Virginia to the Congress of 1775, his personal qualifications pointed him out as the fittest person in the whole country to be invested with the command of any army which the United Colonies might see fit to raise; and it is quite certain that there would have been no hesitation about the appointment, if some political considerations had not been suggested as obstacles. At the moment when the choice was to be made, the scene of actual operations was in Massachusetts, where an army composed of troops wholly raised by the New England colonies, and under the command of General Ward, of that Province, was besieging the enemy in Boston. This army was to be adopted by the Congress into the service of the continent, and serious doubts were entertained by some of the members of the Congress as to the policy of appointing a Southern general to the command of it, and a good deal of delicacy was felt on account of General Ward, who, it was thought, might consider himself injured by such an appointment. On the other hand, there were strong reasons for selecting a general-in-chief from Virginia. That colony had taken the lead, among the Southern provinces, in the cause of the continent, and the appointment seemed to be due to her, if it was to be made upon political considerations. The motives for this policy were deemed sufficient to outweigh the objections arising from the character and situation of the army which the general would, in the first instance, have to command. But after all, it cannot be doubted, that the preëminent qualifications of Washington had far more weight with the majority of the Congress, than any dictates of mere policy, between one part of the Union and another, or any local jealousies or sectional ambition.

Mr. John Adams, whose recently published autobiography contains some statements on this subject, speaks of the existence of a Southern party against a Northern, and a jealousy against a New England army under the command of a New England general, which, he says, he discovered after the Congress had been some time in session, and after the necessity of having an army and a general had become a topic of conversation. (Works, II. 415.) In a letter, also, written by Mr. Adams in 1822 to Timothy Pickering, he states that, on the journey to Philadelphia, he and a party of his colleagues, the delegates from Massachusetts to this Congress, were met at Frankfort by Dr. Rush, Mr. Mifflin, Mr. Bayard, and others of the Philadelphia patriots, who desired a conference with them; that, in this conference, the Philadelphia gentlemen strongly advised the Massachusetts delegates not to come forward with bold measures, or to endeavor to take the lead; and represented that Virginia was the most populous State in the Union, proud of its ancient dominions, and that "they [the Virginians] think they have a right to take the lead, and the Southern States, and the Middle States, too, are too much disposed to yield it to them."

"I must confess," says Mr. Adams, "that there appeared so much wisdom and good sense in this, that it made a deep impression on my mind, and it had an equal effect on all my colleagues." "This conversation," he continues, "and the principles, facts, and motives suggested in it, have given a color, complexion, and character to the whole policy of the United States from that day to this. *Without it, Mr. Washington would never have commanded our armies;* nor Mr. Jefferson have been the author of the Declaration of Independence; nor Mr. Richard Henry Lee the mover of it; nor Mr. Chase the mover of foreign connections. *If I have ever had cause to repent of any part of this policy, that repentance ever has been and ever will be unavailing.* I had forgot to say, nor had Mr. Johnson ever have been the nominator of Washington for general." (Works, II. 512, 513.)

Without impeaching the accuracy of Mr. Adams's recollection, on the score of his age when this letter was written, and without considering here how or why Mr. Jefferson came to be the author of the Declaration of Independence, it is believed that Mr. Adams states other facts, in his autobiography, sufficient to show that motives of policy towards Virginia were *not* the sole or the principal reasons why Washington was elected general. Mr. Adams states in his autobiography, that at the time when he observed the professed jealousy of the South against a New England army under the command of a Northern general, it was very visible to him "that Colonel Washington was their object"; "and," he adds, "so many of our stanchest men were in the plan, that we could carry nothing without conceding it." (Works, II. 415.) When Mr. Adams came, as he afterwards did, to put himself at the head of this movement, and to propose in Congress that the army at Cambridge should be adopted, and that a general should be appointed, he referred directly to Washington as the person whom he had in his mind, and spoke of him as "a gentleman from Virginia who was among us and very well known to all of us, a gentleman whose skill and experience as an officer, whose independent fortune, great talents, and excellent universal character, would command the approbation of all America, and unite the cordial exertions of all the colonies better than any other person in the Union. Mr. Washington, who happened to sit near the door, as soon as he heard me allude to him, from his usual modesty, darted into the library-room." (Works, II. 417.) It is quite clear, therefore, that Mr. Adams put the appointment of Washington, in public, upon his qualifications and character, known all over the Union. He further states, that the subject came under debate, and that nobody opposed the appointment of Washington on account of any personal objection to him; and the only objection which he mentions as having been raised, was on the ground that the army near Boston was all from New England, and that they had a general of their own, with whom they were entirely satisfied. He mentions one of the Virginia delegates, Mr. Pendleton, as concurring in this objection; that Mr. Sherman of Connecticut and Mr. Cushing of Massachusetts also concurred in it, and that Mr. Paine of Massachusetts expressed strong personal friendship for General Ward, but gave no opinion upon the question. Afterwards, he says, the subject being postponed to a future day, "pains were taken out of doors to obtain a unanimity, and the voices were generally so clearly in favor of Washington, that the dissentient members were persuaded to withdraw their opposition, and Mr. Washington was nominated, I believe, by Mr. Thomas Johnson of Maryland, unanimously elected, and the army adopted." (Ibid.)

It is worth while to inquire, therefore, what were the controlling reasons, which so easily and so soon produced this striking unanimity. If it was brought about mainly by the exertions of a Southern against a Northern party, and by the yielding of Northern men to the Virginians from motives of policy, it would not have been accomplished with so much facility, although even a Washington were the candidate of Virginia. Sectional jealousies and sectional parties inflame each other; the struggles which they cause are protracted; and the real merits of men and things are lost sight of in the passions which they arouse. If policy, as a leading or a principal motive, gave to General Washington the great body of the Northern votes, there would have been more dissentients from that policy than any of the accounts authorize us to suppose there were, at any moment, while the subject was under consideration. Nor does the previous conduct of Virginia warrant the belief, that her subsequent exertions in the cause of American liberty were mainly purchased by the honors bestowed upon her great men, or by so much of precedence as was yielded in the public councils to the unquestionable abilities of her statesmen. Some of them had undoubtedly been in favor of measures of conciliation to a late period; and some of them, as Washington, Patrick Henry, and Richard Henry Lee, had been, from an early period, convinced that the sword must decide the controversy. They were perhaps as much divided upon this point, until the army at Boston was adopted, as the leading men of other colonies. But when the necessity of that measure became apparent, it was the peculiar happiness of Virginia to be able to present to the country, as a general, a man whose character and qualifications threw all local and political objects at once into the shade. In order to form a correct judgment, at the present day, of the motives which must have produced a unanimity so remarkable and so prompt, we have only to recollect the previous history of Washington, as it was known to the Congress, at the moment when he shrank from the mention of his name in that assembly.

He was forty-three years of age. From early youth, he had had a training that eminently fitted him for the great part which he was afterwards to play, and which unfolded the singular capacities of his character to meet the extraordinary emergencies of the post to which he was subsequently called. That training had been both in military and in civil life. His military career had been one of much activity and responsibility, and had embraced several brilliant achievements. In 1751, it became necessary to put the militia of Virginia in a condition to defend the frontiers against the French and the Indians. The province was divided into military districts, in each of which an adjutant-general, with the rank of major, was commissioned to drill and inspect the militia. Washington, at the age of nineteen, received the appointment to one of these districts; and in the following year, the province was again divided into four grand military divisions, of which the northern was assigned to him as adjutant general. In 1753, the French crossed the lakes, to establish posts on the Ohio, and were joined by the Indians. Major Washington was sent by the Governor of Virginia to warn them to retire. This expedition was one of difficulty and of delicacy. He crossed the Alleghany Mountains, reached the Ohio, had interviews with the French commander and the Indians, and returned to Williamsburg to make report to the Governor. Of this journey, full of perilous adventures and narrow escapes, he kept a journal, which was published by the Governor; was copied into most of the newspapers of the other colonies; and was reprinted in London, as a document of much importance, exhibiting the views and designs of the French. In 1754, he was appointed, with the rank of lieutenant-colonel, second in command of the provincial troops raised by the Legislature to repel the French invasion. On the first encounter with a party of the enemy under Jumonville, on the 28th of May, 1754, the chief command devolved on Washington, in the absence of his superior. The French leader was killed, and most of his party were taken prisoners. Washington commanded also at the battle of the Great Meadows, and received a vote of thanks for his services from the House of Burgesses. This was in 1754, when he was at the age of twenty-two. During the next year, in consequence of the effect of some new arrangement of the provincial troops, he was reduced from the rank of colonel to that of captain, and thereupon retired from the army, with the consolation that he had received the thanks of his country for the services he had rendered. In 1755, he consented to serve as aide-de-camp to General Braddock, who had arrived from England with two regiments of regular troops. In this capacity he served in the battle of the Monongahela with much distinction. The two other aids were wounded and disabled early in the action, and the duty of distributing the General's orders devolved wholly upon Washington. It was in this battle that he acquired with the Indians the reputation of being under the special protection of the Great Spirit, because he escaped the aim of many of their rifles, although two horses were shot under him, and his dress was perforated by four bullets. His conduct on this occasion became known and celebrated throughout the country; and when he retired to Mount Vernon, as he did soon after, at the age of three-and-twenty, he not only carried with him a decisive reputation for personal bravery, but he was known to have given advice to Braddock, before the action, which all men saw, after it, would, if it had been duly heeded, have prevented his defeat. But he was not allowed to remain long in retirement. In August, 1755, he was appointed commander-in-chief of all the provincial forces of Virginia, and immediately entered upon the duties of reorganizing the old and raising new troops, in the course of which he visited all the outposts along the frontier. Soon afterwards, a dispute about rank having arisen with a person who claimed to take precedence of provincial officers because he had formerly held the King's commission, it became necessary for Colonel Washington to make a visit to Boston, in order to have the point decided by General Shirley, the commander-in-chief of his Majesty's armies in America. He commenced his journey on the 4th of February, 1756, and passed through Philadelphia, New York, New London, Newport, and Providence, and visited the Governors of Pennsylvania and New York. In all the principal cities his character, and his remarkable escape at Braddock's defeat, made him the object of a strong public interest. At Boston, he was received with marked distinction by General Shirley and by the whole society of the town, and the question of rank was decided according to his wishes. General Shirley explained to him the intended operations of the next campaign; and, after an absence from Virginia of seven weeks, he returned to resume his command. The next three years were spent in the duties of this laborious and responsible position, the difficulties and embarrassments of which bore a strong resemblance to those which he afterwards had to encounter in the war of the Revolution. In 1758, he commanded the Virginia troops in the expedition against Fort Duquesne, under General Forbes. Great deference was paid by that officer to his opinions and judgment, in arranging the line of march and order of battle, on this important expedition; for the fate of Braddock was before him. The command of the advanced division, consisting of one thousand men, was assigned to him, with the temporary rank of brigadier. When the army had approached within fifty miles of Fort Duquesne, the French deserted it; its surrender to the English closed the campaign; and in December Washington resigned his commission, and retired to Mount Vernon. What he had been, and what he then was, to the Colony of Virginia, is shown by the Address presented to him by the officers of the provincial troops, on his retirement. "In our earliest infancy," said they, "you took us under your tuition, trained us up in the practice of that discipline which alone can constitute good troops, from the punctual observance of which you never suffered the least deviation. Your steady adherence to impartial justice, your quick discernment, and invariable regard to merit, wisely intended to inculcate those genuine sentiments of true honor and passion for glory, from which the greatest military achievements have been derived, first heightened our natural emulation and our desire to excel. How much we improved by those regulations and your own example, with what alacrity we have hitherto discharged our duty, with what cheerfulness we have encountered the severest toils, especially while under your particular directions, we submit to yourself, and flatter ourselves that we have in a great measure answered your expectations. . . . . . It gives us additional sorrow, when we reflect, to find our unhappy country will receive a loss no less irreparable than our own. Where will it meet a man so experienced in military affairs, one so renowned for patriotism, conduct, and courage? Who has so great a knowledge of the enemy we have to deal with? Who so well acquainted with their situation and strength? Who so much respected by the soldiery? Who, in short, so able to support the military character of Virginia? Your approved love to your King and country, and your uncommon perseverance in promoting the honor and true interest of the service, convince us that the most cogent reasons only could induce you to quit it; yet we, with the greatest deference, presume to entreat you to suspend those thoughts for another year, and to lead us on to assist in the glorious work of extirpating our enemies, towards which so considerable advances have already been made. In you we place the most implicit confidence. Your presence only will cause a steady firmness and vigor to actuate every breast, despising the greatest dangers, and thinking light of toils and hardships, while led on by the man we know and love. But if we must be so unhappy as to part, if the exigencies of your affairs force you to abandon us, we beg it as our last request, that you will recommend some person most capable to command, whose military knowledge, whose honor, whose conduct, and whose disinterested principles we may depend on. Frankness, sincerity, and a certain openness of soul, are the true characteristics of an officer, and we flatter ourselves that you do not think us capable of saying any thing contrary to the purest dictates of our minds. Fully persuaded of this, we beg leave to assure you, that, as you have hitherto been the actuating soul of our whole corps, we shall at all times pay the most invariable regard to your will and pleasure, and shall be always happy to demonstrate by our actions with how much respect and esteem we are," &c.

Washington's marriage took place soon after his resignation (January 6th, 1759), and his civil life now commenced. He had been elected a member of the House of Burgesses, before the close of the campaign, and in the course of the winter he took his seat. Upon this occasion, his inability, from confusion and modesty, to reply to a highly eulogistic address made to him by the Speaker, Mr. Robinson, drew from that gentleman the celebrated compliment, "Sit down, Mr. Washington, your modesty equals your valor, and that surpasses the power of any language that I possess." He continued a member of the House of Burgesses until the commencement of the Revolution, a period of fifteen years. He was not a frequent speaker; but his sound judgment, quick perception, and firmness and sincerity of character, gave him an influence which the habit of much speaking does not give, and which is often denied to eloquence. As the time drew near, when the controversies between the colonies and England began to assume a threatening aspect, he was naturally found with Henry, Randolph, Lee, Wythe, and Mason, and the other patriotic leaders of the colonies. His views concerning the policy of the non-importation agreements were early formed and made known. In 1769, he took charge of the Articles of Association, drawn by Mr. Mason, which were intended to bring about a concert of action between all the colonies, for the purpose of presenting them to the Assembly, of which Mr. Mason was not a member. In 1774, he was chosen a member of the first Virginia Convention, and was by that body elected a delegate to the first Continental Congress, where he was undoubtedly the most conspicuous person present. The second Virginia Convention met in March, 1775, and reëlected the former delegates to the second Continental Congress, from which Washington was removed by his appointment as Commander-in-chief.

There can be no doubt, therefore, that Washington was chosen Commander-in-chief for his unquestionable merits, and not as a compromise between sectional interests and local jealousies.

(The authorities for the statements in this note concerning Washington's history are the biographies by Marshall and Sparks, and the Writings of Washington, edited by the latter.)

CHAPTER III.

1776–1777.

CONTINUANCE OF THE REVOLUTIONARY GOVERNMENT. — DECLARATION OF INDEPENDENCE. — PREPARATIONS FOR A NEW GOVERNMENT. — FORMATION OF THE CONTINENTAL ARMY.

ON the 7th of June, 1776, after the Congress had in fact assumed and exercised sovereign powers with the assent of the people of America, a resolution was moved by Richard Henry Lee of Virginia, and seconded by John Adams of Massachusetts, "That these United Colonies are, and of right ought to be, free and independent states; and that all political connection between them and the state of Great Britain is and ought to be totally suppressed."[1] This resolu-

[1] Richard Henry Lee, the mover of this resolution, was born on the 20th of June, 1732, at Stratford, Westmoreland County, Virginia. His earlier education was completed in England, whence he returned in his nineteenth year. Possessed of a good fortune, he devoted himself to public affairs. At the age of twenty-five, he entered the House of Burgesses, where he became a distinguished advocate of republican doctrines, and a strenuous opponent of the right claimed by Parliament to tax the colonies, of the Stamp Act, and of the other arbitrary measures of the home government, coöperating with Patrick Henry in all his great patriotic efforts. He was the author of the plan adopted by the House of Burgesses in 1773, for the formation of committees of correspondence, to be organized by the colonial legislatures, and out of which grew the

tion was referred to a committee of the whole, and was debated until the 10th, when it was adopted in committee. On the same day, a committee, consisting of five members,[1] was instructed to prepare a declaration "that these United Colonies are, and of right ought to be, free and independent states; that they are absolved from all allegiance to the British crown; and that all political connection between them and the state of Great Britain is, and ought to be, dissolved." The resolution introduced by Mr. Lee on

plan of the Continental Congress. In 1774, he was elected one of the delegates from Virginia to the Congress, in which body, from his known ability as a political writer and his services in the popular cause, he was placed on the committees to prepare the addresses to the King, to the People of Great Britain, and to the People of the Colonies, the last of which he wrote. In the second Congress, he was selected to move the resolution of Independence; and besides serving on other very important committees, he furnished, as chairman of the committee instructed to prepare them, the commission and instructions to General Washington. As mover of the resolution of Independence, he would, according to the usual practice, have been made chairman of the committee to prepare the Declaration; but on the 10th of June, the day when the subject was postponed, he was obliged to leave Congress, and return home for a short time, on account of the illness of some member of his family. He came back to Congress and remained a member until June, 1777, when he went home on account of ill health. In August, 1778, he was again elected a member, and continued to serve until 1780; but from feeble health was compelled to take a less active part than he had taken in former years. He was out of Congress from 1780 until 1784, when he was elected its President, but retired at the end of the year. He was opposed to the Constitution of the United States, but voted in Congress to submit it to the people. After its adoption, he was elected one of the first Senators under it from Virginia, and in that capacity moved and carried several amendments. In 1792, his continued ill health obliged him to retire from public life. He died June 19, 1794.

1 Thomas Jefferson, John Adams, Benjamin Franklin, Roger Sherman, and R. R. Livingston.

the 7th was postponed until the 1st of July, to give time for greater unanimity among the members, and to enable the people of the colonies to instruct and influence their delegates.

The postponement was immediately followed by proceedings in the colonies, in most of which the delegates in Congress were either instructed or authorized to vote for the resolution of Independence; and on the 2d of July that resolution received the assent in Congress of all the colonies, excepting Pennsylvania and Delaware. The Declaration of Independence was reported by the committee, who had been instructed to prepare it, on the 28th of June, and on the 4th of July it received the vote of every colony, and was published to the world.[1]

This celebrated instrument, regarded as a legislative proceeding, was the solemn enactment, by the representatives of all the colonies, of a complete dissolution of their allegiance to the British crown. It severed the political connection between the people of this country and the people of England, and at once erected the different colonies into free and independent states. The body by which this step was taken constituted the actual government of the nation, at the time, and its members had been directly invested with competent legislative power to take it, and had also been specially instructed to do so. The consequences flowing from its adoption were, that the local allegiance of the inhabitants of each

[1] See note at the end of the chapter.

colony became transferred and due to the colony itself, or, as it was expressed by the Congress, became due to the laws of the colony, from which they derived protection;[1] that the people of the country became thenceforth the rightful sovereign of the country; that they became united in a national corporate capacity, as one people; that they could thereafter enter into treaties and contract alliances with foreign nations, could levy war and conclude peace, and do all other acts pertaining to the exercise of a national sovereignty; and finally, that, in their national corporate capacity, they became known and designated as the United States of America. This Declaration was the first national state paper in which these words were used as the style and title of the nation. In the enacting part of the instrument, the Congress styled themselves "the representatives of the United States of America in general Congress assembled"; and from that period, the previously "United Colonies" have been known as a political community, both within their own borders and by the other nations of the world, by the title which they then assumed.[2]

[1] On the 24th of June, 1776, the Congress declared, by resolution, that "all persons abiding within any of the United Colonies, and deriving protection from the laws of the same, owed allegiance to the said laws, and were members of such colony; and that all persons passing through or making a temporary stay in any of the colonies, being entitled to the protection of the laws, during the time of such passage, visitation, or temporary stay, owed, during the same, allegiance thereto." Journals, II. 216.

[2] The title of "The United States of America" was formally assumed in the Articles, of Confederation, when they came to be

On the same day on which the committee for preparing the Declaration of Independence was appointed, another committee, consisting of one member from each colony, was directed "to prepare and digest the form of a confederation to be entered into between these colonies." This committee reported a draft of Articles of Confederation, on the 12th of July, which were debated in Congress on several occasions between that day and the 20th of August of the same year, at which time a new draft was reported, and ordered to be printed. The subject was not again resumed, until the 8th of April, 1777; but, between that date and the 15th of the following November, sundry amendments were discussed and adopted, and the whole of the articles, as amended, were printed for the use of the Congress and the State Legislatures. On the 17th of November, a circular letter was reported and adopted, to be addressed to the Legislatures of the thirteen States, recommending to them "to invest the delegates of the State with competent powers, ultimately, in the name and behalf of the State, to subscribe Articles of Confederation and Perpetual Union of the United States, and to attend Congress for that purpose on or before the 10th day of March next."[1]

adopted. But it was in use, without formal enactment, from the date of the adoption of the Declaration of Independence. On the 9th of September, 1776, it was ordered that in all continental commissions and other instruments, where the words "United Colonies" had been used, the style should be altered to the "United States." Journals, II. 349.

[1] Journals, II. 263, 320; III. 123, 502, 513.

A year and five months had thus elapsed, between the agitation of the subject of a new form of national government, and the adoption and recommendation of a form, by the Congress, for the consideration of the States.[1] During this interval, the affairs of the country were administered by the Revolutionary Congress, which had been instituted, originally, for the purpose of obtaining redress peaceably from the British ministry, but which afterwards became *de facto* the government of the country, for all the purposes of revolution and independence. In order to appreciate the objects of the Confederation, the obstacles which it had to encounter, and the mode in which those obstacles were finally overcome, it is necessary here to take a brief survey of the national affairs during the period beginning with the commencement of the war and the Declaration of Independence, and extending to the date of the submission of the Articles of Confederation to the State Legislatures. From no point of view can so much instruction be derived, as from the position in which Washington stood, during this period. By following the fortunes and appreciating the exertions of him who had been charged with the great military duty of achieving the liberties of the country, and especially by observing his relations with the government that had undertaken the war, we can best understand the fitness of that government for the great task to which it had been called.

[1] From June 11, 1776, to November 17, 1777.

The continental government, which commissioned and sent General Washington to take the command of the army which it had adopted, consisted solely of a body of delegates, chosen to represent the people of the several colonies or states, for certain purposes of national defence, safety, redress, and revolution. When the war had actually commenced, and the United Colonies were engaged in waging it, the Congress possessed, theoretically and rightfully, large political powers, of a vague revolutionary nature; but practically, they had little direct civil power, either legislative or executive. They were obliged to rely almost wholly on the legislatures, provincial congresses and committees, or other local bodies of the several colonies or states, to carry out their plans. When Washington arrived at Cambridge and found the army then encamped around Boston in a state requiring it to be entirely remodelled, he came as the general of a government which could do little more for him than recommend him to the Provincial Congress, to the Committee of Safety, and to the prominent citizens of Massachusetts Bay. The people of the United States, at the present day, surrounded by the apparatus of national power, can form some idea of Washington's position, and of that of the government which he served, from the fact that, when he left Philadelphia to take the command of the army, he requested the Massachusetts delegates to recommend to him bodies of men and respectable individuals, to whom he might apply, to get done, through voluntary coöperation, what was absolutely essential to the existence of that army.[1] In truth, the whole of his residence in Massachusetts during the summer of 1775, and the winter of 1775–6, until he saw the British fleet go down the harbor of Boston, was filled with complicated difficulties, which sprang from the nature of the revolutionary government and the defects in its civil machinery, far more than from any and all other causes. These difficulties required the exertion of great intellectual and physical energy, the application of consummate prudence and forecast, and the patience and fortitude which in him were so happily combined with power. They would have broken down many of the greatest generals whom the world has seen; but it is our good fortune to be able to look back upon his efforts to encounter them as among the more prominent and striking manifestations of the strength of Washington's mind and character, and as among the most valuable proofs of what we owe to him.

On the one side of him was the body of delegates, sitting at Philadelphia, by whom he had been commissioned, who constituted the government of America, and from whom every direction, order, or requisition, concerning national affairs, necessarily proceeded. On the other side were the Provincial Congresses, and other public bodies of the New England colonies, on whom he and the Congress were obliged to rely for the execution of their plans. He was compelled to become the director of this

[1] Sparks's Washington, III. 20, note.

complicated machinery. There were committees of the Congress, charged with the different branches of the public service; but General Washington was obliged to attend personally to every detail, and to suggest, to urge, and to entreat action upon all the subjects that concerned the army and the campaign. His letters, addressed to the President of Congress, were read in that body, and votes or resolutions were passed to give effect to his requests or recommendations. But this was not enough. Having obtained the proper order or requisition, he was next obliged to see that it was executed by the local bodies or magistrates, with whom he not infrequently was forced to discuss the whole subject anew. He met with great readiness of attention, and every disposition to make things personally convenient and agreeable to him; but he found, as he has recorded, a vital and inherent principle of delay, incompatible with military service, in the necessity he was under to transact business through such numerous and different channels.[1] His applications to the Governor of Connecticut for hunting-shirts for the army;[2] to the Governor of Rhode Island for powder;[3] to the Massachusetts Provincial Congress to apprehend deserters and to furnish supplies;[4] and to the New York Provincial Congress to prevent their citizens from trading with the enemy in Boston,[5] — together with the earnest appeals which he was obliged to make on these and many other sub-

[1] Works, III. 20.
[2] Ibid. 46.
[3] Ibid. 47.
[4] Ibid. 55.
[5] Ibid. 56.

jects, which should never have been permitted to embarrass him, — show how feeble were the powers and how defective was the machinery of the government which he served.

But there are two or three topics which it will be necessary to examine more particularly, in order fully to understand the character and working of the revolutionary government. The first of these is the formation of the army.

In order to carry on a war of any duration, it is the settled result of all experience, that the soldier should be bound to serve for a period long enough to insure discipline and skill, and should be under the influence of motives which look to substantial pecuniary rewards, as well as those founded on patriotism. According to Washington's experience, this is as true of officers as it is of common soldiers; and undoubtedly no army can be formed, and kept long enough in the field to be relied upon for the accomplishment of great purposes, if these maxims are neglected in its organization.

Unfortunately, the Revolutionary Congress, at the very commencement of the war, committed the serious error of enlisting soldiers for short periods. When Washington arrived at Cambridge, the army which the Congress had just adopted as the continental establishment consisted of certain regiments, raised on the spur of the moment by the provinces of Massachusetts, New Hampshire, Rhode Island, and Connecticut; acting under their respective officers; regulated by their own militia laws; and, with the exception of those from Massachusetts, under no legal obligation to obey the general then in command. The terms of service of most of these men would expire in the autumn; and as they had enlisted under their local governments for a special object, and had not been in service long enough to have merged their habits of thinking and feeling, as New England citizens, in the character of soldiers, they denied the power of their own governments or of the Congress to transfer them into another service, or to retain them after their enlistments had expired.[1] The army was therefore to be entirely remodelled; or, to speak more correctly, an army was to be formed, by making enlistments under the Articles of War which had been adopted by the Congress, and by organizing new regiments and brigades under officers holding continental commissions. But the greatest difficulties had to be encountered in this undertaking. The continental Articles of War required a longer term of service than any of these troops had originally engaged for, and the rules and regulations were far more stringent than the discipline to which they had hitherto been subjected. There was, moreover, great reluctance, on the part of both officers and men, to serve in regiments consisting of the inhabitants of different colonies. A Connecticut captain would not serve under a Massachusetts colonel; a Massachusetts colo-

[1] Letters of General Washington to the President of Congress, September 21, 1775 (Works, III. 98); October 30, 1775 (Ibid. 137); November 8, 1775 (Ibid. 146).

nel was unwilling to command Rhode Island men; and the men were equally indisposed to serve under officers from another colony, or under any officers, in fact, but those of their own choosing.[1]

In this state of things, a committee, consisting of Dr. Franklin, Mr. Lynch, and Colonel Harrison, was sent by the Congress to confer with General Washington and with the local governments of the New England colonies, on the most effectual method of continuing, supporting, and regulating a continental army.[2] This committee arrived at Cambridge on the 18th of October, and sat until the 24th.[3] They rendered very important services to the commander-in-chief, in the organization of the army; but in forming this first military establishment of the Union, the strange error was committed by the Congress, of enlisting the men for the term of one year only, if not sooner discharged;—a capital mistake, the consequences of which were severely felt throughout the whole war.

There is no reason to suppose that General Washington concurred in the expediency of such short enlistments, then or at any other time; but he was obliged to yield to the pressure of the causes to which the mistake is fairly to be attributed. In fact, we find him, in a short time after the new sys-

[1] Letters of General Washington to Joseph Reed, November 8, 1775 (Works, III. 150); November 28, 1775 (Ibid. 177); and to the President of Congress, December 4, 1775 (Ibid. 184); to Governor Cooke of Connecticut, December 5, 1775 (Ibid. 188).

[2] Journals of Congress, II. 208, September 29, 1775.

[3] Writings of Washington, III. 123, note.

tem had been put into operation, pointing it out as a fatal error, in a letter to the President of Congress.[1] The error may have been owing to the character of the government, to the opinions and prejudices prevailing in Congress, and to the delusive idea, which still lingered in the minds of many of the members, that, although the sword had been drawn, the scabbard was not wholly thrown aside, and that they should be able to coerce the British ministry into a redress of grievances, which might be followed by a restoration of the relations between the colonies and the mother country, upon a constitutional basis. No such idea was entertained by Washington, from the beginning. He entertained no thought of accommodation, after the measures adopted in consequence of the battle of Bunker's Hill.

But at the time of which we are treating, the issue had not been made, as Washington would have made it; and, when we consider the state of things before the Declaration of Independence was adopted, and look attentively at the objects for which the Congress had been assembled, and at the nature of their powers, we may perceive how they came to make the mistake of not organizing a military establishment on a more permanent footing.

The delegates to the first Congress were, as we have seen, sent with instructions, which were substantially the same in all the colonies. These instructions, in some instances, looked to "a redress

[1] February 9, 1776 (Works, III. 278).

of grievances," and in others, to "the recovery and establishment of the just rights and liberties of the colonies"; and the delegates were directed "to deliberate upon wise and proper measures, to be by them recommended to all the colonies," for the attainment of these objects. But with this was coupled the declared object of a "restoration of union and harmony" upon "constitutional principles." We have seen how far this body proceeded towards a revolution. The second, or Revolutionary Congress, was composed of delegates who were originally assembled under similar instructions; but the conflict of arms that had already taken place, between the times of their respective appointments and the date of their meeting, had materially changed the posture of affairs. Powers of a revolutionary nature had been cast upon them, by the force of circumstances; and when they finally resolved to take the field, the character of those powers, as understood and acted upon by themselves, is illustrated by the commission which they issued to their General-in-chief, which embraced in its scope the whole vast object of "the defence of American liberty, and the repelling every hostile invasion thereof," by force of arms, and "by the rules and discipline of war, as herewith given."

It is obvious, therefore, that, at the time when the first continental army was to be formed, the powers of the national government were very broad, although vague and uncertain. There seems to have been no reason, upon principle, why they should not have adopted decrees, to be executed by their own immediate agents, and by their own direct force. But a practical difficulty embarrassed and almost annulled this theoretical and rightful power. The government of the Congress rested on no definite, legislative faculty. When they came to a resolution, or vote, it constituted only a voluntary compact, to which the people of each colony pledged themselves, by their delegates, as to a treaty, but which depended for its observance entirely on the patriotism and good faith of the colony itself. No means existed of compelling obedience from a delinquent colony, and the government was not one which could operate directly upon individuals, unless it assumed the full exercise of powers derived from the revolutionary objects at which it aimed. These powers were not assumed and exercised to their full extent, for reasons peculiar to the situation of the country, and to the character, habits, and feelings of the people.

The people of the colonies had indeed sent their delegates to a Congress, to consult and determine upon the measures necessary to be adopted, in order to assert and maintain their rights. But they had never been accustomed to any machinery of government, or legislation, other than that existing in their own separate jurisdictions. They had imparted to the Congress no proper legislative authority, and no civil powers, except those of a revolutionary character. This revolutionary government was therefore entirely without civil executive officers, fundamental laws, or control over individuals; and the union of the colonies, so far as a union had taken place, was one from which any colony could withdraw at any time, without violating any legal obligation.

In addition to this, the popular feeling on the subject of the grievances existing, and of the measures that ought to be taken for redress, was quite different in the different colonies, before the Declaration of Independence was adopted. The leading patriotic or Whig colonies made common cause with each other, with great spirit and energy, and the more lukewarm followed, but with unequal steps.[1] Virginia had, upon the whole, less to complain of than Massachusetts; but she adopted the whole quarrel of her Northern sister, with the firmness of her Washington and the ardor of her Henry. New York, on the other hand, for a considerable period, and down to the month of January, 1775, stood nearly divided between the Whigs and the Tories, and did not choose its delegates to the second Congress until the 20th of April, — twenty days only before that body assembled.[2]

1 Mr. Jefferson once said to my kinsman, Mr. George Ticknor, that when they had any doubtful and difficult measure to carry in this Congress, they counted the four New England colonies, and Virginia, as *sure;* and then they looked round to see where they could get two more, to make the needful majority.

2 The General Assembly of New York met on the 10th of January, 1775, and by a small majority refused to approve of the non-importation association formed by the first Congress, and also declined to appoint delegates to the second Congress, which was to assemble in May. They adopted, however, a list of grievances, which was substantially the same with that which had been put forth by the first Congress. Towards the close of the session, in the absence of some of the patriotic members, petitions to the King and to Parliament were adopted, which differed somewhat from the principles contained in

One of the most striking illustrations, both of the character of the revolutionary government and of the state of the country, is presented by the proceedings respecting the Loyalists, or, as they were called, the Tories. This is not the place to consider whether the American Loyalists were right or wrong in adhering to the crown. Ample justice is likely to be done, in American history, to the characters and motives of those among them whose characters and motives were pure. From a sense of duty, or from cupidity, or from some motive, good or bad, they made their election to adhere to the public enemy; and they were, therefore, rightfully classed, according to their personal activity and importance, among the enemies of the country, by those whose business it was to conduct its affairs and to fight its battles. General Washington was, at a very early period, of opinion, that the most decisive steps ought to be taken with these persons; and he seems at first to have acted as if it belonged, as in fact it did properly belong, to the commander of the continental forces to determine when and how they should be arrested. He first had occasion to act upon the subject in November, 1775, when he sent Colonel Palfrey, one

their list of grievances, and in which they disapproved "of the violent measures that had been pursued in some of the colonies." But the people of New York generally conformed to the non-importation agreement; and on the 20th of April they met in convention and appointed delegates to the second Congress, "to concert and determine upon such matters as shall be judged most advisable for the preservation and reëstablishment of American rights and privileges." Pitkin's History of the United States, I. 324.

of his aids, into New Hampshire, with orders to seize every officer of the royal government, who had given proofs of an unfriendly disposition to the American cause, and when he had secured them, to take the opinion of the Provincial Congress, or Committee of Safety, in what manner to dispose of them in that Province.[1]

Early in the month of January, 1776, General Washington was led to suppose that the enemy were about to send from Boston a secret expedition by water, for the purpose of taking possession of the city of New York; and it was believed that a body of Tories on Long Island, where they were numerous, were about rising, to join the enemy's forces on their arrival. While Washington was deliberating whether he should be warranted in sending an expedition to check this movement and to prevent the city from falling into the hands of the enemy, without first applying to Congress for a special authority, he received a letter from Major-General Charles Lee, offering to go into Connecticut, to raise volunteers, and to march to the neighborhood of New York, for the purpose of securing the city and suppressing the anticipated insurrection of the Tories.[2] He was in-

1 "I do not mean," the orders continued, "that they should be kept in close confinement. If either of these bodies should incline to send them to any interior towns, upon their parole not to leave them until they are released, it will meet with my concurrence. For the present, I shall avoid giving you the like order in respect to the Tories in Portsmouth; but the day is not far off, when they will meet with this, or a worse fate, if there is not a considerable reformation in their conduct." Writings of Washington, III. 158, 159.

2 Writings of Washington, III. 230, note.

clined to adopt Lee's suggestion, but doubted whether he had power to disarm the people of an entire district, as a military measure, without the action of the civil authority of the Province. Upon this point, he consulted Mr. John Adams, who was then attending the Provincial Congress of Massachusetts. Mr. Adams gave it, unhesitatingly, as his clear opinion, that the commission of the Commander-in-chief extended to the objects proposed in General Lee's letter; and he reminded General Washington, that it vested in him full power and authority to act as he should think for the good and welfare of the service.[1] Lee was thereupon authorized to raise volunteers and to proceed to the city of New York, which he was instructed to prevent from falling into the hands of the enemy, by putting it into the best posture of defence and by disarming all persons upon Long Island and elsewhere, (and, if necessary, by otherwise securing them,) whose conduct and declarations had rendered them justly suspected of designs unfriendly to the views of the Congress.[2] At the same time, General Washington wrote to the Committee of Safety of New York, informing them of the instructions which he had given to General Lee, and requesting their assistance; but without placing Lee under their authority.[3]

It happened, that at this time, while Washington

[1] Writings of Washington, III. 230, note. See also Marshall's Life of Washington, II. 285-287.

[2] Writings of Washington, III. 230.

[3] Ibid., note.

was considering the expediency of sending this expedition, the Congress had under consideration the subject of disarming the Tories in Queen's County, Long Island, where the people had refused to elect members to the Provincial Convention.[1] Two battalions of minute-men had been ordered to enter that county, at its opposite sides, on the same day, and to disarm every inhabitant who had voted against choosing members to the Convention.[2] A part of these orders were suddenly countermanded, and in

[1] Journals of Congress, II. 7–9. January 3, 1776. Congress had, on the 2d of January, passed resolves, recommending to the different assemblies, conventions, and committees or councils of safety, to restrain the Tories, and had declared that they ought to be disarmed, and the more dangerous of them kept in custody. For this purpose, the aid of the continental troops stationed in or near the respective colonies was tendered to the local authorities. Journals, II. 4, 5.

[2] The resolves of the Congress on this subject amounted to an outlawry of the persons against whom they were directed. They were introduced by a preamble, reciting the disaffection of a majority of the inhabitants of Queen's County, evinced by their refusal to elect deputies to the convention of the colony, by their public declaration of a design to remain inactive spectators of the contest, and their general want of public spirit; and declaring, that "those who refuse to defend their country should be excluded from its protection, and prevented from doing it injury." The first resolve then proceeded to declare that all the inhabitants of Queen's County named in a list of delinquents published by the Convention of New York be put out of the protection of the United Colonies, that all trade and intercourse with them cease, and that no inhabitant of that county be permitted to travel or abide in any part of the United Colonies, out of that county, without a certificate from the Convention or Committee of Safety of New York, setting forth that such inhabitant is a friend to the American cause, and not of the number of those who voted against sending deputies to the Convention; and that any inhabitant found out of the county, without such certificate, be apprehended and imprisoned three months. The second resolve declared that any attorney or lawyer

place of the minute-men from Connecticut, three companies were ordered to be detailed for this service from the command of Lord Stirling. This change in the original plan was made on the 10th of January; and when Washington received notice of it from Lee, he seems to have understood it as an abandonment of the whole scheme of the expedition, — a course which he deeply regretted.[1] He thought, that the period had arrived when nothing less than the most decisive measures ought to be pursued; that the enemies of the country

who should commence, prosecute, or defend any action at law, for any inhabitant of Queen's County who voted against sending deputies to the Convention, ought to be treated as an enemy to the American cause. The fourth resolve directed that Colonel Nathaniel Heard, of Woodbridge, N. J., should march, with five or six hundred minute-men, to the western part of Queen's County, and that Colonel Waterbury, of Stamford, Connecticut, with the same number of minute-men, march to the eastern side; that they confer together and endeavor to enter the county on the same day, and that they proceed to disarm every person in the county who voted against sending deputies to the Convention, and cause them to deliver up their arms and ammunition on oath, and confine in safe custody, until further orders, all those who should refuse compliance. These resolves were passed on the 3d of January, 1776, and were reported by a committee on the state of New York. On the 10th of January, on account of "the great distance from Colonel Heard to Colonel Waterbury, and the difficulty of coöperating with each other in their expedition into Queen's County," Congress directed Lord Stirling to furnish Colonel Heard with three companies from his command, who were to join Colonel Heard with his minute-men, and proceed immediately on the expedition; and also directed Heard to inform Waterbury that his services would not be required. Journals, II. 21.

[1] He received this impression from General Lee, who wrote on the 16th of January and informed him that Colonel Waterbury had "received orders to disband his regiment, and the Tories are to remain unmolested till they are joined by the King's assassins." Sparks's Life of Gouverneur Morris, I. 75.

were sufficiently numerous on the other side of the Atlantic, and that it was highly important to have as few internal ones as possible. But supposing that Congress had changed their determination, he directed Lee to disband his troops so soon as circumstances would in his judgment admit of it.[1] Lee was at this time at Stamford in Connecticut, with a body of about twelve hundred men, whom he had raised in that colony, preparing to march to New York to execute the different purposes for which he had been detached. On the 22d of January, — the day before the date of General Washington's letter to him directing him to disband his forces, — he had written to the President of Congress, urging in the strongest terms the expediency of seizing and disarming the Tories;[2] and he immediately communicated to Washington the fact of his having done so. Washington wrote again on the 30th, informing Lee that General Clinton had gone from Boston on some expedition with four or five hundred men; that there was reason to believe that this expedition had been sent on the application of Tryon, the royal Governor of New York, who, with a large body of the inhabitants, would probably join it; and that the Tories ought, therefore, to be disarmed at once, and the principal persons among them seized. He also expressed the hope that Congress would empower General Lee to act conformably to both their wishes; but

[1] Letter to General Lee, January 23, 1776. Writings of Washington, III. 255.

[2] Marshall's Life of Washington, II., Appendix, xvii.

that, if they should order differently, their directions must be obeyed.[1]

General Washington was mistaken in supposing that Congress had resolved to abandon the expedition against the Tories of Queen's County. That expedition had actually penetrated the county, under Colonel Heard, who had arrested nineteen of the principal inhabitants and conducted them to Philadelphia. Congress directed them to be sent to New York, and delivered to the order of the Convention of that Colony, until an inquiry could be instituted by the Convention into their conduct, and a report thereon made to Congress.[2]

This destination of the prisoners had become necessary, in consequence of the local fears and jealousies excited by the approach of General Lee to the city of New York, at the head of a force designed to prevent it from falling into the possession of the enemy. The inhabitants of the city were not a little alarmed at the idea of its becoming a post to be contended for; and the Committee of Safety wrote to General Lee earnestly deprecating his approach.[3] Lee replied to them, and continued his march, inclosing their letter to Congress. It was received in that body on the 26th, and a committee of three members was immediately appointed to repair to New York, to consult and advise with the Council of Safety of

[1] Letter to General Lee, January 31, 1776. Writings of Washington, III. 275.

[2] February 6, 1776. Journals, II. 51.

[3] Sparks's Life of Gouverneur Morris, I. 75, 76. They wished to "save appearances with the [enemy's] ships of war, till at least the month of March."

the Colony, and with General Lee, respecting the defence of the city.[1] The Provincial Congress of New York were in session at the time of the arrival of this committee,[2] and, in consequence of the temper existing in that body and in the local committees, the Continental Congress found themselves obliged to recede from the course which they had taken of disarming the Tories of Queen's County by their own action, and to submit the whole subject again to the colonial authorities everywhere, by a mere recommendation to them to disarm all persons, within their respective limits, notoriously disaffected to the American cause.[3]

Thus, after having resolved on the performance of a high act of sovereignty, which was entirely within the true scope of their own powers, and eminently necessary, the Congress was obliged to content itself with a recommendation on the subject to the colonial authorities; not only because it felt itself, as a government, far from secure of the popular cooperation in many parts of the country, but because it had not finally severed the political tie which had bound the country to the crown of Great Britain, and because it had no civil machinery of its own, through which its operations could be conducted.

Another topic, which illustrates the character of the early revolutionary government, is the entire absence, at the period now under consideration, of a

[1] January 26, 1776. Journals, II. 39.

[2] January 30.

[3] March 14, 1776. Journals, II. 91.

proper national tribunal for the determination of questions of Prize; — a want which gave General Washington great trouble and embarrassment, during his residence at Cambridge and for some time afterwards. As this subject is connected with the origin of the American Navy, a brief account may here be given of the commencement of naval operations by the United Colonies.

When General Washington arrived at Cambridge, no steps had been taken by the Continental Congress towards the employment of any naval force whatever. In June, 1775, two small schooners had been fitted out by Rhode Island, to protect the waters of that Colony from the depredations of the enemy; and in the same month, the Provincial Congress of Massachusetts resolved to provide six armed vessels; but none of them were ready in the month of October.[1] In the early part of that month, the first movement was made by the Continental Congress towards the employment of any naval force. General Washington was then directed to fit out two armed vessels, with all possible despatch, to sail for the mouth of the St. Lawrence, in order to intercept certain ships from England bound to Quebec with powder and stores. He was to procure these vessels from the government of Massachusetts.[2] The authorities of Massachusetts had then made no such

[1] Letter of General Washington to the President of Congress.

[2] Resolve passed October 5, 1775. Journals of Congress, II. 197.

provision; but in the latter part of August, General Washington had, on the broad authority of his commission, proceeded to fit out six armed schooners, to cruise in the waters of Massachusetts Bay, so as to intercept the enemy's supplies coming into the port of Boston. One of them sailed in September, and in the course of a few weeks they were all cruising between Cape Ann and Cape Cod.[1]

On the 17th of September, 1775, the town of Falmouth in Massachusetts (now Portland in Maine) was burnt by the enemy. This act stimulated the Continental Congress to order the fitting out of two armed vessels on the 26th of October, and of two

[1] These vessels were fitted out from the ports of Salem, Beverly, Marblehead, and Plymouth. They were officered and manned chiefly by sea-captains and sailors who happened to be at that time in the army. They sailed under instructions from General Washington, to take and seize all vessels in the ministerial service, bound into or out of Boston, having soldiers, arms and ammunition, or provisions on board, and to send them into the nearest port, under a careful prize-master, to wait his further directions. The first person commissioned in this way by the Commander-in-chief was Captain Nicholas Broughton of Marblehead, who sailed in the schooner Hannah, fitted out at Beverly; and in his instructions he was described as "a captain in the army of the United Colonies of North America," and was directed to take the command of "a detachment of said army, and proceed on board the schooner Hannah, lately fitted out, &c. at the continental expense." Another of these vessels, called the Lee, was commanded by Captain John Manly. The names of three others of them were the Harrison, the Washington, and the Lynch. The name of the sixth vessel is not known, but the names of the four other captains were Selman, Martindale, Coit, and Adams. (Writings of Washington, III. 516.) When Washington received directions from the President of Congress to send two vessels to the mouth of the St. Lawrence, he wrote, on the 12th of October, that one of these vessels was then out, and that two of them would be despatched as directed, immediately. (Ibid., III. 124.) In the course of a few weeks, they were all out.

others, on the 30th. It also stimulated the Massachusetts Assembly to issue letters of marque and reprisal, and to pass an act establishing a court to try and condemn all captures made from the enemy, by the privateers and armed vessels of that Colony.

In the autumn of this year, therefore, there were two classes of armed vessels cruising in the waters of Massachusetts: one consisting of those sailing under the continental authority, and the other consisting of those sailing under the authority of the Massachusetts Assembly. Captures were made by each, and some of those sailing under the continental authority were quite successful. Captain Manly, commanding the Lee, took, in the latter part of November, a valuable prize, with a large cargo of arms, ammunition, and military tools; and several other captures followed before any provision had been made for their condemnation, — a business which was thus thrown entirely upon the hands of General Washington.

The court established by the Legislature of Massachusetts, at its session in the autumn of 1775, for the trial and condemnation of all captures from the enemy, was enabled to take cognizance only of captures made by vessels fitted out by the Province, or by citizens of the Province. As the cruisers fitted out at the continental expense did not come under this law, General Washington early in November called the attention of Congress to the necessity of establishing a court for the trial of prizes made by continental authority.[1] On the 25th of November, the Congress passed resolves ordering all trials of prizes to be held in the court of the colony into which they should be brought, with a right of appeal to Congress.[2] But these resolves do not seem to have been, for a considerable period of time, communicated to General Washington; for, during the months of November, December, and January, he supposed it to be necessary for him to attend personally to the adjudication of prizes made by continental vessels,[3] and it was not until the early part of February that the receipt of the resolves of Congress led to a resort to the jurisdiction of the admiralty court of Massachusetts. When, however, this was done, an irreconcilable difference was found to exist between the resolves of Congress and the law of the Colony respecting the proceedings; the trials were stopped for a long time, to enable the General Court of Massachusetts to alter their law, so as to make it conform to the resolves; and in

1 Letter to the President of Congress, November 11, 1775. Writings of Washington, III. 154.

2 Journals, I. 260.

3 On the 4th of December, he repeated his former recommendation to the President of Congress. (Writings of Washington, III. 184.) On the 26th of December, he wrote to Richard Henry Lee, in Congress, begging him to use his influence in having a court of admiralty or some power appointed to hear and determine all matters relative to captures; saying, "You cannot conceive how I am plagued on this head, and how impossible it is for me to hear and determine upon matters of this sort, when the facts, perhaps, are only to be ascertained at ports forty, fifty, or more miles distant, without bringing the parties here [Cambridge] at great trouble and expense. At any rate, my time will not allow me to be a competent judge of this business." Ibid., III. 217.

the mean while, many of the captors, weary of the law's delay, applied, without waiting for the decisions, for leave to go away, which General Washington granted.[1] As late as the 25th of April, 1776, there had been no trials of any of the prizes brought into Massachusetts Bay. At that date, General Washington wrote to the President of Congress, from New York, that some of the vessels which he had fitted out were laid up, the crews being dissatisfied because they could not obtain their prize-money; that he had appealed to the Congress on the subject; and that, if a summary way of proceeding were not resolved on, it would be impossible to have the continental vessels manned. At this time Captain Manly and his crew had not received their share of the valuable prize taken by them in the autumn previous.[2]

Another remarkable defect in the revolutionary government was found in the mode in which it undertook to supply the means of defraying the public expenses. It was a government entirely without revenues of any kind; for, in constituting the Congress, the colonies had not clothed their delegates with power to lay taxes, or to establish imposts. At the time when hostilities were actually commenced, the commerce of the country was almost totally annihilated; so that if the Congress had possessed power to derive a revenue from commerce, little could

[1] Letter to the President of Congress, February 9, 1776. Ibid., III. 282. Letter to Joseph Reed, February 10, 1776. Ibid., III. 284.

[2] Ibid., III. 370.

have been obtained for a long period after the commencement of the war. But the power did not exist; money in any considerable quantity could not be borrowed at home; the expedient of foreign loans had not been suggested; and consequently the only remaining expedient to which the Congress could resort was, like other governments similarly situated, to issue paper money. The mode in which this was undertaken to be done was, in the first instance, to issue two millions of Spanish milled dollars, in the form of bills, of various denominations, from one dollar to eight dollars each, and a few of twenty dollars, designed for circulation as currency. The whole number of bills which made up the sum of $2,000,000 was 403,800.[1] The next emission amounted to $1,000,000, in bills of thirty dollars each, and was ordered on the 25th of July.[2] When the bills of the first emission were prepared, it would seem to have been the practice to have them signed by a committee of the members; but this was found so inconvenient, from the length of time during which it withdrew the members from the other business of Congress, that, when the second emission

[1] This was the emission ordered on the 23d of June, 1775. There were *forty-nine thousand* bills of each denomination from one dollar to eight dollars, inclusive, and *eleven thousand eight hundred* bills of the denomination of twenty dollars. The form of the bills was as follows (Journals, I. 126): —

CONTINENTAL CURRENCY.

No. Dollars.

This Bill entitles the Bearer to receive Spanish milled Dollars, or the value thereof in Gold or Silver, according to the Resolutions of the Congress, held at Philadelphia on the 10th day of May, A. D. 1775.

[2] Journals, I. 177.

was ordered, a committee of twenty-eight citizens of Philadelphia was appointed for the purpose, and the bills were ordered to be signed by any two of them.[1] At this time, no continental Treasurers had been appointed.[2]

Such a clumsy machinery was poorly adapted to the supply of a currency demanded by the pressing wants of the army and of the other branches of the public service. The signers of the bills were extremely dilatory in their work. In September, 1775, the paymaster and commissary, at Cambridge, had not a single dollar in hand, and they had strained their credit, for the subsistence of the army, to the utmost; the greater part of the troops were in a state not far from mutiny, in consequence of the deduction which had been made from their stated allowance; and there was imminent danger, if the evil were not soon remedied, and greater punctuality observed, that the army would absolutely break up. In November, General Washington deemed it highly desirable to adopt a system of advanced pay, but the unfortunate state of the military chest rendered it impossible. There was not cash sufficient to pay the troops for the months of October and November. Through the months of December and January, the signing of the bills did not keep pace with the demands of the army, notwithstanding General Washington's urgent remonstrances; and in February his

[1] Journals, I. 126, 177. The signers of the bills were allowed a commission of one dollar and one third of a dollar on each thousand of the bills signed by them. Ibid.

[2] Ante, p. 35.

wants became so pressing, that he was obliged to borrow twenty-five thousand pounds of the Province of Massachusetts Bay, in order that the recruiting service might not totally cease.[1]

These facts show significantly, that, before the Declaration of Independence, scarcely any progress had been made towards the formation of a national government with definite powers and appropriate departments. In matters of judicature, and in measures requiring executive functions and authority, the Congress were obliged to rely almost entirely upon the local institutions and the local civil machinery of the different colonies; while, in all military affairs, the very form of the revolutionary government was unfavorable to vigor, despatch, and consistent method. There were also causes existing in the temper and feelings of many of the members of that government, both before and after the Declaration of Independence, which, at times, prevented the majority from acting with the decision and energy demanded by the state of their affairs. Many excellent and patriotic men in the Congress of 1775–6, while they concurred fully in the necessity for resistance to the measures of the British ministry, and had decided, or were fast deciding, that a separation must take place, still entertained a great jealousy of standing armies. This jealousy began to exhibit itself very soon after the appointment of the Commander-in-chief, and was never wholly without influ-

[1] Writings of Washington, III. 104, 167, 173, 178, 283.

ence in the proceedings of Congress during the entire period of the war. It led to a degree of reliance upon militia, which, in the situation of the colonies, was too often demonstrated to be a weak and fatal policy.[1]

[1] Writings of Washington, III. 278; IV. 115; V. 328. Mr. Sparks has preserved an anecdote, which shows the perpetuation of this feeling about standing armies, and evinces also that Washington possessed more humor than has been generally attributed to him. In the Convention for forming the Constitution of the United States, some member proposed to insert a clause in the Constitution, limiting the army of the United States to *five thousand men*. General Washington, who was in the chair, observed that he should not object to such a clause, if it were so amended as to provide that no enemy should ever presume to invade the United States with more than *three thousand*.

NOTE TO PAGE 51.

ON THE DECLARATION OF INDEPENDENCE.

THE Declaration of Independence was drawn by Thomas Jefferson; and the circumstances under which he was selected for this honorable and important task have been for more than a quarter of a century somewhat in doubt, and that doubt has been increased by the recent publication of a part of the Works of Mr. John Adams. The evidence on the subject is to be derived chiefly from statements made by both of these eminent persons in their memoirs, and in a letter written by each of them. We have seen, in a former note, that in 1822 Mr. Adams declared, that had it not been for a conversation which occurred in 1775, before the meeting of the Congress of that year, between himself and his Massachusetts colleagues and certain of the Philadelphia "sons of liberty," in which the Massachusetts members were advised to concede precedence to Virginia, from motives of policy, and but for the principles, facts, and motives suggested in that conversation, many things would not have happened which did occur, and among them, that Mr. Jefferson never would have been the author of the Declaration of Independence. In regard to the same speculation, concerning the election of Washington as Commander-in-chief, I have ventured, on Mr. Adams's own authority, to suggest doubts whether that election ought now to be considered to have turned upon motives which Mr. Adams made so prominent in 1822. In regard to the authorship of the Declaration of Independence, I shall only endeavor to state fairly and fully the conflicting evidence, in order that the reader may judge what degree of weight ought to be assigned to the cause, *without* which Mr. Adams supposed Mr. Jefferson would not have been selected to draft it.

Mr. Jefferson, as it appeared when his writings came to be published in 1829, wrote in 1821, when at the age of seventy-seven, a memoir of some of the public transactions in which he had been engaged. At this time, he had in his possession a few notes of the debates which took place in Congress on the subject of Independence, and which he made at the time. These notes he inserted bodily, as they stood, in his memoir, and they are so printed. (Jefferson's Works, I. 10-14.) They are easily distinguishable from the text of the memoir, but they do not appear to throw any especial light upon the fact now in controversy; although, as Mr. Jefferson, in 1823, when writing on this subject, supported his recollection by "written notes, taken at the moment and on the spot," it is proper to allow that those notes may in some way have aided his memory, although we cannot now see in what way they did so. He made this latter reference in a letter which he wrote to Mr. Madison, in reply to the statements in Mr. Adams's letter to Timothy Pickering, under date of August 6, 1822. (Jefferson's Works, IV. 375, 376.)

At or near the beginning of the present century, Mr. Adams, then about sixty-six, wrote an autobiography, which has recently been published [1850], and in which he gave an account of the authorship of the Declaration. In 1822, when about eighty-six, Mr. Adams wrote the letter to Mr. Pickering, which called forth Mr. Jefferson's contradiction in his letter to Mr. Madison, under date of August 30, 1823. (Adams's Works, II. 510-515.) Mr. Jefferson, in his memoir written in 1821, states simply that the committee for drawing the Declaration desired him to do it; that he accordingly wrote it, and that, being approved by the committee, he reported it to the Congress on Friday, the 28th of June, when it was read and ordered to lie on the table; and that on Monday, the 1st of July, the Congress, in committee of the whole, proceeded to consider it. "The pusillanimous idea," he continues, "that we had friends in England worth keeping terms with, still haunted the minds of many. For this reason, those passages which conveyed censures on the people of England were struck out, lest they should give them offence.

The clause, too, reprobating the enslaving the inhabitants of Africa, was struck out in complaisance to South Carolina and Georgia, who had never attempted to restrain the importation of slaves, and who, on the contrary, wished to continue it. Our Northern brethren, also, I believe, felt a little tender under those censures; for though their people had very few slaves themselves, yet they had been pretty considerable carriers of them to others. . The debates having taken up the greater parts of the 2d, 3d, and 4th days of July, were, on the evening of the last, closed." (Jefferson's Works, I. 14, 15.)

In Mr. Adams's autobiography, the following account is given: — "The Committee of Independence were Thomas Jefferson, John Adams, Benjamin Franklin, Roger Sherman, and Robert R. Livingston. Mr. Jefferson had been now about a year a member of Congress, but had attended his duty in the house a very small part of the time, and, when there, had never spoken in public. During the whole time I sat with him in Congress, I never heard him utter three sentences together. It will naturally be inquired how it happened that he was appointed on a committee of such importance. There were more reasons than one. Mr. Jefferson had the reputation of a masterly pen; he had been chosen a delegate in Virginia, in consequence of a very handsome public paper which he had written for the House of Burgesses, which had given him the character of a fine writer. Another reason was, that Mr. Richard Henry Lee was not beloved by the most of his colleagues from Virginia, and Mr. Jefferson was set up to rival and supplant him. This could be done only by the pen, for Mr. Jefferson could stand no competition with him or any one else in elocution and public debate. . . . . . The committee had several meetings, in which were proposed the articles of which the Declaration was to consist, and minutes made of them. The committee then appointed Mr. Jefferson and me to draw them up in form, and clothe them in a proper dress. The sub-committee met, and considered the minutes, making such observations on them as then occurred, when Mr. Jefferson desired me to take them to my lodgings, and make the draft. This I declined, and gave several reasons for declining: 1. That he was a Virginian, and I a Massachusettensian. 2. That he was a Southern man, and I a Northern one. 3. That I had been so obnoxious for my early and constant zeal in promoting the measure, that any draft of mine would undergo a more severe scrutiny and criticism in Congress than one of his composition. 4. And lastly, and that would be reason enough if there were no other, I had a great opinion of the elegance of his pen, and none at all of my own. I therefore insisted that no hesitation should be made on his part. He accordingly took the minutes. and in a day or two produced to me his draft. Whether I made or suggested any corrections I remember not. The report was made to the committee of five, by them examined, but whether altered or corrected in any thing, I cannot recollect. But, in substance, at least, it was reported to Congress, where, after a severe criticism, and striking out several of the most oratorical paragraphs, it was adopted on the 4th of July, 1776, and published to the world." (Adams's Works, II. 511–515.)

The account in Mr. Adams's letter to Mr. Pickering is as follows:— "You inquire why so young a man as Mr. Jefferson was placed at the head of the committee for preparing a Declaration of Independence? I answer, it was the Frankfort advice to place Virginia at the head of every thing. Mr. Richard Henry Lee might be gone to Virginia, to his sick family, for aught I know; but that was not the reason of Mr. Jefferson's appointment. There were three committees appointed at the same time. One for the Declaration of Independence, another for preparing Articles of Confederation, and another for preparing a treaty to be proposed to France. Mr. Lee was chosen for the Committee of Confederation, and it was not thought convenient that the same person should be upon both. Mr. Jefferson came into Congress in June, 1775, and brought with him a reputation for literature, science, and a happy talent of composition. Writings of his were handed about, remarkable for their peculiar felicity of expression. Though a silent member in Congress, he was so prompt, frank, explicit, and decisive upon committees and in conversation, — not even Samuel Adams was more so, — that he soon seized upon my heart; and upon this occasion I gave him my vote, and did all in my power to procure the votes of others. I think he had one more vote than any other, and that placed him at the head of the committee. I had the next highest number, and that placed me second. The committee met, discussed the subject, and then appointed Mr. Jefferson and me to make the draft, I suppose because we were the two first on the list. The sub-committee met. Jefferson proposed to me to make the draft. I said, 'I will not.' 'You should do it.' 'O, no.' 'Why will you not? You ought to do it.' 'I will not.' 'Why?' 'Reasons enough.' 'What can be your reasons?' 'Reason first, — You are a Virginian, and a Virginian ought to appear at the head of this business. Reason second, — I am obnoxious, suspected, and unpopular. You are very much otherwise. Reason third, — You can write ten times better than I can.' 'Well,' said Jefferson, 'if you are decided, I will do as well as I can.' 'Very well. When you have drawn it up, we will have a meeting.'

"A meeting we accordingly had, and conned the paper over. I was delighted with its high tone and the flights of oratory with which it abounded, especially that concerning negro slavery, which, though I knew his Southern brethren would never suffer to pass in Congress, I certainly never would oppose. There were other expressions which I would not have inserted, if I had drawn it up, particularly that which called the King tyrant. I thought this too personal; for I never believed George to be a tyrant in disposition and in nature; I always believed him to be deceived by his courtiers on both sides of the Atlantic, and in his official capacity only, cruel. I thought the expression too passionate, and too much like scolding, for so grave and solemn a document; but as Franklin and Sherman were to inspect it afterwards, I thought it would not become me to strike it out. I consented to report it, and do not now remember that I made or suggested a single alteration.

"We reported it to the committee of five. It was read, and I do not remember that Franklin or Sherman criticized any thing. We were all in haste. Congress was impatient, and the instrument was reported, as I believe, in Jefferson's handwriting, as he first drew it. Congress cut off about a quarter of it, as I expected they would; but they obliterated some of the best of it, and left all that was exceptionable, if any thing in it was. I have long wondered that the original draft has not been published. I suppose the reason is, the vehement philippic against negro slavery.

"As you justly observe, there is not an idea in it but what had been hackneyed in Congress for two years before. The substance of it is contained in the declaration of rights and the violation of those rights, in the Journals of Congress, in 1774. Indeed, the essence of it is contained in a pamphlet, voted and printed by the town of Boston, before the first Congress met, composed by James Otis, as I suppose, in one of his lucid intervals, and pruned and polished by Samuel Adams."

Mr. Jefferson, on the contrary, in his letter to Mr. Madison, says: — "These details are quite incorrect. The committee of five met; no such thing as a sub-committee was proposed, but they unanimously pressed on myself alone to undertake the draft. I consented; I drew it; but, before I reported it to the committee, I communicated it *separately* to Doctor Franklin and Mr. Adams, requesting their correction, because they were the two members of whose judgments and amendments I wished most to have the benefit, before presenting it to the committee; and you have seen the original paper now in my hands, with the corrections of Doctor Franklin and Mr. Adams interlined in their own handwritings. Their alterations were two or three only, and merely verbal. I then wrote a fair copy, reported it to the committee, and from them, unaltered, to Congress. This personal communication and consultation with Mr. Adams he has misremembered into the actings of a sub-committee. Pickering's observations, and Mr. Adams's in addition, 'that it contained no new idea, that it is a commonplace compilation, its sentiments hackneyed in Congress for two years before, and its essence contained in Otis's pamphlet,' may all be true. Of that I am not to be the judge. Richard Henry Lee charged it as copied from Locke's Treatise on Government. Otis's pamphlet I never saw, and whether I had gathered my ideas from reading or reflection I do not know. I know only that I turned to neither book nor pamphlet while writing it. I did not consider it as any part of my charge to invent new ideas altogether, and to offer no sentiment which had ever been expressed before. Had Mr. Adams been so restrained, Congress would have lost the benefit of his bold and impressive advocations of the rights of revolution. For no man's confident and fervid addresses, more than Mr. Adams's, encouraged and supported us through the difficulties surrounding us, which, like the ceaseless action of gravity, weighed on us by night and by day. Yet, on the same ground, we may ask what of these elevated thoughts was new, or can be affirmed never before to have entered the conceptions of man?

"Whether, also, the sentiment of Independence, and the reasons for declaring it, which make so great a portion of the instrument, had been hackneyed in Congress for two years before the 4th of July, 1776, or this dictum of Mr. Adams be another slip of memory, let history say. This, however, I will say for Mr. Adams, that he supported the Declaration with zeal and ability, fighting fearlessly for every word of it. As to myself, I thought it a duty to be, on that occasion, a passive auditor of the opinions of others, more impartial judges than I could be of its merits or demerits. During the debate I was sitting by Doctor Franklin, and he observed that I was writhing a little under the acrimonious criticisms on some of its parts; and it was on that occasion, that, by way of comfort, he told me the story of John Thomson, the hatter, and his new sign." (Jefferson's Works, IV. 376.)

The substantial point of difference in these two accounts of the same transaction, relates to the action of the committee in designating the person or persons who were to prepare the draft of a Declaration. Mr. Adams states that Mr. Jefferson and himself were appointed a sub-committee to prepare it; Mr. Jefferson states that he alone was directed by the committee to write the Declaration. This question is not important, since Mr. Adams's version does not in the least impair Mr. Jefferson's claim to the authorship of the instrument. The latter, it must be allowed, gracefully parries the criticisms of Mr. Adams, by a noble allusion to the eloquence which sustained his compatriots in the difficulties and embarrassments that surrounded them, and which they did not think of analyzing, for the purpose of tracing the exact originality of its sentiments.

It is proper to add, that Mr. Jefferson's account is confirmed by the original manuscript draft of the Declaration, a fac-simile of which was published in 1829, in the fourth volume of his Works, exhibiting the corrections and interlineations made by Dr. Franklin and Mr. Adams in their respective handwritings. These emendations were not important.

The reasons assigned by Mr. Adams for the selection of Mr. Jefferson as the writer of the Declaration are so numerous, that it is difficult to determine which of them he intended should be regarded as the principal or decisive one. In the autobiography, he states that there were more reasons than one why Mr. Jefferson was appointed on a committee of such importance. He assigns two reasons: one, Mr. Jefferson's reputation as a writer, and the other, the desire of his Virginia colleagues to have Mr. Jefferson supplant Mr. Richard Henry Lee. In his letter to Mr. Pickering, Mr. Adams gives as the reason why Mr. Jefferson was placed at the head of the committee, that it was "the Frankfort advice to place Virginia at the head of every thing"; but he also adds, that Mr. Jefferson brought with him to Congress "a reputation for literature, science, and a happy talent of composition," and that this reputation had then been sustained by writings "remarkable for their peculiar felicity of expression." As in the case of Washington, therefore, it would seem that there were reasons of eminent fitness and qualification for the duty assigned; and certainly the Declaration of Independence itself fully justifies the selection. Few state papers have ever been written with more skill, or greater adaptation to the purposes in view. Whether its sentiments were purely original with its author, or were gathered from the political philosophy which had become familiar to the American mind, through the great discussions of the time, it must for ever remain an imperishable monument of his power of expression, and his ability to touch the passions, as well as to address the reason, of mankind. It would be inappropriate to apply to its style the canons of modern criticism. Its statements of political truth, taken in the sense in which they were manifestly intended, can never be successfully assailed. With regard to the passage concerning slavery, we may well conceive that both Northern and Southern men might have felt the injustice of the terrible denunciation with which he charged upon *the King* all the horrors, crimes, and consequences of the African slave-trade, and in which he accused him of exciting the slaves to insurrection, and "to purchase the liberty of which *he* had deprived them by murdering the people upon whom *he* had obtruded them." Mr. Jefferson, in drawing up the list of our national accusations against the King, obviously intended to refer to him as the representative of the public policy and acts of the mother country; and it is true that the imperial government was, and must always remain, responsible for the existence of slavery in the colonies. But this was not one of the grievances to be redressed by the Revolution; it did not constitute one of the reasons for aiming at independence; and there was no sufficient ground for the accusation that the government of Great Britain had knowingly sought to excite general insurrections among the slaves. The rejection of this passage from the Declaration shows that the Congress did not consider this charge to be as tenable as all their other complaints certainly were.

CHAPTER IV.

JULY, 1776 — NOVEMBER, 1777.

CONSEQUENCES OF THE DECLARATION OF INDEPENDENCE. — REORGANIZATION OF THE CONTINENTAL ARMY. — FLIGHT OF THE CONGRESS FROM PHILADELPHIA. — PLAN OF THE CONFEDERATION PROPOSED.

WHEN the Declaration of Independence at length came, it did not in any way change the form of the revolutionary government. It created no institution, and erected no civil machinery. Its political effect has already been described. Its moral effect, both upon the members of the Congress and upon the country, was very great, inasmuch as it put an end alike to the hope and the possibility of a settlement of the controversy upon the principles of the English Constitution, for it made the colonies free, sovereign, and independent states. Men who had voted for such a measure, and who had put their signatures to an instrument which the British Parliament or the Court of King's Bench could have had no difficulty in punishing as treasonable, could no longer continue to feed themselves on "the dainty food of reconciliation."[1] Thenceforward, there was

[1] Washington's Writings, III. 403.

no retreat. The colonies might be conquered, overrun, and enslaved; but this, or the full and final establishment of their own sovereignty, were the sole alternatives. The consequence was, that the Declaration was followed by a greater alacrity on the part of the whole body of the Congress to adopt vigorous and decisive measures, than had before prevailed among them.

But there was one feeling which the Declaration did not dispel, and another to which it immediately gave rise, both of which were unfavorable to concentrated, vigorous, and effective action on the part of the revolutionary government. The Declaration of Independence did not dissipate the unreasonable and ill-timed jealousy of standing armies, which gave way, at last, only when the country was in such imminent peril that Washington felt it to be his duty to ask for extraordinary powers, to be conferred upon himself. It was followed, too, as an immediate consequence, by that jealousy with regard to State rights, and that adhesion to State interests, which have existed in our system from that day to the present, and are not entirely separable from it. As the Declaration made the colonies sovereign and independent, and was followed by the formation of State governments, before the creation of any well-defined national system, State sovereignty became at once an ever-present cause of embarrassment to the Congress, in whose proceedings entire delegations sometimes made the interests of the country bend to the interests of their own State, to a mischievous extent.

To explain these observations, we must recur again to the history of the army, and to the efforts of Washington to have the military establishment put into a safe and efficient condition.

After the evacuation of Boston by the British forces, General Washington proceeded, at once, with the continental army to the city of New York, where he arrived on the 13th of April, 1776. The loss of the battle of Long Island on the 27th of August, and the extreme improbability of his being able to hold the city against the superior forces by which it had been invested through the entire summer, made it necessary for him to appeal once more to the Congress for the organization of a permanent army, capable of offering effectual resistance to the enemy. The establishment formed at Cambridge in the autumn previous was to continue for one year only; it was about to be dissolved; and in the month of September General Washington was compelled to abandon the city of New York to the enemy. Before he withdrew from it, he addressed a letter to the President of Congress, on the 2d of September, in which he told that body explicitly that the liberties of the country must of necessity be greatly hazarded, if not entirely lost, should their defence be left to any but a permanent standing army; and that, with the army then under his command, it was impossible to defend and retain the city.[1] On the 20th

[1] Writings of Washington, IV. 72.

of the same month, he again wrote, expressing the opinion that it would be entirely impracticable to raise a proper army, without the allowance of a large and extraordinary bounty.[1]

At length, when he had retreated to the Heights of Haerlem, and found himself surrounded by a body of troops impatient of restraint, because soon to be entitled to their discharge, and turbulent and licentious, because they had never felt the proper inducements which create good conduct in the soldier, he made one more appeal to the patriotism and good sense of the Congress. Few documents ever proceeded from his pen more wise, or evincing greater knowledge of mankind, or a more profound apprehension of the great subject before him, than the letter which he then wrote concerning the reorganization of the army.[2]

Before this letter was written, however, urged by his repeated requests and admonished by defeat, the Congress had adopted a plan, reported by the Board of War, for the organization of a new army, to serve during the war. A long debate preceded its adoption, but the resolves were at length passed on the 16th of September, 1776.[3] They authorized the enlistment of a body of troops, to be divided into eighty-eight battalions, and to be enlisted as soon as possible. These battalions were to be raised by the States; a certain number being assigned to each State

[1] Writings of Washington, IV. 100.

[2] Letter to the President of Congress, Washington's Writings, IV. 110. September 24, 1776.

[3] Journals, II. 357.

as its quota. The highest quota, which was 15, was assigned to the States of Virginia and Masschusetts, respectively. Pennsylvania had 12; North Carolina, 9; Maryland and Connecticut, 8 each; South Carolina, 6; New York and New Jersey, 4 each; New Hampshire, 3; Rhode Island, 2; and Delaware and Georgia, 1 each. The inducements to enlist were a bounty of twenty dollars and one hundred acres of land to each non-commissioned officer or soldier; and to the commissioned officers, the same bounty in money, with larger portions of land.[1] The States were to provide arms and clothing for their respective quotas, and the expense of clothing was to be deducted from the pay.[2] Although the officers were to be commissioned by the Continental Congress, each State was to appoint the officers of its own battalions, from the colonel to those of the lowest grade, inclusive. A circular letter was addressed by Congress to each State, urging its immediate attention to the raising of these troops; and a committee of three members of the Congress was sent to the headquarters of General Washington, to confer with him on the subject.[3]

Two serious defects in this plan struck the Commander-in-chief, as soon as it was laid before him; but the resolves had been passed, and passed with

[1] 500 acres to a colonel; 450 to a lieutenant-colonel; 400 to a major; 300 to a captain; 200 to a lieutenant; and 150 to an ensign.

[2] Journals, II. 357. Subsequently, by a resolve passed November 12 (1776), the option was given to enlist for the war or for three years, taking away the land bounty from those who enlisted for the latter period only. Ibid. 454.

[3] Ibid.

difficulty, before he had an opportunity specifically to point out the mistakes. In the first place, by giving the appointment of the officers to the States, any central system of promoting or placing the officers then serving on the continental establishment according to their characters and deserts was rendered impossible. The resolutions of Congress did not even recommend these officers to the consideration of their respective States. They were left to solicit their appointments at a distance, or to go home and make personal application. Those who chose to do the latter were more likely to get good places than those who remained at their posts; but they were also less likely to be deserving of important commissions than those who stayed with the army. To expect that a proper attention would be paid to the claims of men of real merit, under such a system, — whether they had or had not been in service before, — or that the army when brought together would be found to be officered on a uniform principle, exhibiting an adaptation of character to station, was, in Washington's view, to expect that local authorities would not be influenced by local attachments, and that merit would make its way, in silence and absence, against personal importunity and bold presumption.

But Washington saw no remedy for these evils, except by opening a direct communication with the States, through which he might exert some influence over their appointments. He immediately suggested to the Congress, that each State should send a commission to the army, with authority to appoint all the officers of the new regiments. Congress passed a resolve recommending this step to the States, and advising that the Commander-in-chief should be consulted in making the appointments; that those officers should be promoted who had distinguished themselves for bravery and attention to their duties; that no officer should be appointed who had left his station without leave; and that all the officers to be appointed should be men of honor and known abilities, without particular regard to their having been in service before.[1] This was but a partial remedy for the defects of the system. Several of the States sent such a commission to act with the Commander-in-chief; but many of them were tardy in making their appointments, and finally the Congress authorized General Washington to fill the vacancies.

Another and a dangerous defect in this plan was, that the continental pay and bounty on enlistment were fixed so low, that some of the States, in order to fill up their quotas, deemed it expedient to offer a further pay and bounty to their own men. This was done immediately by the States of Connecticut and Massachusetts. The consequence was likely to be, that, if the quotas of some States were raised before the fact became known that other States had increased the pay and the bounty, some regiments would, when the army came together, be on higher pay than others, and jealousy, impatience, and mu-

[1] Journals, II. 403. October 8, 1776.

tiny must inevitably follow. Knowing that a different pay could not exist in the same army without these consequences, General Washington remonstrated with the Governor of Connecticut, arrested the proceedings of the commissioners of that State and of Massachusetts, and prevented them from publishing their terms, until the sense of the Congress could be obtained.[1] That body, on receiving from him another strong representation on the subject, passed a resolve augmenting the pay.

Still, the system, notwithstanding these efforts to amend it, worked ill. The appointment of the officers by the States was incapable of being well managed; the pay and bounty, even after they were increased, were insufficient; and the whole scheme of raising a permanent army was entered upon at too late a period to be effectually accomplished. As late as the middle of November, so little had been done, that the whole force on one side of the Hudson, opposed to Howe's whole army, did not exceed two thousand men of the established regiments; while, on the other side, there was a force not much larger to secure the passes into the Highlands.[2] "I am wearied almost to death," said the Commander-in-chief, in a private letter, "with the retrograde motion of things, and I solemnly protest that a pecuniary reward of twenty thousand pounds a year would not induce me to undergo what I do; and

[1] Writings of Washington, IV.173. [2] Ibid. 183, 184.

after all, perhaps, to lose my character, as it is impossible, under such a variety of distressing circumstances, to conduct matters agreeably to public expectation, or even to the expectations of those who employ me, as they will not make proper allowances for the difficulties their own errors have occasioned."[1]

There are few pages in our history so painful as those on which are recorded the complaints extorted from Washington, at this period, by the trials of his situation. That he, an accomplished soldier, who had retired with honor from the late war with France to his serene Mount Vernon; who had left it again, to stake life, and all that makes life valuable, on the new issue of his country's independence; who asked no recompense and sought no object but her welfare, should have been compelled to pass into the dark valley of the retreat through New Jersey, with all its perplexities, dangers, and discouragements, — its cruel exertions and its humiliating reverses, — without a powerful and energetic government to lean upon, and with scarcely more than Divine assistance to which to turn, presents, indeed, to our separate contemplation, a disheartening and discreditable fact. But no trials are appointed to nations, or to men, without their fruits. The perplexities and difficulties which surrounded Washington in the early part of the Revolution contributed, undoubtedly, to give him that profound civil wisdom, that knowledge of our civil wants, and that

[1] Writings of Washington, IV. 184.

influence over the moral sense of the country, which were afterwards so beneficently felt in the establishment of the Constitution. The very weakness of the government which he served became in this manner his and our strength. Without the trials to which it subjected him, it may well be doubted whether we should now possess that tower of strength, — that security against distracted counsels and clashing interests, — which exist for us in the character and services of that extraordinary man.

It is not necessary to sketch the scene or to follow the route of General Washington's retreat through New Jersey, except as they illustrate the subject of this work, — the constitutional history of the country. Its remarkable military story is well known. On the 23d of November, four days after the date of the letter to his brother above quoted, he was at Newark, with a body of troops whose departure was near at hand, and for supplying whose places no provision had been made. The enemy were pressing on his rear, and in order to impress upon Congress the danger of his situation, he sent General Mifflin to lay an exact account of it before them.[1] On the 28th, he marched out of Newark in the morning, and Lord Cornwallis entered it on the afternoon of the same day. On the 30th, he was at Brunswick, endeavoring, but with little success, to raise the militia; — the terms of service of the Jersey and Maryland brigades expiring on that day. On the

[1] Writings, IV. 190.

1st of December, his army numbered only four thousand men, and the enemy were pushing forward with the greatest energy.[1] On the 5th, he resolved to march back to Princeton; but neither militia nor regulars had come in, and it was too late to prevent an evil, which he had both foreseen and foretold.[2] On the 8th, he crossed the Delaware.[3] On the 12th, he saw his little handful of men still further decrease, and now, without succors from the government, or spirited exertions on the part of the people, the loss of Philadelphia—"an event," said he, "which will wound the heart of every virtuous American"—rose as a spectre in his path.[4] On the 16th, as he moved on, gathering all the great energies of his character to parry this deep disgrace, concentrating every force that remained to him towards the defence of the city, and animating and directing public bodies, in a tone of authority and command, he once more urged the Congress to discard all reliance upon the militia, to augment the number of the regular troops, and to strain every nerve to recruit them.[5] Finally,—being still in doubt whether Howe did not intend an attack on Philadelphia, before going into winter quarters,—with less than three thousand men fit for duty, to oppose a well-appointed army of ten or twelve thousand, and surrounded by a population rapidly submitting to the enemy, — he felt that the time had come, when to his single hands must be given all the military authority and power which the Continental

1 Ibid. 197.
2 Ibid. 202.
3 Ibid. 206.
4 Ibid. 211.
5 Ibid. 225.

Union of America held in trust for the liberties of the country. On the 20th of December, therefore, he wrote to the President of Congress a memorable letter, asking for extraordinary powers, but displaying at the same time all the modesty and high principle of his character.[1]

To this appeal Congress at once responded, in a manner suited to the exigency. On the 27th of December, 1776, they passed a resolution, vesting in General Washington ample and complete power to raise and collect together, in the most speedy and effectual manner from all or any of the United States, sixteen battalions of infantry, in addition to those already voted; to appoint the officers of these battalions; to raise, officer, and equip three regiments of artillery and a corps of engineers, and to establish their pay; to apply to any of the States for such aid of their militia as he might judge necessary; to form such magazines of provisions, and in such places, as he should think proper; to displace and appoint all officers under the rank of brigadier-general; to fill up all vacancies in every other department of the American army; to take, wherever he might be, whatever he might want for the use of the army, if the inhabitants would not sell it, allowing a reasonable price for the same; to arrest and confine persons who should refuse to receive the continental currency, or were otherwise disaffected to the American cause; and to return to the States of which

[1] Writings, IV. 232.

such persons were citizens their names and the nature of their offences, together with the witnesses to prove them. These powers were vested in the Commander-in-chief for the space of six months from the date of the resolve, unless sooner revoked by the Congress.[1]

The powers thus conferred upon General Washington were in reality those of a military dictatorship; and in conferring them, the Congress acted upon the maxim that the public safety is the supreme law. They acted, too, as if they were the proper judges of the exigency, and as if the powers they granted were then rightfully in their hands. But it is a singular proof of the unsettled and anomalous condition of the political system of the country,

[1] Journals, II. 475. A committee, at the head of which was Robert Morris, was appointed to transmit this resolve to General Washington, and in their letter they said: "We find by these resolves that your Excellency's hands will be strengthened by very ample powers; and a new reformation of the army seems to have its origin therein. Happy it is for this country, that the general of their forces can safely be intrusted with the most unlimited power, and neither personal security, liberty, nor property be in the least degree endangered thereby." In his reply, the General said to the committee: "Yours of the 31st of last month inclosed to me sundry resolves of Congress, by which I find they have done me the honor to intrust me with powers, in my military capacity, of the highest nature, and almost unlimited in extent. Instead of thinking myself freed from all *civil* obligations, by this mark of their confidence, I shall constantly bear in mind, that, as the sword was the last resort for the preservation of our liberties, so it ought to be the first thing laid aside when those liberties are firmly established. I shall instantly set about the most necessary reforms in the army; but it will not be in my power to make so great a progress as if I had a little leisure time upon my hands." Writings of Washington, IV. 257, 552.

and of the want of practical authority in the continental government, that, in three days after the adoption of the resolves conferring these powers, the Congress felt it necessary to address a letter to the Governors of the States, apologizing for this step. Nor was their letter a mere apology. It implied a doubt whether the continental government possessed a proper authority to take the steps which the crisis demanded, and whether the execution of all measures did not really belong to the States, the Congress having only a recommendatory power. "Ever attentive," their letter declared, "to the security of civil liberty, Congress would not have consented to the vesting of such powers in the military department as those which the inclosed resolves convey to the continental Commander-in-chief, if the situation of public affairs did not require, at this crisis, a decision and vigor which distance and numbers deny to assemblies far removed from each other and from the seat of war." The letter closed, by requesting the States to use their utmost exertions to further such levies as the general might direct, in consequence of the new powers given him, and to make up and complete their quotas as formerly settled.[1]

Strictly examined, therefore, the position taken by the Congress was, that a crisis existed demanding the utmost decision and vigor; that the measures necessary to meet it, such as the raising of troops and the compulsory levying of supplies, belonged to the

[1] Writings of Washington, IV. 551.

States; but that, the State governments being removed from each other and from the seat of war, the Congress confers upon the continental general power to do things which in reality it belongs to the States to do. In this there was a great inaccuracy, according to all our present ideas of constitutional power. But still the action of the Congress expresses and exhibits their real situation. It contains a contradiction between the true theory of their revolutionary powers and the powers which they could in fact practically exercise. Upon principle, it was just as competent to the Congress to take the steps required by the exigency, as it was to adjudge them to the States; and it was just as competent to the Congress to do any thing directly, as to confer a power to do it on their general. But the jealousies of the States, the habits of the country, and the practical working of the existing institutions, had never permitted the full exercise of the revolutionary powers which properly resided in the hands of the Congress. The true theory of their situation was limited by practical impossibilities; and an escape from contradictions became impossible. It was perceived that the States would neither pass laws or resolves for the summary raising of forces and levying of supplies, nor allow this to be done by committees or commissioners of Congress; but it was believed that they would acquiesce in its being done by General Washington, out of respect for his character, for his abilities and his motives, and from conviction that he alone could save the country.

The expectations of the Congress were not disappointed. It was felt throughout the country, that such powers could be lodged in the hands of Washington without danger. The States in general acquiesced in the necessity and propriety of this measure, and there was little disposition to encroach upon or to complain of the authority conferred. To this acquiescence, however, there were exceptions.[1]

The period which now followed was a part of the interval during which the Articles of Confederation were pending in Congress. We have seen that the plan of a confederation was reported to that body in July, 1776, and finally adopted for recommendation to the States in November, 1777. But soon after the extraordinary powers had been conferred upon General Washington, the attendance of the members began to diminish, and several of the most eminent and able men, who had hitherto served, retired from Congress. In January, 1777, there were no delegations present from the States of Delaware and New York;[2] and in February, the absence of many distinguished men, whose counsels had been of vast importance, made a striking deficiency. The formation of the State governments, and the local affairs of the States, absorbed for a time, with a few important exceptions, the best civil talent in the country.[3]

1 Writings of Washington, IV. 551.

2 Journals, III. 35.

3 "We have now to lament," said Robert Morris, in a private letter to General Washington, under date of February 27th, 1777, "the absence from the public councils of America of Johnson, Jay, R. R. Livingston, Duane, Deane, W. Livingston, Franklin, Dickinson, Harrison, Nelson, Hooper,

While the personal efficiency and wisdom of the Congress thus sensibly declined, no change took place in the nature of their powers, or in their relations to the States, that would impart greater vigor to their proceedings. The delegations of many of the States were renewed in the winter of 1776 – 7; but there was a great diversity, and in some cases a great vagueness, in their instructions.[1] In such a state of things,

Rutledge, and others not less conspicuous, without any proper appointments to fill their places, and this at the very time they are most wanted, or would be so, if they had not very wisely supplied the deficiency by delegating to your Excellency certain powers, that they durst not have intrusted to any other man. But what is to become of America, and its cause, if a constant fluctuation is to take place among its counsellors, and at every change we find reason to view it with regret?" Writings of Washington, IV. 340, note.

1 Massachusetts, in December, 1776, renewed the credentials of John Hancock, Samuel Adams, John Adams, Robert Treat Paine, Elbridge Gerry, Francis Dana, and James Lovell, giving power to any three or more of them, with the delegates from the other American States, to concert, direct, and order such further measures as shall to them appear best calculated for the establishment of right and liberty to the American States, upon a basis permanent and secure against the power and art of the British administration; for prosecuting the present war, concluding peace, contracting alliances, establishing commerce, and guarding against any future encroachments and machinations of their enemies; with power to adjourn, &c. (Journals, IV. 14.) New Hampshire in the same month sent William Whipple, Josiah Bartlett, and Mathew Thornton, making any one of them a full delegation, without any other instructions than "to represent" the State in the Continental Congress for one year, and allowing only two of them to attend at a time. (Ibid. 41.) Virginia in the same month appointed Mann Page, in the room of George Wythe, with the same general instructions "to represent" the State. (Ibid. 42.) North Carolina in the same month appointed William Hooper, Joseph Hewes, and Thomas Burke, and invested them "with such powers as may make any act done by them, or any of them, or consent given in the said Congress in behalf of this State, obligatory upon every inhabitant thereof." (Ibid. 37.) South Carolina chose

— with no uniform rule prescribing the powers of the Congress, and with some uncertainty in that body itself with regard to its authority to confer upon the Commander-in-chief the powers with which he was now invested, — however general might be the readiness of the country to acquiesce in their necessity, it is not surprising that State jealousy was sometimes aroused, or that it should have been unreasonable in some of its manifestations.

A striking instance of this jealousy occurred upon the occasion of a proclamation issued by General Washington at Morristown, on the 25th of January, 1777. Sir William Howe had published a proclamation in New Jersey, offering protection to such of the inhabitants as would take an oath of allegiance to the King. Many of the substantial farmers of

Arthur Middleton, Thomas Hayward, Jr., and Henry Laurens, with power "to concert, agree to, and *execute* every measure which one or all of them should judge necessary for the defence, security, or interest of this State in particular, and of America in general." (Ibid. 53.) Connecticut sent Roger Sherman, Samuel Huntington, Eliphalet Dyer, Oliver Wolcott, Richard Law, and William Williams, "to consult, advise, and resolve upon measures necessary to be taken and pursued for the defence, security, and preservation of the rights and liberties of the said United States, and for their common safety"; but requiring them "of such their proceedings and resolves to transmit authentic copies from time to time to the General Assembly of this State." (Ibid. 5.) Of the other States, Pennsylvania, Rhode Island, New York, New Jersey, Maryland, and Georgia, which renewed their delegations somewhat later in the year, instructed them simply "to represent" the State in the Continental Congress; and Delaware empowered its delegates, on behalf of the State, "to concert, agree to, and execute any measure which they, together with a majority of the Continental Congress, should judge necessary for the defence, security, interest, and welfare of that State in particular, and America in general." (Ibid. 64, 315, 171, 169, 395, 54, 403, 86.)

the country had availed themselves of this offer, and had received protections from the British general. The English and Hessian troops, however, made no distinction between friends and foes, but frequently committed great outrages both upon person and property. The resentment of the population would have restored them to the patriot side; but many who had taken the oath of allegiance felt, or affected, in consequence, scruples of conscience.

General Washington therefore issued a counter-proclamation, commanding all persons who had received the enemy's protection to repair to head-quarters, or to some general officer of the army, and to surrender their protections and take an oath of allegiance to the United States; — allowing thirty days for those who preferred to remain under the protection of Great Britain to withdraw within the enemy's lines. This was considered in some quarters as an undue exercise of power. The idea of an oath of allegiance to the United States, before the Confederation was formed, was regarded by many as an absurdity. Allegiance, it was said, was due exclusively to the State of which a man was an inhabitant; the States alone were sovereign; and it was for each State, not for the United States, which possessed no sovereignty, to exact this obligation. The Legislature of New Jersey were disposed to treat General Washington's proclamation as an encroachment on their prerogatives: and one of the delegates of that State in Congress denounced it as improper.[1]

[1] This was Mr. Abraham Clark, one of the signers of the Declara-

This feeling was shared by other members; but it is not to be doubted, that the proceeding was a legitimate exercise of the authority vested in the Commander-in-chief. He had been expressly empowered to arrest and confine persons disaffected to the American cause; and the requiring them to attend at his head-quarters was clearly within the scope of this authority. Moreover, although no confederation or political union of the States had been formed under a written compact, yet the United States were waging war, as a government regularly constituted by its representatives in a congress, for the very purpose of carrying on such war. They had an army in the field, whose officers held continental commissions, and were paid by a continental currency. They were exercising certain of the attributes of sovereignty as a belligerent power; and in that capacity they had a complete right to exact such an obligation not to aid the enemy, as would separate their friends from their foes. It was a military measure; and the tenor of the proclamation shows that General Washington exacted the oath in that relation. To pause at such a moment, and to consider nicely how much sovereignty resided in each of the States, and how much or how little belonged to the United States, was certainly a great refinement. But it marks the temper of the times, and the extreme jealousy with which all continental power and authority were watched at that period.[1]

tion of Independence. Mr. Sparks has preserved a curious letter written by this gentleman on the subject. Writings of Washington, IV. 298.

[1] The whole of this alarm evi-

We have seen that the powers conferred upon General Washington authorized him to raise, in the most speedy and effectual manner, sixteen battalions of infantry, in addition to those before voted by Congress, three regiments of artillery, and a corps of engineers; and also to apply to any of the States for

dently arose from the use of the words "oath of allegiance" in General Washington's proclamation. Probably this phrase was used by him as a convenient description of the obligation which he intended to exact. He did not use it as a jurist, but as a general and a statesman. In a letter written by him on the 5th of February (1777) to the President of Congress, desiring that body to urge the States to adopt an oath of fidelity, he said: "From the first institution of civil government, it has been the national policy of every precedent state to endeavor to engage its members to the discharge of their public duty by the obligation of some oath"; and he then observes, with his characteristic wisdom, that "an oath is the only substitute that can be adopted to supply the *defect of principle.*" He advised that every State should fix upon some oath or affirmation of allegiance, to be tendered to all the inhabitants without exception, and to outlaw those that refused it. (Writings, IV. 311, 312.) Afterwards, when the Legislative Council of New Jersey — where some of the people had refused to take the oath required by his proclamation — applied to him to explain the nature of the oath, and to be furnished with a copy of it, that they might know whether it was the oath prescribed by the General Assembly of that State, he informed them that he had prescribed no form, and had reverted to none prescribed by them; that his instructions to the brigadiers who attended to that duty were, to insist on nothing more than an obligation in *no manner to injure the States;* and that he had left the form to his subordinates; but that if he had known of any form adapted to the circumstances of the inhabitants, he would certainly have ordered it. (Ibid. 319, note.) This explanation makes it quite certain, that what General Washington called in his proclamation an oath of allegiance was merely a military exaction of an obligation in favor of a belligerent power against the enemy; and his advice on the subject of a general civil oath of allegiance, to be exacted by the States, shows that he understood the niceties of the subject as well as any casuist in or out of Congress. This topic may be dismissed by reverting here to the fact, that in February, 1778, Congress prescribed an oath or

the aid of their militia when wanted.[1] At the period when he addressed himself to this great undertaking of forming a new army, for the third time, the existing force which he had with him in and around New Jersey was about to be dissolved. The additional regiments of the regular line were to be raised by the States, and upon them alone could he depend for the supply of a new army, with which to commence the campaign in the spring of 1777. He had labored, he said, ever since he had been in the service, to discourage all kinds of local attachments and distinctions of country, denominating the whole by the greater name of AMERICAN; but he had found it impossible to overcome prejudices.

Two causes especially embarrassed his efforts in the formation of the new army; and both of them show how powerful were the centrifugal forces of our system at that period, and how little hold that great central name had taken upon the people of the different States. One of these causes was the persistence of some of the States in giving extra bounties to encourage enlistments into their quotas of the original eighty-eight battalions not yet raised. The bounty allowed by Congress was twenty dollars to every soldier enlisting into the new establishment for

affirmation, to be taken by the officers of the army, and all others holding office under Congress, which was simply a renunciation of allegiance to the King of Great Britain, an acknowledgment of the independence of the United States, and a promise to support, maintain, and defend them against King George III. and his successors, and to serve the United States in the office mentioned with fidelity, and the best skill and understanding of the party taking the oath. Journals, IV. 49.

[1] Ante, p. 100

three years or during the war. The additional bounty offered by Massachusetts was sixty-six dollars and two thirds. There was thus an inducement of eighty-six dollars and two thirds offered to the men then in the service of the United States, not to reënlist in their old regiments, as fast as their time of service expired, but to go to Massachusetts and enlist in the fresh quotas which were forming in that State, and which were to be afterwards mustered into the continental service. The same inconsiderate and unpatriotic policy was pursued in all the Eastern States, and before the spring opened, the consequences began to be felt in the state of the new continental battalions which General Washington was endeavoring to procure from some of the Middle States, and in which he would not sanction the allowance of an extra bounty, regarding it as an indirect breach of the union, and of the agreement entered into by the delegates of the States in Congress to give a bounty of twenty dollars only for service in the continental army.[1] The month of April arrived, and he had not received a man of the new levies, except a few hundreds from Jersey, Pennsylvania, and Virginia, while the few old regiments which remained, after the dissolution of the army in January, were reduced to a handful of men, the enemy being in great force, and making every preparation to seize upon Philadelphia.

Nor did the allowance of these irregular bounties

[1] Letter to General Knox, February 11, 1777. Writings, IV. 316.

help the States, in raising the old levies, as had been anticipated. They rather caused the soldiers to set a high price upon themselves, and to hold back from enlisting; while the second cause, to which I have alluded, as embarrassing the Commander-in-chief, was a great hinderance to his efforts to plan and carry out a campaign, having for its object the general benefit of the whole Union.

This cause was the inability of many local authorities to comprehend the necessity of such a campaign. General Washington was, at this period, harassed by numerous applications to allow the troops, which had been raised in the States for the service of the continent, to remain for the defence of particular neighborhoods against incursions of the enemy. Nothing, he said on one of these occasions, could exceed the pleasure which he should feel, if he were able to protect every town and every individual on the continent. But as this was a pleasure which he never should realize, and as the continental forces were wanted to meet and counteract the main designs of the enemy on the principal theatre of the war, he could not consent to divide them and detach them to every point where the enemy might possibly attempt an impression; "for that," he added, "would be in the end to destroy ourselves and subjugate our country."[1]

From the operation of these and other causes connected with the political system of the country, the army with which Washington was obliged to take

[1] Letter to Governor Trumbull, May 11, 1777. Writings, IV. 413. See also Letter to Major-General Stephen, May 24, 1777. Ibid. 431.

the field, in the spring of 1777, did not exceed five thousand seven hundred and thirty-eight effective men, exclusive of a small body of cavalry and artillery.[1] The consequence was, a necessary reliance upon militia, to a great extent, throughout that summer. The battle of the Brandywine, fought with an effective force of only eleven thousand men, including militia, against a thoroughly disciplined army of fifteen thousand British and Hessian troops, and fought for the city of Philadelphia as a stake, was lost on the 11th of September.[2] The Congress broke up on the 18th. Sir William Howe took possession of the city on the 26th; and on the 27th, the Congress reassembled at Lancaster. In a few days, they removed to Yorktown, where their sessions continued to be held for several months.

The position in which they found themselves, amid the dark clouds which lowered around their cause, seems to have recalled to their recollection the Articles of Confederation, which had lain slumbering upon their table since the 8th of April. On that day, they had resolved that the report should be

[1] Marshall's Life of Washington, III. 102.

[2] The exact numbers of the troops on both sides, in this battle, are not known. Sir William Howe estimated the American force at 15,000, including militia; and this number is given in the Annual Register. But the effective force of the American army was always, at this period of the war, considerably less than the total number; and Chief Justice Marshall states it to have been, on this occasion, 11,000, including militia. The Annual Register gives the number of the royal army brought into action as 15,000. Marshall supposes it to have been 18,000, when they landed on the shores of the Chesapeake. Marshall's Life of Washington, III. 140, 141. Annual Register for 1777, XX. 127.

taken into consideration on the following Monday, and that two days in each week should be employed on the subject, until it had been wholly discussed. When the Monday came, it was postponed; and it was only after they had been driven from Philadelphia by the approach of the enemy, that they seem to have fully realized the fact, that, without a more perfect union and a more efficient government, the country could not be saved. As soon as they had reassembled at Yorktown, after the urgent business of the moment had been attended to, they passed a resolve, on the 2d of October, that the Articles of Confederation be taken into consideration the next day, at eleven o'clock. The discussion did not actually commence, however, until the 7th of October; but from that day it was continued until the 17th of November, when the Articles, as they afterwards went into operation, were adopted for recommendation to the States, and a circular letter was addressed to the several legislatures, submitting the plan of a confederacy, and urging its adoption.

We are now approaching the period when the American people began to perceive that something more was necessary to their safety and happiness than the formation of State governments; — when they found, or were about to find, that some digested system of national government was essential to the great objects for which they were contending; and that, for the formation of such a government, other arrangements than the varying instructions of different colonies or states to a body of delegates were indispensable. The previous illustrations, drawn from the civil and military history of the country, have been employed to show the character and operation of the revolutionary government, the end of which is drawing near. For we have seen that the great purpose of that government was to secure the independence of each of these separate communities or states from the crown of Great Britain; that it was instituted by political societies having no direct connection with each other except the bond of a common danger and a common object; and that it was formed by no other instrumentality, and possessed no other agency, than a single body of delegates assembled in a congress. For certain great purposes, and in order to accomplish certain objects of common interest, a union of the people of the different States had indeed taken place, bringing them together to act through their representatives; but this union was now failing, from the want of definite powers; from the unwillingness of the people of the country to acquiesce in the exercise of the general revolutionary powers with which it was impliedly clothed; and from the want of suitable civil machinery. In truth, the revolutionary government was breaking down, through its inherent defects, and the peculiar infelicity of its situation. Above all, it was breaking down from the want of a civil executive to take the lead in assuming and exercising the powers implied from the great objects for which it was contending. Its legislative authority, although defined in no written instruments or public charters, was sufficient, under its implied general powers, to have enabled it to issue decrees, directing the execution, by its own agents, of all measures essential to the national safety. But this authority was never exercised, partly because the States were unwilling to execute it, but chiefly because no executive agency existed to represent the continental power, and to enforce its decrees.

It is a singular circumstance, that, while the revolutionary government was left to conduct the great affairs of the continent through the mere instrumentality of a congress of delegates, and was thus failing for the want of departments and powers, the States were engaged in applying those great principles in the organization and construction of popular governments, under which they may be formed with rapidity and ease, and which are capable of the most varied adaptation to the circumstances and wants of a free people.

The suppression of the royal authority throughout the colonies, by virtue of the resolve of the Continental Congress passed on the 10th of May, 1776, rendered necessary the formation of local governments, capable at once of answering the ends of political society, and of continuing without interruption the protection of law over property, life, and public order. Fortunately, as we have seen, the previous constitutions of all the colonies had accustomed the people, to a great extent, to the business of government; and, when the recommendation of the Continental Congress to the several colonies to adopt such governments as would best conduce to their happiness and safety was made immediately after the first effusion of blood, it was addressed to civil societies, in which the people had, in different modes, been long accustomed to witness and to exercise the functions of legislation, and in all of which there were established forms of law, of judicature, and of executive power.

The new political situation in which they now found themselves required, in many of the colonies, but little departure from these ancient institutions. The chief innovation necessary was, to bring into practical working the authority of the people, in place of that of the crown of England, as the source of all political power. The changes requisite to effect this were of course to be made at once; the materials for these changes existed everywhere, in the representative institutions which had been long a part of the system of every colony since the first settlement of the country. Thus, as we have seen, in all the provincial, the proprietary, and the charter governments, the freemen of the colony had been accustomed to be represented in the government, in some form; and although those governments, with a few exceptions, were under the direct or indirect restraint of the crown, and could all be reached and controlled by the exercise of arbitrary power, the practice of representation, through popular elections, was everywhere known and familiar. The old constitutions of some of the colonies had also been highly democratic, admitting an election of the executive, as well as of the legislature, directly by the people;[1] while, in others, where the executive was appointed by the crown, the second or less numerous branch of the legislature had been elected by the people, either directly, or indirectly through the popular assembly. The foundations, therefore, for popular governments existed in all the colonies, and furnished the means for substituting the new source of political power, the will of the people, in the place of that of an external sovereign.

But there were other materials, also, for the formation of regular and balanced governments, with nearer approaches to perfection and with far greater completeness than a mere democracy can afford to any people, however familiar they may be with the exercise and the practice of government. The people of these colonies had been so trained as to be able to apply those principles in the construction and operation of government which enable it to work freely, successfully, and wisely, while resting on a popular basis. They were able to see, that the whole of what is meant and understood by government is comprehended in the existence and due operation of legislative, executive, and judicial powers.[2] They had lived under political arrangements, in which these powers had been distributed so as to keep them for the most part distinct from each other, and so as

[1] Connecticut and Rhode Island.

[2] See John Adams's letter to R. H. Lee.

to mark the proper limitations of each. If, in some instances, the same individuals had exercised more than one of these powers, the distinctions between the departments, and the principles which ought to regulate such distinctions, had become known. The people of the colonies, in general, therefore, saw that nothing was so important, in constructing a government with popular institutions, as to balance each of these departments against the others, so as to leave to neither of them uncontrolled and irresponsible power. In general, too, they understood, and had always been accustomed to the application of that other fundamental principle, essential to a well-regulated liberty, the division of the legislative power between two separate chambers, having distinct origins and of distinct constructions.[1]

[1] Three of the colonies, namely, New Hampshire, South Carolina, and Virginia, proceeded to form constitutions of government before the Declaration of Independence was adopted, under a special recommendation given to each of them by Congress, in the latter part of the year 1775, addressed to the provincial convention, advising them "to call a full and free representation of the people, to establish such a form of government as in their judgment will best promote the happiness of the people, and most effectually secure good order in the province during the continuance of the present dispute between Great Britain and the colonies." (Journals, I. 231, 235, 279.) In New Hampshire, this suggestion was carried out in January, 1776, by the representatives of the people, who had first met as a Provincial Congress of deputies from the towns, and then assumed the name and authority of a "house of representatives," or "assembly" of the Colony; in which capacity they proceeded to elect twelve persons from the several counties, to form a distinct branch of the legislature, as a council. The council were to elect their own presiding officer. All acts and resolves, to be valid, were required to pass both branches; all public officers, except clerks of courts, were to be appointed by the two houses, and all money bills were to originate in the popular

But none of these ideas were applied, or were yet thought of being applied, to the construction of a government for the United States; and it is therefore at this period that we are to observe the slow progress making, through disaster and trial, to those great discoveries which led the way to the Constitution, and that we are to mark the first of those failures by which the people of America learnt the bitter wisdom of experience. For the fate of the revolutionary government presents the first illustration in our history of the complete futility of a federative union, whose operation as a government should

branch. In case the dispute with Great Britain should continue longer than the year 1776, and the general Congress should not give other instructions, it was provided that the council should be chosen by the people of each county, in a mode to be prescribed by the council and house. This form of government continued through the Revolution, and until the year 1790, when a new constitution was formed. (Pitkin's History of the United States, II. 294.) In South Carolina, the Provincial Congress likewise resolved itself a "general assembly," and elected a legislative council, from their own body. By these two bodies, acting jointly, an executive, styled a president, a commander-in-chief, and a vice-president, was chosen. The legislative authority was vested in the president and the two houses. The judiciary were elected by the two houses and commissioned by the president, and were to hold their offices during good behavior, subject to removal on the address of both houses. This form of government remained until June, 1790, when a new constitution was formed by a convention. On the 15th of May, 1776, the Provincial Convention of Virginia proceeded to prepare a declaration of rights and a constitution. The latter declared that the legislative, executive, and judiciary departments ought to be distinct and separate, and divided the legislative department into two branches, the house of delegates and the senate, to be called "the General Assembly of Virginia." The members of the house of delegates were chosen from each county, and one from the city of Williamsburg and one from the borough of Norfolk. The senate consisted of twenty-four members, chosen from as many districts. A governor and

consist merely in agreeing upon measures in a general council, leaving the execution of those measures to the separate members of the confederacy. But this first illustration, we shall soon see, was not sufficient to establish this truth in the convictions of the American people.

Another and a severer trial awaited them. They were not only to be taught once more that a mere federative union was a rope of sand, but they were also to be taught, that a government instituted upon this principle for the purposes of a war, in which the separate members of the confederacy had a common

council of state were chosen annually by joint ballot of both houses. The legislature appointed the judges, who were commissioned by the governor, and held their offices during good behavior. Massachusetts was one of the colonies whose situation rendered it necessary to defer the formation of a constitution for several years. The transition in that colony from the government of the King to a government of the people took place in the latter part of the year 1774 and the beginning of 1775. The occurrences which led the House of Representatives to resolve themselves into a Provincial Congress have been stated in the text of a previous chapter (ante, p. 26). This body, which assumed the control of the affairs of the colony in October, 1774, first assembled at Cambridge, where they continued in session until the 10th of December, and then dissolved themselves, having first appointed a *Committee of Safety* to manage the public concerns, until a new Congress should be assembled. On the 1st of February, 1775, a new Provincial Congress met at Cambridge, adjourned to Concord, and thence to Watertown, and were dissolved on the 23d of May. On the 16th of May, they wrote to the Continental Congress, requesting their advice on "taking up and exercising the powers of civil government." In their letter they said, "As the sword should in all free states be subservient to the civil powers, and as it is the duty of the magistrate to support it for the people's necessary defence, we tremble at having an army, although consisting of our own countrymen, established here, without a civil power to provide for and control them." On the 9th of June, the Continental Congress passed a resolve, recom-

interest, would not answer the exigencies of a country like this, in time of peace. They were to learn, by a trying experience, that the vast concerns of peace are far more complex than the concerns of war; that there were important functions of government to be discharged upon this continent, which only national power and national authority can accomplish, and that those functions are essential, not only to the prosperity and happiness of this nation, but to the continued existence of republican liberty within the States themselves. They were to learn this through a state of things verging upon anarchy; amidst the decay of public virtue; the conflict of sec-

mending the election of a new General Assembly, under the directions of the Provincial Congress, and that the Assembly, when chosen, should exercise the powers of government, until a governor of the King's appointment would consent to govern the Colony according to its charter. (Journals, I. 115.) Meanwhile, a third Provincial Congress met at Watertown, on the 31st of May, and sat until the 19th. The new General Assembly of the Province, called "the General Court," after its ancient usage, met in the mode provided by the charter, and elected a council. These two branches continued to administer the government, as nearly in the spirit of the charter as might be, without a governor, until 1780, when a convention was called and a constitution framed, similar in all its main features to the present constitution of the State. The constitutions of the other States were formed under the general recommendation of the resolve of Congress of May 10th, 1776, addressed to all the colonies, which contemplated the formation of permanent governments, and dissolved the allegiance of the people to the crown of Great Britain. The constitutions of New Jersey, Maryland, Delaware, and North Carolina were formed in 1776, and that of New York in April, 1777; all having three branches, the legislative, the executive, and the judiciary, and all having a legislature consisting of two houses. The constitution of Georgia was formed in 1789, after the same general model. That of Pennsylvania was formed in 1776, with a legislature consisting of a single branch, but with the like division of the legislative, executive, and judicial departments.

tional interests; and the almost total dissolution of the bands by which society is held together. In this state of things was to be at last developed the fundamental idea on which the Constitution of the United States now rests, — the political union of the *people* of the United States, as distinguished from a union of the *States* of which they are citizens.

We have, therefore, now reached the first stage in the constitutional history of the country. What has thus far been stated comes to a single point, the earliest great illustration of the radical defects in a purely federative union. The next stage which succeeds presents the second illustration of this important truth.

CHAPTER V.

NOVEMBER, 1777—MARCH, 1781.

ADOPTION OF THE ARTICLES OF CONFEDERATION.—CESSIONS OF WESTERN TERRITORY.—FIRST POLITICAL UNION OF THE STATES.

WE have now to examine the period which intervened between the recommendation of the Confederation by Congress, in November, 1777, and its final adoption by all the States, in March, 1781;—a period of three years and a half. The causes which protracted the final assent of the States to the new government, and the mode in which the various objections were at length obviated, are among the most important topics in our constitutional history. But, before they are examined, the order of events by which the Confederation finally became obligatory upon all the States should here be stated.

The last clause of the Articles of Confederation directed that they should be submitted to the legislatures of all the States to be considered; and if approved of by them, they were advised to authorize their delegates to ratify the instrument in Congress; upon which ratification, it was to become binding and conclusive. On the 20th of June, 1778, a call was made in Congress for the report of the delegations on the action of their several States, and on the 26th of the same month a form of ratification was adopted for signature. On the 9th of July, the ratification was signed by the delegates of eight States; New Hampshire, Massachusetts, Rhode Island, Connecticut, New York, Pennsylvania, Virginia, and South Carolina. North Carolina ratified the Articles on the 21st of July; Georgia on the 24th; New Jersey on the 26th of November; Delaware on the 5th of May, 1779; Maryland on the 1st of March, 1781. On the 2d of March, 1781, Congress met under the Confederation.

Undoubtedly one of the causes which deferred the full adoption of the Confederation to so late a period after it was proposed, was the absence from Congress of many of the most important and able men, whose attention had hitherto been devoted to the affairs of the continent, but who began to be occupied with local affairs, soon after the extraordinary powers were conferred upon General Washington. In October, 1777, Hancock left the chair of Congress, for an absence of two months; and the votes on a resolution of thanks to him, for his services as presiding officer, show a great paucity of talent in Congress at that moment.[1] Twenty-two members only were pres-

[1] Hancock retired on the 31st of October, for a short absence, after an unremitted service of two years and five months in the chair. A vote of thanks was moved, as soon as he had concluded his address; but before the question was put, it was moved "to resolve as the opinion of Congress, that it is improper to thank

ent, and of these the only names much known to fame, at that time or since, were those of Samuel Adams, John Adams, and Elbridge Gerry of Massachusetts, the two Lees of Virginia, Hayward and Laurens of South Carolina, and Samuel Chase of Maryland. Franklin, Arthur Lee, and Silas Deane were then in France. Patrick Henry was Governor of Virginia. Mr. Jefferson was in the legislature of Virginia, having left Congress in September, in order, as he has himself recorded, to reform the legislation of the State, which, under the royal government, was, he says, full of vicious defects.[1] Mr. Madison was also in the legislature of his native State, a young man of great promise, but unknown at that time as a continental statesman. He entered Congress in March, 1780.

In the year 1778, when the delegations were called upon for reports on the action of their several States upon the Confederation, and when the first objections to the Articles were to be encountered, Hancock had returned to Congress. Samuel Adams and Elbridge Gerry were among his colleagues from Massachusetts. Mr. John Adams was in Europe, as Commissioner of the United States to the Court of France. Dr. Franklin was still abroad. Richard Henry Lee of Virginia, Mr. Laurens and Mr. Hayward of South Carolina, Roger Sherman, Samuel Huntington, and Oliver

any president for the discharge of the duties of that office"; and it is a curious fact, that on this motion the States were equally divided. The previous motion was then put, and five States voted in the affirmative, three in the negative, and the delegation of one State was divided. Journals, III. 465–467

[1] Writings of Jefferson, I. 29.

Wolcott of Connecticut, and Robert Morris of Pennsylvania, were present. The rest of the members, with one brilliant exception, were not men of great distinction, influence, or capacity. That exception was Gouverneur Morris, who came into Congress in January of this year, with a somewhat remarkable youthful reputation, acquired in the public councils of New York.

When this Congress is compared with that of the year 1776, and it is remembered that the Declaration of Independence bears the names of John Adams and Robert Treat Paine of Massachusetts, Francis Hopkinson of New Jersey, Benjamin Rush and Dr. Franklin of Pennsylvania, Cæsar Rodney of Delaware, Samuel Chase of Maryland, George Wythe, Thomas Jefferson, and Benjamin Harrison of Virginia, William Hooper of North Carolina, and Edward Rutledge and Arthur Middleton of South Carolina, — none of whom were now present, — we perceive at once a striking difference in the two bodies. This difference was not unobserved by those who were then deeply interested in watching the course of public affairs. More than once it filled Washington with dark forebodings;[1] and in the early part of the year 1778, it had attracted the notice of Hamilton, whose vigilant comprehension surveyed the whole field of public affairs, and detected the causes of every danger that threatened the health of the body politic.[2]

1 Writings of Washington, V. 326, 327, 350.

2 "America once had a representation that would do honor to

The objections made by the legislatures of several of the States to the Articles of Confederation were found, when examined, to consist almost entirely of propositions for mere verbal amendments, chiefly for the purpose of rendering the instrument more clear. All of these amendments were rejected. Some of the

any age or nation. The present falling off is very alarming and dangerous. What is the cause? and How is it to be remedied? are questions that the welfare of these States requires should be well attended to. The great men who composed our first council, — are they dead, have they deserted the cause, or what has become of them? Very few are dead, and still fewer have deserted the cause: they are all, except the few who still remain in Congress, either in the field, or in the civil offices of their respective States; far the greater part are engaged in the latter. The only remedy, then, is to take them out of these employments, and return them to the places where their presence is infinitely more important. Each State, in order to promote its own internal government and prosperity, has selected its best members to fill the offices within itself, and conduct its own affairs. Men have been fonder of the emoluments and conveniences of being employed at home; and local attachment, falsely operating, has made them more provident for the particular interests of the States to which they belonged, than for the common interests of the Confederacy. This is a most pernicious mistake, and must be corrected. However important it is to give form and efficiency to your interior constitutions and police, it is infinitely more important to have a wise general council; otherwise, a failure of the measures of the Union will overturn all your labors for the advancement of your particular good, and ruin the common cause. You should not beggar the councils of the United States to enrich the administration of the several members. Realize to yourself the consequences of having a Congress despised at home and abroad. How can the common force be exerted, if the power of collecting it be put in weak, foolish, and unsteady hands? How can we hope for success in our European negotiations, if the nations of Europe have no confidence in the wisdom and vigor of the great continental government? This is the object on which their eyes are fixed; hence it is, America will derive its importance or insignificance in their estimation." Letter by Hamilton to George Clinton, written from the head-quarters of the army, February 13, 1778. Writings of Washington, V. 508.

States objected to the rule for apportioning the taxes and forces to be raised by the States for the service of the Union; but Congress rejected every proposition to alter it, as it was believed to be impossible that any other rule should be agreed upon.

But there was an objection made by the State of New Jersey, which should be particularly noticed here, because it foreshadowed the great idea which the Constitution of the United States afterwards embodied. This objection was, that the Articles of Confederation contained no provision by which the foreign trade of the country would be placed under the regulation of Congress. The sixth of the Articles of Confederation declared, that no State should levy any imposts or duties, which might interfere with any stipulations entered into by the United States with any foreign power pursuant to the treaties already proposed to the courts of France and Spain; while the ninth article declared that no treaty of commerce should be made by the United States, whereby the legislative power of the respective States should be restrained from imposing such imposts and duties on foreigners as their own people were subjected to, or from prohibiting the exportation or importation of any species of goods or commodities whatsoever. The effect of these provisions was simply to restrain the States from laying imposts which would interfere with the then proposed treaties; in all other respects, the foreign trade of each State was left to be regulated by State legislation.

The legislature of New Jersey, in a very able memorial, laid before Congress on the 25th of June, 1778, declared that the sole and exclusive power of regulating the trade of the United States with foreign nations ought to be clearly vested in the Congress, and that the revenue arising from duties and customs ought to be appropriated to the building and support of a navy for the protection of trade and the defence of the coasts, and to other public and general purposes, for the common benefit of the States. They suggested that a great security would be derived to the Union, from such an establishment of a common and mutual interest.[1] But this suggestion was both premature and tardy. It was premature, because the States had not yet learned that their control over foreign commerce must be surrendered, if they would avoid the evils of perpetual conflict with each other; and it came too late, because the Articles of Confederation were practically incapable of

[1] Journals, IV. 269, 270. This wise and well-considered document contained many other very important suggestions; among which was that of an oath, test, or declaration to be taken by the delegates in Congress, previous to their admission to their seats. "It is indeed to be presumed," said the memorial, "that the respective States will be careful that the delegates they send to assist in managing the general interests of the Union, take the oaths to the government from which they derive their authority: but as the United States, collectively considered, have interests as well as each particular State, we are of opinion, that some test or obligation, binding upon each delegate while he continues in the trust, to consult and pursue the former as well as the latter, and particularly to assent to no vote or proceeding which may violate the general confederation, is necessary. The laws and usages of all civilized nations evince the propriety of an oath on such occasions, and the more solemn and important the deposit, the more strong and explicit ought the obligation to be."

amendment, at the period when the suggestion was made.[1]

The great obstacle, however, to the adoption of the Confederation, which delayed the assent of several of the smaller States for so long a period, was the claim of some of the larger States to the vacant lands lying within what they considered their rightful boundaries. The boundaries of the great States, as fixed by their charters derived from the crown of England, extended, in terms, "to the South Sea," and each of these States, as successor, by the Revolution, to the crown, with regard to territorial sovereignty, claimed to own both the jurisdiction and the property of all the crown lands within its limits. This claim was strenuously resisted by Rhode Island, Delaware, New Jersey, and Maryland. They insisted that Congress ought to have the right to fix the boundaries of the States whose charters stretched to such an indefinite extent into the Western wilderness, and that the unoccupied lands ought to be the property of the whole Union; since, if the independence of the country should be finally established, those lands would have been conquered from the crown of England by the common blood and treasure of all the States. The effect of a tacit recognition of the claims of the great States upon the welfare of such a State as Maryland, through the absence from the Articles of Confedera-

[1] Three States only voted in favor of adopting any of the suggestions made by New Jersey: six voted against them, and one was divided. Journals, IV. 272.

tion of any provision on the subject, was strikingly exhibited, by its legislature, in certain instructions to their delegates in Congress, which were laid before that body on the 21st of May, 1779. They pointed out two consequences likely to result from a confirmation of the claim which Virginia had set up to an extensive and fertile country; the one would be, they said, directly injurious to Maryland, while the other would be inconsistent with the letter and spirit of the proposed Confederation. They supposed, on the one hand, that a sale by Virginia of only a small proportion of these lands would draw into her treasury vast sums of money, enabling her to lessen her taxes, and thereby to drain the less wealthy neighboring State of its most useful inhabitants, which would cause it to sink, in wealth and consequence, in the scale of the confederated States. On the other hand, they suggested that Virginia might, and probably would, be obliged to divide its territory, and to erect a new State, under the auspices and direction of the elder, from whom it would receive its form of government, to whom it would be bound by some alliance, and by whose counsels it would be influenced. They declared that, if this were to take place, it would be inconsistent with the letter and spirit of the Confederation already proposed; that, if it were to result in the establishment of a sub-confederacy, an *imperium in imperio*, the State possessed of this extensive dominion must then either submit to all the inconveniences of an overgrown and unwieldy government, or suffer the authority of Congress to interpose at a future time, and lop off a part of its territory to be erected into a new and free state, and admitted into a confederation on such conditions as should be settled by nine States. If, they asked, it should be necessary for the happiness and tranquillity of a State thus overgrown, that Congress should, at some future time, interfere and divide its territory, why should the claim to that territory be now made and insisted upon? Policy and justice, they urged, alike required, that a country, — unsettled at the commencement of the war, claimed by the British crown and ceded to it by the treaty of Paris, — if wrested from the common enemy by the blood and treasure of the thirteen States, should be considered as a common property, subject to be parcelled out by Congress into free, convenient, and independent governments, in such manner and at such times as their wisdom might thereafter direct. Coolly and dispassionately considering the subject, weighing probable inconveniences and hardships against the sacrifice of just and essential rights, they then instructed their delegates to withhold the assent of Maryland to the Confederation, until an article or articles could be obtained in conformity with these views.[1]

Against this proposition, the State of Virginia, which had already ratified the Articles of Confederation, so remonstrated, that there appeared to be no prospect of reconciling the difficulty. At this juncture the State of New York came forward, and by an

[1] Secret Journals, I. 433.

act of its legislature, passed on the 19th of February, 1780, authorized its delegates in Congress to limit the western boundaries of the State, and ceded a portion of its public lands for the use and benefit of such of the United States as should become members of the federal alliance. The motives upon which this concession was expressly made had reference to the formation of the Union, by removing, as far as depended upon the State of New York, the impediment which had so long prevented it.[1]

After they had received official notice of this act, by a report made on the 6th of September, 1780, Congress pressed upon the other States, similarly situated, the policy of a liberal surrender of a portion of their territorial claims, as they could not be preserved entire without endangering the stability of the general confederacy; — reminding them how indispensably necessary it was to establish the Federal Union on a fixed and permanent basis, and on principles acceptable to all its respective members, — how essential it was to public credit and confidence, to the support of the army, to the vigor of the national councils, to tranquillity at home, to reputation abroad, and to the very existence of the people of America as a free, sovereign, and independent people. At the same time, they earnestly requested the legislature of the State of Maryland to accede to the Confederation.[2]

That State was not without examples of patriotic confidence among her smaller sister States. As

[1] Secret Journals, I. 440. [2] Ibid. 442.

early as the 20th of November, 1778, New Jersey had led the way to a generous trust on the part of the States which still remained out of the Union. She declared that the Articles of Confederation were in divers respects unequal and disadvantageous to her, and that her objections were of essential moment to the welfare and happiness of her people; yet, convinced of the present necessity of acceding to the confederacy proposed, feeling that every separate and detached interest ought to be postponed to the general good of the Union, and firmly believing that the candor and justice of the several States would, in due time, remove the inequality of which she complained, she authorized her delegates to accede to the Confederation.[1]

Delaware followed with not unequal steps. On the 1st of February, 1779, she declared that, although she was justly entitled to a right, in common with the other members of the Union, to that extensive tract of country lying to the westward of the frontiers of the United States, gained by the blood and treasure of all, and therefore proper to become a common estate, to be granted out on terms beneficial to all; yet, for the same reasons, and from the same motives with those announced by New Jersey, and with a like faith in the sense of justice of her great confederates, she ratified the Articles of Confederation.[2]

These examples were not without influence upon

[1] Secret Journals, I. 421. [2] Ibid. 424.

the councils of patriotic Maryland. On the 30th of January, 1781, her legislature passed an act, the preamble of which commences with these memorable words: "Whereas it hath been said, that the common enemy is encouraged, by this State not acceding to the Confederation, to hope that the union of the sister States may be dissolved; and they therefore prosecute the war in expectation of an event so disgraceful to America; and our friends and illustrious ally are impressed with an idea, that the common cause would be promoted by our formally acceding to the Confederation: This General Assembly, conscious that this State hath, from the commencement of the war, strenuously exerted herself in the common cause, and fully satisfied that, if no formal confederation were to take place, it is the fixed determination of this State to continue her exertions to the utmost, agreeable to the faith pledged in the Union; — from an earnest desire to conciliate the affection of the sister States, to convince all the world of our unalterable resolution to support the independence of the United States, and the alliance with his most Christian Majesty, and to destroy for ever any apprehension of our friends, or hope in our enemies, of this State being again united to Great Britain; — Be it enacted," &c. The act then proceeded to adopt and ratify the Articles of Confederation, relying on the justice of the other States to secure the interests of the whole in the unoccupied Western territory.[1]

[1] Secret Journals, I. 445.

As soon as this act of Maryland was laid before Congress, the joyful news was announced to the country, that the Union of the States was consummated under the written instrument, which had been so long projected. The same month which saw the completion of this Union witnessed a cession by Virginia to the United States of all her claims to lands northwest of the river Ohio; but the cession was not finally completed and accepted until the month of March, 1784. This vast territory, now the seat of prosperous and powerful States, came into the possession of the United States, under a provision made by Congress, that such lands should be disposed of for the common benefit of the United States, and should be settled and formed into distinct republican States, to become members of the Federal Union, with the same rights of sovereignty, freedom, and independence as the other States.

The historian who may, in any generation, record these noble acts of patriotism and concession, should pause and contemplate the magnitude of the event with which they were connected. He should pause, to render honor to the illustrious deeds of that great community, which first generously withdrew the impediment of its territorial claims; and to the no less gallant confidence of those smaller States, which trusted to the future for the final and complete removal of the inequality of which they complained. He should render honor to the State of New York, for the surrender of a territory to which she believed her legal title to be complete;

a title which nothing but the paramount equity of the claims of the whole Confederacy ought to have overcome. That equity she acknowledged. She threw aside her charters and her title-deeds; she ceased to use the language of royal grants, and discarded the principle of succession. She came forth from among her parchments into the forum of conscience, in presence of the whole American people; and — recognizing the justice of their claim to territories gained by their common efforts — to secure the inestimable blessings of union, for their good and for her own, she submitted to the national will the determination of her western boundaries, and devoted to the national benefit her vast claims to unoccupied territories.

Equal honor should be rendered to New Jersey, to Delaware, and to Maryland. The two former, without waiting for the action of a single State within whose reputed limits these public domains were situate, trusted wholly to a future sense of justice, and ratified the Union in the confidence that justice would be done. The latter waited; but only until she saw that the common enemy was encouraged, and that friends were disheartened, by her reserve. Seeing this, she hesitated no longer, but completed the union of the States before Virginia had made the cession, which afterwards so nobly justified the confidence that had been placed in her.[1]

[1] After the Confederation had thus been formed, by subsequent cessions of their claims by the other States, to use the language of Mr. Justice Story, "this great source of national dissension was at last dried up."

The student of American constitutional history, therefore, cannot fail to see, that the adoption of the first written constitution was accomplished through great and magnanimous sacrifices. The very foundations of the structure of government since raised rest upon splendid concessions for the common weal, made, it is true, under the stern pressure of war, but made from the noblest motives of patriotism. These concessions evince, the progress which the people of the United States were then making towards both a national character and a national feeling. They show that, while there were causes which tended to keep the States apart, — the formation of State constitutions, the conflicting interests growing out of the inequalities of these different communities, and the previous want of a national legislative power, — there were still other causes at work, which tended to draw together the apparently discordant elements, and to create a union in which should be bound together, as one nation, the populations which had hitherto known only institutions of a local character. The time was indeed not come, when these latter tendencies could entirely overcome the former. It was not until the trials of peace had tested the strength and efficiency of a system formed under the trials of war, — when another and a severer conflict between national and local interests was to shake the republic to its centre, — that a national government could be formed, adequate to all the exigencies of both. Still, the year 1781 saw the establishment of the Confederation, caused by the necessities of military defence against an invading enemy. But it was accomplished only through the sacrifice of great claims; and the fact that it was accomplished, and that it led the way to our present Constitution, proves at once the wisdom and the patriotism of those who labored for it.

The great office of the Confederation, in our political history, will be a proper topic for consideration, after the analysis of its provisions. But we should not omit to observe here, that, when the union of the States was thus secured, the motives on which it was formed, and the concessions by which it was accompanied and followed, created a vast obstacle to any future dissolution. The immediate object of each State was to obtain its own independence of the crown of Great Britain, through the united, and therefore more powerful, action of all the States. But, in order to effect such a union, that immense territory, over which, in the language of Maryland, "free, convenient, and independent governments" were afterwards to be formed, was to be ceded in advance, or to be impliedly promised to be ceded, to the use and benefit of the whole confederacy. A confederacy of states, which had become possessed of such a common property, was thus bound together by an interest, the magnitude and force of which cannot now be easily estimated. The Union might incur fresh dangers of dissolution, after the war had ceased; its frame of government and its legislative power might prove wholly inadequate to the national wants in time of peace; the public faith might be prostrated, and the national arm enfeebled; — still, while the Confederacy stood as the great trustee of property large enough for the accommodation of an empire, a security existed against its total destruction. No State could withdraw from the Confederation, without forfeiting its interest in this grand public domain; and no human wisdom could devise a satisfactory distribution of property, ceded as a common fund for the common benefit of sovereign States, without any fixed ratio of interest in the respective beneficiaries, and without any clear power in the government of the Confederation to deal with the trust itself.[1]

[1] One of the great inducements to the adoption of the Constitution of the United States was to give the general government adequate constitutional power to dispose of the Western territory and to form new States out of it. Congress, under the Confederation, had no express authority to do this, although they proceeded both to dispose of the lands and to erect new States, by the Ordinance of 1787. See The Federalist, No. 38, 42, 43. Story's Commentaries on the Constitution, III. 184 – 190, 1st edition.

CHAPTER VI.

Nature and Powers of the Confederation.

The nature of the government established by the Articles of Confederation can be understood only by an analysis of their provisions. For this purpose, the instrument must here be examined with reference to three principal topics: first, the union which it established between the different members of the Confederacy; second, the form of the government which it created; and third, the powers which it conferred, or omitted to confer, upon that government.

I. The parties to this instrument were free, sovereign, and independent political communities, — each possessing within itself all the powers of legislation and government, over its own citizens, which any political society can possess. But, by this instrument, these several States became united together for certain purposes. The instrument was styled, "Articles of Confederation and Perpetual Union between the States," and the political body thus formed was entitled "The United States of America." The Articles declared — as would, indeed, be implied, in such circumstances, without any express declaration —

that each State retained its sovereignty, freedom, and independence, and every power, jurisdiction, and right not expressly delegated by the instrument itself to the United States in Congress assembled. The nature and objects of this union were described as a firm league of friendship between the States, for their common defence, the security of their liberties, and their mutual and general welfare; and the parties bound themselves to assist each other against all force offered to or attacks made upon them, or any of them, on account of religion, sovereignty, trade, or under any pretence whatever.

It was also provided, that the free inhabitants of each State should be entitled to all the privileges of free citizens in the several States;[1] that there should be an open intercourse and commerce between the different States; that fugitives from justice from one State to another should be delivered up; and that full faith and credit should be given in each State to the records, acts, and judicial proceedings of every other State.[2]

II. The government established by the Articles of Confederation consisted of a single representative

[1] That is to say, that a citizen of any State might go and reside in any other State, and be there entitled to all the privileges of a citizen of that State.

[2] The meaning of this is, that, on the production in any State of a law passed or of a judgment rendered in any other State, properly authenticated, it should be admitted that such a law had been passed or such a judgment rendered in the State whose act it purported to be, and that all the legal consequences should follow.

body, called a General Congress. In this body were vested all the powers, executive, legislative, and judicial, granted to the United States. The members of it were to be chosen by the States, in such manner as the legislature of each State might determine; no State to be represented by more than seven delegates, or by less than two. No delegate was eligible for more than three years in a period of six; and no delegate could hold any office of emolument under the United States. Each State was to maintain its own delegates, and in the determination of questions, the voting was to be by States, each State having one vote.

III. It should be remembered, that the objects and purposes of the Confederation related chiefly to the defence of the States against external attacks; and it was, therefore, as it purported to be, a league for mutual defence and protection, through the combined powers of the whole, operating in certain forms and under certain restrictions. For the manner in which this new authority was to be exercised, we are to look at the powers conferred upon "the United States in Congress assembled." These powers related to external and to internal affairs.

With regard to the external relations of the country, Congress was invested with the sole and exclusive right of determining on peace and war, unless in case of an invasion of a State by enemies, or an imminent danger of invasion by Indians; of sending and receiving ambassadors; of entering into treaties and alliances, under the limitation that no treaty of commerce could be made, which would have the effect to restrain the legislature of any State from imposing such imposts and duties on foreigners as their own people were subjected to, or which would operate to prohibit the exportation or importation of any commodity whatever. Congress was also invested with power to deal with all captures and prizes made by the land or naval forces of the United States; to grant letters of marque and reprisal in times of peace; and to establish courts for the trial of piracies and felonies committed on the high seas, and for determining appeals in cases of capture.

With regard to internal affairs, Congress was invested with power to decide, in the last resort, on appeal, all disputes between two or more States, concerning boundary, jurisdiction, or any other cause; and also all controversies concerning land-titles, where the parties claimed under different grants of two or more States before the settlement of their jurisdiction; but no State was to be deprived of territory for the benefit of the United States. Congress was also invested with the sole and exclusive right and power of regulating the alloy and value of coin struck by their authority, or by that of any of the United States; of fixing the standard of weights and measures throughout the United States; of regulating the trade and managing all affairs with the Indians, who were not members of any State, provided that the legislative authority of any State, within its own limits, should not be infringed or violated;

of establishing and regulating post-offices from one State to another, and exacting postage to defray the expenses; of appointing all officers of the land forces in the service of the United States, and of making rules for the government and regulation of the land and naval forces, and directing their operations.

Congress was also invested with power to appoint a "committee of the States," to sit in the recess of Congress, to consist of one delegate from each State, and other committees and civil officers, to manage the general affairs under their direction; to appoint one of their number to preside, but authorizing no person to serve in the office of president more than one year in a term of three years; to ascertain and appropriate the necessary sums for the public service; to borrow money and emit bills on the credit of the United States; to build and equip a navy; and to agree upon the number of land forces and make requisitions upon each State for its quota, in proportion to the numbers of white inhabitants in such State. The legislature of each State was to appoint the regimental officers, enlist the men, and clothe, arm, and equip them, at the expense of the United States.

Such were the powers conferred upon Congress by the Articles of Confederation. But the restrictions imposed, in the same instrument, greatly qualified and weakened, and in fact almost rendered nugatory, the greater part of them. It was expressly provided, that Congress should never engage in a war; nor grant letters of marque or reprisal in time of peace;

nor enter into any treaties or alliances; nor coin money or regulate its value; nor ascertain the sums of money necessary for the public purposes; nor emit bills; nor borrow money on the credit of the United States; nor appropriate money; nor agree upon the number of vessels for the navy, or the number of land or sea forces to be raised; nor appoint a commander-in-chief of the army or navy; — unless nine States should assent to the same. The Committee of the States authorized to sit during the recess of Congress could not do any of these things, for the assent of nine States could not be delegated.

The revenues of the country were left by the Articles of Confederation wholly in the control of the separate States. It was provided, that all charges of war, and all other expenses for the common defence or general welfare, should be defrayed out of a common treasury; but this treasury was to be supplied, not by taxes, duties, or imposts, levied by or under the authority of Congress, but by taxes to be laid and levied by the legislatures of the several States, within such time as might be fixed by Congress. The amount to be furnished by each State was in proportion to the value of the land within its limits granted or surveyed, and the buildings and improvements thereon, to be estimated according to the mode prescribed by Congress. The sole means, therefore, which the Confederation gave to Congress of supplying the treasury of the United States, was to vote what sum was wanted, and to call upon the legislature of each State to pay in its proportion within a given time. The commerce of the country was left entirely within the control of the State legislatures; rendering it the commerce of thirteen different States, each of which could levy what duties it saw fit upon all exports and imports, provided they did not interfere with any treaties then proposed, or touch the property of the United States, or that of any other State. The United States had no power of taxation, direct or indirect.

The Articles of Confederation were also entirely without any provision for enforcing the measures which they authorized Congress to adopt for the general welfare of the Union. It was declared in the instrument, that every State should abide by the determinations of Congress on all the questions over which the instrument gave that body control; that the Articles should be inviolably observed by every State; that the Union should be perpetual; and that no alterations should be made in any of the Articles, unless agreed to by Congress, and confirmed by the legislature of every State. But these declarations, however strong and emphatic in their terms, only made the Confederation in fact, as in name, a league or compact between sovereign States; for it gave the government of the Union no power to enforce its own measures or laws by process upon the persons of individuals, and consequently any party to the instrument could infringe any or all of its provisions, without any other consequence than a resort to arms by the general Confederacy, which would have been civil war.

These, with some restrictions upon the power of the States in regard to the making of treaties, engaging in war, sending ambassadors, and some other topics, were the main provisions of the Articles of Confederation; and under the government thus constituted, the United States, on the second day of March, 1781, entered upon a new era of civil polity, and commenced a new existence, under somewhat happier auspices than they had known before.

It will be seen, in the further development of the period which followed the establishment of this Confederation, down to the calling of the Convention which framed the Constitution, that what I have called the great office of the Confederation, in our political system, was indeed a function of vast importance to the happiness of the American people, but, at the same time, was one that was necessarily soon fulfilled, to be followed by a more perfect organization for the accomplishment of the objects and the satisfaction of the wants which it brought in its train. This office of the Confederation was, to demonstrate to the people of the American States the practicability and necessity of a more perfect union. The Confederation showed to the people of these separate communities, that there were certain great purposes of civil government, which they could not discharge by their separate means; that independence of the crown of Great Britain could not be achieved by any one of them, unassisted by all the rest; that no one of them, however respectable in population or resources, could be received and dealt with, by the governments of the world, as a nation among nations; — but that, by union among themselves, by some political tie, which should combine all their resources in the hands of one directing power, and make them, in some practical sense, one people, it was possible for them to achieve their independence, and take a place among the nations. The Confederation made it manifest, that these consequences could be secured. It did not, indeed, answer all the purposes, or accomplish all the objects, which had been designed or hoped from it: it was defective as a means; but it taught the existence of an end, and demonstrated the possibility of reaching that end, by showing that in some form, and for some purposes, a union of the States was both possible and necessary. It thus made the permanent idea of union familiar to the people of the different States. It did more than this. It created a larger field for statesmanship, by creating larger interests, to be managed by that higher order of men, who could rise above local concerns and sectional objects, and embrace within the scope of their vision the happiness and welfare of a continent. It introduced to men's minds the great ideas of national power and national sovereignty, as the agencies that were to work out the difficult results, which no local power could accomplish; and, although these ideas were at first vague and indefinite, and made but a slow and difficult progress against influences and prejudices of a narrower kind, they were planted in the thoughts of men, to ripen into maturity and strength in the progress of future years. When the eagle grasped in his talons the united shafts of power, and unfurled the scroll which taught that one people could be formed out of many communities, the destiny of America was ascertained.[1]

[1] The armorial bearings of the United States were adopted on the 20th of June, 1782. Journals, VII. 395.

BOOK II.

THE CONSTITUTIONAL HISTORY OF THE UNITED STATES, FROM THE ADOPTION OF THE ARTICLES OF CONFEDERATION, IN 1781, TO THE PEACE OF 1783.

CHAPTER I.

1781-1783.

Requisitions. — Claims of the Army. — Newburgh Addresses. — Peace proclaimed. — The Army disbanded.

The interval of time which extends from the adoption of the Articles of Confederation to the initiatory steps for the formation of the Constitution, must, for our purpose, be divided into two periods; that which preceded and that which followed the peace of 1783; in both of which the defects of the Confederation were rapidly developed, and in both of which efforts were made to supply those defects, by an enlargement of the powers of Congress. Our attention, however, will be confined, in the present Book, to the first of these periods.

Congress assembled, under the Confederation, on the 2d of March, 1781, and the Treaty of Peace, which put an end to the war and admitted the independence of the United States, was definitively signed on the 3d of September, 1783, and was ratified and proclaimed by Congress on the 14th of January, 1784.

Notwithstanding the solemn engagements into which the States had entered with each other, under the Articles of Confederation, the prospect of bringing the war to a close, through a compliance with those obligations, was exceedingly faint, at the commencement of the campaign of 1782. The United States had made a treaty of alliance with the king of France, in 1778;[1] and in pursuance of that treaty, six thousand French troops arrived at Newport in July, 1780, and in the spring of 1781 joined the American army near New York. The presence in the country of a foreign force, sent hither by the ancient rival of England, to assist the people of the United States in their contest for independence, encouraged an undue reliance upon external aid. Many of the States became culpably remiss in complying with the requisitions of Congress; and, although they had so recently authorized Congress to make requisitions, both for men and money, and had provided the form in which they were to be made, the adoption of the Articles of Confederation had very little tendency to render the States prompt to discharge the obligations which they imposed. In October and November, 1781, Congress called upon the States to raise their several quotas of eight millions of dollars, for the use of the United States, and recommended to them to lay taxes for raising these quotas separate from those laid for their own particular use, and to pass acts directing the collectors of the taxes, intended for the use of the United States, to pay the same directly into the treasury of the

[1] The treaty was concluded at Paris, February 6, 1778, and was ratified by Congress on the 5th of May. Journals, IV. 256, 257.

Union.[1] In December of the same year, Congress also called upon the States, with great urgency, to complete their quotas of troops for the next campaign.[2]

The aid of Washington was invoked, to influence the action of the States upon these requisitions. On the 22d of January, 1782, he addressed a circular letter to the governors of the States, to be laid before their respective legislatures, on the subject of finance; reminding them how the whole army had been thrown into a ferment twelve months before, for the want of pay and a regular supply of clothing and provisions; warning them that the recent successes in Virginia, by the capture of Lord Cornwallis's army, might have a fatal tendency to cool the ardor of the country in the prosecution of the war; assuring them that a vigorous prosecution of that war could alone secure the independence of the United States; and urging them to adopt such measures as would insure the prompt payment of the sums which Congress had called for.[3] A few days afterwards, he addressed a similar letter to the States, on the subject of completing their quotas of troops, in which he told them that the continuance or termination of the war now rested on their vigor and decision; and that, even if the enemy were, in consequence of their late reverses, disposed to treat, nothing but a decidedly superior force could enable us boldly to claim our

1 Resolves of October 30 and November 2, 1781. Journals, VII. 167, 169.

2 Resolves of December 10, 1781. Journals, VII. 190.

3 Writings, VIII. 226.

rights and dictate the terms of pacification. "And soon," he said, "might that day arrive, and we might hope to enjoy all the blessings of peace, if we could see again the same animation in the cause of our country inspiring every breast, the same passion for freedom and military glory impelling our youths to the field, and the same disinterested patriotism pervading every rank of men, that was conspicuous at the commencement of this glorious revolution; and I am persuaded that only some great occasion was wanting, such as the present moment exhibits, to rekindle the latent sparks of that patriotic fire into a generous flame, to rouse again the unconquerable spirit of liberty, which has sometimes seemed to slumber for a while, into the full vigor of action."[1]

Notwithstanding these urgent appeals, the spring of 1782 arrived, and the summer passed away, without any substantial compliance by the States with the requisitions of Congress for either men or money. When Washington arrived in camp, in May, to commence the campaign that was to extort from the British government — now in the hands of a new ministry, supposed to be more favorable to peace — the terms which he hoped might be procured, there were less than ten thousand men in the Northern army; and their numbers were not much increased during the summer.[2] Great and dangerous discontents now existed in the army, both among officers

[1] Writings, VIII. 232, 235.

[2] Sparks's Life of Washington, p. 380.

and soldiers, concerning the arrearages of pay; for, as the prospects of peace became brighter, it seemed to become more and more probable, that the army would ultimately be disbanded without adequate provision for its claims, and that officers and men would be thrown penniless upon the world, unpaid by the country whose independence they had achieved.

At this period there occurred the famous proceedings of the officers, called the Newburgh Addresses, on the subject of half-pay; and since the claims of the officers and soldiers, as public creditors of the United States, are intimately connected with the constitutional history of the country, it is needful to give here a brief account of them.

The pay of the officers in the Revolutionary army was originally established upon so low a scale, that men with families dependent upon them could feel little inducement to remain long in a service, the close of which was to be rewarded only with a patent for a few hundred acres of land in some part of the Western wilderness. In the year 1778, it had become apparent to Washington, that something must be done to avert the consequences of the mistaken policy on which Congress had acted with reference to the army; and while at Valley Forge, — that scene of dreadful suffering by the army, — he wrote on this subject to the President of Congress the first of a series of most able and instructive letters, which extend through the five following years.[1]

[1] Letter of April 10, 1778. Writings of Washington, V. 312.

On the 17th of April, after this first letter had been laid before Congress, a resolution was moved, that an establishment of half-pay be made for officers, who should serve during the war; to begin after its conclusion.[1] Four days afterwards, the sense of the house was taken on the question, whether there should be any provision made for the officers after the conclusion of the war, and the affirmative was carried, by the votes of eight States against four.[2] On the 26th of April, a proposition, that half-pay be granted for life, to commence at the close of the war, passed by a majority of one State; six States voting in the affirmative, five in the negative, and one being divided.[3] The next day, the value of this vote was destroyed by a resolution, which provided that the United States should have the right to redeem the half-pay for life, by giving to the officer entitled six years' half-pay;[4] and on the 15th of May, Congress substituted for the whole scheme a provision of half-pay for seven years, taking away the option of half-pay for life.[5]

This miserable and vacillating legislation shows the unpopularity of the scheme of such an establishment, although demanded alike by considerations of

[1] Journals, IV. 221.

[2] Ibid. 228, 229. The States which voted in the negative were Rhode Island, Connecticut, New Jersey, and South Carolina.

[3] Ibid. 243. The States voting in the negative were Massachusetts, Rhode Island, Connecticut, New Jersey, and South Carolina. The State whose vote was divided was Pennsylvania.

[4] Ibid. 244. Under this resolve, each officer was entitled to receive half-pay annually, for the term of seven years after the conclusion of war, if living.

[5] Ibid. 288.

justice and policy.[1] The spirit which, for a time, actuated a large part of the people of this country towards the men who were suffering so much in the cause of national independence, evinces an extreme jealousy for the abstract principles of civil liberty, unmitigated by the generous virtues of justice and gratitude. This spirit was duly represented in Congress. The main arguments employed out of doors were, that pensions were contrary to the maxims and spirit of our institutions; that to grant half-pay for life to the officers was establishing a privileged class of men, who were to live upon the public for the rest of their days; and that the officers entered the service on the pay and inducements originally offered, without any promise or prospect of such a reward. This kind of impracticable adherence to a principle, working in this instance the greatest injustice and leading ultimately to a breach of public faith, was the principal cause that prolonged the war, and made it cost so much suffering, so much blood, and so much treasure. The people of the United States adhered so tenaciously to the principles and axioms of freedom, that, even when they had undertaken a war for their own security and independence against a foreign foe, they would not establish a government with the power of direct taxation, or organ-

[1] On the 21st of April, in the resolution reported by a committee, the words "an establishment of half-pay for life" were, on motion, changed to "a provision of half-pay"; — an amendment which reveals very plainly the character of the popular objections. Journals, IV. 228.

ize an army with suitable rewards for service. The want of such a power in their government led to the enormous emissions of paper money, which brought with them a long train of sufferings and disasters, ending at last in national bankruptcy. The want of justice to the army placed the civil liberty of the country in imminent danger, and finally led to the cruel oppression of men, whose valor had first won, and whose patriotism then saved it from destruction.

In the six months which followed the vote of the 15th of May, 1778, the provision which it had made was found to be wholly inadequate, and General Washington, then at Philadelphia, again earnestly pressed the subject upon the attention of Congress. On the 11th of August, 1779, a report from a committee on this subject being under consideration, a motion was made to amend it, by inserting a provision that the half-pay granted by the resolve of the 15th of May, 1778, be extended so as to continue for life; and this motion was carried by a vote of eight States against four.[1] On the 17th, Congress resolved that the consideration of that part of the report for extending the half-pay be postponed, and that it be recommended to the several States that had not already adopted measures for that purpose, to make such further provision for the officers and soldiers enlisted for the war, who should continue in service till the establishment of peace, as would be an adequate compensation for their dangers, losses, and hardships, either

[1] Journals, V. 312.

by granting to the officers half-pay for life and proper rewards to the soldiers, or in such other manner as might appear most expedient to the legislatures of the several States.[1]

Before the passage of this resolve, the State of Pennsylvania had placed her officers upon an establishment of half-pay for life, and with the happiest consequences. But no other State followed her example; and in the autumn of 1780, it became necessary for Washington to apply to Congress again.[2] At length, in consequence of his earnest and repeated appeals, a resolve was passed, on the 21st of October, that the officers who should continue in service to the end of the war should be entitled to half-pay during life, to commence from the time of their reduction.[3]

From this time, therefore, the officers of the army continued in the service, relying upon the faith of the country, as expressed in the vote of the 21st of October, 1780, and believing, until they saw proof to the contrary, that the public faith thus pledged to them would be observed.[4] But they were destined to a severe disappointment; and one of the causes of that disappointment was the adoption of the Articles of Confederation. The very change in the constitutional position of the country, from which the most happy results were anticipated, and which undoubt-

1 Ibid. 316, 317.

2 Writings of Washington, VII. 165, 246.

3 Journals, VI. 336.

4 See General Washington's letter to General Sullivan (in Congress), November 20, 1780. Writings, VII. 297.

edly cemented the Union, became the means by which they were cheated of their hopes. The Congress of 1780, which had pledged to them a half-pay for life, was the Revolutionary Congress; but the Congress which was to redeem this pledge was the Congress of the Confederation, which required a vote of nine States for an appropriation of money, or a call upon the States for their proportions. When the vote granting the half-pay for life was passed, there were less than nine States in favor of the measure; and after the Confederation was established, the delegates of the States which originally opposed the provision could not be brought to consider it in its true light,—that of a compact with the officers. It was even contended that the vote, having passed before the Confederation was signed and acted upon, was not obligatory upon the Congress under the Confederation, as that instrument required the votes of nine States for an appropriation of money. In this manner, men deluded themselves with the notion, that a change in the form of a government, or in the constitutional method of raising money to discharge the obligations of a contract, can dissolve those obligations, or alter the principles of justice on which they depend. The States in the opposition to the measure refused to be coerced, as they were pleased to consider it, and in the autumn of 1782, the officers became convinced that they had nothing to hope for from Congress, but a reference of their claims to their several States.[1]

[1] See the letter of General Lincoln, Secretary at War, to Washington, cited by Mr. Sparks, VIII. 356.

In November, 1782, preliminary and eventual articles of peace were agreed upon between the United States and Great Britain, by their plenipotentiaries. Nothing had been done by Congress for the claims of the army, and it seemed highly probable that it would be disbanded without even a settlement of the accounts of the officers, and if so, that they would never receive their dues. Alarmed and irritated by the neglect of Congress; destitute of money and credit and of the means of living from day to day; oppressed with debts; saddened by the distresses of their families at home, and by the prospect of misery before them, — they presented a memorial to Congress in December, in which they urged the immediate adjustment of their dues, and offered to commute the half-pay for life, granted by the resolve of October, 1780, for full pay for a certain number of years, or for such a sum in gross, as should be agreed on by their committee sent to Philadelphia to attend the progress of the memorial through the house. It is manifest from statements in this document, as well as from other evidence, that the officers were nearly driven to desperation, and that their offer of commutation was wrung from them by a state of public opinion little creditable to the country. They recited their hardships, their poverty, and their exertions in the cause; and all that they said was fully borne out by their great commander, in his personal remonstrances with many of the members of Congress. The officers asserted, that many of their brethren, who had retired on the half-pay promised by the resolve of 1780, were not only destitute of any effectual provision, but had become objects of obloquy; and they referred with chagrin to the odious view in which the citizens of too many of the States endeavored to place those who were entitled to that provision.

But, from the prevailing feeling in Congress and in the country, nothing better was to be expected than a compromise in place of the discharge of a solemn obligation; and this feeling no American historian should fail to record and to condemn. If these men had borne only the character of public creditors, a state of public feeling which drove them into a compromise of their claims ought always to be severely reprehended. But, beyond the capacity of public creditors, they were the men who had fought the battles which liberated the country from a foreign yoke; who had endured every extremity of hardship, every form of suffering, which the life of a soldier knows; who had stood between the common soldiery and the civil power; and often, at the hazard of their lives, preserved that discipline and subordination which the civil power had done too much to hazard. They were, in a word, the men of whom their commander said, that they had exhibited more virtue, fortitude, self-denial, and perseverance, than had perhaps been then paralleled in the history of human enthusiasm.

Painful, therefore, as it is, this lesson, of the wrong that may be done by a breach of public faith, must be read. It lies open on the page of history, and is the case of those to whose right arms the people of this country owe the splendid inheritance of liberty. All real palliations should be sought for and admitted. The country was poor: no proper system of finance had been, or could be, developed by a government which had no power of taxation; and the ideas and feelings of the people of many of the States were provincial, and without the liberality and enlargement of thought which comes of intercourse with the world. But, after every apology has exhausted its force, the conscientious student of history must mark the dereliction from public duty; must admit what the public faith required; and must observe the dangerous consequences which attend, and must ever attend, the breach of a public obligation.

The immediate consequences which followed, in this instance, were predicted by General Washington, who gave the clearest warning, in advance of the officers' memorial, of the hazards that would attend the further neglect of their claims. But his warning seems to have been unheeded, or to have made but little impression against the prevailing aversion to touch the unpopular subject of half-pay. The committee of the officers were in attendance upon Congress during the whole winter, and early in March, 1783, they wrote to their constituents that nothing had been done.

At this moment, the predicament in which Washington stood, in the double relation of citizen and soldier, was critical and delicate in the extreme. In the course of a few days, all his firmness and patriotism, all his sympathies as an officer, on the one side, and his fidelity to the government on the other, were severely tried. On the 10th of March, an anonymous address was circulated among the officers at Newburgh, calling a meeting of the general and field officers, and of one officer from each company, and one from the medical staff, to consider the late letter from their representatives at Philadelphia, and to determine what measures should be adopted to obtain that redress of grievances which they seemed to have solicited in vain. It was written with great ability and skill.[1] It spoke the language of injured feeling; it pointed directly to the sword, as the remedy for injustice; and it spoke to men who were suffering keenly under public ingratitude and neglect. Its eloquence and its passion fell, therefore, upon hearts not insensible, and a dangerous explosion seemed to be at hand. Washington met the crisis with firmness, but also with conciliation. He issued orders forbidding an assemblage at the call of an anonymous paper, and directing the officers to assemble on Saturday, the 15th, to hear the report of their committee, and to deliberate what further measures ought to be adopted as most rational and best calcu-

1 The "Newburgh Addresses" were written by John Armstrong, (afterwards General Armstrong,) then a young man, and aide-de-camp to General Gates, with the rank of Major. (Sparks's Life of Gouverneur Morris, I. 253. United States Magazine for January 1, 1823, New York.) The style of these papers, considering the period when they appeared, is remarkably good. They are written with great point and vigor of expression and great purity of English. For the purpose for which they were designed, — a direct appeal to feeling, — they show the hand of a master.

lated to obtain the just and important object in view. The senior officer in rank present was directed to preside, and to report the result to the Commander-in-chief.

On the next day after these orders were issued, a second anonymous address appeared from the same writer. In this paper, he affected to consider the orders of General Washington, assuming the direction of the meeting, as a sanction of the whole proceeding which he had proposed. Washington saw, at once, that he must be present at the meeting himself, or that his name would be used to justify measures which he intended to discountenance and prevent. He therefore attended the meeting, and under his influence, seconded by that of Putnam, Knox, Brooks, and Howard, the result was the adoption of certain resolutions, in which the officers, after reasserting their grievances, and rebuking all attempts to seduce them from their civil allegiance, referred the whole subject of their claims again to the consideration of Congress.

Even at this distant day, the peril of that crisis can scarcely be contemplated without a shudder. Had the Commander-in-chief been other than Washington, had the leading officers by whom he was surrounded been less than the noblest of patriots, the land would have been deluged with the blood of a civil war. But men who had suffered what the great officers of the Revolution had suffered, had learned the lessons of self-control which suffering teaches. The hard school of adversity in which they had passed so many years made them sensible to an appeal which only such a chief as Washington could make; and, when he transmitted their resolves to Congress, he truly described them as "the last glorious proof of patriotism which could have been given by men who aspired to the distinction of a patriot army; not only confirming their claim to the justice, but increasing their title to the gratitude, of their country."[1]

The effect of these proceedings was the passage by Congress of certain resolves, on the 22d of March, 1783, commuting the half-pay for life to five years' full pay after the close of the war, to be received, at the option of Congress, in money, or in such securities as were given to other creditors of the United States.[2] On the 4th of July, the accounts of the army were ordered to be made up and adjusted, and certificates of the sums due were required to be given in the form directed by the Superintendent of the Finances. On the 18th of October, a proclamation was issued, disbanding the army.

From this time, the officers passed into the whole mass of the creditors of the United States; and although they continued to constitute a distinct class among those creditors, the history of their claims is to be pursued in connection with that of the other

[1] March 18, 1783. Writings, VIII. 396.

[2] The resolves gave the option to lines of the respective States, and not to the officers individually in those lines, to accept or refuse the commutation. Journals, VIII. 162.

public debts of the country. The value of the votes which fixed their compensation, and paid them in public securities, depended, of course, upon the ability of the government to redeem the obligations which it issued. The general financial powers of the Union, therefore, under the Confederation, must now be considered.

CHAPTER II.

1781-1783.

Financial Difficulties of the Confederation. — Revolutionary Debt. — Revenue System of 1783.

It is not easy to ascertain the amount of the public debt of the United States, at the time when the Confederation went into operation. But on the 1st of January, 1783, it amounted to about forty-two millions of dollars. About eight millions were due on loans obtained in France and Holland, and the residue was due to citizens of the United States. The annual interest of the debt was a little more than two million four hundred thousand dollars.[1]

[1] The debt due to the crown of France was ascertained in 1782 to be eighteen millions of livres; and by the contract entered into by the United States with the king of France, on the 16th of July, 1782, the principal of this debt was to be paid in twelve annual instalments of one million five hundred thousand livres each, in twelve years, to commence from the third year after a peace, at the royal treasury in Paris. The interest was payable annually, at the time and place stipulated for the payment of the instalments of the principal, at five per cent. The king generously remitted the arrears of interest due at the date of the contract. There was also due to the king of France ten millions of livres, borrowed by him of the States-General of the Netherlands for the use of the United States, and the payment of which he had guaranteed. This sum was to be paid in Paris, in ten annual instalments of one million of livres each, commencing on the 5th of November, 1787. The interest on this loan was payable in Paris imme-

The Confederation had no sooner gone into operation, than it was perceived by many of the principal statesmen of the country, that its financial powers were so entirely defective, that Congress would never be able, under them, to pay even the interest on the public debt. Indeed, before the Confederation was finally ratified, so as to become obligatory upon all the States, on the 3d of February, 1781, Congress passed a resolve, recommending to the several States, as indispensably necessary, to vest a power in Congress to levy for the use of the United States a duty of five per cent. *ad valorem*, at the time and place of importation, upon all foreign goods and merchandise imported into any of the States; and that the money arising from such duties should be appropriated to the discharge of the principal and interest of the debts already then contracted, or which might be contracted, on the faith of the United States, for the support of the war; the duties to be continued until the debts should be fully and finally discharged.

diately, and the first payment of interest became due on the 5th of November, 1782. There was also due to the Farmers-General of France one million of livres, and to the king six millions of livres, on a loan for the year 1783; making in the whole thirty-eight millions of livres, or $ 7,037,037, due in France. There was also due to money-lenders in Holland $ 671,000; for money borrowed by Mr. Jay in Spain, $ 150,000; and a year's interest on the Dutch loan of ten millions of livres, amounting to $ 26,848; — making the whole foreign debt $ 7,885,085. The domestic debt amounted to $ 34,115,290. Five millions of this were due to the army, under the commutation resolves of March, 1783. The residue was held by other citizens, or consisted of arrears of interest. The whole debt of the United States was estimated at $ 42,000,375, and the annual interest of this sum was $ 2,415,956.

It was at this time that the office of Superintendent of the Finances was established, and Robert Morris was unanimously elected by Congress to fill it. He was an eminent merchant of Philadelphia, of known financial skill, devoted to the cause of the country, and possessed of very considerable private resources, which he more than once sacrificed to the public service. Under his administration, it is more than probable that, if the States had complied with the requisitions of Congress, the war would have been brought to a close at an earlier period. But there was scarcely any compliance with those requisitions, and, contemporaneously with this neglect, the proposal to vest in Congress the power to levy duties met with serious opposition. On the 30th of October, 1781, Congress made a requisition upon the States for eight millions of dollars, to meet the service of the ensuing year. In January, 1783, one year and three months from the date of this requisition, less than half a million of this sum had been received into the treasury of the United States. After a delay of nearly two years, one State entirely refused its concurrence with the plan of vesting in Congress a power to levy duties, another withdrew the assent it had once given, and a third had returned no answer.

The State which refused to grant this power to Congress was Rhode Island. On the 6th of December, 1782, Congress determined to send a deputation to that State, to endeavor to procure its assent to this constitutional change. The increasing discontents of the army, the loud clamors of the public creditors, the extreme disproportion between the current means and the demands of the public service, and the impossibility of obtaining further loans in Europe unless some security could be held out to lenders, made it necessary for Congress to be especially urgent with the legislature of Rhode Island. But, at the moment when the deputation was about to depart on this mission, the intelligence was received that Virginia had repealed the act by which she had previously granted to Congress the power of laying duties, and the proposal was therefore abandoned for a time.[1] But the leading persons then in Congress — who saw the ruin impending over the country; who were aware that the whole amount of money which Congress had received, to carry on the public business for the year then just expiring, was less than two millions of dollars,[2] while the three branches of feeding, clothing, and paying the army exceeded five millions of dollars per annum, exclusive of all other departments of the public service; and who were equally aware that no means whatever existed of paying the interest on the public debts — resolved still to persevere in their endeavors to procure the establishment

[1] Mr. Madison (under the date of December 24, 1782) says, that, on the receipt of this intelligence, "the most intelligent members were deeply affected, and prognosticated a failure of the impost scheme, and the most pernicious effects to the character, the duration, and the interests of the Confederacy. It was at length, notwithstanding, determined to persist in the attempt for permanent revenue, and a committee was appointed to report the steps proper to be taken." Debates in the Congress of the Confederation, Elliot, I. 17.

[2] $ 1,545,818$\frac{30}{90}$ was the whole amount.

of revenues equal to the purpose of funding all the debts of the United States.

Among these persons, Hamilton and Madison were the most active; and the part which they took, at this period, in the measures for sustaining the sinking credit of the country, and the efforts which they made, are among the less conspicuous, but not less important services, which those great men performed for their country. Another plan was devised, after the failure of that of 1781, for investing Congress with a power to derive a revenue from duties, and, in April, 1783, its promoters procured for it the almost unanimous consent of Congress. This plan recommended the States to vest in Congress the power of levying certain duties upon goods imported into the country, partly specific and partly *ad valorem;* the proceeds of such duties to be applied to the discharge of the interest or principal of the debts incurred by the United States for supporting the war. The duties were to be collected by collectors appointed by the States, but accountable to Congress. It also recommended to the States to establish, for a term of twenty-five years, substantial and effectual revenues, exclusive of the duties to be levied by Congress for supplying their proportions of fifteen millions of dollars annually, for the same purpose; and that, when this plan had been acceded to by all the States, it should be considered as forming a mutual compact, irrevocable by one or more of them without the consent of the whole. It was also proposed that the rule of proportion fixed by the Confederation should be changed from the basis of real estate to the basis of population.

This plan was sent out to the States, accompanied by an address, prepared by Mr. Madison, in which the necessity of the measure was urged with much ability and force. Annexed to this paper were various documents, exhibiting the nature and origin of the public debts, and the meritorious characters of the various public creditors; the whole of the Newburgh Addresses, and the proceedings of the officers; the contracts made with the king of France; and a very able answer by Hamilton to the objections of Rhode Island. No stronger and more direct appeal was ever made to the sense of right of any people. Never was the cause of national honor, public faith, and public safety more powerfully and eloquently set forth.[1]

[1] On the final question, as to the revenue system, Hamilton voted against it. His reasons were given in a letter to the Governor of New York, under date of April 14, 1783. They were, "First, that it does not designate the funds (except the impost) on which the whole interest is to arise; and by which (selecting the capital articles of visible property) the collection would have been easy, the funds productive, and necessarily increasing with the increase of the country. Secondly, that the duration of the funds is not coextensive with the debt, but limited to twenty-five years, though there is a moral certainty that in that period the principal will not, by the present provision, be fairly extinguished. Thirdly, that the nomination and appointment of the collectors of the revenue are to reside in each State, instead of, at least, the nomination being in the United States; the consequence of which will be, that those States which have little interest in the funds, by having a small share of the public debt due to their own citizens, will take care to appoint such persons as are the least likely to collect the revenue." Still, he urged the adoption of the plan by his own State, "because it is her interest, at all events, to promote the payment of the public debt in continental funds, indepen-

And when we consider the various classes of the public creditors, at the close of the war, and remember that the debts of the country had been contracted for the great purpose of establishing its independence, and that there was scarcely a creditor who had not some claim to the gratitude of the country, we cannot but be astonished that such an appeal as was then made should have fallen, as it did, unheeded upon the legislatures and people of many of the States. In the first place, the debts were due to an ally, the generous king of France, who had loaned to the American people his armies and his treasures; who had added to his loans liberal donations; and whose very contracts for repayment contained proof of his magnanimity. In the next place, they were due to that noble band of officers and soldiers, who had fought the battles of their country, and who now asked only such a portion of their dues as would enable them to retire, with the means of daily bread, from the field of victory and glory into the

dent of the general considerations of union and propriety. I am much mistaken, if the debts due from the United States to the citizens of the State of New York do not considerably exceed its proportion of the necessary funds; of course, it has an immediate interest that there should be a continental provision for them. But there are superior motives that ought to operate in every State, — the obligations of national faith, honor, and reputation. Individuals have been too long already sacrificed to the public convenience. It will be shocking, and, indeed, an eternal reproach to this country, if we begin the peaceable enjoyment of our independence by a violation of all the principles of honesty and true policy. It is worthy of remark, that at least four fifths of the domestic debt are due to the citizens of the States from Pennsylvania, inclusively, northward." Life of Hamilton, II. 185, 186.

bosom of peace and privacy, and such effectual security for the residue of their claims, as their country was unquestionably able to provide. In the last place, they were due partly to those citizens of the country who had lent their funds to the public, or manifested their confidence in the government by receiving transfers of public securities from those who had so lent, and partly to those whose property had been taken for the public service.[1]

The United States had achieved their independence. They were about to take rank among the nations of the world. As they should meet this crisis, their character would be determined. The rights for which they had contended were the rights of human nature. These rights had triumphed, and now formed the basis of the civil polity of thirteen independent States. The forms of republican government were therefore called upon to justify themselves by their fruits. The higher qualities of national character — justice, good faith, honor, gratitude — were called upon to display an example, that would save the cause of republican liberty from reproach and disgrace.[2]

But, unhappily, the establishment of peace tended to weaken the slender bond which held the Union together, by turning the attention of men to the internal affairs of their own States. The advantage and the necessity of giving the regulation of foreign commerce to the general government, if perceived at

[1] Address. [2] Ibid.

all, was perceived only by a few leading statesmen. The commercial States fancied that they profited by a condition of things which enabled them as importers to levy contribution on their neighbors. The people did not as yet perceive, that, without some central authority to regulate the whole trade alike, the clashing regulations of rival States would sooner or later destroy the Confederacy. Nor were they willing to be taxed for the payment of the public debts. The people of the United States had not yet begun to feel, that such a burden is to be borne as one of the first of public and social duties. That part of the financial plan of 1783, which required from the States a pledge of internal revenues for twenty-five years, met with so much opposition, that Congress was obliged to abandon it, and to confine its efforts to that part of the scheme which related to the duties on imports. In 1786, all the States, except New York, had complied with the latter part of the plan; but the refusal of that State rendered the whole of it inoperative, and no resource remained to Congress, after the close of the war, but the old method of making requisitions on the States, under the rule of the Confederation.[1]

[1] With what success this was attended may be seen from the fact, that, from the year 1782 to the year 1786, Congress made requisitions on the States for the purpose of paying the interest on the public debts, of more than six millions of dollars, and on the 31st of March, 1787, about one million only of this sum had been received. The interest of the debt due to domestic creditors remained wholly unpaid; money was borrowed in Europe to pay the interest on the foreign loans; and the domestic debt sunk to so low a value, that it was often sold for one tenth of its nominal amount.

At the return of peace, therefore, the Confederation had had a trial of two years and six months, as a government for purposes of war. It was for these purposes, mainly, that it was established; being in fact, as it was in name, a league of friendship between sovereign States, for their common defence, the security of their liberties, and their mutual and general welfare; the parties to which had bound themselves by it to assist each other against all external attacks. Doubtless the framers of the Confederation contemplated its duration beyond the period of the war; for, besides the perpetual character of the Union, which it sought and professed to establish, it had certain functions which were manifestly to be exercised in peace as well as in war. These functions, however, were few. The government was framed during a revolutionary war, for the purposes of that war, and it went into operation while the war was still waged; taking the place and superseding the powers of the Revolutionary Congress, under which the war had been commenced and prosecuted.

A written constitution, with a precise and well-defined mode of operation, had thus succeeded to the vague and indefinite, but ample, powers of the earlier government. But in the very modes of its operation, there was a monstrous defect, which distorted the whole system from the true proportions and character of a government. It gave to the Confederation the power of contracting debts, and at the same time withheld from it the power of paying them. It created a corporate body, formed by the Union and known as the United States, and gave to it the faculty of borrowing money and incurring other obligations. It provided the mode in which its treasury should be supplied for the reimbursement of the public creditor. But over the sources of that supply, it gáve the government contracting the debts no power whatever. Thirteen independent legislatures granted or withheld the means which were to enable the general government to pay the debts which the general constitution had enabled it to contract, according to their own convenience or their own views and feelings as to the purposes for which those debts had been incurred. Yet the debts were wholly national in their character, and by the nation they were to be discharged. But, by the operation of the system under which the nation had undertaken to discharge its obligations, the duty of performance was parcelled out among the various subordinate corporations of States, and the country was thus placed in the position of an empire whose power was at the mercy of its provinces, and was sure to be controlled by provincial objects and ideas.

A government thus situated, engaged in the prosecution of a war, perpetually borrowing, but never paying, and scarce likely ever to pay, was in a position to prosecute that war with far less than the real energies and resources of the nation: and it stands the recorded opinion of him who conducted his country through the whole struggle, and without whom it could not, under this defective system, have achieved its independence, that the war would have terminated sooner, and would have cost vastly less both of blood and treasure, if the government of the Union had possessed the power of direct or indirect taxation.[1] But the government of the Confederation was one that trusted too much to the patriotism and sense of honor of the different populations of the different States. The moral feelings of a people will prompt to high and heroic deeds; will impel them with irresistible force and energy to the accomplishment of the great objects of liberty and happiness; and will develop in individuals the highest capacity for endurance that human nature can display. They did so in the American Revolution. The annals of no people, struggling for liberty, exhibit more of the virtues of fortitude, self-denial, and an ardent love of freedom, than ours exhibit, especially in the earlier stages of the contest. But any *feelings* are an unsafe and uncertain reliance for the regular and punctual operations of civil government. The fiscal concerns of a nation, left to depend principally upon the prevailing sentiments of justice, honor, and gratitude, — upon the connection between these sentiments and that passion for liberty which animated the earlier struggles for national independence, — are exposed to great hazards. If an appeal to the feelings of a people constitutes the principal ground of security for the public creditor, other feelings may intervene, which will lead to a

[1] General Washington's letter to Hamilton, March 31, 1783. Writings, VIII. 409, 410. Circular Letter to the Governors of the States, on disbanding the army. Ibid. 439, 451.

denial of the justice of the claim; for it is the very nature of such an appeal to submit the whole question of obligation and duty to popular determination. That government alone is likely to discharge the just obligations of any people, which possesses both the power to declare what those obligations are, and the power to levy the means of payment, without a reference of either point to popular sentiment.

The history of the Confederation contains abundant proofs of the soundness of this position. At the close of the war, a debt of more than forty millions of dollars was due from the United States to various classes of creditors, and the whole of it had been contracted either by the government of the Confederation, or by its predecessors, for whose contracts the Confederation was expressly bound, by the Articles, to provide. This debt could not be discharged without a grant of internal revenues from the States, and without a grant of the power to collect other revenues from the external trade of the country. The appeal that was made by the government in order to obtain these grants was addressed almost wholly to the moral sentiments of the people of the different States; the time had scarcely arrived, although rapidly approaching, for an appeal to those interests which were involved in the surrender to the general government of the power of regulating foreign commerce;[1] and consequently the arguments

[1] None of the documents, connected with the Address to the People of the United States, issued by Congress in 1783, discussed the question as one of direct interest and advantage, except Hamilton's

addressed to the sense of justice and the feeling of gratitude were answered by discussions of the propriety, justice, and reasonableness of some of the claims, for which the States were thus called upon to provide, as existing debts of the country, not without the hope, entertained in some quarters, of involving the whole in confusion and final rejection.[2]

The design of the framers of the revenue system of 1783 was twofold; first, to do justice to the creditors of the country, by procuring adequate power to fund the public debts; and second, to strengthen and consolidate the national government, by means of those debts and of the various interests which would be combined in the great object of their liquidation. They foresaw, on the approach of peace, that to leave these debts to be provided for by the States individually would lead to a separation of interests fatal to the continuance of the Union; but that to make the United States responsible for the whole of them would be to create a bond of union, that would

answer to the objections of Rhode Island. The Address itself appealed entirely to considerations of honor, justice, and good faith. Hamilton's paper, however, showed with great perspicacity, that the proposed impost would not be unfavorable to commerce, but the contrary; that it would not diminish the profits of the merchant, being too moderate in amount to discourage the consumption of imported goods, and therefore that it would not diminish the extent of importations; but that, even if it had this tendency, it was a tendency in the right direction, because it would lessen the proportion of imports to exports, and incline the balance in favor of the country. But the great question of yielding the control of foreign commerce to the Union, *for the sake of uniformity of regulation*, was not touched in any of these papers. The time for it had not arrived.

[2] See note at the end of this chapter.

be effectual and operative, after the external pressure of war, which had hitherto held the States together, should have been removed. For this purpose, they undoubtedly availed themselves of the discontents of the army, a class of the public creditors the justice of whose claims there was immediate danger in denying. There is no reason to suppose that these discontents were promoted by any one concerned in giving direction to the action of Congress. But before the crisis had been reached in the "Newburgh Addresses," it was perceived to be extremely important to prevent the army from turning away from the general government, as their debtor, to look to their respective States; and, after the imminent hazard of that moment had passed, the claims of the army were used, and used most rightfully, to impress upon the States the necessity of yielding to Congress the powers necessary to do justice.[1]

In the proposal of this scheme of finance, involving, as it did, a material change in the operation of the existing constitution of the country, there was great wisdom; and it was eminently fortunate that it went forth before the advent of peace, to be considered and acted upon by the States. The system of the Confederation had utterly failed to supply the means of sustaining the public credit of the Union, and the consciousness of that failure tended to produce a resolution of the Union into its component elements, the States. Men had begun to abandon the hope of

[1] See note on page 194.

paying the debts of the country; or, if they were to be paid at all, they had begun to look to the States, in their individual capacities, as the ultimate debtors, to whom at least a part of the claims was to be referred. Had the country been permitted to pass from a state of war to a state of peace, without the suggestion and proposal of a definite system for funding these debts on continental securities, the Union would at once have been exhausted of all vitality. The Confederation, left to discharge the functions which belonged to it in peace, without the power of relieving the burdens which it had entailed upon the country during the war, would have been everywhere regarded as a useless machine, the purposes of which — poorly answered in the period of its greatest activity — had entirely ceased to exist. Congress would have been attended by delegates from few of the States, if attended at all;[1] and the rapid decay of the Union would have been marked by the feeble,

[1] As it was, the approach of peace had reduced the attendance upon Congress below the constitutional number of States necessary to ratify the treaty, when it was received. On the 23d of December, 1783, a resolve was passed, "That letters be immediately despatched to the executives of New Hampshire, Connecticut, New York, New Jersey, South Carolina, and Georgia, informing them that the safety, honor, and good faith of the United States require the immediate attendance of their delegates in Congress; that there have not been during the sitting of Congress at this place [Annapolis] more than seven States represented, namely, Massachusetts, Rhode Island, Pennsylvania, Delaware, Maryland, Virginia, and North Carolina, and most of those by only two delegates; and that the ratification of the definitive treaty, and several other matters, of great national concern, are now pending before Congress, which require the utmost despatch, and to which the assent of at least nine States is necessary." (Journals, IX. 12.)

spasmodic, and unsuccessful efforts of some of them to discharge so much of the general burdens as could have been assigned to them in severalty; the open repudiation of others; and the final confusion and loss of the whole mass of the debts, in universal bankruptcy, poverty, and disgrace.

But the comprehensive scheme of 1783, although never adopted, saved the imperfect Union that then existed from the destruction to which it was hastening. It saved it for a prolonged, though feeble existence, through a period of desperate exhaustion. It saved it, by ascertaining the debts of the country, fixing their national character, and proposing a national system for their discharge. It directed the attention of the States to the advantage and the necessity of giving up to the Union some part of the imposts that might be levied on foreign commodities, and thus led the way to that grand idea of uniformity of regulation, which was afterwards developed as the true interest of communities, which, from their geographical and moral relations, constitute in fact but one country.

It is not intended, however, in assigning this influence to the revenue system proposed in 1783, to suggest that it contained the germ of the present Constitution. It was an essentially different system. It proposed the enlargement of the powers of Congress, as they existed under the Confederation, only by the grant to the United States of the right to collect certain duties on foreign importations, for the limited period of twenty-five years, to be applied to the discharge of the debts contracted for the purposes of the war, but to be collected by officers appointed by the States, although amenable to Congress; and the levy and collection by the States of certain internal taxes, during the same limited term, for the purpose of raising certain proportionate sums, to be paid over to the United States, for the same object. So far, therefore, as this system suggested any new powers, there is a wide difference between its features and principles and those of an entire and irrevocable surrender to the Union of the whole subject of taxing and regulating foreign commerce. But the influence of this proposal upon the country, during the four years which followed, is to be measured by the evident necessities which it revealed, and by the means to which it pointed for their relief; — means which, though never applied, and, if applied, would have proved inadequate, still showed, through the period of increasing weakness in the Union, the high obligations which rested upon the country, and which could be discharged only by the preservation of the Union.

NOTE TO PAGE 185.

ON THE HALF-PAY FOR THE OFFICERS OF THE REVOLUTION.

In Connecticut, the opposition to the plan of enabling Congress to fund the public debts arose from the jealousy with which the provision of half-pay for the officers of the army had always been regarded in that State. In October, 1783, Governor Trumbull, in an address to the Assembly declining a reëlection, had spoken of the necessity of enlarging the powers of Congress, and of strengthening the arm of the government. A committee reported an answer to this address, which contained a paragraph approving of the principles which the Governor had inculcated, but it was stricken out in the lower house. Jonathan Trumbull, Jr., who had been one of Washington's aids, thus wrote to him concerning the rejection of this paragraph : "It was rejected, lest, by adopting it, they should seem to convey to the people an idea of their concurring with the political sentiments contained in the address; so exceedingly jealous is the spirit of this State at present respecting the powers and the engagements of Congress, arising principally from their aversion to the half-pay and commutation granted to the army; principally, I say, arising from this cause. It is but too true, that some few are wicked enough to hope, that, by means of this clamor, they may be able to rid themselves of the whole public debt, by introducing so much confusion into public measures as shall eventually produce a general abolition of the whole." (Writings of Washington, IX. 5, note.) It appears from the Journals of Congress, that in November, 1783, the House of Representatives of Connecticut sent some remonstrance to Congress respecting the resolution which had granted half-pay for life to the officers, which was referred to a committee, to be answered. In the report of this committee it was said, that "the resolution of Congress referred to appears by the yeas and nays to have been passed according to the then established rules of that body in transacting the business of the United States; the resolution itself had public notoriety, and does not appear to have been formally objected against by the legislature of any State till after the Confederation was completely adopted, *nor till after the close of the war*." These words were stricken out from the report by a vote of six States against one, two States declining to vote. The journal gives no further account of the matter. (Journals, IX. 79. March 12, 1784.)

In Massachusetts, the half-pay had always been equally unpopular. The legislature of that State, on the 11th of July, 1783, addressed a letter to Congress, to assign, as a reason for not agreeing to the impost duty, the grant of half-pay to the officers. The tone of this letter does little credit to the State.

"*Commonwealth of Massachusetts.*

"Boston, July 11, 1783.

"SIR:—

"The Address of the United States in Congress assembled has been received by the legislature of the Commonwealth of Massachusetts; and, while they consider themselves as bound in duty to give Congress the highest assurance that no measures consistent with their circumstances, and the constitution of this government and the Federal Union, shall remain unattempted by them to furnish those supplies which justice demands, and which are necessary to support the credit and honor of the United States, they find themselves under a necessity of addressing Congress in regard to the subject of the half-pay of the officers of the army, and the proposed commutation thereof; with some other matters of a similar nature, which produce among the people of this Commonwealth the greatest concern and uneasiness, and involve the legislature thereof in no small embarrassments. The legislature have not been unacquainted with the sufferings, nor are they forgetful of the virtue and bravery, of their fellow-citizens in the army; and while they are sensible that justice requires they should be fully compensated for their services and sufferings, at the same time it is most sincerely wished that they may return to the bosom of their country, under such circumstances as may place them in the most agreeable light with their fellow-citizens. Congress, in the year 1780, resolved, that the officers of the army, who should continue therein during the war, should be entitled to half-pay for life; and at the same time resolved, that all such as should retire therefrom, in consequence of the new arrangement which was then ordered to take place, should be entitled to the same benefit; a commutation of which half-pay has since been proposed. The General Court are sensible that the United States in Congress assembled are, by the Confederation, vested with a discretionary power to make provision for the support and payment of the army, and such civil officers as may be necessary for managing the general affairs of the United States; but in making such provision, due regard ever ought to be had to the welfare and happiness of the people, the rules of equity, and the spirit and general design of the Confederation. We cannot, on this occasion, avoid saying, that, with due respect, we are of opinion those principles were not duly attended to, in the grant of half-pay to the officers of the army; that being, in our opinion, a grant of more than an adequate reward for their services, and inconsistent with that equality which ought to subsist among citizens of free and republican States. Such a measure appears to be calculated to raise and exalt some citizens in wealth and grandeur, to the injury and oppression of others, even if the inequality which will happen among the officers of the army, who have performed from one to eight years' service, should not be taken into consideration. The observations which have been made with regard to the officers of the army will in general apply to the civil officers appointed by Congress, who, in our opinion, have been allowed much larger salaries than are consistent with the state of our finances, the rules of equity, and a proper regard to the public good. And, indeed, if the United States were in the most wealthy and prosperous circumstances, it is conceived that economy and moderation, with respect to grants and allowances, in opposition to the measures which have been adopted by monarchical and luxurious courts, would most highly conduce to our reputation, even in the eyes of foreigners, and would cause a people, who have been contending with so much ardor and expense for republican constitutions and freedom, which cannot be supported without frugality and virtue, to appear with dignity and consistency; and at the same time would, in the best manner, conduce to the public happiness. It is thought to be essentially necessary, especially at the present time, that Congress should be expressly informed, that such measures as are complained of are extremely opposite and irritating to the principles and feelings which the people of some Eastern States, and of this in particular, inherit from their ancestry. The legislature cannot without horror entertain the most distant idea of the dissolution of the Union which subsists between the United States, and the ruin which would inevitably ensue thereon; but with great pain they must observe, that the extraordinary grants and allowances which Congress have thought proper to make to their civil and military officers have produced such effects in this Commonwealth as are of a threatening aspect. From these sources, and particularly from the grant of half-pay to the officers of the army, and the proposed commutation thereof, it has arisen, that the General Court has not been able hitherto to agree in granting to the United States an impost duty, agreeable to the recommendation of Congress; while the General Assembly at the same time have been deeply impressed with a sense of the necessity of speedily adopting some effectual measures for supplying the continental treasury, for the restoration of the public credit, and the salvation of the country; — and propose, as the present session is near terminating, again to take the subject of the impost duty into consideration early in the next. From these observations, you may easily learn the difficult and critical situation the legislature is in, and they rely on the wisdom of Congress to adopt and propose some measure for relief in this extremity.

"In the name and by order of the General Court,

"We are your Excellency's most obedient humble servants,

"SAMUEL ADAMS,
President of the Senate.
"TRISTRAM DALTON,
Speaker of the House of Representatives.

"HIS EXCELLENCY THE PRESIDENT OF CONGRESS."

This letter was thought worthy an answer, and accordingly a report upon it was brought in by Mr. Madison, and adopted in Congress, containing among other things the following: —

"Your committee consider the measure of Congress as the result of a deliberate judgment, framed on a general view of the interests of the Union at large. They consider it to be a truth, that no State in this Confederacy can claim (more equitably than an individual in a society) to derive advantages from a Union, without conforming to the judgment of a constitutional majority of those who compose it; still, however, they conceive it will be found no less true, that, if a State every way so important as Massachusetts should withhold her solid support to constitutional measures of the Confederacy, the result must be a dissolution of the Union; — and then she must hold herself as alone responsible for the anarchy and domestic confusion that may succeed, and for exposing all these confederated States (who at the commencement of the late war leagued to defend her violated rights) an easy prey to the machinations of their enemies, and the sport of European politics; and therefore they are of opinion, that Congress should still confide that a free, enlightened, and generous people will never hazard consequences so perilous and alarming, and in all circumstances rely on the wisdom, temper, and virtue of their constituents, which (guided by an all-wise Providence) have ever interposed to avert impending evils and misfortunes. Your committee beg leave further to observe, that, from an earnest desire to give satisfaction to such of the States as expressed a dislike to the half-pay establishment, a sum in gross was proposed by Congress, and accepted by the officers, as an equivalent for their half-pay. That your committee are informed, that such equivalent was ascertained on established principles which are acknowledged to be just, and adopted in similar cases; but that if the objections against the commutation were ever so valid, yet, as it is not now under the arbitration of Congress, but an act finally adopted, and the national faith pledged to carry it into effect, they could not be taken into consideration. With regard to the salaries of civil officers, it may be observed, that the necessaries of life have been very high during the war: hence it has happened that even the salaries complained of have not been found sufficient to induce persons properly qualified to accept of many important offices, and the public business is left undone." (Journals of Congress, VIII. 379 – 385. September 25, 1783.)

NOTE TO PAGE 186.

ON THE NEWBURGH ADDRESSES.

There was a period in this business, when the officers would have accepted from Congress a recommendation to their several States for the payment of their dues. Their committee, consisting of General McDougall, Colonel Brooks of Massachusetts, and Colonel Ogden of New Jersey, arrived in Philadelphia about the 1st of January. In their memorial to Congress, they abstained from designating the funds from which they desired satisfaction of their demands, because their great object was to get a settlement of their accounts and an equivalent for the half-pay established. But they were, in fact, at one time, impressed with the belief that their best, and indeed their only security, was to be sought for in funds to be provided by the States, under the recommendation of Congress. This plan would have involved a division of the army into thirteen different parts, leaving the claims of each part to be satisfied by its own State: a course that would unquestionably have led to the rejection of their demands in some States, and probably in many. To prevent this, there is little doubt that the influence of those members of Congress who wished to promote their interests, and to identify them with the interests of the other public creditors, was used; and by the middle of February the committee of the officers became satisfied, that the army must unitedly pursue a common object, insisting on the grant of revenues to the general government, adequate to the liquidation of all the public debts. (Letter of Gouverneur Morris to General Greene, February 15, 1783. Life, by Sparks, I. 250.) The point, however, which they continued to urge, was the commutation; and upon this they encountered great obstacles. The committee of Congress to whom their memorial was referred went into a critical examination of the principles of annuities, in order to determine on an equivalent for the half-pay for life, promised by the resolve of 1780. The result was a report, declaring that six years' full pay was the proper equivalent. This report was followed by a declaratory resolve, which was passed, "that the troops of the United States, in common with all the creditors of the same, have an undoubted right to expect security; and that Congress will make every effort to obtain, from the respective States, substantial funds, adequate to the object of funding the whole debt of the United States, and will enter upon an immediate and full consideration of the nature of such funds, and the most likely mode of obtaining them." The remainder of the report, however, was referred to a new committee of five, the number of years being considered too many. The second committee reported five years' whole pay as an equivalent, after another calculation of annuities; but the approval of nine States could not be obtained. A desire was then expressed by some of the members, who were opposed both to the commutation and the half-pay, to have more time for consideration, and this was granted.

This was the position of the matter on the 8th of February, when the committee of the officers wrote to General Knox on the part of the army. They stated that "Massachusetts, New York, Pennsylvania, Virginia, North and South Carolina were for the equivalent; New Hampshire, Rhode Island, Connecticut, and Jersey against it. There is some prospect of getting one more of these States to vote for the commutation. If this is accomplished, with Maryland and Delaware, the question will be carried; whenever it is, as the report now stands, it will be at the election of the line, as such, to accept of the commutation or retain their claim to the half-pay, Congress being determined, that no alteration shall take place in the emolument held out to the army but by their consent. This rendered it unnecessary for us to consult the army on the equivalent for half-pay. The zeal of a great number of members of Congress to get continental funds, while a few wished to have us referred to the States, induced us to conceal what funds we wished or expected, lest our declaration for one or the other might retard a settlement of our accounts, or a determination on the equivalent for half-pay. Indeed, some of our best friends in Congress declared, however desirous they were to have our accounts settled, and the commutation fixed, as well as to get funds, yet they would oppose referring us to the States for a settlement and security, till all prospect of obtaining continental funds was at an end. Whether this is near or not, as commutation for the half-pay was one of the principal objects of the address, the obtaining of that is necessary, previous to our particularizing what fund will be most agreeable to us: this must be determined by circumstances. If Congress get funds, we shall be secured. If not, the equivalent settled, a principle will be established, which will be more acceptable to the Eastern States than half-pay, if application must be made to them. As it is not likely that Congress will be able to determine soon on the commutation, (for the reasons above mentioned,) it is judged necessary that Colonel Brooks return to the army, to give them a more particular detail of our prospects than can be done in the compass of a letter." (Writings of Washington, VIII. 553, 554.)

Two classes of persons existed at this time in Congress, of very different views; the one attached to State, the other to continental politics; the one strenuous advocates for funding the public debts upon solid securities, the other opposed to this plan, and finally yielding to it only in consequence of the clamors of the army and the other public creditors. The advocates for continental funds, convinced that nothing could be done for the public credit by any other measures, determined to blend the interests of the army and those of the other creditors in their scheme, in order to combine all the motives that could operate upon different descriptions of men in the different States. Washington, who naturally regarded the interests of the army as the first object in point of importance, and who had not given his attention so much to the general financial affairs of the country, seems to have thought it unadvisable to bring the claims of the army before the States, in connection with the other public debts. On the 4th of March, he wrote to Hamilton (then in Congress), that "the just claims of the army ought, and it is to be hoped will, have their weight with every sensible legislature in the United States, if Congress point to their demands, and show, if the case is so, the reasonableness of them, and the impracticability of complying with them without their aid. In any other point of view, it would in my opinion be impolitic to introduce the army on the tapis, lest it should excite jealousy and bring on its concomitants. The States surely cannot be so devoid of common sense, common honesty, and common policy, as to refuse their aid on a full, clear, and candid representation of facts from Congress; more especially if these should be enforced by members of their own body, who might demonstrate what the inevitable consequences of failure will lead to." (Writings, VIII. 390.)

But while the advocates of the continental system were maturing their plans, new difficulties arose, in consequence of the proceedings of the officers at Newburgh, and of the jealousies which the army began to entertain. Among the resolutions adopted by the officers was one, which expressed their unshaken confidence in the justice of Congress and the country, and their conviction that Congress would not disband them, until their accounts had been liquidated, and adequate funds established for their payment. But Congress had no constitutional power, under the Confederation, to demand funds of the States; and to determine that the army should be continued in service until the States granted the funds, which it was intended to recommend, would be to determine that it should remain a standing army in time of peace, until the States should comply with the recommendation. On the other hand, Congress had no present means of paying the army, if they were to disband them. This dilemma rendered it necessary to evade for a short time any explicit declaration of the purposes of Congress as to disbanding the army; and hence arose a jealousy, on the part of the army, that they were to be used as mere puppets to operate upon the country, in favor of a general revenue system. Washington himself communicated the existence of these suspicions to Hamilton, on the 4th of April, advising that the army should be disbanded as soon as possible, consulting its wishes as to the mode. He also intimated that the Superintendent of the Finances, Robert Morris, was suspected to be at the bottom of the scheme of keeping the army together, for the purpose of aiding the adoption of the revenue system.

Hamilton's reply explains the position of the whole matter, and the motives and purposes of those with whom he acted. "But the question was not merely how to do justice to the creditors, but how to restore public credit. Taxation in this country, it was found, could not supply a sixth part of the public necessities. The loans in Europe were far short of the balance, and the prospect every day diminishing; the court of France telling us, in plain terms, she could not even do as much as she had done; individuals in Holland, and everywhere else, refusing to part with their money on the precarious tenure of the mere faith of this country, without any pledge for the payment either of principal or interest. In this situation, what was to be done? It was essential to our cause that vigorous efforts should be made to restore public credit; it was necessary to combine all the motives to this end, that could operate upon different descriptions of persons in the different States. The necessity and discontents of the army presented themselves as a powerful engine. But, sir, these gentlemen would be puzzled to support their insinuations by a single fact. It was indeed proposed to appropriate the intended impost on trade to the army debt, and, what was extraordinary, by gentlemen who had expressed their dislike to the principle of the fund. I acknowledge I was one that opposed this, for the reasons already assigned, and for these additional ones: *that* was the fund on which we most counted to obtain further loans in Europe; it was necessary we should have a fund sufficient to pay the interest of what had been borrowed and what was to be borrowed. The truth was, these people in this instance wanted to play off the army against the funding system. As to Mr. Morris, I will give your Excellency a true explanation of his conduct. He had been for some time pressing Congress to endeavor to obtain funds, and had found a great backwardness in the business. He found the taxes unproductive in the different States; he found the loans in Europe making a very slow progress; he found himself pressed on all hands for supplies; he found himself, in short, reduced to this alternative, — either of making engagements which he could not fulfil, or declaring his resignation in case funds were not established by a given time. Had he followed the first course, the bubble must soon have burst; he must have sacrificed his credit and his character, and *public* credit, already in a ruined condition, would have lost its last support. He wisely judged it better to resign; this might increase the embarrassments of the moment, but the necessity of the case, it was to be hoped, would produce the proper measures, and he might then resume the direction of the machine with advantage and success. He also had some hope that his resignation would prove a stimulus to Congress. He was, however, ill-advised in the publication of his letters of resignation. This was an imprudent step, and has given a handle to his personal enemies, who, by playing upon the passions of others, have drawn some well-meaning men into the cry against him. But Mr. Morris certainly deserves a great deal from his country. I believe no man in this country but himself could have kept the money machine going during the period he has been in office. From every thing that appears, his administration has been upright as well as able. The truth is, the old leaven of Deane and Lee is at this day working against Mr. Morris. He happened in that dispute to have been on the side of Deane, and certain men can never forgive him. . . . . . The matter, with respect to the army, which has occasioned most altercation in Congress, and most dissatisfaction in the army, has been the half-pay. The opinions on this head have been two: one party was for referring the several lines to their States, to make such commutation as they should think proper; the other, for making the commutation by Congress, and funding it on continental security. I was of this last opinion, and so were all those who will be represented as having made use of the army as our puppets. Our principal reasons were: — First, by referring the lines to their respective States, those which were opposed to the half-pay would have taken advantage of the officers' necessities to make the commutation short of an equivalent. Secondly, the inequality which would have arisen in the different States when the officers came to compare, (as has happened in other cases,) would have been a new source of discontent. Thirdly, such a reference was a continuance of the old, wretched State system, by which the ties between Congress and the army have been nearly dissolved, — by which the resources of the States have been diverted from the common treasury and wasted: a system which your Excellency has often justly reprobated. I have gone into these details to give you a just idea of the parties in Congress. I assure you, upon my honor, sir, I have given you a candid statement of facts, to the best of my judgment. The men against whom the suspicions you mention must be directed, are in general the most sensible, the most liberal, the most independent, and the most respectable characters in our body, as well as the most unequivocal friends to the army; in a word, they are the men who think continentally." (Life of Hamilton, II. 162 – 164.)

CHAPTER III.

1781–1783.

OPINIONS AND EFFORTS OF WASHINGTON AND OF HAMILTON. — DECLINE OF THE CONFEDERATION

THE proposal of the revenue system went forth to the country, although not in immediate connection, yet nearly at the same time, with those comprehensive and weighty counsels which Washington addressed to the States, when the great object for which he had entered the service of his country had been accomplished, and he was about to return to a private station. His relations to the people of this country had been peculiar. He had been, not only the leader of their armies, but, in a great degree, their civil counsellor; for although he had rarely, if ever, gone out of the province of his command to give shape or direction to constitutional changes, yet the whole circumstances of that command had constantly placed him in contact with the governments of the States, as well as with the Congress; and he had often been obliged to interpose the influence of his own character and opinions with all of them, in order that the civil machine might not wholly cease to move. At the moment when he was about to lay aside the sword, he saw very clearly that there were certain principles of conduct which must be called into action in the States, and among the people of the States, for the preservation of the Union. He, and he alone, could address to them with effect the requisite words of admonition, and point out the course of safety and success. This great service, the last act of his revolutionary official life, was performed with all the truth and wisdom of his character, before he proceeded to resign into the hands of Congress the power which he had held so long, and which he now surrendered with a virtue, a dignity, and a sincerity, with which no such power has ever been laid down by any of the leaders of revolutions whom the world has seen.

His object in this Address was not so much to urge the adoption of particular measures, as to inculcate principles which he believed to be essential to the welfare of the country. So clearly, however, did it appear to him, that the honor and independence of the country were involved in the adoption of the revenue system which Congress had recommended, that he did not refrain from urging it as the sole means by which a national bankruptcy could be averted, before any different plan could be proposed and adopted.

But how far, at this time, any other or further plans, for the formation of a better constitution, had been formed, or how far any one perceived both the vicious principle of the Confederation and the means of substituting for it another and more efficient power, we can judge only by the published writings of the Revolutionary statesmen. It is quite certain that at this period Washington saw the defects of the Confederation, as he had seen them clearly, and suffered under them, from the beginning. He saw that in the powers of the States, which far exceeded those of the Continental Congress, lay the source of all the perplexities which he had experienced in the course of the war, and of almost the whole of the difficulties and distresses of the army; and that to form a new constitution, which would give consistency, stability, and dignity to the Union, was the great problem of the time. He saw, also, that the honor and true interest of this country were involved in the development of continental power; that local and State politics were destined to interfere with the establishment of any more liberal and extensive plan of government, which the circumstances of the country required, as they had perpetually weakened the bond by which the Union had thus far been held together; and that such local influences would make these States the sport of European policy. He predicted, moreover, that the country would reach, if it reached at all, some system of sufficient capabilities, only through mistakes and disasters, and through an experience purchased at the price of further difficulties and distress. Such were his general views, at the close of the war.[1]

But there was one man in the country who had looked more deeply still into its wants, and who

[1] Letter to Hamilton, March 31, 1783. Writings, VIII. 409. Letter to Lafayette, April 5, 1783. Ibid. 411. Address to the States, June 8, 1783. Ibid. 439.

had formed in his enlarged and comprehensive mind the clearest views of the means necessary to meet them, even before the Confederation had been practically tried. A reorganization of the government had engaged the attention of Hamilton, as early as 1780; and, with his characteristic penetration and power, he saw and suggested what should be the remedy.

He entertained the opinion, at this time, as he had always entertained it, that the discretionary powers originally vested in Congress for the safety of the States, and implied in the circumstances and objects of their assembling, were fully competent to the public exigencies. But their practice, from the time of the Declaration of Independence through all the period that preceded the establishment of the Confederation, had accustomed the country to doubts of their original authority, and had at last amounted to a surrender of the ground from which they might have exercised it. No remedy, therefore, remained, applicable to the circumstances, and capable of rescuing the affairs of the country from their deplorable situation, but to vest in Congress, expressly and by a direct grant, the powers necessary to constitute an efficient government and a solid, coercive union. The project then before the country, in the Articles of Confederation, had been designed to accomplish what the revolutionary government had failed to do. But it was manifestly destined to fail in its turn; for it left an uncontrollable sovereignty in the States, capable of defeating the beneficial exercise of the very powers which it undertook to confer upon Congress.

It made the army, not a unit, formed and organized by a central and supreme authority, and looking up to that authority alone, but a collection of several armies, raised by the several States. It gave to the State legislatures the effective power of the purse, by withholding all certain revenues from Congress. It proposed to introduce no method and energy of administration; and without an executive, it left every detail of government to be managed by a deliberative body, whose constitution rendered it fit for none but legislative functions.

Under these circumstances, it was Hamilton's advice, before the Confederation took effect, that Congress should plainly, frankly, and unanimously confess to the States their inability to carry on the contest with Great Britain, without more ample powers than those which they had for some time exercised, or those which they could exercise under the Confederation; and that a convention of all the States be immediately assembled, with full authority to agree upon a different system. He suggested that a complete sovereignty should be vested in Congress, except as to that part of internal police which relates to the rights of property and life among individuals, and to raising money by internal taxes, which he admitted should be regulated by the State legislatures. But in all that relates to war, peace, trade, and finance, he maintained that the sovereignty of Congress should be complete; that it should have the entire management of foreign affairs, and of raising and officering armies and navies; that it should have the entire regulation of trade, determining with what countries it should be carried on, laying prohibitions and duties, and granting bounties and premiums; that it should have certain perpetual revenues of an internal character, in specific taxes; that it should be authorized to institute admiralty courts, coin money, establish banks, appropriate funds, and make alliances offensive and defensive, and treaties of commerce. He recommended also that Congress should immediately organize executive departments of foreign affairs, war, marine, finance, and trade, with great officers of state at the head of each of them.[1]

[1] These suggestions were made by Hamilton, in a letter of great ability, written in 1780, while he was still in the army, to James Duane, a member of Congress from New York. It was not published until it appeared in his Life, I. 284. At its close, he says: "I am persuaded a solid confederation, a permanent army, a reasonable prospect of subsisting it, would give us treble consideration in Europe, and produce a peace this winter. *If a convention is called, the minds of all the States and the people ought to be prepared to receive its determinations by sensible and popular writings*, which should conform to the views of Congress. There are epochs in human affairs when *novelty* is useful. If a general opinion prevails that the old way is bad, whether true or false, and this obstructs or relaxes the operations of the public service, a change is necessary, if it be but for the sake of change. This is exactly the case now. 'T is an universal sentiment, that our present system is a bad one, and that things do not go right on this account. The measure of a convention would revive the hopes of the people, and give a new direction to their passions, which may be improved in carrying points of substantial utility. The Eastern States have already pointed out this mode to Congress: they ought to take the hint, and anticipate the others." What is here said of the action of the Eastern States probably refers, not to any suggestion of a convention to revise the powers of the general government, but to a convention of committees of the Eastern States, which first assembled at Hartford and afterwards at Boston, in No

Hamilton's entry into Congress in 1782 marks the commencement of his public efforts to develop the idea of a general government, whose organs should act directly, and without the intervention of any State machinery. He first publicly propounded this idea in the paper which he prepared, as chairman of a committee, to be addressed to the legislature of Rhode Island, in answer to the objections of that State to the revenue system proposed in 1781. One of these objections was, that the plan proposed to introduce into the State officers unknown and unaccountable to the State itself, and therefore that it was against its constitution. From the prevalence of this notion, we may see how difficult it was to create the idea of a national sovereignty, that would consist with the sovereignty of the States, and would work in its appropriate sphere harmoniously with the State institutions, because directed to a different class of objects. The nature of a federal constitution was little understood. It was apparent that the exercise of its powers must affect the internal police of its component members, to some extent; but it was not well understood that political sovereignty is capable of partition, according to the character of its subjects, so that powers of one class may be imparted to a federal, and powers of another class remain in a State

vember, 1779, and in August, 1780, *for regulating the prices of commodities.* Journals of Congress, V. 406; VI. 271, 331, 392. But the writer may have had in his mind the convention which had just assembled in Massachusetts to form the constitution of that State. I am aware of no public proposal, as early as 1780, of a general convention to remodel the Confederacy.

constitution, without destroying the sovereignty of the latter. Hamilton presented this view, and at the same time pointed out, that, unless the constitution of a State expressly prohibited its legislature from granting to the federal government new power to appoint officers for a special purpose, to act within the State itself, it was competent to the legislative authority of the State to communicate such power, just as it was competent to it originally to enter into the Confederation.[1]

[1] "It is not to be presumed," he said, "that the constitution of any State means to define and fix the precise numbers and descriptions of all officers to be permitted in the State, excluding the creation of any new ones, whatever might be the necessity derived from that variety of circumstances incident to all political institutions. The legislature must always have a discretionary power of appointing officers, not expressly known to the constitution, and this power will include that of authorizing the federal government to make the appointments in cases where the general welfare may require it. The denial of this would prove too much; to wit, that the power given by the Confederation to Congress, to appoint all officers in the post-office, was illegal and unconstitutional. The doctrine advanced by Rhode Island would perhaps prove also that the federal government ought to have the appointment of no internal officers whatever; a position that would defeat all the provisions of the Confederation, and all the purposes of the union. The truth is, that no federal constitution can exist without powers that in their exercise effect the internal police of the component members. It is equally true, that no government can exist without a right to appoint officers for those purposes which proceed from, and concentre in, itself; and therefore the Confederation has expressly declared, that Congress shall have authority to appoint all such 'civil officers as may be necessary for managing the general affairs of the United States under their direction.' All that can be required is, that the federal government confine its appointments to such as it is empowered to make by the original act of union, or by the subsequent consent of the parties; unless there should be express words of exclusion in the constitution of a State, there can be no reason to doubt that it is within the compass of legislative discretion to communicate that authority. The propriety

In the same paper, also, he urged the necessity of vesting the appointment of the collectors of the proposed revenue in the general government, because it was designed as a security to creditors, and must therefore be general in its principle and dependent on a single will, and not on thirteen different authorities. This was the earliest suggestion of the principle, that, in exercising its powers, the federal government ought to act directly, through agents of its own appointment, and thus be independent of State negligence or control. When the debate came on in January, 1783, upon the new project of a revenue system, he again urged the necessity of strengthening the federal government, through the influence of

of doing it upon the present occasion, is founded on substantial reasons. The measure proposed is a measure of necessity. Repeated experiments have shown, that the revenue to be raised within these States is altogether inadequate to the public wants. The deficiency can only be supplied by loans. Our applications to the foreign powers on whose friendship we depend, have had a success far short of our necessities. The next resource is to borrow from individuals. These will neither be actuated by generosity nor reasons of state. 'T is to their interest alone we must appeal. To conciliate this, we must not only stipulate a proper compensation for what they lend, but we must give security for the performance. We must pledge an ascertained fund, simple and productive in its nature, general in its principle, and at the disposal of a single will. There can be little confidence in a security under the constant revisal of thirteen different deliberatives. It must, once for all, be defined and established on the faith of the States, solemnly pledged to each other, and not revocable by any without a breach of the general compact. 'T is by such expedients that nations whose resources are understood, whose reputations and governments are erected on the foundation of ages, are enabled to obtain a solid and extensive credit. Would it be reasonable in us to hope for more easy terms, who have so recently assumed our rank among the nations? Is it not to be expected, that individuals will be cautious in lending their money to a people in our circumstances, and

officers deriving their appointments directly from Congress; — a suggestion that was received at the moment with pleasure by the opponents of the scheme, because it seemed to disclose a motive calculated to touch the jealousy rather than to propitiate the favor of the States. But the temporary expedients of the moment always pass away. The great ideas of a statesman like Hamilton, earnestly bent on the discovery and inculcation of truth, do not pass away. Wiser than those by whom he was surrounded, with a deeper knowledge of the science of government and the wants of the country than all of them, and constantly enunciating principles which extended far beyond the temporizing policy of the hour,

that they will at least require the best security we can give? We have an enemy vigilant, intriguing, well acquainted with our defects and embarrassments. We may expect that he will make every effort to instil diffidences into individuals, and in the present posture of our internal affairs he will have too plausible ground on which to tread. Our necessities have obliged us to embrace measures, with respect to our public credit, calculated to inspire distrust. The prepossessions on this article must naturally be against us, and it is therefore indispensable we should endeavor to remove them, by such means as will be the most obvious and striking. It was with these views Congress determined on a general fund; and the one they have recommended must, upon a thorough examination, appear to have fewer inconveniences than any other. It has been remarked as an essential part of the plan, that the fund should depend on a single will. This will not be the case, unless the collection, as well as the appropriation, is under the control of the United States; for it is evident, that, after the duty is agreed upon, it may, in a great measure, be defeated by an ineffectual mode of levying it. The United States have a common interest in a uniform and equally energetic collection; and not only policy, but justice to all the parts of the Union, designates the utility of lodging the power of making it where the interest is common. Without this, it might in reality operate as a very unequal tax." Journals of Congress, VIII. 153.

the smiles of his opponents only prove to posterity how far he was in advance of them.[1]

The efforts of Hamilton to effect a change in the rule of the Confederation, as to the ratio of contribution by the States to the treasury of the Union, also evince both the defects of the existing government and the foresight with which he would have obviated them, if he could have been sustained. The rule of the Confederation required that the general treasury should be supplied by the several States in proportion to the value of all lands within each State, granted or surveyed, with the buildings and improvements thereon, to be estimated according to such mode as Congress should from time to time direct and appoint; the taxes for paying such proportion to be laid and levied by the State legislatures, within the time fixed by Congress. But Congress had never appointed any mode of ascertaining the valuation of lands within the States. The first requisition called for after the Confederation took effect was appor-

[1] He said, as an additional reason for the revenue being collected by officers under the appointment of Congress, that, "as the energy of the federal government was evidently short of the degree necessary for pervading and uniting the States, it was expedient to introduce the influence of officers deriving their emoluments from, and consequently interested in supporting the power of Congress." Upon this Mr. Madison observes: "This remark was imprudent, and injurious to the cause it was intended to serve. This influence was the very source of jealousy which rendered the States averse to a revenue under collection, as well as appropriation, of Congress. All the members of Congress who concurred in any degree, with the States in this jealousy, smiled at the disclosure. Mr. Bland, and still more Mr. Lee, who were of this number, took notice, in private conversation, that Mr. Hamilton had let out the secret." Elliot's Debates, I. 35.

tioned among the several States without any valuation, — provision being made by which each State was to receive interest on its payments, as far as they exceeded what might afterwards be ascertained to be its just proportion, when the valuation should have been made.[1] At the outset, therefore, a practical inequality was established, which gave rise to complaints and jealousies between the States, and increased the disposition to withhold compliance with the requisitions. The dangerous crisis in the internal affairs of the country which attended the approach of peace, had arrived in the winter and spring of 1783, and nothing had ever been done to carry out the rule of the Confederation, by fixing upon a mode of valuation. When the discussion of the new measures for sustaining the public credit came on, three courses presented themselves, with regard to this part of the subject; — either, first, to change the principle of the Confederation entirely; or, secondly, to carry it out by fixing a mode of valuation, at once; or, thirdly, to postpone the attempt to carry it out, until a better mode could be devised than the existing state of the country then permitted.

Hamilton's preference was for the first of these courses, as the one that admitted of the application of those principles of government which he was endeavoring to introduce into the federal system; for he saw that in the theory of the Confederation there was an inherent inequality, which would constantly

[1] March 18 and 23, 1781. Journals, VII. 56, 67.

increase in practice, and which must either be removed, or destroy the Union. He maintained, that, where there are considerable differences in the relative wealth of different communities, the proportion of those differences can never be ascertained by any common measure; that the actual wealth of a country, or its ability to pay taxes, depends on an endless variety of circumstances, physical and moral, and cannot be measured by any one general representative, as *land*, or *numbers;* and therefore that the assumption of such a general representative, by whatever mode its local value might be ascertained, would work inevitable inequality. In his view, the only possible way of making the States contribute to the general treasury in an equal proportion to their means, was by general taxes imposed under continental authority; and it is a striking proof of the comprehensive sagacity with which he looked forward, that, while he admitted that this mode would, for a time, produce material inequalities, he foresaw that balancing of interests which would arise in a continental legislation, and would relieve the hardships of one tax in a particular State by the lighter pressure of another bearing with proportional weight in some other part of the Confederacy.[1]

Accordingly, after an attempt to postpone the consideration of a mode of carrying out the Confederation, he made an effort to have its principle changed, by substituting specific taxes on land and houses, to

[1] Life of Hamilton, II. 50-57.

be collected and appropriated, as well as the duties, under the authority of the United States, by officers to be nominated by Congress, and approved by the State in which they were to exercise their functions, but accountable to and removable by Congress.[1] These ideas, however, as he himself saw, were not agreeable to the spirit of the times, and his plan was rejected. After many fruitless projects had been suggested and discussed, for making the valuation required by the Confederation, — some of them proposing that it should be done by commissioners appointed by the United States, and some by commissioners appointed by the States, — it was determined to propose no other change in the principle of making requisitions on the States, than to substitute population in the place of land, as the rule of proportion.[2]

1 March 20, 1783. Journals, VIII. 157 - 159.

2 The census was to be of "the whole number of white and other free citizens and inhabitants, of every age, sex, and condition, including those bound to servitude for a term of years, and three fifths of all other persons not comprehended in the foregoing description, except Indians, not paying taxes, in each State; which number shall be triennially taken and transmitted to the United States in Congress assembled, in such mode as they shall direct and appoint." When the Articles of Confederation were framed and adopted in Congress, a valuation of land as the rule of proportion was adopted instead of numbers of inhabitants, in consequence of the impossibility of compromising the different ideas of the Eastern and Southern States as to the rate at which slaves should be counted; the Eastern States of course wishing to have them counted in a near ratio to the whites, and the Southern States wishing to diminish that ratio. Numbers would have been preferred by the Southern States to land, if half their slaves only could have been taken; but the Eastern States were opposed to this estimate. (Elliot's Debates, I. 79.) In 1783, when it was proposed to change the rule of proportion from land to numbers, the first compromise suggested (by Mr. Wolcott of Connecticut) was

Equally extensive and important were his views on the subject of a peace establishment, for which he saw the necessity of providing, as the time approached when the Confederation would necessarily be tested as a government for the purposes of peace. To adapt a constitution, whose principal powers were originally designed to be exercised in a state of war, to a state of peace, for which it possessed but few powers, and those not clearly defined, was a problem in the science of government of a novel character. It might prove to be an impossible task; for on applying the constitutional provisions to the real wants and necessities of the country, it might turn out that the Confederation was in some respects destitute of the capacity to provide for them; and in undertaking to carry out its actual and sufficient powers, which had never hitherto been exercised, opposition might spring up, from State jealousy and local policy, which, in the real weakness of the federal government, would be as effectual a barrier as the want of constitutional authority. Still the effort was to be made; and Hamilton approached the subject with all the sagacity and statesmanship for which he was so distinguished.

He saw that the Confederation contained provisions which looked to the continuance of the Union after the war had terminated, and that these pro-

to include only such slaves as were between the ages of sixteen and sixty; this was found to be impracticable; and it was agreed on all sides, that, instead of fixing the proportion by ages, it would be best to fix it in absolute numbers, and the rate of three fifths was agreed upon. (Ibid. 81, 82.)

visions required practical application, through a machinery which had never been even framed. The Articles of Confederation vested in Congress the exclusive management of foreign relations; but the department of foreign affairs had never been properly organized. They also gave to Congress the exclusive regulation of trade and intercourse with the Indian nations; but no department of Indian affairs had been established with properly defined powers and duties. Nothing had been done to carry out the provision for fixing the standard of weights and measures throughout the United States, or to regulate the alloy and value of coin. Above all, the great question of means, military and naval, for the external and internal defence of the country during peace, for the preservation of tranquillity, the protection of commerce, the fulfilment of treaty stipulations, and the maintenance of the authority of the United States, had not been so much as touched. To regulate these important subjects was the design of a committee, at the head of which Hamilton was placed; and his earliest attention was directed to the most serious and difficult of them, — the provision for a peace establishment of military and naval forces.[1]

The question whether the United States could constitutionally maintain an army and navy, in time of peace, was, under the Articles of Confederation, not free from difficulty; but it became of imminent practical importance, under the treaty of peace. That

[1] Life of Hamilton, II. 204-212.

treaty provided for an immediate withdrawal of the British forces from all posts and fortifications within the United States; and it became at once an important question, whether these posts and fortifications — especially those within certain districts, the jurisdiction and property of which had not been constitutionally ascertained — should be garrisoned by troops of the United States, or of the States within which they were situated. There was also territory appertaining to the United States, not within the original claim of the United States. The whole of the Western frontier required defence. The navigation of the Mississippi and the lakes, and the rights of the fisheries and of foreign commerce, all belonging to the United States, and depending on the laws of nations and treaty stipulations, demanded the joint protection of the Union, and could not with propriety be left to the separate establishments of the States.

But the Articles of Confederation contained no express provision for the establishment and maintenance of any military and naval forces during peace. They empowered the United States, generally, (and without mention of peace or war,) to build and equip a navy, and to agree upon the number of land forces to be raised, and to call upon the States to furnish their quotas. But they also declared that no vessels of war should be kept up by any State in time of peace, except such number only as should be deemed necessary by Congress for the defence of such State or its trade; and that no body of forces should be kept up by any State in time of peace, except such number only as Congress should deem requisite to garrison the posts necessary for the defence of such State. This provision might be construed to imply, that, in time of peace, the general defence was to be provided for by the forces of each State, and, in time of war, by those of the Union. But it was the opinion of Hamilton, that the restrictions on the powers of the States, with regard to maintaining forces during peace, could not with propriety be said to contain any directions to the United States, or to contravene the positive power vested in the latter to raise both sea and land forces, without mention of peace or war. He strengthened this view by the capital inconvenience of the contrary construction, and by the manifest necessities of the country, which could only be provided for by the power of the Union. If the United States could have neither army nor navy, until war had been declared, they would be obliged to begin to create both at the very moment when both were needed in actual hostilities; and, if the States were to be intrusted with the defence of the country in time of peace, that defence would be left to thirteen different armies and navies, under the direction of as many different governments.[1]

He contemplated, therefore, the formation of a peace establishment, to consist of certain corps of infantry, artillery, cavalry, engineers, and dragoons;[2] a

[1] Ibid.

[2] He proposed that the States should transfer to Congress the right to appoint the regimental officers, and that the men should be enlisted under continental direction.

general survey, preparatory to the adoption of a general system of land fortifications; the establishment of arsenals and magazines, and the erection of founderies and manufactories of arms. He advised the establishment of ports and maritime fortifications, and the formation and construction of a navy; and his report embraced also a plan for classing and disciplining the militia.

[1] That the subject of a peace establishment originated with Hamilton is certain, from the fact that early in April, soon after the appointment of the committee, he wrote to General Washington, wishing to know his sentiments at large on such institutions of every kind for the interior defence of the States as might be best adapted to their circumstances. (Writings of Washington, VIII. 417.) Washington wrote to all the principal officers of the army then in camp, for their views, and from the memoirs which they presented to him an important document was compiled, which was forwarded by him to the committee of Congress. In one of these memoirs Colonel Pickering suggested the establishment of a military academy at West Point. "If any thing," he said, "like a military academy in America be practicable at this time, it must be grounded on the permanent military establishment of our frontier posts and arsenals, and the wants of the States, separately, of officers to command the defences of their sea-coasts. On this principle, it might be expedient to establish a military school, or academy, at West Point. And that a competent number of young gentlemen might be induced to become students, it might be made a rule, that vacancies in the standing regiments should be supplied from thence; those few instances excepted where it would be just to promote a very meritorious sergeant. For this end, the number which shall be judged requisite to supply vacancies in the standing regiment might be fixed, and that of the students, who are admitted with an exception of filling them, limited accordingly. They might be allowed subsistence at the public expense. If any other youth desired to pursue the same studies at the military academy, they might be admitted, only subsisting themselves. Those students should be instructed in what is usually called military discipline, tactics, and the theory and practice of fortification and gunnery. The commandant and one or two other officers of the standing regiment, and the engineers, making West Point their

In all this design, Hamilton pursued the purpose, which he had long entertained, of strengthening and consolidating the Union, and guarding against its dissolution, by providing the means necessary for its defence. Federal, rather than State provision for the defence of every part of the Confederacy, in peace as well as in war, seemed to him essential. He thought, that the general government should have exclusively the power of the sword, and that each State should have no forces but its militia.[1] But his

general residence, would be the masters of the academy; and the inspector-general superintend the whole." (Ibid.) The subject of a peace establishment was made one of the four principal topics on which Washington afterwards enlarged in his circular letter to the States, in June; but his suggestions related chiefly to a uniform organization of the militia throughout the States. He subsequently had several conferences with the committee of Congress, on the whole subject, but nothing was done. (Vide note, infra.)

[1] Life of Hamilton, II. 214–219. The State of New York precipitated the constitutional question, by demanding that the Western posts within her limits should be garrisoned by troops of her own, and by instructing her delegates in Congress to obtain a declaration, conformably to the sixth article of the Confederation, of the number of troops necessary for that purpose. Hamilton forbore to press this application while the general subject of a peace establishment was under consideration. But the doubts that arose as to the constitutional power of Congress to raise an army for the purposes of peace, and the urgency of the case, made it necessary to adopt a temporary measure with regard to the frontier posts, and to direct the commander-in-chief to garrison them with a part of the troops of the United States which had enlisted for three years. This was ordered on the 12th of May. Soon after, the mutiny of a portion of the new levies of the Pennsylvania line occurred, which drove Congress from Philadelphia to Princeton, on the 21st of June. At Princeton, they remained during the residue of the year, but with diminished numbers and often without a constitutional quorum of States. In September, General Washington wrote to Governor Clinton: "Congress have come to no determination yet respecting a peace establishment, nor am I able to say when they will. I have lately had a conference with a com-

great plans were arrested, partly in consequence of the doubts entertained on the point of constitutional power, and partly by reason of the great falling off of the attendance of members in Congress. At the very time when this important subject was under consideration, Congress were driven from Philadelphia, by the mutiny of a handful of men, whom they could not curb at the moment without the aid of the local authorities, and that aid was nôt promptly and efficiently given.[1]

mittee on this subject, and have reiterated my former opinions: but it appears to me, that there is not a sufficient representation to discuss great national points; nor do I believe there will be, while that honorable body continue their sessions at this place. The want of accommodation, added to a disinclination in the Southern delegates to be farther removed than they formerly were from the centre of the empire, and an aversion in the others to give up what they conceive to be a point gained by the late retreat to this place, keep matters in an awkward situation, to the very great interruption of national concerns. Seven States, it seems, by the Articles of Confederation, must agree, before any place can be fixed upon for the seat of the federal government; and seven States, it is said, never will agree; consequently, as Congress came here, here they are to remain, to the dissatisfaction of the majority and a great let to business, having none of the public offices about them, nor any place to accommodate them, if they were brought up; and the members, from this or some other cause, are eternally absent."

[1] Mr. Madison has given the following account of this occurrence: — "On the 19th of June, Congress received information from the Executive Council of Pennsylvania, that eighty soldiers, who would probably be followed by others, were on the way from Lancaster to Philadelphia, in spite of the expostulations of their officers, declaring that they would proceed to the seat of Congress and demand justice, and intimating designs against the Bank. A committee, of which Colonel Hamilton was chairman, was appointed to confer with the executive of Pennsylvania, and to take such measures as they should find necessary. After a conference, the committee reported that it was the opinion of the executive that the militia of Philadelphia would probably not

Convinced, at length, that no temporary expedients would meet the wants of the country, and that a radical reform of its constitution could alone preserve the Union from dissolution, Hamilton surveyed the Confederation in all its parts, and determined to lay before the country its deep defects, with a view to the establishment of a government with proper departments and adequate powers. In this examination, he applied to the Confederation the approved maxims of free government, which had been made famil-

be willing to take arms before they should be provoked by some actual outrage; that it would hazard the authority of government to make the attempt; and that it would be necessary to let the soldiers come into the city, if the officers who had gone out to meet them could not stop them. The next day the soldiers arrived in the city, led by their sergeants, and professing to have no other object than to obtain a settlement of accounts, which they supposed they had a better chance for at Philadelphia than at Lancaster. On the 21st, they were drawn up in the street before the State-House, where Congress were assembled. The Executive Council of the State, sitting under the same roof, was called on for the proper interposition. The President of the State (Dickinson) came in and explained the difficulty of bringing out the militia of the place for the suppression of the mutiny. He thought that, without some outrages on persons or property, the militia could not be relied on. General St. Clair, then in Philadelphia, was sent for, and desired to use his interposition, in order to prevail on the troops to return to the barracks. But his report gave no encouragement. In this posture of things, it was proposed by Mr. Izard that Congress should adjourn. Colonel Hamilton proposed that General St. Clair, in concert with the Executive Council of the State, should take order for terminating the mutiny. Mr. Reed moved that the General should endeavor to withdraw the mutineers, by assuring them of the disposition of Congress to do them justice. Nothing, however, was done. The soldiers remained in their position, occasionally uttering offensive words and pointing their muskets at the windows of the hall of Congress. At the usual hour of adjournment the members went out, without obstruction; and the soldiers retired to their barracks. In the evening Congress reassembled, and appoint-

iar in the formation of the State constitutions, and which point to the distinct separation of the legislative, executive, and judicial functions. The Confederation vested all these powers in a single body, and thus violated the principles on which the government of nearly every State in the Union was founded. It had no federal judicature, to take cognizance of matters of general concern, and especially of those in which foreign nations and their subjects were concerned; and thus national treaties, the national faith, and the public tranquillity were exposed to the conflict of local regulations against the powers vested in the Union. It gave to Congress the power of ascertaining and appropriating the sums necessary for the public expenses, but withheld all control over either the imposition or collection of the taxes by which they were to be raised, and thus made the inclinations, not the abilities, of the respective States, the criterion of their contributions to the common expenses of the Union. It authorized Congress to borrow money, or emit bills, on the credit of the United States, without the power of providing funds to secure the repayment of the money, or the redemption of the bills emitted.

ed a committee to confer anew with the executive of the State. This conference produced nothing but a repetition of the doubts concerning the disposition of the militia to act, unless some actual outrage were offered to persons or property, the insult to Congress not being deemed a sufficient provocation. On the 24th, the efforts of the State authority being despaired of, Congress were summoned by the President to meet at Trenton." (Elliot's Debates, I. 92–94.) The mutiny was afterwards suppressed by marching troops into Pennsylvania under Major-General Howe. (Journals, VIII. 281.)

It made no proper or competent provision for interior or exterior defence; for interior defence, because it allowed the individual States to appoint all regimental officers of the land forces, and to raise the men in their own way, while at the same time an ambiguity rendered it uncertain whether the defence of the country in time of peace was not left to the particular States, both by sea and land; — for exterior defence, because it authorized Congress to build and equip a navy, without providing any compulsory means of manning it.

It failed to vest in the United States a general superintendence of trade, equally necessary both with a view to revenue and regulation.

It required the assent of nine States in Congress to matters of principal importance, and of seven to all others except adjournments from day to day, and thus subjected the sense of a majority of the people of the United States to that of a minority, by putting it in the power of a small combination to defeat the most necessary measures.

Finally, it vested in the federal government the sole direction of the interests of the United States in their intercourse with foreign nations, without empowering it to pass *all general laws* in aid and support of the laws of nations; thus exposing the faith, reputation, and peace of the country to the irregular action of the particular States.[1]

Having thus fully analyzed for himself the nature

[1] Life of Hamilton, II. 230–237.

of the existing constitution, Hamilton proposed to himself the undertaking of inducing Congress freely and frankly to inform the country of its imperfections, which made it impossible to conduct the public affairs with honor to themselves and advantage to the Union; and to recommend to the several States to appoint a convention, with full powers to revise the Confederation, and to adopt and propose such alterations as might appear to be necessary, which should be finally approved or rejected by the States.[1]

But he was surrounded by men, who were not equal to the great enterprise of guiding and enlightening public sentiment. He was in advance of the time, and far in advance of the men of the time. He experienced the fate of all statesmen, in the like position, whose ideas have had to wait the slow development of events, to bring them to the popular comprehension and assent. He saw that his plans could not be adopted; and he passed out of Congress to the pursuits of private life, recording upon them his conviction, that their public proposal would have failed for want of support.[2]

There was in fact a manifest indisposition in Congress to propose any considerable change in the principle of the government. Hence, nothing but the revenue system, with a change in the rule by which a partition of the common burdens was to be made, was publicly proposed. Although this system was a

[1] Life of Hamilton, II. 230-237.

[2] Ibid

great improvement upon that of the Confederation, it related simply to revenue, in regard to which it proposed a reform, not of the principle of the government, but of the mode of operation of the old system; for it embraced only a specific pledge by the States of certain duties for a limited term, and not a grant of the unlimited power of levying duties at pleasure. There was confessedly a departure from the strict maxims of national credit, by not making the revenue coextensive with its object, and by not placing its collection in every respect under the authority charged with the management and payment of the debt which it was designed to meet.[1]

These relaxations were a sacrifice to the jealousies of the States; and they show that the time had not come for a change from a mere federative union to a constitutional government, founded on the popular will, and therefore acting by an energy and volition of its own.

The temper of the time was wholly unfavorable to such a change. The early enthusiasm with which the nation had rushed into the conflict with England, guided by a common impulse and animated by a national spirit, had given place to calculations of local interest and advantage; and the principle of the Confederation was tenaciously adhered to, while the events which accompanied and followed the peace were rapidly displaying its radical incapacity. The

[1] See the Address to the States, accompanying the proposed revenue system, April 26, 1783, from the pen of Mr. Madison. Journals, VIII. 194–201.

formation of the State governments, and the consequent growth and importance of State interests, which came into existence with the Confederation, and the fact that the Confederation was itself an actual diminution of the previous powers of the Union, may be considered the chief causes of the decline of a national spirit. That spirit was destined to a still further decay, until the conflict of State against State, and of section against section, by shaking the government to its foundation, should reveal both the necessity for a national sovereignty and the means by which it could be called into life.

As a consequence and proof of the decline of national power, it is worthy of observation, that, at the close of the year 1783, Congress had practically dwindled to a feeble junto of about twenty persons, exercising the various powers of the government, but without the dignity and safety of a local habitation. Migrating from city to city and from State to State, unable to agree upon a seat of government, from jealousy and sectional policy; now assembling in the capitol of a State, and now in the halls of a college; at all times dependent upon the protection and even the countenance of local authorities, and without the presence of any of the great and powerful minds who led the earlier counsels of the country, this body presented a not inadequate type of the decaying powers of the Union.[1] At no time in the

[1] The first Continental Congress was called to meet at Philadelphia, that being the nearest to the centre of the Union of any of the principal cities in the United States. Succeeding Congresses had been

history of the Confederation, had all the States been represented at once; and the return of peace seemed

held there, with the exception of the period when the city was in the possession of the enemy, in the year 1777, until, on the 21st of June, 1783, in consequence of the mutiny of the soldiers, the President was authorized to summon the members to meet at Trenton, or Princeton, in New Jersey, "in order that further and more effectual measures may be taken for suppressing the present revolt, and maintaining the dignity and authority of the United States." On the 30th, Congress assembled at Princeton, in the halls of the college, which were tendered by its officers for their use. In August, a proposition was made to return to Philadelphia, and that, on the second Monday in October, Congress should meet at Annapolis, unless in the mean time it had been ordered otherwise. But this was not agreed to. A committee was then appointed (in September), "to consider what jurisdiction may be proper for Congress in the place of their permanent residence." This seems to have been followed by propositions from several of the States, from New York to Virginia inclusive, respecting a place for the permanent residence of Congress, although the Journal does not state what they were. A question was then taken (October 6), in which State buildings should be provided and erected for the residence of Congress, beginning with New Hampshire and proceeding with all the States in their order. Each State was negatived in its turn. The highest number of votes given (by States) were for New Jersey and Maryland, which had four votes each. A resolution was then carried, "that buildings for the use of Congress be erected on or near the banks of the Delaware, provided a suitable district can be procured on or near the banks of said river, for a federal town; and that the right of soil, and an exclusive or such jurisdiction as Congress may direct, shall be vested in the United States"; and a committee was appointed, to repair to the falls of the Delaware, to view the country, and report a proper district for this purpose. A variety of motions then followed, for the selection of a place of temporary residence, but none was adopted. On the 17th of October, a proposition was made by a delegate of Massachusetts (Mr. Gerry), to have buildings provided for the alternate residence of Congress in two places, with the idea of "securing the mutual confidence and affection of the States, and preserving the federal balance of power"; but the question was lost. Afterwards, the following resolution was agreed to: "Whereas, there is reason to expect that the providing buildings for the alternate residence of Congress in two places will be productive of the most salutary effects, by securing

likely to reduce the entire machinery of the government to a state of complete inaction.[1]

The Confederation, at the close of the war, is found to have accomplished much, and also to have failed to accomplish much more. It had effected the cession of the public lands to the United States; for although that cession was not completed until after the peace, still the arch on which the Union was ultimately to rest for whatever of safety and perpetuity remained for it through the four following years, was deposited in its place, when the Confederation was established. It had also placed the United States, as a nation, in a position to contract some alliances with foreign powers. It had finished the war; it had achieved the independence of the nation; and had given peace to the country. It had thus demonstrated the value of the Union, although its defective construction aided the development of

the mutual confidence and affections of the States, *Resolved*, That buildings be likewise erected, for the use of Congress, at or near the lower falls of the Potomac, or Georgetown, provided a suitable district on the banks of the river can be procured for a federal town, and the right of soil, and an exclusive jurisdiction, or such as Congress may direct, shall be vested in the United States; and that until the buildings to be erected on the banks of the Delaware and Potomac shall be prepared for the reception of Congress, their residence shall be alternately, at equal periods of not more than one year and not less than six months, in Trenton and Annapolis; and the President is hereby authorized and directed to adjourn Congress on the twelfth day of November next, to meet at Annapolis on the twenty-sixth day of the same month, for the despatch of public business." (Journals of Congress from June to November, 1783.)

1 Report of a committee appointed to devise means for procuring a full representation in Congress, made November 1, 1783. Journals, VIII. 480-482.

tendencies which weakened and undermined its strength.

But its imperfect performance of the great tasks to which it had been called, displayed its inherent defects. It had often been unequal to the purpose of effectually drawing forth the resources of its members for the common welfare and defence. It had often wanted an army adequate to the protection and proportioned to the abilities of the country. It had, therefore, seen important posts reduced, others imminently endangered, and whole States and large parts of others overrun by small bodies of the enemy; — had been destitute of sufficient means of feeding, clothing, paying, and appointing its troops, and had thus exposed them to sufferings for which history scarcely affords a parallel. It had been compelled to make the administration of its affairs a succession of temporary expedients, inconsistent with order, economy, energy, or a scrupulous adherence to public engagements. It found itself, at the close of the war, without any certain means of doing justice to those who had been the principal supporters of the Union; — to an army which had bravely fought, and patiently suffered, — to citizens and to foreigners, who had cheerfully lent their money, — and to others who had contributed property and personal service to the common cause. It was obliged to rely, for the last hope of doing that justice, on the precarious concurrence of thirteen distinct legislatures, the dissent of either of which might defeat the plan, and leave the States, at an early period of their existence, involved in all the disgrace and mischiefs of violated faith and national bankruptcy.[1]

While, therefore, the United States emerged from the war, which for seven long years had wasted the energies and drained the resources of the people, with national independence, dark and portentous clouds gathered about the dawn of peace, as the future opened before them. The past had been crowned with victory; — dearly bought, but not at too dear a price, for it brought with it the vast boon of civil liberty. But the dangers and embarrassments through which that victory had been achieved made it apparent that the government of the country was unequal to its protection and prosperity. That government was now called to assume the great duties of peace, without the acknowledged power of maintaining either an army or a navy, and without the means of combining and directing the forces and wills of the several parts to a general end; without the least control over commerce; without the power to fulfil a treaty; without laws acting upon individuals; and with no mode of enforcing its own will, but by coercing a delinquent State to its federal obligations by force of arms. How it met the great demands upon its energy and durability which its new duties involved, we are now to inquire.

[1] Hamilton's proposed Resolutions; Life, II. 230 – 230 – 237.

BOOK III.

THE CONSTITUTIONAL HISTORY OF THE UNITED STATES, FROM THE PEACE OF 1783 TO THE FEDERAL CONVENTION OF 1787.

CHAPTER I.

JANUARY, 1784 — MAY, 1787.

DUTIES AND NECESSITIES OF CONGRESS. — REQUISITIONS ON THE STATES. — REVENUE SYSTEM OF 1783.

THE period which now claims our attention is that extending from the Peace of 1783 to the calling of the Convention which framed the Constitution, in 1787. It was a period full of dangers and difficulties. The destinies of the Union seemed to be left to all the hazards arising from a defective government and the illiberal and contracted policy of its members. Patriotism was generally thought to consist in adhesion to State interests, and a reluctance to intrust power to the organs of the nation. The national obligations were therefore disregarded; treaty stipulations remained unfulfilled; the great duty of justice failed to be discharged; rebellion raised a dangerous and nearly successful front; and the commerce of the country was exposed to the injurious policy of other nations, with no means of counteracting or escaping from its effects. At length, the people of the United States began to see danger after they had felt it, and the growth of sounder views and higher principles of public conduct gave to the friends of order, public faith, and national security a controlling influence in the country, and enabled the men, who had won for it the blessings of liberty, to establish for it a durable and sufficient government.

Four years only elapsed, between the return of peace and the downfall of a government which had been framed with the hope and promise of perpetual duration; — an interval of time no longer than that during which the people of the United States are now accustomed to witness a change of their rulers, without injury to any principle or any form of their institutions. But this brief interval was full of suffering and peril. There are scarcely any evils or dangers, of a political nature, and springing from political and social causes, to which a free people can be exposed, which the people of the United States did not experience during this period. That these evils and dangers did not precipitate the country into civil war, and that the great undertaking of forming a new and constitutional government, by delegates of the people, could be entered upon and prosecuted, with the calmness, conciliation, and concession essential to its success, is owing partly to the fact that the country had scarcely recovered from the exhausting effects of the Revolutionary struggle; but mainly to the existence of a body of statesmen, formed during that struggle, and fitted by hard experience to build up the government. But before their efforts and their influences are explained, the period which developed the necessity for their interposition must be described.

He who would know what the Constitution of the United States was designed to accomplish, must understand the circumstances out of which it arose.

On the 3d of November, 1783, a new Congress, according to annual custom, was assembled at Annapolis, and attended by only fifteen members, from seven States. Two great acts awaited the attention of this assembly; — both of an interesting and important character, both of national concern. The one was the resignation of Washington; a solemnity which appealed to every feeling of national gratitude and pride, and which would seem to have demanded whatever of pomp and dignity and power the United States could display. The other was a legislative act, which was to give peace to the country, by the ratification of the Treaty. Several weeks passed on, and yet the attendance was not much increased. Washington's resignation was received, at a public audience of seven States, represented by about twenty delegates;[1] and on the same day letters were de-

[1] The Journals give the following account of General Washington's resignation: —

"According to order, his Excellency the Commander-in-chief was admitted to a public audience, and being seated, the President, after a pause, informed him that the United States in Congress assembled were prepared to receive his communications; whereupon he arose and addressed as follows: 'MR. PRESIDENT, — The great events on which my resignation depended having at length taken place, I have now the honor of offering my sincere congratulations to Congress, and of presenting myself before them to surrender into their hands the trust committed to me, and to claim the indulgence of retiring from the service of my country. Happy in the confirmation of our independence and sovereignty, and pleased with the opportunity afforded the United States of becoming a respectable nation, I resign with satisfaction the appointment I accepted with diffidence; a diffidence in my abilities to ac-

spatched to the other States, urging them, for the safety, honor, and good faith of the United States, to require the immediate attendance of their mem-

complish so arduous a task; which, however, was superseded by a confidence in the rectitude of our cause, the support of the supreme power of the Union, and the patronage of Heaven. The successful termination of the war has verified the most sanguine expectations; and my gratitude for the interposition of Providence, and the assistance I have received from my countrymen, increases with every review of the momentous contest. While I repeat my obligations to the army in general, I should do injustice to my own feelings not to acknowledge, in this place, the peculiar services and distinguished merits of the gentlemen who have been attached to my person during the war. It was impossible the choice of confidential officers to compose my family should have been more fortunate. Permit me, sir, to recommend in particular those who have continued in the service to the present moment, as worthy of the favorable notice and patronage of Congress. I consider it an indispensable duty to close this last act of my official life by commending the interests of our dearest country to the protection of Almighty God, and those who have the superintendence of them to his holy keeping. Having now finished the work assigned me, I retire from the great theatre of action, and, bidding an affectionate farewell to this august body, under whose orders I have so long acted, I here offer my commission, and take my leave of all the employments of public life.' He then advanced and delivered to the President his commission, with a copy of his address, and having resumed his place, the President (Thomas Mifflin) returned him the following answer: 'Sir, — The United States in Congress assembled receive with emotions too affecting for utterance the solemn resignation of the authorities under which you have led their troops with success through a perilous and doubtful war. Called upon by your country to defend its invaded rights, you accepted the sacred charge, before it had formed alliances, and whilst it was without funds or a government to support you. You have conducted the great military contest with wisdom and fortitude, invariably regarding the rights of the civil power through all disasters and changes. You have, by the love and confidence of your fellow-citizens, enabled them to display their martial genius, and transmit their fame to posterity. You have persevered, till these United States, aided by a magnanimous king and nation, have been enabled, under a just Providence, to close the war in freedom, safety, and independence; on which happy event we sincerely join you in congratulations. Hav-

bers.[1] It was not, however, until the 14th of January that the Treaty could be ratified by the constitutional number of nine States; and, when this took place, there were present but three-and-twenty members.[2]

It should undoubtedly be considered, that, from the nature and form of the government, the delegates in Congress had in some sense an ambassadorial character, and were assembled as the representatives of sovereign States. But with whatever dignity, real or fictitious, they may be considered as having been clothed, the government itself was one that created a constant tendency to the neglect of its functions, and therefore produced great practical evils. The Articles of Confederation provided that delegates should be annually appointed by the States, to meet in Congress on the first Monday in November in every year; and although they also gave to Congress the power of ad-

ing defended the standard of liberty in this New World, having taught a lesson useful to those who inflict and to those who feel oppression, you retire from the great theatre of action with the blessings of your fellow-citizens, but the glory of your virtues will not terminate with your military command; it will continue to animate remotest ages. We feel with you our obligations to the army in general, and will particularly charge ourselves with the interests of those confidential officers who have attended your person to this affecting moment. We join you in commending the interests of our dearest country to the protection of Almighty God, beseeching him to dispose the hearts and minds of its citizens to improve the opportunity afforded them of becoming a happy and respectable nation. And for you we address to him our earnest prayers that a life so beloved may be fostered with all his care; that your days may be happy as they have been illustrious; and that he will finally give you that reward which this world cannot give." Journals, IX. 12, 13. December 22, 1783.

1 Ibid.

2 Journals, IX. 30. January 14, 1784.

journment for a recess, during which the government was to be devolved on a Committee of the States, they fixed no period for the termination of a session. While the war lasted, it had been both customary and necessary for the old Congress, and for its successors under the Confederation, to be perpetually in session; and this practice was continued after the peace, with very short intervals of Committees of the States, partly from habit, and partly in consequence of the reduction of the delegations to the lowest constitutional number. This rendered despatch impossible, by putting it in the power of a few members to withhold from important matters the constitutional concurrence of nine States. Without any reference to population by the Articles of Confederation, not less than two nor more than seven delegates were allowed to each State; and by casting the burden of maintaining its own delegates upon each State, they created a strong motive for preferring the smaller number, and often for not being represented at all. This motive became more active after the peace, when the immediate stimulus of hostilities was withdrawn; and it was at the same time accompanied, in most of the States, by a great jealousy of the powers of Congress, a disinclination to enlarge them, and a prevalent feeling that each State was sufficient unto itself for all the purposes of government.[1] The consequence was, that the Congress of the Confederation, from the ratification of the Treaty of Peace to

[1] See Washington's letter to Governor Harrison, of the date of January 18, 1784. Writings, IX. 11.

the adoption of the Constitution, although entitled to ninety-one members, was seldom attended by one third of that number; and the state of the representation was sometimes so low, that one eighth of the whole number present could, under the constitutional rule, negative the most important measures.[1]

Such was the government which was now called to provide for the payment of at least the interest on the public debts, and to procure the means for

[1] Twenty-three members voted on the ratification of the Treaty, January 14, 1784. On the 19th of April of the same year, the same number being present, eleven States only being represented, and nine of these having only two members each, the following resolution was passed: "*Resolved*, That the legislatures of the several States be informed, that, whilst they are respectively represented in Congress by two delegates only, such a unanimity for conducting the most important public concerns is necessary as can be rarely expected; that if each of the thirteen States should be represented by two members, five out of twenty-six, being only a fifth of the whole, may negative any measures requiring the voice of nine States; that of eleven States now on the floor of Congress, nine being represented by only two members from each, it is in the power of three out of twenty-five, making only one eighth of the whole, to negative such a measure, notwithstanding that by the Articles of Confederation the dissent of five out of thirteen, being more than one third of the number, is necessary for such a negative; that in a representation of three members from each State, not less than ten of thirty-nine could so negative a matter requiring the voice of nine States; that, from facts under the observation of Congress, they are clearly convinced that a representation of two members from the several States is extremely injurious, by producing delays, and for this reason is likewise much more expensive than a general representation of three members from each State; that therefore Congress conceive it to be indispensably necessary, and earnestly recommend, that each State, at all times when Congress are sitting, be hereafter represented by three members at least; as the most injurious consequences may be expected from the want of such representation." At the time when the report of the Convention, transmitting the Constitution, was received (September 28, 1787), there were thirty-three members in attendance, from twelve States. Rhode Island was not represented.

its own support; to carry out the Treaty of Peace, and secure to the country its advantages; to complete the cessions of the Western lands, and provide for their settlement and government; to guard the commerce of the country against the hostile policy of other nations; to secure to each State the forms and principles of a republican government; to extend and secure the relations of the country with foreign powers; and to preserve and perpetuate the Union. By tracing the history of its efforts and its failures with regard to these great objects, we may understand the principal causes which brought about the conviction on the part of the people of the United States, that another and a stronger government must take the place of the Confederation.

It was ascertained in April, 1784, that a sum exceeding three millions of dollars would be wanted to pay the arrears of interest, and to meet the interest and current expenses of the public service for the year.[1] Two sources only could be looked to for this supply. It must either be obtained by requisitions on the States, according to the old rule of the Confederation, or from the new duties and taxes proposed by the revenue system of 1783. But that proposal was still under the consideration of the State legislatures; some of them having as yet acceded to the impost only, and others having decided neither on the impost nor on the supplementary taxes. Some time must therefore elapse before the final confirmation of this

[1] The sum reported by a committee, and finally agreed to be necessary, was $ 3,812,539.33. Journals, IX. 171. April 27, 1784.

system, even if its final confirmation were probable; and, after it should have been confirmed, further time would be requisite to bring it into operation. It was quite clear, therefore, that other measures must be resorted to. Requisitions presented the sole resource. But in what mode were they to be made? The preceding Congress had offered two recommendations to the States on the subject of the rule of the Confederation, which directed that the quotas of the several States should be apportioned according to the value of their lands. The Congress of 1783, in order to give this rule a fair trial, had recommended to the States to make returns of their lands, buildings, and inhabitants;[1] but, apprehending that the insufficiency of the rule would immediately show itself, they had followed this recommendation with another, to change the basis of contribution from land to numbers of inhabitants.[2] Both of these propositions were still under the consideration of the State legislatures, and four States only had acceded to them.[3] A new requisition, therefore, if made at all, must be made under the old rule of the Confederation, and with entirely imperfect means of making it with justice and equality. It was found, however, that large arrears were still due from the States, of the old requisitions made during the war.[4] A new call upon them to pay one half of these arrears, deducting therefrom the

1 Journals, VIII. 129. February 17, 1783.

2 Ibid. 198. April 26, 1783.

3 Connecticut, New Jersey, Pennsylvania, and South Carolina.

4 Of the old requisition of $8,000,000, made October 30, 1781, only $1,486,511.71 had been paid by all the States before December 31, 1783.

amount of their payments to the close of the year, would, if complied with, produce a sum nearly sufficient for the wants of the government. This resource was accordingly tried.[1]

In the year 1785, three millions, it was ascertained, would be required for the service of the year. A renewed call was made for the remaining unpaid moiety of the old requisition of eight millions, and for the whole of the old requisition of two millions; but, considering that the public faith required Congress to continue their annual demand for money, they issued a new requisition for three millions, and adjusted it according to the best information they could obtain.[2]

In the year 1786, a sum of more than three millions was wanted for the current demands on the treasury, and a new requisition was made for it, under the old rule of the Confederation.[3] Two of the States, Rhode Island and New Jersey, thereupon passed acts, making their own paper currency receivable on all arrears of taxes due to the United States, and proposing to pay their quotas in such currency.[4]

1 Journals, IX. 171–179. April 27, 1784.

2 Journals, X. 325–334. September 27, 1785.

3 Journals, XI. 167. August 2, 1786.

4 Ibid. 224. September 18, 1786. Upon this attempt of Rhode Island and New Jersey to pay their proportions in their own paper currency, the report of a committee declared, "That, to admit the receipt of bills of credit, issued under the authority of an individual State, in discharge of their specie proportions of a requisition, would defeat its object, as the said bills do not circulate out of the limits of the State in which they are emitted, and because a paper medium of any State, however well funded, cannot, either in the extensiveness of its circulation, or in the course of its ex-

But the entire inadequacy of this source of supply to maintain the federal government, and to discharge the annual public engagements, had now become but too apparent. From the 1st of November, 1781, to the 1st of January, 1786, less than two and a half millions of dollars had been received from requisitions made during that period, amounting to more than ten millions.[1] For the last fourteen months of that interval, the average receipts from requisitions amounted to less than four hundred thousand dollars per annum, while the interest alone due on the foreign debt was more than half a million; and, in the course of each of the nine following years, the average sum of one million, annually, would become due by instalments on the principal of that debt.[2] In addition to this, the interest on the domestic debt; the security of the navigation and commerce of the country against the Barbary powers; the immediate protection of the people dwelling on the frontier from the savages; the establishment of military magazines in different parts of the Union, quite indispensable to the public safety; the maintenance

change, be equally valuable with gold and silver. That if the bills of credit of the States of Rhode Island and New Jersey were to be received from those States in discharge of federal taxes, upon the principles of equal justice, bills emitted by any other States must be received from them also in payment of their proportions, and thereby, instead of the requisitions yielding a sum in actual money, nothing but paper would be brought into the federal treasury, which would be wholly inapplicable to the payment of any part of the interest or principal of the foreign debt, or the maintenance of the government of the United States."

[1] Journals, XI. 34–40. February 15, 1786.

[2] Ibid.

of the federal government at home, and the support of the public servants abroad, — each and all depended upon the contribution of the States under the annual requisitions, and were each and all likely to be involved in a common failure and ruin.[1]

There can be no doubt that the continuance of the practice of making requisitions, after the proposal of the revenue system of 1783, had some tendency to prevent the adoption of that system by the States. But there was no other alternative within the constitutional reach of Congress; and in the mean time, the revenue system, submitted as it necessarily was to the legislatures of thirteen different States, was, as far as it was assented to, embarrassed with the most discordant and irreconcilable provisions. It was ascertained in February, 1786, that seven of the States had granted the impost part of the system, in such a manner, that, if the other six States had made similar grants, the plan of the general impost might have been immediately put into operation.[2] Two of the other States had also granted the impost, but had embarrassed their grants with provisos, which suspended their operation until all the other States should have passed laws in full conformity with the whole system.[3] Two other States had fully acceded to the system in all its parts;[4] but four others had not decided in favor of any part of it.[5]

[1] Journals, XI. 34-40. February 15, 1786.

[2] New Hampshire, Massachusetts, Connecticut, New Jersey, Virginia, North Carolina, and South Carolina.

[3] Pennsylvania and Delaware.

[4] Delaware and North Carolina.

[5] Rhode Island, New York, Maryland, and Georgia.

No member of the Confederacy had, at this time, suggested to Congress any reasonable objection to the principles of the system; and the contradictory provisions by which their assent to it had been clogged, present a striking proof of the inherent difficulties of obtaining any important constitutional change from the legislatures of the States. The government was founded upon a principle, by which all its powers were derived from the States in their corporate capacities; in other words, it was a government created by, and deriving its authority from, the governments of the States. They alone could change the fundamental law of its organization; and they were actuated by such motives and jealousies, as rendered a unanimous assent to any change a great improbability. Still, the Congress of 1786 hoped that, by a clear and explicit declaration of the true position of the country, the requisite compliance of the States might be obtained. They accordingly made known, in the most solemn manner, the public embarrassments, and declared that the crisis had arrived, when the people of the United States must decide whether they were to continue to rank as a nation, by maintaining the public faith at home and abroad; or whether, for want of timely exertion in establishing a general revenue, they would hazard the existence of the Union, and the great national privileges which they had fought to obtain.[1]

[1] The report on this occasion (February 15, 1786), drawn by Rufus King, declared, "that the requisitions of Congress for eight years past have been so irregular in their operation, so uncertain in

Under the influence of this urgent representation, all the States, except New York, passed acts granting the impost, and vesting the power to collect it in Congress, pursuant to the recommendations of 1783, but upon the condition that it should not be in force until all the States had granted it in the same manner. The State of New York passed an act,[1] reserving to itself the sole power of levying and collecting the impost; making the collectors amenable to and removable by the State, and not by Congress; and making the duties receivable in specie or bills of credit, at the option of the importer. Such a departure from the plan suggested by Congress, and adopted by the other States, of course made the whole system inoperative in the other States, and there remained no possibility of procuring its adoption, but by inducing the State of New York to reconsider its determination. All hope of meeting the public engagements, and of carrying on the government, now turned upon the action of a single State.

The principal argument made use of, by those who

their collection, and so evidently unproductive, that a reliance on them in future as a source from whence moneys are to be drawn to discharge the engagements of the Confederacy, definite as they are in time and amount, would be not less dishonorable to the understandings of those who entertain such confidence, than it would be dangerous to the welfare and peace of the Union. The committee are therefore seriously impressed with the indispensable obligation that Congress are under, of representing to the immediate and impartial consideration of the several States the utter impossibility of maintaining and preserving the faith of the federal government by temporary requisitions on the States, and the consequent necessity of an early and complete accession of all the States to the revenue system of the 18th of April, 1783."

[1] May 4, 1786.

supported the conduct of New York, was, that Congress, being a single body, might misapply the money arising from the duties. An answer to this pretence, from the pen of Hamilton, declared that the interests and liberties of the people were not less safe in the hands of those whom they had delegated to represent them for one year in Congress, than they were in the hands of those whom they had delegated to represent them for one or four years in the legislature of the State; that all government implies trust, and that every government must be trusted so far as it is necessary to enable it to attain the ends for which it is instituted, without which insult and oppression from abroad, and confusion and convulsion at home, must ensue.[1] The real motive, however, with those who ruled the counsels of New York at this period, was a hope of the commercial aggrandizement of the State; and the jealousies and fears of national power, which were widely prevalent, were diligently employed to defeat the system proposed by Congress.

After the passage of the act of New York, and the adjournment of the legislature, Congress earnestly recommended to the executive of that State to convene the legislature again, to take into its consideration the recommendation of the revenue system, for the purpose of granting the impost to the United States, in conformity with the grants of other States, so as to enable the United States to carry it into immediate effect.[2] The Governor declined to accede to

[1] Life of Hamilton, II. 385.

[2] August 11, 1786.

this recommendation.[1] Congress repeated it, declaring that the critical and embarrassed state of the finances required that the impost should be carried into immediate operation, and expressing their opinion, that the occasion was sufficiently important and extraordinary for them to request that the legislature should be specially convened.[2] The executive of New York again refused the request of Congress, and the fate of the impost system remained suspended until the meeting of the legislature, at its regular session in January, 1787. It was never adopted by that State, and consequently never took effect.

[1] The ground of his refusal was, "that he had not the power to convene the legislature before the time fixed by law for their stated meeting, except upon '*extraordinary occasions*,' and as the present business had already been particularly laid before them, and so recently as at their last session received their determination, it cannot come within that description." Life of Hamilton, II. 389.

[2] August 23, 1786.

CHAPTER II.

1784–1787.

INFRACTIONS OF THE TREATY OF PEACE.

THE Treaty of Peace, ratified on the 14th of January, 1784, contained provisions of great practical and immediate importance. One of its chief objects, on the part of the United States, was, of course, to effect the immediate withdrawal of the British troops, and of every sign of British authority, from the country whose independence it acknowledged. A stipulation was accordingly introduced, by which the King bound himself, with all convenient speed, and without causing any destruction, or carrying away any negroes or other property of the American inhabitants, to withdraw all his armies, garrisons, and fleets from the United States, and from every post, place, and harbor within the same. Although the ratification of the Treaty was followed by the departure of the British forces from the Atlantic coast, many important posts in the Western country, within the incontestable limits of the United States, with a considerable territory around each of them, were still retained.[1]

[1] Secret Journals of Congress, IV. 186, 187.

On the part of England, it was of great consequence to secure to British subjects the property, and rights of property, of the enjoyment of which the state of hostilities had deprived them. A war between colonies and the parent state, which had sundered the closest intimacies of social and commercial intercourse, involved of necessity vast private interests. There were two large classes of English creditors, whose interests required protection; the British merchants to whom debts had been contracted before the Revolution, and the Tories, who had been obliged to depart from the United States, leaving debts due to them, and landed property, which had been seized. Clear and explicit stipulations were inserted in the Treaty, in order to protect these interests. It was provided that creditors on either side should meet with no lawful impediments to the recovery of the full value in sterling money of all *bona fide* debts contracted before the date of the Treaty.[1] It was also agreed, that Congress should earnestly recommend to the legislatures of the respective States to provide for the restitution of all estates, rights, and properties, which had been confiscated, belonging to real British subjects, and to persons resident in districts in the possession of his Majesty's arms, and who had not borne arms against the United States; that persons of any other description should have free liberty to go into any of the States, and remain for the period of twelve months unmolested

[1] Article IV.

in their endeavors to obtain the restitution of their property and rights which had been confiscated; that Congress should recommend to the States a reconsideration and revision of all their confiscation laws, and a restoration of the rights and property of the last-mentioned persons, on their refunding the *bona fide* price which any purchaser might have given for them since the confiscation. It was also agreed, that all persons having any interest in confiscated lands, either by debts, marriage settlements, or otherwise, should meet with no lawful impediment in the prosecution of their just rights.[1]

It was further provided, that there should be no future confiscations made, nor any prosecutions commenced against any person on account of the part he might have taken in the war, and that no person should, on that account, suffer any future loss or damage, either in person, liberty, or property, and that those who might be in confinement on such charges, at the time of the ratification of the Treaty in America, should be immediately set at liberty, and the prosecutions be discontinued.[2]

These provisions related to a great subject, with which, in the existing political system of this country, it was difficult to deal. The action of the States, with regard to some of the interests involved in these stipulations, had been irregular from an early period of the war. The Revolutionary Congress, on the commencement of hostilities, had suffered the oppor-

[1] Article V.

[2] Article VI.

tunity of asserting their rightful control over the subject of alien interests, except as to property found on the high seas, to pass away; and the consequence was, that the States had, on some points, usurped an authority which belonged to the Union. A Union, founded in compact, and vesting the rights of war and peace in Congress, was formed in 1775; and from that time the Colonies, or, as they afterwards became, States, were never rightfully capable of passing laws to sequester or confiscate the debts or property of a national enemy.[1] After the great acts of national sovereignty which took place in 1775 – 6, a British subject could not, with any propriety, be considered as the enemy of Massachusetts, or of Virginia; he was the enemy of the United States, and by that authority alone, as the belligerent, was his property, in strictness, liable to be seized, or the debts due to him sequestered. But neither the Revolutionary Congress, nor that of the Confederation, appear to have ever exercised the power of confiscating the debts or property of British subjects, within the States, or to have recommended such confiscation to the States themselves.[2] On the other hand, they did not interfere when the States saw fit to do it.

With regard to those inhabitants of the States who, adhering to the British crown, had abandoned the country, and left property behind them, it cannot so clearly be affirmed that the States should not have

[1] See the Report made to Congress on this subject by Mr. Jay, Secretary of Foreign Affairs, October, 1786. Secret Journals, IV. 209.

[2] Ibid.

dealt with their persons or property. Congress, as we have seen, at an early period of the war, committed the whole subject of restraining the persons of the Tories to the Colonies or States; and as Congress never assumed or exercised any jurisdiction over their property, it was of course left to be dealt with by the legislatures of the States, to whom Congress had declared that their several inhabitants owed allegiance.[1] But as these persons, by adhering to the crown, might claim of the crown the rights and protection of British subjects, the propriety of confiscating or withholding their property would remain for solution, at the negotiation of the Treaty of Peace, as a question of general justice and equity, rather than of public law.

The interests of both of these classes of persons were too important to be overlooked. Three millions sterling were due from the inhabitants of the Colonies to merchants in Great Britain, at the commencement of the war. At the return of peace, the laws of five of the States were found either to prohibit the recovery of the principal, or to suspend its collection, or to prohibit the recovery of interest, or to make land a good payment in place of money.[2]

[1] Resolve of June 24, 1776. Journals, II. 216. Ante, p. 52, note.

[2] An act passed by the legislature of Massachusetts, November 9, 1784, suspended judgment for interest on British debts, until Congress should have put a construction upon the Treaty declaring that it was due. An act of the State of New York, of July 12, 1782, restrained the collection of debts due to persons within the enemy's lines. Pennsylvania, soon after the peace, passed a law restraining the levy of executions. Virginia, at the time of the peace, had existing laws inhibiting the recovery of British debts. South

The purpose of the Treaty was to declare, that all *bona fide* debts, contracted before the date of the Tréaty, and due to citizens of either country, remained unextinguished by the war; and consequently, that interest, when agreed to be paid, or payable by the custom, or demandable as damages for delay of payment, was justly due. Over this whole subject of foreign debts, the national sovereignty, of right, had exclusive control; for confiscation of the property of a national enemy belongs exclusively to the power exercising the rights of war; and therefore whatever State laws might have been passed during the war, exercising rights which belonged to the national sovereign, they could have no validity when that sovereign came to resume its control over the subject, and to stipulate that the right of confiscation, if it ever existed, should not be exercised. The State laws, however, existed, and remained in conflict with the Treaty, for several years, producing consequences to which we shall presently advert.

The fifth article of the Treaty was infringed by an act passed by the State of New York, authorizing actions for rent to be brought by persons who had been compelled to leave their lands and houses by the enemy, against those who had occupied them while the enemy were in possession, and declaring that no military order or command of the enemy should be pleaded in justification of such occupation.[1]

Carolina had made land a good payment, in place of money. (See Mr. Jay's Report.)

[1] Passed March 17, 1783. Secret Journals, IV. 267.

The sixth article was also violated by an act of the same State, which made those inhabitants who had adhered to the enemy, if found within the State, guilty of misprision of treason, and rendered them incapable of holding office, or of voting at elections.[1]

The powers of the government were entirely inadequate to meet this state of things. The Confederation gave to the United States in Congress assembled the sole and exclusive right of determining on peace and war, and of entering into treaties and alliances. The nature of the sovereignty thus established made a treaty the law of the land, and binding upon every member of the Union; but there existed no means of enforcing the obligation. If the legislatures of the States passed laws restraining or interfering with the provisions of a treaty, Congress could only declare that they ought to be, and recommend that they should be, repealed. The simple and effectual intervention of a national judiciary, clothed with the power of declaring void any State legislation that conflicted with the national sovereignty, and of giving the means of enforcing all rights which that sovereignty had guaranteed by compact with a foreign power, did not exist. Resort, it is true, could be had to the State tribunals; and, on one memorable occasion, such resort was had to them with success. But the legislative power assailed the independence of the judiciary, and indignantly declared a decision, made with fairness by a competent tribunal, subver-

[1] Passed May 12, 1784, after the Treaty had been ratified. Secret Journals, IV. 269-274.

sive of law and good order, because it recognized the paramount authority of a treaty over a statute of the State.[1]

The effect of such State legislation upon the relations of the two countries was direct and mischievous. The Treaty of Peace was designed, and was adapted, to produce a fair and speedy adjustment of those relations, upon principles of equity and justice. But its obligations were reciprocal, and it could not execute itself. It was made, on the one side, by a power capable of performing, but also capable of waiting for the performance of the obligations which rested upon the other contracting party. On the other side, it was made by a power possessed of very imperfect means of performance, yet standing in constant need of the benefit which a full compliance with its obligations would insure. After the lapse of three years from the signature of the preliminary articles, and of more than two years from that of the definitive Treaty, the military posts in the Western country were still held by British garrisons, avowedly on account of the infractions of the Treaty on our part. The Minister

[1] This happened in New York, in a case under the "Trespass Act," where a suit was brought in the Mayor's Court of the City of New York, "to recover the rents of property held by the defendant under an order of Sir Henry Clinton. Hamilton, in the defence of this case, contended, with great power, that the act was a violation of the Treaty, and the court sustained his position. But the legislature passed resolves, declaring the decision to be subversive of law and good order, and recommending the appointing power "to appoint such persons Mayor and Recorder of New York as will govern themselves by the known law of the land." Life of Hamilton, II. 244, 245.

of the United States at St. James's was told, in answer to his complaints, that one party could not be obliged to a strict observance of the engagements of a treaty, and the other remain free to deviate from its obligations; and that whenever the United States should manifest a real determination to fulfil their part of the Treaty, Great Britain would be ready to carry every article of it into complete effect.[1] An investigation of the whole subject, therefore, became necessary, and Congress directed the Secretary of Foreign Affairs to make inquiry into the precise state of things. His report ascertained that the fourth and fifth articles of the Treaty had been constantly violated on our part by legislative acts still in existence and operation; that on the part of England, the seventh article had been violated, by her continuing to hold the posts from which she had agreed to withdraw her garrisons, and by carrying away a considerable body of negroes, the property of American inhabitants, at the time of the evacuation of New York.[2]

The serious question recurred, — what was to be done? The United States had neither committed nor approved of any violation of the Treaty; but an appeal was made to their justice, relative to the conduct of particular States, for which they were obliged

[1] Mr. John Adams was sent as the first Minister of the United States to the Court of St. James's in 1785. He received this reply to a memorial which he addressed to the British government, on the subject of the Western posts, in February, 1786. Secret Journals, IV. 187.

[2] Secret Journals, IV. 209.

eventually to answer. They could only resolve and recommend; and accordingly, after having declared that the legislatures of the States could not, of right, do any thing to explain, interpret, or limit the operation of a treaty, Congress recommended to the States to pass a general law, repealing all their former acts that might be repugnant to the Treaty, and leaving to their courts of justice to decide causes that might arise under it, according to its true intent and meaning, by determining what acts contravened its provisions.[1] This recommendation manifestly left the interests of the Union exposed to two hazards; the one, that the legislatures of the States might not pass the repealing statute, which would submit the proper questions to their courts, and the other, that their courts might not decide with firmness and impartiality between the policy of the State, on the one hand, and the interests of foreigners and obnoxious Tories, on the other.

But this was all that could be done, and partial success only followed the effort. Most of the States passed acts, in compliance with the recommendation of Congress, to repeal their laws which prevented the recovery of British debts.[2] But the State of Virginia, although it passed such an act, suspended its operation, until the Governor of the State should issue a proclamation, giving notice that Great Britain had delivered up the Western posts, and was

[1] March 21, 1787.

[2] New Hampshire, Massachusetts, Rhode Island, Connecticut, Delaware, Maryland, Virginia, and North Carolina passed such acts.

taking measures for the further fulfilment of the Treaty, by delivering up the negroes belonging to the citizens of that State, which had been carried away, or by making compensation for their value.[1] The two countries were thus brought to a stand, in their efforts to adjust the matters in dispute, and the Western posts remained in the occupation of British garrisons, inflaming the hostile temper of the Indian tribes, and enhancing the difficulty of settling the vacant lands in the fertile region of the Great Lakes.[2]

[1] Pitkin's History of the United States, II. 198.

[2] Marshall's Life of Washington, V. 67, 68.

CHAPTER III.

1786–1787.

No Security afforded by the Confederation to the State Governments. — Shays's Rebellion in Massachusetts, and its Kindred Disturbances.

No federative government can be of great permanent value, which is not so constructed that it may stand, in some measure, as the common sovereign of its members, able to protect them against internal disorders, as well as against external assaults. The Confederation undertook but one of these great duties. It was formed at a time when the war with England was the great object of concern to the revolted Colonies, and when they felt only the exigencies which that war created. Hence its most important powers, as well as its leading purpose, concerned the common cause of resistance to a foreign domination. A federal league of States independent of each other, formed principally for mutual defence against a common enemy, was all that succeeded to the general superintending power of the British crown, by which the internal affairs of each of them had always been regulated and controlled, in the last resort. When the tie was broken by which they had been held to the parent state, each of them created for itself a new government, resting for its basis on the popular will, and deriving its authority directly from the people; but none of them provided for the creation of a power, external to itself, which might stand as the guarantor and protector of their new institutions, and secure the principles on which they rested against violence and overthrow. Yet the constitutions thus formed, from their peculiar nature, eminently needed the safeguards which such a power could afford.

These constitutions were admirably constructed. They contained principles imperfectly known to the ancient governments; found in modern times only in the government of England; and applied there with far less consistency and completeness. They embraced the regular distribution of political power into distinct departments; legislative checks and balances, by means of two coördinate branches of the legislature; a judiciary in general holding office during good behaviour; and the representation of the people in the legislature, by deputies of their own actual election, in which the theory of such representation was more perfectly carried into practice than it had ever been in the country from which it was derived. But the fundamental principle on which they all rested, and without which they could not maintain existence, required means of defence. They were established upon the great doctrine, that it is the right of every political society to govern itself, and for the purposes of such self-government, to create such constitutions and ordain such fundamental laws as its own judgment and its own intelligent choice may find best suited to its own interests. But society can act only by an expression of the aggregate will of its members; and as there may be members who dissent from the views and determinations of the great mass of society, and it is therefore necessary to decide with whom the power of compelling obedience resides, — since there must be obedience in order that there may be peace, — nature and reason have determined that this power is to reside with a majority of the members. The American constitutions, therefore, are founded wholly upon the principle, that a majority expresses the will of the whole society, and may establish, change, and abrogate forms of government at its pleasure.[1] It follows, as a necessary deduction from this fundamental doctrine, that so soon as society has acted in the formation and establishment of a government, upon this principle, no change can take place, but

[1] Gibbon, with that graceful satire which knew how to hit two objects with the same stroke of his pen, describes hereditary monarchy as "an expedient which deprives the multitude of the dangerous, and indeed the ideal, power of giving themselves a master." The historian of the Decline and Fall began to publish his great work, just as the American Revolution burst upon the world. Since that sentence was penned, the experiment of a system, by which the multitude give to themselves a master, in the constitutional organs of their own will, has had a fair trial. We may not say that its trial is past, or that the system is established beyond the possibility of further dangers. But we may with a just pride point to its escape, in the days of its first establishment and greatest danger, and to the securities which the Constitution of the United States now affords, against similar perils, when they threaten the constitutions of the States.

by a new expression of the will of society through the voice of a majority; and whether a majority desires or has actually decreed a change, is a fact that must be made certain, and can only be made certain in one of two modes, — either by the evidence and through the channels which the society has previously ordained for this purpose, or by the submission of all its members to a violent and successful revolution.

The first constitution of Massachusetts did not designate any mode in which it was to be amended or changed. But no peaceable change can take place in any government founded on the expressed will of a majority of the people, consistently with the principle on which it had been established, until it has been ascertained, in some mode, that a change is demanded by the same authority. The vital importance of ascertaining this fact with precision was not so clearly perceived, at that early period, as it is now.

Seizing upon the newly established doctrine, which made them the sources of all political power, the people did not at once apprehend the rule which preserves and upholds that power, and makes the doctrine itself both practicable and safe. Hence, when troubles arose, individuals were led to suppose that they had only to declare a grievance, to demand a change, and to compel a compliance with their demand by force. So far as they reasoned at all, they persuaded themselves that, as their government was the creation of the people, by their own direct act, bodies of the people could assemble in their primary capacity, and, by obstructing any of its functions which they connected with a particular grievance, produce a reform, which the people have always a right to make. By overlooking, in this manner, the only safe and legitimate mode in which the popular will can be really ascertained, they passed into the mischiefs of anarchy and rebellion, mistaking the voices of a minority for the ascertained will of society.

To these tendencies, the recently established governments of New England, where the spirit of liberty was most vigorous, could oppose no efficient check; while, in any open outbreak, they were without any external defender, on whose power they could lean. The Confederation succeeded to the Revolutionary Congress, as we have more than once had occasion to observe, with less power than its predecessor might have exercised. It was formed by a written constitution, yet it was, strictly speaking, scarcely a government. It was a close union of the States; but it was a union from which all powers had been jealously withheld which would have enabled it to interfere with vigor and success between an insurgent minority of the people of a State and its lawful rulers. The Revolutionary Congress was once possessed of such large, indefinite powers, that, upon principles of public necessity, it might have assumed, in a great emergency, to hold a direct relation to the internal concerns of any Colony. It was, in fact, looked to, in some degree, for direction in the formation of the State governments, after it had broken the bonds of colonial allegiance to the English crown; and it might very properly have undertaken to support the governments whose establishment it had recommended. But such a relation between the early States and the continental power, though it certainly existed in 1776, was soon lost in the independent and jealous attitude which they began to occupy, and the Union rapidly assumed a position, where the character of sovereignty which it appeared to wear when it promulgated the Declaration of Independence was scarcely to be discerned. At no period in the history of the Confederation did it act upon the internal concerns or condition of a State. Its written articles of union hardly admitted of a construction which would have enabled it to do so, and certainly contained no express delegation of such a power.

At the same time, some of the State governments, during the period of which we are treating, were singularly exposed to the dangers of anarchy. None of them had any standing forces of any consequence, three years after the peace, and the New England States had no military forces whatever but their militia. No State could call upon its neighbors for aid in quelling an insurrection, for their militia would not have obeyed the summons, if it had been issued; and no State could call upon the federal government, in such an emergency, with any certainty of success in the application.[1]

[1] A power to interfere in the internal concerns of a State could only have been exercised by a broad construction of the third of the Ar-

In such a state of things, the year 1786 witnessed an insurrection in Massachusetts of a very dangerous character, which, from the fortunate circumstance that her counsels were then guided by a man of singular energy and firmness of character, she was just able to subdue. The remote causes of this insurrection lie too far from the path of our main subject to be more than summarily stated.

At the close of the Revolutionary war, the State of Massachusetts was oppressed with an enormous debt. At the breaking out of that war, the debt of the Colony was less than one hundred thousand pounds. The private debt of the State, in the year 1786, was one million three hundred thousand

ticles of Confederation, which was in these words: "The said States hereby severally enter into a firm league of friendship with each other, for their common defence, the security of their liberties, and their mutual and general welfare; binding themselves to assist each other against all force offered to or attacks made upon them, or any of them, on account of religion, sovereignty, trade, or any other pretence whatever." When this is compared with the clear and explicit provision in the Constitution, by which it is declared that "the United States shall guarantee to every State in this Union a republican form of government," there can be no wonder that a doubt was felt in the Congress of 1786 – 87 as to their powers upon this subject. It is true that the Massachusetts delegation, when they laid before Congress the measures which had been taken by the State government to suppress the insurrection, expressed the confidence of the legislature that the firmest support and most effectual aid would have been afforded by the United States, had it been necessary, and asserted that such support and aid were expressly and solemnly stipulated by the Articles of Confederation. (Journals, XII. 20. March 9, 1787.) But this was clearly not the case; and it was not generally supposed in Congress that the power existed by implication. All that was done by Congress towards raising troops, at the time of the insurrection, was done for the *ostensible* purpose of protecting the frontiers against an Indian invasion, as we shall see hereafter.

pounds, besides two hundred and fifty thousand pounds due to the officers and soldiers of the State line of the Revolutionary army. The State's proportion of the federal debt was not less than one million and a half of pounds.[1] According to the customary mode of taxation, one third of the whole debt was to be paid by the ratable polls, which scarcely exceeded ninety thousand.[2] The Revolution had made the people of Massachusetts familiar with the great general doctrines of liberty and human rights; but it had given them little insight into the principles of revenue and finance, and little acquaintance with the rules of public economy. No sufficient means, therefore, to relieve the people from direct taxation, by encouraging a revival of trade and at the same time drawing from it a revenue, were devised by the legislature. The exports of the State, moreover, had suffered a fearful diminution. The fisheries, which had been a fruitful source of prosperity to the colony, had been nearly destroyed by the war, and the markets of the West Indies and of Europe were now closed to the products of this lucrative industry, by which wealth had formerly been drawn from the wastes of the ocean. The State had scarcely any other commodity to exchange for the precious metals in foreign commerce. Its agriculture yielded only a scanty support to its population, if it yielded so much; its manufactures were in a languishing condition; and its carrying trade had been driven from

[1] Minot's History of the Insurrection, p. 6. [2] Ibid.

the seas during the war, and was afterwards annihilated by the oppressive policy of England, which succeeded the Peace. The people were every year growing poorer than they had been the year before, and taxes, onerous taxes, beyond their resources and always odious, were pressing upon them with a constantly increasing accumulation, from which the political state of the country seemed to promise no relief.[1]

But the demand of the tax-gatherer was not the sole burden which individuals had to encounter. Private debts had accumulated during the war, in almost as large a ratio as the public obligations. The collection of such debts had been generally suspended, while the struggle for political freedom was going on; but that struggle being over, creditors necessarily became active, and were often obliged to be severe. Suits were multiplied in the courts of law beyond all former precedent, and the first effect of this sudden influx of litigation was to bring popular odium upon the whole machinery of justice. In a state of society approaching so nearly to a democracy, the class of debtors, if numerous, must be politically formidable. They had begun to be so before the close of the war. Their clamors and the supposed necessity of the case led the legislature, in 1782, to a violation of principle, in a law known as the Tender Act, by which executions for debt might be satisfied by certain articles of property, to be taken at an appraisement. This law was limited in its operation to

[1] See the next chapter for some particulars respecting the trade of Massachusetts.

one year; but in the course of that year it taught the debtors their strength, and gave the first signal for an attack upon property. A levelling, licentious spirit, a restless desire for change, and a disposition to throw down the barriers of private rights, at length broke forth in conventions, which first voted themselves to be the people, and then declared their proceedings to be constitutional. At these assemblies, the doctrine was publicly broached, that property ought to be common, because all had aided in saving it from confiscation by the power of England. Taxes were voted to be unnecessary burdens, the courts of justice to be intolerable grievances, and the legal profession a nuisance. A revision of the constitution was demanded, in order to abolish the Senate, reform the representation in the House, and make all the civil officers of the government eligible by the people.

A passive declaration of their grievances did not, however, content the disaffected citizens of Massachusetts. They proceeded to enforce their demands. The courts of justice were the nearest objects for attack, as well as the most immediately connected with the chief objects of their complaints. Armed mobs surrounded the court-houses in several counties, and sometimes effectually obstructed the sessions of the courts. These acts were repeated, until, in the autumn of 1786, the insurrection broke out in a formidable manner in the western part of the State. The insurgents actually embodied, and in arms against the government, in the month of December, in the counties of Worcester and Hampshire, numbered about fifteen hundred men, and were headed by one Daniel Shays, who had been a captain in the continental army.[1]

The executive chair of the State was at that time filled by James Bowdoin; a statesman, firm, prudent, of high principle, and devoted to the cause of constitutional order. In the first stages of the disaffection, he had been thwarted by a House of Representatives, in which the majority were strongly inclined to sympathize with the general spirit of the insurgents; but the Senate had supported him. Afterwards, when the movement grew more dangerous, the legislature became more reconciled to the use of vigorous means to vindicate the authority of the government, and a short time before it actually took the form of an armed and organized rebellion against the Commonwealth, they had encouraged the Governor to use the powers vested in him by the constitution to enforce obedience to the laws. The Executive promptly met the emergency. A body of militia was marched against the insurgents, and by the middle of February they were dispersed or captured, with but little loss of life.

The actual resources of the State, however, to meet an emergency of this kind, were feeble and few. A voluntary loan, from a few public-spirited individuals, supplied the necessary funds, of which the treasury of the State was wholly destitute.[2] At one time, so general was the prevalence of discontent, even

[1] Minot's History of the Insurrection, p. 82 et seq.

[2] Governor Bowdoin's Speech to the Legislature, February 3, 1787.

among the militia on whom the government were obliged to rely, that men were known openly to change sides in the field, when the first bodies of troops were called out.[1] Had the government of the State been in the hands of a person less firm and less careless of popularity than Bowdoin, it would have been given up to anarchy and civil confusion. The political situation of the country did not seem to admit of an application to Congress for direct assistance, and there is no reason to suppose that such an application would have been effectively answered, if it had been made.[2]

When the news of the disturbances in Massachusetts, in the autumn of 1786, was received in Congress, it happened that intelligence from the Western country indicated a hostile disposition on the part of several Indian tribes against the frontier settlements. A resolve was unanimously adopted, directing one thousand three hundred and forty additional troops to be raised, for the term of three years, for the protection and support of the States bordering on the Western territory and the settlements on and near the Mississippi, and to secure and facilitate the surveying and selling of the public lands.[3] From the fact that the whole of these troops were ordered to be raised by the four New England States, and

1 Minot.

2 In the spring of 1786, the State had asked the loan from Congress of sixty pieces of field artillery. The application was refused, by the negative vote of six States out of eight, one being divided, and the delegation from Massachusetts alone supporting it. Journals, XI. 65-67. April 19, 1786.

3 Journals, XI. 258. October 30, 1786.

one half of them by the State of Massachusetts, and from other circumstances, it is quite apparent that the object assigned was an ostensible one, and that Congress intended by this resolve to strengthen the government of that State and to overawe the insurgents.[1] But this motive could not be publicly announced. The enlistment went on very slowly, however, until February, when a motion was made by Mr. Pinckney of South Carolina to stop it altogether, upon the ground that the insurrection in Massachusetts, the real, though not the ostensible, object of the resolve, had been crushed. Mr. King of Massachusetts earnestly entreated that the federal enlistments might be permitted to go on, otherwise the greatest alarm would be felt by the government of the State and its friends, and the insurrection might be rekindled. Mr. Madison advised that the proposal to rescind the order for the enlistments should be suspended, to await the course of events in Massachusetts. At the same time, he admitted that it would be difficult to reconcile an interference of Congress in the internal controversies of a State with the tenor of the Articles of Confederation.[2] The whole subject was postponed, and the direct question of the power of Congress was not acted upon. In the Con-

[1] It was well understood, for instance, in the legislature of Virginia, that this was the real purpose; for Mr. Madison says that this consideration inspired the ardor with which they voted, towards their quota of the funds called for to defray the expenses of this levy, a tax on tobacco, which would scarcely have been granted for any other purpose, as its operation was very unequal. Elliot's Debates, V. 95. February 19, 1787.

[2] Ibid.

vention which framed the Constitution, it was very early declared, that the Confederation had neither constitutional power, nor means, to interfere in case of a rebellion in any State.[1]

This generation can scarcely depict to itself the alarm which these disturbances spread through the country, and the extreme peril to which the whole fabric of society in New England was exposed. The numbers of the disaffected in Massachusetts amounted to one fifth of the inhabitants in several of the populous counties. Their doctrines and purposes were embraced by many young, active, and desperate men in Rhode Island, Connecticut, and New Hampshire, and the whole of this faction in the four States was capable of furnishing a body of twelve or fifteen thousand men, bent on annihilating property, and cancelling all debts, public and private.[2]

But this great peril was not without beneficial consequences. It displayed, at a critical moment, when a project of amending the Federal Constitution for other purposes was encountering much opposition, a more dangerous deficiency than any to which the public mind had hitherto been turned. While thoughtful and considerate men were speculating upon the causes of diminished prosperity and the general feebleness of the system of government, a gulf suddenly yawned beneath their feet, threatening

1 Ibid. 127.

2 This was the estimate of their numbers formed by General Knox, on careful inquiry, and by him given to General Washington. See a letter from General Washington to Mr. Madison. Works, IX. 207.

ruin to the whole social fabric. It was but a short time before, that the people of this country had shed their blood to obtain constitutions of their own choice and making. Now, they seemed as ready to overturn them as they had once been to extort from tyranny the power of creating and erecting them in its place. It was manifest, that to achieve the independence of a country is but half of the great undertaking of liberty; — that, after freedom, there must come security, order, the wise disposal of power, and great institutions on which society may repose in safety. It was clear, that the Federal Union alone could certainly uphold the liberty which it had gained for the people of the States, and that, to enable it to do so, it must become a government.[1]

From his retreat at Mount Vernon, Washington observed the progress of these disorders with intense anxiety. To him, they carried the strongest evidence of a want of energy in the system of the Federal Union. They did more than all things else to convince him that "a liberal and energetic constitution, well checked and well watched to prevent encroachments, might restore us to that degree of respectability and consequence to which we had the fairest prospect of attaining."[2] He was kept accu-

[1] Washington, writing to Henry Lee in Congress, October 31, 1786, says: "You talk, my good sir, of employing influence to appease the present tumults in Massachusetts. I know not where that influence is to be found, or, if attainable, that it would be a proper remedy for the disorders. *Influence* is not *government*. Let us have a government by which our lives, liberties, and properties will be secured, or let us know the worst at once.' Works, IX. 204.

[2] Ibid. 208.

rately informed of the state of things in New England, and the probability that he would be obliged to come forward, and take an active part in the support of order against civil discord, was directly intimated to him.[1] He had foreseen the possibility of this; but the successful issue of the struggle relieved him from the contemplation of this painful task, and left to him only the duty of giving the whole weight of his influence and presence in the Convention, which was to assemble in the following May, for the revision of the Federal Constitution.

1 Ibid. 221.

CHAPTER IV.

ORIGIN AND NECESSITY OF THE POWER TO REGULATE COMMERCE.

AMONG all the causes which led to the establishment of the Constitution of the United States, there is none more important, and none that is less appreciated at the present day, than the inability of the Confederation to manage the foreign commerce of the country. We have seen that, when the Articles of Confederation were proposed for adoption by the States, the State of New Jersey remonstrated against the absence of all provision for placing the foreign trade of the States under the regulation of the federal government. But this remonstrance was without effect, and the instrument went into operation in 1781, with no other restriction upon the powers of the States to regulate trade according to their pleasure, than a prohibition against levying imposts or duties which would interfere with the treaties then proposed. While the war continued, the subject was of comparatively little importance. But the return of peace found this country capable of becoming a great commercial, as well as agricultural nation; and it could not be overlooked, that its government possessed very inadequate means for establishing such relations with foreign powers as would best develop its resources and conduce to its internal harmony and prosperity. How early this great interest had attracted the attention of those who were most capable of enlarged and statesmanlike views of the actual nature of the Union and the wants of the States, there are perhaps as yet before the world no sufficient means of determining. We know, however, that, before the peace, Hamilton saw clearly that it was essential for the United States to be vested with a general superintendence of trade, both for purposes of revenue and regulation; that he foresaw the encouragement of our own products and manufactures, by means of general prohibitions of particular articles and a judicious arrangement of duties, and that this could only be effected by a central authority; and that the due observance of any commercial treaty which the United States might make with a foreign power could not be expected, if the different States retained the regulation of their own trade, and thus held the practical construction of treaties in their own hands.[1]

But it does not appear that, among the other principal statesmen of the Revolution, these ideas had made much progress, until the entire incapacity of the Confederation to negotiate advantageous commercial treaties, for want of adequate power to en-

[1] Life of Hamilton, II. 233, 234. See also his resolutions on the defects of the federal government, intended to be offered in Congress in 1783, and especially the eighth resolution. Works of Hamilton, II. 269.

force them, had displayed the actual weakness of its position, and the oppressive measures of other countries had taught them that there was but one remedy for such evils. Then, indeed, they saw that the United States could have a standing as a commercial power among the other powers of the world, only when their representatives could be received and dealt with as the representatives of one, and not of thirteen sovereignties; and that, if the measures of other countries, injurious to the trade of America, were to be counteracted at all, it must be by a power that could prohibit access to all the States alike, or grant it as to all, as circumstances might require.[1]

[1] Hamilton himself, in some papers which he published in 1781, under the title of The Continentalist, gave the general sum of American statesmanship and its opportunities, down to that period. The events of the next seven years gave it a wonderful development. "It would be the extreme of vanity in us," said he, "not to be sensible that we began this revolution with very vague and confined notions of the practical business of government. To the greater part of us, it was a novelty; of those who under the former constitution had had opportunities of acquiring experience, a large proportion adhered to the opposite side, and the remainder can only be supposed to have possessed ideas adapted to the narrow colonial sphere in which they had been accustomed to move, not of that enlarged kind suited to the government of an independent nation. There were, no doubt, exceptions to these observations; — men in all respects qualified for conducting the public affairs with skill and advantage; — but their number was small; they were not always brought forward in our councils; and when they were, their influence was too commonly borne down by the prevailing torrent of ignorance and prejudice. On a retrospect, however, of our transactions, under the disadvantages with which we commenced, it is perhaps more to be wondered at, that we have done so well, than that we have not done better. There are, indeed, some traits in our conduct, as conspicuous for sound policy as others for magnanimity. But, on the other hand, it must also be confessed, there have been many false steps, many chimerical

The actual commercial relations of the United States with other countries, when the peace took place, were confined to treaties of amity and commerce with France, Sweden, and the Netherlands; the two latter transcending, in some degree, the powers of the Confederation. In 1776, the Revolutionary Congress had adopted a plan of treaties to be proposed to France and Spain, which contemplated that the subjects of each country should pay no duties in the other except such as were paid by natives, and should have the same rights and privileges as natives in respect to navigation and commerce.[1] When a treaty of amity and commerce came to be concluded with France, in 1778, the footing on which the subjects of the two countries were placed, in the dominions of each other, was that of the most favored nations, instead of that of natives.[2] The Articles of Confederation, proposed in 1777, and finally ratified in March, 1781, reserved to the States the right of levying duties and imposts, excepting only such as would interfere with any treaties that might be made "pursuant to the treaties proposed to France and Spain." The United States could therefore constitutionally complete these two

projects and Utopian speculations, in the management of our civil as well as of our military affairs. A part of these were the natural effects of the spirit of the times, dictated by our situation. An extreme jealousy of power is the attendant on all popular revolutions, and has seldom been without its evils. It is to this source we are to trace many of the fatal mistakes, which have so deeply endangered the common cause; particularly that defect which will be the object of these remarks, — a want of power in Congress." Works, II. 186.

1 Secret Journals, II. 7, 8.

2 Ibid. 59.

treaties, and such as were dependent upon them, but no others which should have the effect of restraining the legislatures of the States from prohibiting the exportation or importation of any species of goods or merchandise, or laying whatever duties or imposts they thought proper.[1]

In 1782, negotiations were entered into for a similar treaty with the States General of the Netherlands. When the instructions to Mr. Adams to negotiate this treaty were under consideration in Congress, it was recollected that the French treaty contained a stipulation, the effect of which would enable the heirs of the subjects of either party, dying in the territories of the other, to inherit real property, without obtaining letters of naturalization.[2] The doubt suggested itself, — as it well might, — whether such an indefinite license to aliens to possess real property within the United States, was not an encroachment upon the rights of the States. It seems to have been expected, when the French treaty was entered into, that the States would acquiesce in this provision, on account of the peculiar relations of this country to

1 Articles of Confederation, Art. VI., IX. The expression in the *sixth* article was: "No State shall lay any imposts, &c. that shall in-interfere with any stipulations in treaties entered into by the United States with any king, prince, or state, *in pursuance of* any treaties already proposed by Congress to the court of France and Spain." The *ninth* article saved to the States the general power of levying duties and laying prohibitions.

2 Secret Journals, II. 65, 66. Art. XIII. of the Treaty of Amity and Commerce with France. The expression employed was, "goods movable and immovable," and the right of succession was given, *ab intestato*, without first obtaining letters of naturalization.

France, and because of the saving clause in the Articles of Confederation in favor of the treaties to be made with that power and with Spain.[1] But such a stipulation as this was clearly not within the meaning of that clause; and it was received with great repugnance by many of the States.[2] In the treaty with the Netherlands, it was proposed to insert a similar provision; but it was found to be extremely improbable that the States would comply with a similar engagement with another power. The language was therefore varied, so as to give the privilege of inheritance only as to the "effects" of persons dying in the country; — an expression which would probably exclude real property, but which might possibly be construed to include it.[3]

With regard to duties and imposts, the Dutch treaty contained the same stipulation as the French, putting the subjects of either power on the footing of the most favored nations, and thereby holding out to the subjects of the United Provinces the promise of an equality, under the laws of the United States, with the subjects of France.[4] The same stipulation was inserted in a treaty subsequently made at Paris with the King of Sweden.[5]

If these stipulations were supposed or intended to

[1] See a report on this *projet* of the treaty, made by Mr. Madison, July 17, 1782. Secret Journals, II. 142-144.

[2] Ibid.

[3] Art. VI. of the Treaty of Amity and Commerce with the Netherlands, executed by Mr. Adams at the Hague, October 8, 1782. Journals, VIII. 96.

[4] Ibid., Art. II., III.

[5] April 3, 1783. Journals, VIII. 386-398.

be binding upon the States, so as to restrain them from adopting, within their respective jurisdictions, any other rule than that fixed by the French treaty, for the subjects of the United Provinces and the King of Sweden, it is quite clear that the Articles of Confederation gave no authority to Congress to make them. They could have no effect, therefore, in producing a uniformity of regulation throughout the United States, with regard to the trade with Sweden and the Netherlands.

The relations of the United States with Great Britain were, however, far more important, than their relations with Sweden or Holland. When the war was drawing to a close, and the provisional articles of peace had been agreed upon, a measure was in preparation in England, under the auspices of Mr. Pitt, designed as a temporary arrangement of commercial intercourse between Great Britain and the United States, and which would have enabled the government of this country to have formed a treaty so advantageous, that the States would doubtless have conformed their legislation to its provisions. That great statesman perceived, that it was extremely desirable to establish the intercourse of the two countries on the most enlarged principles of reciprocal benefit, and his purpose was, by a provisional arrangement, to evince the disposition of England to be on terms of amity with the United States, preparatory to the negotiation of a treaty.[1]

[1] Mr. Pitt's bill was brought in in March, 1783, and he went out of office immediately afterwards.

But the administration, in which he was then Chancellor of the Exchequer, went out of office immediately after he had proposed this measure, and their successors, following a totally different line of policy, procured an act of Parliament authorizing the King in Council to regulate the commercial intercourse between the United States and Great Britain and her dependencies.[1]

Mr. Pitt's bill was designed to admit the vessels and subjects of the United States into all the ports of Great Britain, in the same manner as the subjects and vessels of other independent sovereign states, and to admit merchandise and goods, the growth, produce, or manufacture of this country, under the same duties and charges as if they were the property of British subjects, imported in British vessels. It also proposed to establish an entirely free trade between the United States and the British islands, colonies, and plantations in America. The new administration, on the contrary, believing that this would encourage the American marine, to the ruin of that of Great Britain, and would deprive the latter of a monopoly in the consumption of her colonies, and in their carrying trade, resolved to reverse this entire policy. In this course, they were encouraged by the views which they took of the internal situation of this country, and which were, to a great extent, justified by the fact. They believed that we could not act, as a nation, upon questions of commerce; that

[1] April, 1783

the climates, the staples, and the manners of the States were different, and their interests therefore opposite; and that no combination was likely to take place, from which England would have reason to fear retaliation. They supposed, that, inasmuch as the Confederation had no power to make any but general treaties, and as the States had reserved to themselves nearly every power concerning the regulation of trade, no treaty could be made that would be binding upon all the States; and that, if treaties should become necessary, they must be made with the States respectively. But they denied that treaties were necessary, and maintained that it would be unwise to enter at present into any arrangements by which they might not wish afterwards to be bound. They determined, therefore, to deal with this country as a collection of rival States, with each of which they could make their own terms, after the pressure of their policy, and the impossibility of escaping from its effects, had begun to be felt. They accordingly began, by excluding from the British West Indies, under Orders in Council, the whole American marine, and by prohibiting fish, and many important articles of our produce, from being carried there, even in British vessels.[1]

At the termination of the war, the foreign commerce of the United States was capable of great ex-

[1] July, 1783. Their idea was, that, if the American States should choose to send consuls, they should be received, and consuls sent to them in return · that each State would soon enter into all necessary regulations with the consul, and that nothing more was necessary. See Lord Sheffield's Observations on American Commerce.

pansion. It consisted of three important branches,— the trade of the Eastern, that of the Middle, and that of the Southern States; each of which required at once the means of reaching foreign markets. The rice and indigo of the South might be carried to Europe. The Middle States might export to Europe tobacco, tar, wheat, and flour; and to the West Indies, pork, beef, bread, flour, lumber, tar, and iron. The Eastern States might supply the markets of Europe with spars, ship-timber, staves, boards, fish, and oil, and those of the West Indies with lumber, pork, beef, live cattle, horses, cider, and fish. The whole of these great interests of course received a sudden and almost fatal blow from the English Orders in Council, and no means whatever existed of countervailing their effects, but such as each State could provide for its own people, by its own legislation.

Congress, however, awoke to the perception of an efficient and appropriate remedy, of a temporary character, and prepared to apply it, through an amendment of their powers. For the purpose of meeting the policy of Great Britain with similar restrictions on her commerce, they recommended to the States to vest in Congress, for the term of fifteen years, authority to prohibit the vessels of any power, not having treaties of commerce with the United States, from importing or exporting any commodities into or from any of the States, and also with the power of prohibiting, for a like term, the subjects of any foreign country, unless authorized by treaty, from importing into the United States any merchandise not the produce or manufacture of such country.[1] There was already before the States, as we have seen, in the revenue system of 1783, a proposal to them to vest in Congress power to levy certain duties on foreign commodities, for the same period; and if these two grants of power had been made, and made promptly, by the States, Congress would have possessed, for a time, an effectual control over commerce, and the practical means of forming suitable commercial treaties.

But the proposal of the 30th of April, 1784, met with a tardy and reluctant attention among the States. Only one of them had acted upon it, as late as the following February, when the delegates for Maryland laid before Congress an act of that State upon the subject.[2] New Hampshire was the next State to comply, in the succeeding June.[3] In the mean time, however, Congress prepared to prosecute negotiations in Europe, trusting to the chances of an enlargement of their powers, in pursuance of their recommendation. Accordingly, they proceeded, in the spring of 1784, to appoint a commission to negotiate commercial treaties, and settled the principles on which such treaties were to be formed. The leading principle then determined on was, that each party to the treaty should have a right to carry their own produce, manufactures, and merchandise

[1] April 30, 1784.

[2] February 14. 1785. Journals, X. 53.

[3] By an act passed June 22–23, 1785; laid before Congress October 10, 1785. Ibid. 353.

in their own bottoms to the ports of the other, and to take thence the produce, manufactures, and merchandise of the other, paying, in both cases, such duties only as were paid by the most favored nation. The resolves appointing the commission also contained a very explicit direction, that "the United States, in all such treaties, and in every case arising under them, should be considered as one nation, upon the principles of the Federal Constitution."[1] Yet the Federal Constitution did not, at that very moment, make the United States one nation for this purpose. Its principles gave to Congress no authority which could prevent the States from prohibiting any exportations or importations whatever, as to their respective territories; and the validity of these treaties, thus proposed to be negotiated with fifteen European powers, depended altogether upon the precarious assent of the thirteen States to the alterations in the principles of the Federal Constitution which Congress had proposed.

That assent was not likely to be given, so as to become effectual for the purposes for which it had been asked. The action of the States was found, in the spring of 1786, to present a mass of incongrui-

[1] The commission consisted of Mr. John Adams, then at the Hague, Dr. Franklin, then in France, and Mr. Jefferson, then in Congress. Mr. Jefferson sailed from Boston on the 5th of July, and arrived in Paris on the 6th of August, 1784. (Works, I. 49.) The powers with whom they were to negotiate commercial treaties were Russia, Austria, Prussia, Denmark, Saxony, Hamburg, Great Britain, Spain, Portugal, Genoa, Tuscany, Rome, Naples, Venice, Sardinia, and the Ottoman Porte. Secret Journals, III. 484-489. May 7, 1784.

ties, which rendered the whole scheme of thus increasing the federal powers almost hopeless. Four of the States had passed laws, conforming substantially to the recommendations of Congress, but restraining their operation until the other States should have complied.[1] Three of the States had passed the requisite acts, and had fixed different periods at which they were to take effect.[2] One State had granted full powers to regulate its trade, by restrictions or duties, for fifteen years, with a proviso that the law should be suspended until all the other States had done the same.[3] Another State had granted power, for twenty-five years, to regulate trade between the respective States, and to prohibit or regulate the importation only of foreign goods in foreign vessels, but restricting the operation of the act until the other States had passed similar laws.[4] Still another State had granted powers like the last, but without limitation of time, and with the proviso that, when all the other States had made the same grants, it should become an Article of the Confederation.[5] The three remaining States had passed no act upon the subject.[6] Upon these conflicting and irreconcilable provisions, Congress could take no other action, than to call the attention of the States again to the original proposal, and request them to revise their laws.[7]

1 Massachusetts, New York, New Jersey, and Virginia.

2 Connecticut, Pennsylvania, and Maryland.

3 New Hampshire.

4 Rhode Island.

5 North Carolina.

6 Delaware, South Carolina, and Georgia.

7 See a report made in Congress, March 3, 1786. Journals, XI. 41.

While this discordant legislation was manifesting at home the entire impracticability of amending the Federal Constitution by means of the separate action of the State legislatures, the commissioners abroad were engaged in efforts, nearly as fruitless, to negotiate the treaties which they had been instructed to make. The commission was opened at Paris on the 13th of August, 1784, and its objects announced to the different governments. France was not disposed to change the existing relations. England perceived the real want of power in the federal government, and recognized nothing in the commission but the fact that it had been issued by Congress, while the separate States had conferred no powers upon either Congress or the commissioners.[1] Prussia alone entered into a

[1] The Duke of Dorset, the English Ambassador at Paris, wrote to the commissioners (March 26, 1785) as follows: "Having communicated to my court the readiness you expressed in your letter to me of the 9th of December to remove to London, for the purpose of treating upon such points as may materially concern the interests, both political and commercial, of Great Britain and America; and having at the same time represented that you declared yourselves to be fully authorized and empowered to negotiate, I have been, in answer thereto, instructed to learn from you, gentlemen, what is the real nature of the powers with which you are invested, — whether you are merely commissioned by Congress, or whether you have received separate powers from the respective States. A committee of North American merchants have waited upon his Majesty's principal Secretary of State for Foreign Affairs, to express how anxiously they wished to be informed upon this subject; repeated experience having taught them in particular, as well as the public in general, how little the authority of Congress could avail in any respect, where the interest of any one individual State was even concerned, and particularly so where the concerns of that State might be supposed to militate against such resolutions as Congress might think proper to adopt. The apparent determination of the respective States to reg-

treaty, upon some of the principles laid down in the commission, and soon after it was executed, the commissioners ceased to do any thing whatever.[1]

During the period which elapsed from the Treaty of Peace with England to the assembling of the Convention at Annapolis, the legislation of the different States, designed to protect themselves against the policy of England, was of course without system or concert, and without uniformity of regulation. At one time duties were made extravagantly high; at another, competition reduced them below the point at which any considerable revenue could be derived. At one time, the States acted in open hostility to each other; at another, they contemplated commercial leagues, without regard to the prohibition contained in the Articles of Confederation. No steady system was pursued by any of them, and the inefficacy of State legislation became at length so apparent, that a conviction of the necessity of new powers in Congress forced itself upon the public mind.

ulate their own separate interests renders it absolutely necessary, towards forming a permanent system of commerce, that my court should be informed how far the commissioners can be duly authorized to enter into any engagements with Great Britain, which it may not be in the power of any one of the States to render totally fruitless and ineffectual." Diplomatic Correspondence, II. 297.

[1] Jefferson's Works, I. 50, 51. The whole proceedings of this commission may be found in the Diplomatic Correspondence, II. 193 – 346.

CHAPTER V.

1783–1787.

THE PUBLIC LANDS.—GOVERNMENT OF THE NORTHWESTERN TERRITORY.—THREATENED LOSS OF THE WESTERN SETTLEMENTS.

THE Confederation, although preceded by a cession of Western territory from the State of New York for the use of the United States, contained no grant of power to Congress to hold, manage, or dispose of such property. There had been, while the Articles of Confederation were under discussion in Congress, a proposal to insert a provision, giving to Congress the sole and exclusive right and power to ascertain and fix the western boundary of such States as claimed to the Mississippi or the South Sea, and to lay out the land beyond the boundary so ascertained into separate and independent States, from time to time, as the numbers and circumstances of the inhabitants might require.[1] This proposal was negatived by the vote of every State except Maryland and New Jersey.[2] Its rejection caused the adoption of the Confederation to be postponed for a period of more than two years after it was submitted to the States.[3] Virginia

[1] October 15, 1777. Secret Journals, I. 328.

[2] Ibid.

[3] See the account of the adop-

had set up claims to an indefinite extent of territory, stretching far into the Western wilderness, which were looked upon with especial jealousy by Maryland; and when the Articles of Confederation came before the legislature of that State for consideration, the absence of any provision vesting in the Union any control over these claims, or any power to ascertain and fix the western boundaries of the great States, became at once a cause of irritation and alarm. The steps taken by Maryland to have this power introduced into the Articles have already been detailed.[1] But the Articles could not be amended. Congress could only make efforts to remove this impediment to their adoption, by recommending to the States to cede their territorial claims to the Union. The first step which they took, for this purpose, was to recommend to the State of Virginia, and all the other States similarly situated, not to make sales of unappropriated lands during the continuance of the war.[2] This was followed by a full consideration of the subject presented by the objections of Maryland and the remonstrance of Virginia. Declining to reopen the question of the merits or policy of attempting to engraft the proposed power upon the Confederation, Congress deemed it more advisable to endeavor to procure a surrender of a portion of the territorial claims of the several States.[3] In pressing a recommendation to this effect, they were greatly aided by

tion of the Confederation, ante, pp. 131 - 141.

[1] Ante, pp. 131 - 136.

[2] October 30, 1779. Journals, V. 401, 402.

[3] September 6, 1780.

the course of the State of New York, which had already authorized its delegates in Congress to limit its western boundaries, and to cede a portion of its vacant lands to the United States.[1] They then immediately declared, by resolve, the purposes for which such cessions were to be held. The territories were to be disposed of for the common benefit of the United States; to be settled and formed into distinct republican States, which should become members of the Federal Union, and have the same rights of sovereignty, freedom, and independence as the other States. Each State so formed was to contain a suitable extent of territory, not less than one hundred, nor more than one hundred and fifty miles square; the necessary expenses incurred by any State in acquiring the territory ceded, were to be reimbursed; and the lands were to be granted or settled at such times, and under such regulations, as should thereafter be agreed upon by the United States in Congress assembled, or any nine or more of them.[2]

The cessions were made under the guaranties of this resolve. Strictly speaking, there was no express constitutional power under which Congress could thus act, either before or after the adoption of the Articles of Confederation. Before that period, if the United States could acquire and hold lands, for any purpose, it could only be by the common attribute of sovereignty belonging to every government. Per-

[1] February 19, 1780. [2] October 10, 1780.

haps this power existed, by implication, in the revolutionary government; but the compact which was to constitute the new government contained no authority for the establishment of new States within the limits of the Union. But when, aside from the Articles of Confederation, and before they had been adopted, the Revolutionary Congress undertook, in 1780, to hold out these inducements to the States, as motives for their adoption of that instrument, and these motives were acted upon and the cessions made, it must be taken that the territory came rightfully into the possession of the United States. Whether the adoption of the Articles, containing no power for the government of such territories, or for the admission of new States into the Union, did not place the new government in a position where, if it acted at all, it would act beyond the scope of its constitutional authority, certainly admitted of grave question.[1] But the acquisition of the territory itself rested upon acts, which were so directly and expressly connected with the establishment of the new Union under the Confederation, as to make the acquisition itself part of the fundamental conditions of that Union, and the principal guaranty of its continuance. Among the declared purposes for which these acquisitions were made, was that of forming them into new States, to be admitted into the Union; and as all the States acquiesced in and embraced this purpose, they may be said to have conferred

[1] The Federalist.

upon Congress an implied power to legislate to carry it into effect. Still, the want of an express authority in the Articles thus to deal with acquired territory was afterwards felt and insisted upon, as the Confederation drew towards the close of its career.[1]

Virginia, in 1781, offered to make a cession to the United States of her title to lands northwest of the Ohio, upon certain conditions, which were not satisfactory, and the subject had not been acted upon in Congress when the revenue system of 1783 was adopted for recommendation to the States. Looking to the prospect of vacant lands, as a means of hastening the extinguishment of the public debts, as well as of establishing the harmony of the Union, Congress accompanied the recommendation of the revenue system by new solicitations to the States which had made no cessions of their public lands, or had made them in part only, to comply fully with the former recommendations. This drew from the State of New Jersey, apprehensive that the offer of Virginia might be accepted, a remonstrance against the cession proposed by that State, as partial, unjust, and illiberal.[2] Congress again took the subject into consideration, examined the conditions which the legislature of Virginia had annexed to their proposed grant, declared some of them inadmissible, and stated the conditions on which the cession could be received.[3] Virginia complied with the terms proposed by Congress,

[1] Ibid.

[2] June 20, 1783.

[3] September 13, 1783.

and upon those terms ceded to the United States all right, title, and claim, both of soil and jurisdiction, which the State then had to the territory within the limits of its charter, lying to the northwest of the river Ohio. That magnificent region, in which now lie the powerful States of Ohio, Indiana, Illinois, Michigan, and Wisconsin, became the property of the United States, by a grant of twenty lines, executed in Congress by Thomas Jefferson and three of his colleagues, on the 1st day of March, 1784.[1]

Soon after this cession had been completed, Congress passed a resolve for the regulation of the territory that had been or might be ceded to the United States, for the establishment of temporary and permanent governments by the settlers, and for the

[1] The granting part of the deed of cession, exclusive of its recitals, is as follows: "That we, the said Thomas Jefferson, Samuel Hardy, Arthur Lee, and James Munroe, by virtue of the power and authority committed to us by the act of the said General Assembly of Virginia before recited, and in the name and for and on behalf of the said Commonwealth, do by these presents convey, transfer, assign, and make over unto the United States in Congress assembled, for the benefit of the said States, Virginia inclusive, all right, title, and claim, as well of soil as of jurisdiction, which the said Commonwealth hath to the territory or tract of country within the lines of the Virginia charter, situate, lying, and being to the northwest of the river Ohio, to and for the uses and purposes, and on the conditions, of the said recited act." The cession was made with the reservation of such a portion of the territory ceded, between the rivers Scioto and Little Miami, as might be required to make up the deficiencies of land on the south side of the Ohio, called the Green River lands, reserved for the Virginia troops on continental establishment. (Journals, IX. 47-49.) Subsequently, the act of cession was altered, so as to admit of the formation of not more than five, nor less than three States, of a size more convenient than that described in the act of cession and in the resolve of October 10, 1780. (Journals, XI. 139, 140. July 9, 1786.)

admission of the new States thus formed into the Union.[1] This resolve provided, that the territory which had been or might be ceded to the United States, after the extinguishment of the Indian title, and when offered for sale by Congress, should be divided into separate States, in a manner specified; that the settlers on such territory, either on their own petition or on the order of Congress, should receive authority to form a temporary government; and that when there should be twenty thousand free inhabitants within the limits of any of the States thus designated, they should receive authority to call a convention of representatives to establish a permanent constitution and government for themselves, provided that both the temporary and permanent governments should be established on these principles, as their basis: — 1. That they should for ever remain a part of the Confederacy of the United States of America. 2. That they should be subject to the Articles of Confederation and the acts and ordinances of Congress, like the original parties to that instrument. 3. That they should in no case interfere with the disposal of the soil by Congress. 4. That they should be subject to pay a part of the federal debts, present and prospective, in the same measure of apportionment with the other States. 5. That they should impose no tax upon lands, the property of the United States. 6. That their respective governments should be republican. 7. That the lands of

[1] April 23, 1784. Journals, IX. 153.

non-resident proprietors should not be taxed higher than those of residents, in any new State, before its delegates had been admitted to vote in Congress.

The resolve also contained a provision, which appears to have been designed to meet the want of constitutional power, under the Articles of Confederation, relative to the admission of new States. It was declared, that whenever any of the States thus formed should have as many free inhabitants as the least numerous of the thirteen original States, it should be admitted by its delegates into Congress on an equal footing with the original States, provided the assent of so many States in Congress should be first obtained, as might at the time be competent to such admission. It was further declared, that, in order to adapt the Articles of Confederation to the condition of Congress when it should be thus increased, it should be proposed to the original States, parties to that instrument, to change the rule, which required a vote of nine States, to a vote of two thirds of all the States in Congress; and that when this change had been agreed upon, it should be binding upon the new States.

After the establishment of a temporary government, and before its admission into the Union, each of the new States was to have the right to keep a member in Congress, with the privilege of debating, but not of voting. It was also provided, that measures not inconsistent with the principles of the Confederation, and necessary for the preservation of peace and good order among the settlers in any of the said new States, until they had assumed a temporary government, might, from time to time, be taken by the United States in Congress assembled.

These provisions were to stand as a charter of compact and as fundamental constitutions between the thirteen original States and each of the new States thus described, unalterable from and after the sale of any part of the territory of such State, but by the joint consent of the United States in Congress assembled, and of the particular State to be affected.[1]

New and urgent recommendations followed the passage of this resolve, pressing the States to consider that the war was now happily brought to a close, by the services of the army, the supplies of property by citizens, and loans of money by citizens and foreigners, constituting a body of creditors who had a right to expect indemnification, and that the vacant territory was an important resource for this great object.[2]

The subject does not seem to have again occupied the attention of Congress until the spring of the following year, when a proposition was introduced and committed, to exclude slavery and involuntary servitude, otherwise than in punishment of crimes, from the States described in the resolve of April 23d, 1784, and to make this provision part of the compact established by that resolve.[3]

Soon afterwards, a cession was made by Massa-

1 April 23, 1784. Journals, IX. 153.

2 April 29, 1784. Journals, IX. 184.

3 This proposition was introduced by Rufus King, March 16, 1785, and was committed by the votes of *eight* States against *four*.

chusetts of all its right and title, both of soil and jurisdiction, to the Western territory lying within the limits of the charter of that State.[1] In the succeeding month, Congress adopted an ordinance for ascertaining the mode of disposing of the Western lands to settlers.[2] In the course of the next year, the cession by Connecticut was made, after various negotiations, with a reservation to that State of the property in a considerable tract of country, since called the Connecticut Reserve, lying to the south of Lake Erie, and now embraced within the State of Ohio.[3]

Before this transaction had been completed, it had become manifest, from the knowledge that had been obtained of the country northwest of the Ohio, that it would be extremely inconvenient to lay it out into States of the extent and dimensions described in the resolve of October 10, 1780, under which the cession of Virginia had been made; and the legislature of that State were accordingly asked to modify their

1 April 19, 1785.

2 May 20, 1785.

3 September 14, 1786. Journals, XI. 221 - 223. The deed of cession, and the act of Connecticut recited in it, do not disclose this reservation. The territory ceded is described by certain lines which include less than the whole claim of Connecticut. It appears from the Journals, under the date of May 22 - 26, 1786, and from various propositions considered between those dates, that the State of Connecticut claimed to own a larger extent of territory than she proposed to cede; and by way of compromise, her claim was so far acceded to, that Congress agreed to accept of a cession of less than the whole. The reservation embraced about six millions of acres. See Sparks's Washington, IX. 178, note, where it appears that the right of the State to this territory was considered very feeble at the time.

act of cession, so as to enable Congress to lay out the territory into not more than five nor less than three States, as the situation and circumstances of the country might require.[1] This suggestion was complied with.[2]

A cession by South Carolina then followed, of all its claim to lands lying towards the river Mississippi;[3] but no other cessions were made to the United States under the Confederation; those of Georgia and North Carolina having been made after the adoption of the Constitution.[4]

It appears, therefore, that, with the exception of the claims of South Carolina to territory lying due west from that State towards the river Mississippi, the United States, before the 13th of July, 1787, had become possessed of the title to no other territory than that which had been surrendered to them by the States of New York, Virginia, Massachusetts, and Connecticut. The great mass of this territory was that embraced within the cession of Virginia, and lying to the northwest of the river Ohio; and after the whole title to this region, with the exception of some reserved tracts, had become complete in the United States, it was subject to the resolves of 1780 and of 1784. The provisions of the resolve of 1784, however, were soon seen to be inconvenient and inapplicable to the pressing wants of this region. Immediate legislation was plainly demanded for this

1 July 9, 1786.

2 December 30, 1788.

3 August 9, 1789.

4 That of North Carolina was made February 25, 1790, and that of Georgia, April 24, 1802.

territory, which could not wait the slow process of forming first temporary and then permanent governments, as had been contemplated by that resolve. Congress had had cast upon it the administration of an empire, exterior to the Confederation, and rapidly filling with people, in which the rights and tenure of property, the preservation of order and tranquillity, and the shaping of its political and social destinies, required instant legislation. This legislation was therefore provided in the celebrated Ordinance for the Government of the Northwestern Territory, enacted July 13, 1787, which was designed to supersede and in terms directly repealed the resolve of 1784. As this fundamental law for a new and unsettled country — at that time a novel undertaking — must always be regarded with interest in every part of the world, and as it lies at the foundation of the civil polity of a sixth part of these United States, its principles and provisions should be carefully examined.

The territory was, for the purposes of temporary government, constituted one district, subject to be divided into two, as future circumstances might require. An equal distribution of property among the children of persons dying intestate, with a life estate to the widow in one third of the real and personal estate, was made the law of the territory, until it should be altered by its legislature. Persons of full age were empowered to dispose of their estates by a written will, executed in the presence of three witnesses. Real estates were authorized to be conveyed by deed, executed by a person of full age, acknowledged and attested by two witnesses. Both wills and deeds were required to be registered. Personal property was transferable by delivery.

The civil government of the territory was to consist of executive, legislative, and judicial branches. A Governor was to be appointed from time to time by Congress, and to be commissioned for three years, subject to removal; but he was to reside in the district, and to have a freehold estate there in one thousand acres of land, while in the exercise of his office. A Secretary was also to be appointed from time to time by Congress, and to be commissioned for four years, subject to removal, but to reside in the district, and to have a freehold estate there in five hundred acres of land, while in the exercise of his office. There was also to be appointed a court of common law jurisdiction, to consist of three judges, any two of whom should form a court; they were to reside in the district, and to have each a freehold estate there in five hundred acres of land, while in the exercise of their office; their commissions to continue in force during good behavior.

The Governor and Judges, or a majority of them, were to adopt and publish in the district such laws of the original States, criminal and civil, as might be necessary and best suited to the circumstances of the district, to be in force in the district until the organization of the General Assembly, unless disapproved by Congress, to whom, from time to time, they should be reported; — but the legislature, when constituted, were to have authority to alter them as they should think fit.

Magistrates and other civil officers were to be appointed by the Governor, previous to the organization of the General Assembly, for the preservation of peace and good order. After the organization of the General Assembly, the powers and duties of magistrates and other civil officers were to be regulated and defined by the legislature, but their appointment was to remain with the Governor.

For the prevention of crimes and injuries, the laws to be adopted or made were to have force in all parts of the district, and for the execution of process, criminal and civil, the Governor was to make proper divisions of the territory, and to lay out the portions where the Indian titles had been extinguished, from time to time, into counties and townships, subject to future alteration by the legislature.

As soon as there should be five thousand free male inhabitants, of full age, in the district, upon giving proof thereof to the Governor, they were to receive authority to elect representatives from their counties or townships, to represent them in the General Assembly. For every five hundred male inhabitants, there was to be one representative; and so on progressively the right of representation was to increase, until the number of representatives should amount to twenty-five, after which their numbers and proportions were to be regulated by the legislature. The qualifications of a representative were to be previous citizenship in one of the United States for three years, and residence in the district, or a residence of three years in the district, with a fee-simple estate, in either case, of two hundred acres of land within the district. The qualifications of electors were to be a freehold in fifty acres of land in the district, previous citizenship in one of the United States, and residence in the district, or the like freehold and two years' residence in the district.

The Ordinance then proceeded to state certain fundamental articles of compact between the original States and the people and States in the territory, which were to remain unalterable, except by common consent. The first provided for freedom of religious opinion and worship. The second provided for the right to the writ of *habeas corpus;* for trial by jury; for a proportionate representation in the legislature; for judicial proceedings according to the course of the common law; for offences not capital being bailable; for fines being moderate, and punishments not cruel nor unusual; for no man's being deprived of his liberty or property, but by the judgment of his peers or the law of the land; for full compensation for property taken or services demanded for the public; and that no law should ever be made, or have force in the territory, that should in any manner whatever interfere with or affect private contracts or engagements, previously formed, *bona fide* and without fraud. The third provided for the encouragement of religion and education, for schools, and for good faith towards the rights and property of the Indian tribes. The fourth provided that the territory and the States to be formed therein should for ever remain a part of the Confederacy, subject to the constitutional authority of Congress; that the inhabitants should be liable to be taxed proportionately for the public expenses; that the legislature in the territory should never interfere with the primary disposal of the soil by Congress, nor with their regulations for securing the title to purchasers; that no tax should be imposed on lands, the property of the United States; that non-resident proprietors should not be taxed more than residents; and that the navigable waters leading into the Mississippi and St. Lawrence, and the carrying-places between them, should be common highways and for ever free.

The fifth provided, that there should be formed in the territory not less than three, nor more than five States, with certain boundaries; and that whenever any of the States should contain sixty thousand free inhabitants, such State should be (and might be before) admitted by its delegates into Congress, on an equal footing with the original States in all respects whatever, and should be at liberty to form a permanent constitution and State government, provided it should be republican, and in conformity with these articles of compact.

The sixth provided, that there should be neither slavery nor involuntary servitude in the territory, otherwise than in the punishment of crimes; but that fugitives owing service in other States might be reclaimed.

American legislation has never achieved any thing more admirable, as an internal government, than this comprehensive scheme. Its provisions concerning the distribution of property, the principles of civil and religious liberty which it laid at the foundation of the communities since established under its sway, and the efficient and simple organization by which it created the first machinery of civil society, are worthy of all the praise that has ever attended it. It was not a plan devised in the closet, upon theoretical principles of abstract fitness. It was a constitution of government drawn by men who understood, from experience, the practical working of the principles which they undertook to embody. Those principles were, it is true, to be applied to a state of society not then formed; but they were taken from states of society in which they had been tried with success. The equal division of property; general, not universal suffrage, but a suffrage guarded by some degree of interest in society; representative government; the division of the three grand departments of political power; freedom of religious opinion and worship; the *habeas corpus*, trial by jury, and the course of the common law; the right to be bailed for offences not capital, and the prohibition of immoderate fines and cruel or unusual punishments; the great principle of compensation for property or service demanded by the public, and the legislative inviolability of contracts; the encouragement of schools and the means of education,—were all taken from the ancient or recent constitutions of States, from which the greater part of the inhabitants of the new territory would necessarily come. A community founded on these principles was predestined to prosperity and happiness.

But it was in the provisions of the Ordinance relative to the admission into the Union of the new States to be formed upon this territory, that the relation between the existing government of the United States and its great dependency was afterwards found to involve serious difficulties. The Union was at that time a confederacy of thirteen States, originally formed mainly with reference to the exigencies of the war; and, although the Articles of Confederation had been ratified under circumstances which gave to the United States the authority to acquire this property, they had vested in Congress no power to enlarge the Confederacy by the admission of new States. Yet the Ordinance undertook to declare that new States should be admitted into the Congress of the United States on an equal footing with the existing States in all respects whatever, without proposing to submit that question to the original parties to the Confederacy.

It does not appear from contemporary evidence that this difficulty attracted public attention, at the time of the passage of the Ordinance. In the year 1787, the Confederation was laboring under far more pressing and alarming defects than the want of strict constitutional power to create new States. Public attention was consequently more engaged with the consideration of evils which affected the prosperity of the original States themselves, than with the destiny of the new communities, or the method by which they were to be brought into the Union. It was not immediately perceived, also, that a property, capable at no distant day of becoming a vast mine of wealth to the United States, as a great and independent revenue, had come under the management of a single body of men, constituted originally without reference to such a trust, and with no declared constitutional provisions for its administration. When, however, the Constitution was in the process of formation, the necessity for provisions under which Congress could dispose of the public lands, and by which new States could be admitted into the Union, was at once felt and conceded on all sides.[1]

Far more serious difficulties, however, attended the management by the Confederation of the interests of the Western country;—difficulties which commenced immediately after the Peace, and continued to increase, until the course taken by Congress had nearly lost to the Union the whole of that immense region which now pours its commerce down the Mississippi and its great tributary waters. These difficulties sprang from the inherent weakness of the federal government,—from the absolute incapacity of Congress, constituted as it was, to deal wisely, safely, and efficiently with the foreign relations of the country and its internal affairs, under the delicate and critical circumstances in which it was then placed. After the Treaty of Peace, the Western settlements, flanked by the dependencies of Great Britain at the north and of

[1] See Mr. Madison's notes of the Debates in the Confederation. Elliot, V. 128, 157, 190, 211, 376, 381

Spain at the south, and rapidly filling with a bold, adventurous, and somewhat lawless population, whose ties of connection with the Eastern States were almost sundered by the remoteness of their position and the difficulties of communication, stood upon a pivot, where accident might have thrown them out of the Union. This population found themselves seated in a luxuriant and fertile country, capable of a threefold greater production than the States eastward of the Alleghany and Appalachian Mountains, and intersected by natural water communications of the most ample character, all tending to the great highway of the Mississippi. A soil richer than any over which the Anglo-Saxon race had hitherto spread itself upon this continent, in any of its temperate climes; large plains and meadows, capable, without labor, of supporting millions of cattle; and fields destined to vie with the most favored lands on the globe in the production of wheat, were already accumulating upon the banks of their great rivers a weight of produce far beyond the necessities of subsistence, and loudly demanding the means of reaching the markets of the world. The people of the Atlantic States knew little of the resources or situation of this country. They valued it chiefly as a means of paying the public debts by the sale of its lands; but until they were in imminent danger of losing it, from the inefficiency of the national government, they had little idea of the supreme necessity of securing for it an outlet to the sea, if they would preserve it to the Union.

Washington, in the autumn of 1784, after his retirement to Mount Vernon, made a tour into the Western country, for the express purpose of ascertaining by what means it could be most effectually bound to the Union. The policy of opening communications eastward, by means of the rivers flowing through Virginia to the Atlantic Ocean struck him at once. On his return, he addressed a letter to the Governor of the State, in which he recommended the appointment of a commission, to make a survey of the whole means of natural water communication between Lake Erie and the tide-waters of Virginia. He does not seem at this time to have considered the navigation of the Mississippi as of great importance; but he thought rather that the opening of that river would have a tendency to separate the Western from the Eastern States.[1] A year later, he held a clear opinion, that its navigation ought not at present to be made an object by the United States, but that their true policy was to open all the possible avenues be-

[1] His recommendation contemplated a survey of James River and the Potomac, from tide-water to their respective sources; then to ascertain the best portage between those rivers and the streams capable of improvement which run into the Ohio; then to traverse and survey those streams to their junction with the Ohio; then, passing down the Ohio to the mouth of the Muskingum, to ascend that river to the carrying-place to the Cuyahoga; then down the Cuyahoga to Lake Erie, and thence to Detroit. He also advised a survey of Big Beaver Creek, and of the Scioto, and of all the waters east and west of the Ohio, which invited attention by their proximity and the ease of land transportation between them and the James and Potomac Rivers. "These things being done," he said, "I shall be mistaken if prejudice does not yield to facts, jealousy to candor, and finally, if reason and nature, thus aided, do not dictate what is right and proper to be done." (Writings of Washington, IX. 65.) This suggestion was adopted, and a commission appointed.

tween the Atlantic States and the Western territory, and that, until this had been done, the obstructions to the use of the Mississippi had better not be removed.[1] Those obstructions, however, involved the hazard of a loss of the territory to which the navigation of that river had already become extremely important. Their nature is, therefore, now to be explained.

The Treaty of Peace with Great Britain recognized, as the southern boundary of the United States, a line drawn from a point where the thirty-first degree of north latitude intersected the river Mississippi, along that parallel due east to the middle of the river Appalachicola; thence along the middle of that river to its junction with the Flint River; thence in a straight line to the head of St. Mary's River; and thence down the middle of that river to the Atlantic Ocean.[2] At the time of the negotiation of this treaty West Florida was in the possession of Spain; and a secret article was executed by the British and American plenipotentiaries, which stipulated that in case Great Britain, at the conclusion of a peace with Spain, should recover or be put in possession of West Florida, the north boundary between that province and the United States should be a line drawn from the mouth of the river Yassous, where it unites with the river Mississippi, due east to the river Appalachicola.[3] The treaty also stipulated, that the navigation of the Mississippi, from its source to the

[1] Writings, IX. 63, 117–119. August 22, 1785.

[2] Article II. Journals, IX. 26.

[3] Executed November 30, 1782. Secret Journals, III. 338.

ocean, should for ever remain free and open to the subjects of Great Britain and the citizens of the United States.[1]

When the treaty came to be ratified and published, in 1784, the Spanish government was already acquainted with this secret article. Justly assuming that no treaty between Great Britain and the United States could settle the boundaries between the territories of the latter power and those of Spain, or give of itself a right to navigate a river passing wholly through their dominions, they immediately caused it to be signified to Congress, that, until the limits of Louisiana and the two Floridas should be settled and determined, by an admission on the part of Spain that they had been rightfully described in the Treaty with England, they must assert their territorial claims to the exclusive control of the river; and also, that the navigation would under no circumstances be conceded, while Spain held the right to its control.[2] To accommodate these difficulties, Congress resolved to send Mr. Jay, their Secretary of Foreign Affairs, to Spain; but his departure was prevented by the arrival in the United States of Don Diego Guardoqui, as Minister from Spain, charged with the negotiation of a treaty.[3]

Preparatory to this negotiation, the first instruction which Mr. Jay received from Congress was, to

[1] Article VIII. Journals, IX. 29.

[2] June 25, 1784. Communicated to Congress November 19, 1784. Secret Journals, III. 517, 518.

[3] Guardoqui arrived and was recognized July 2, 1785. Secret Journals, III. 563.

insist upon the right of the United States to the territorial boundaries and the free navigation of the Mississippi, as settled by their treaty with Great Britain.[1] Upon this point, however, the Spanish Minister was immovable. A long negotiation ensued, in which he evinced entire readiness to make a liberal commercial treaty with the United States, conceding to their trade very important advantages; but at the same time refusing the right to use the Mississippi. Such a treaty was regarded as extremely important to the United States. There was scarcely a single production of this country that could not be advantageously exchanged in the Spanish European ports for gold and silver. The influence of Spain in the Mediterranean, with Portugal, with France, with the States of Barbary, and the trade with her Canaries and the adjacent islands, rendered a commercial alliance with her of the utmost importance. That importance was especially felt by the Eastern and Middle States, whose influence in Congress thus became opposed to the agitation of the subject of opening the Mississippi.[2] Indeed, the prevailing opinion in Congress, at this time, was for not insisting on the right of navigation as a necessary requisite in the treaty with Spain; and there were some important and influential persons in that body ready to agree to the abandonment of the right, rather than defer longer a free and liberal system of trade

[1] August 25, 1785. Secret Journals, III. 585, 586.

[2] See the communication made by Mr. Jay to Congress, August 3, 1786. Secret Journals, IV. 43.

with a power able to give conditions so advantageous to the United States.[1] The Eastern States considered a commercial treaty with Spain as the best remedy for their distresses, which flowed, as they believed, from the decay of their commerce. Two of the Middle States joined in this opinion. Virginia, on the other hand, opposed all surrender of the right.[2]

In this posture of affairs, Mr. Jay proposed to Congress a middle course. Believing, as Washington continued to believe,[3] that the navigation of the

[1] Henry Lee, then in Congress, wrote to Washington on the 3d of July, 1786, as follows: "Your reasoning is perfectly conformable to the prevalent doctrine on that subject in Congress. We are very solicitous to form a treaty with Spain for commercial purposes. Indeed, no nation in Europe can give us conditions so advantageous to our trade as that kingdom. The carrying business they are like ourselves in, and this common source of difficulty in adjusting commercial treaties between other nations does not apply to America and Spain. But, my dear General, I do not think you go far enough. Rather than defer longer a free and liberal system of trade with Spain, why not agree to the exclusion of the Mississippi? This exclusion will not, cannot, exist longer than the infancy of the Western emigrants. Therefore, to these people what is now done cannot be important. To the Atlantic States it is highly important; for we have no prospect of bringing to a conclusion our negotiations with the court of Madrid, but by yielding the navigation of the Mississippi. Their Minister here is under positive instructions on that point. In all other arrangements, the Spanish monarch will give to the States testimonies of his regard and friendship. And I verily believe, that, if the above difficulty should be removed, we should soon experience the advantages which would flow from a connection with Spain." (Writings of Washington, IX. 173, note.)

[2] Washington's Writings, IX. 205, 206, note.

[3] Washington had not changed his opinion, at the time of these negotiations. On the 18th of June, 1786, he wrote to Henry Lee, in answer to his letter above quoted: "The advantages with which the inland navigation of the rivers Potomac and James is pregnant, must strike every mind that reasons upon the subject; but there is, I perceive, a diversity of sentiment respecting the benefits and

Mississippi was not at that time very important, and that it would not become so for twenty-five or thirty years, he suggested that the treaty should be limited to that period, and that one of its articles should stipulate, that the United States would forbear to use the navigation of the river below their territories to the ocean. It was supposed that such a forbearance, carrying no surrender of the right, would, at the expiration of the treaty, leave the whole subject in as favorable a position as that in which it now stood. Besides, the only alternative to obtaining such an article from Spain was to make war with her, and enforce the opening of the river. The experiment, at

consequences which may flow from the free and immediate use of the Mississippi. My opinion of this matter has been uniformly the same; and no light in which I have been able to consider the subject is likely to change it. It is, neither to relinquish nor to push our claim to this navigation, but in the mean while to open *all* the communications which Nature has afforded between the Atlantic States and the Western territory, and to encourage the use of them to the utmost. In my judgment, it is matter of very serious concern to the well-being of the former to make it the interest of the latter to trade with them; without which, the ties of consanguinity, which are weakening every day, will soon be no bond, and we shall be no more, a few years hence, to the inhabitants of that country, than the British and Spaniards are at this day; not so much, indeed, because commercial connections, it is well known, lead to others, and united are difficult to be broken. These must take place with the Spaniards, if the navigation of the Mississippi is opened. Clear I am, that it would be for the interest of the Western settlers, as low down the Ohio as the Big Kenhawa, and back to the Lakes, to bring their produce through one of the channels I have named; but the way must be cleared, and made easy and obvious to them, or else the ease with which people glide down streams will give a different bias to their thinking and acting. Whenever the new States become so populous and so extended to the westward as really to need it, there will be no power which can deprive them of the use of the Mississippi. Why, then, should we

least, it was argued, would do no injury, and might produce much good.[1]

These arguments prevailed, so far as to cause a change in Mr. Jay's instructions, by a vote, which was deemed by him sufficient to confer authority to obtain such an article as he had suggested, but which was clearly unconstitutional. Seven States against five voted to rescind the instructions of August 25, 1785, by which the Secretary had been directed to insist on the right of navigation, and not to conclude or sign any treaty until he had communicated it to Congress.[2] Mr. Jay accordingly agreed with the

prematurely urge a matter which is displeasing, and may produce disagreeable consequences, if it is our interest to let it sleep? It may require some management to quiet the restless and impetuous spirits of Kentucky, of whose conduct I am more apprehensive in this business than I am of all the opposition that will be given by the Spaniards." (IX. 172, 173.)

On the 26th of July of the same year, he again wrote to the same gentleman, expressing the same opinions; and on the 31st of October, he said that these sentiments "are controverted by only one consideration of weight, and that is, the operation which the occlusion of the river may have on the minds of the Western settlers, who will not consider the subject in a relative point of view, or on a comprehensive scale, and may be influenced by the demagogues of the country to acts of extravagance and desperation, under the popular declamation, that their interests are sacrificed." In July, 1787, he retained the same views as to the true policy of the different sections of the country interested in this question, but admitted that, from the spirit manifested at the West, it had become a moot point to determine, when every circumstance was brought into view, what was best to be done. (IX. 172, 180, 205, 261.)

1 See Mr. Jay's reasoning, Secret Journals, IV. 53, 54.

2 August 29, 1786. Secret Journals, IV. 109, 110. The States which voted to rescind these instructions were New Hampshire, Massachusetts, Rhode Island, Connecticut, New York, New Jersey, Pennsylvania, and Maryland; Virginia, North and South Carolina, and Georgia, voted not to rescind. Another resolution was carried on the following day (August 30), by

Spanish Minister on an article which suspended the use of the Mississippi, without relinquishing the right asserted by the United States.[1]

While these proceedings were going on, and before the vote of seven States in Congress had been obtained in favor of the present suspension of this difficult controversy, an occurrence took place at Natchez, which aroused the jealousy of the whole West. A seizure was made there, by the Spanish authorities, of certain American property, which had been carried down the river for shipment or sale at New Orleans.[2] The owner, returning slowly in the autumn to his home, in the western part of North Carolina, by a tedious land journey through Kentucky, detailed everywhere the story of his wrongs and of the loss of his adventure. The news of this seizure, as it circulated up the valley from below, encountered the intelligence coming from the eastward, that Congress proposed to surrender the present use of the Mississippi. Alarm and indignation fired the whole population of the Western settlements. They believed themselves to be on the point of being sacrificed to the commercial policy of the

the votes of seven States, instructing the Secretary to insist on the territorial limits or boundaries of the United States, as fixed in the Treaty with Great Britain, and not to form any treaty with the Spanish Minister, unless those boundaries were acknowledged and secured. Ibid. 111-116.

[1] This agreement was made between the 29th of August, the date of the rescinding resolution, and the 6th of October, 1786. See Mr. Jay's communication to Congress under the latter date, Secret Journals, IV. 297-301.

[2] This seizure was made on the 6th of June, 1786. Secret Journals, IV. 325.

Atlantic States; and, feeling that they stood in the relation of colonists to the rest of the Union, they held language not unlike that which the old colonies had held towards England, in the earlier days of the great controversy.

They surveyed the magnificent region which they were subduing from the dominion of Nature; — the inexhaustible resources of its soil already yielding an abundance, which needed only a free avenue to the ocean to make them rich and prosperous; — and they felt that the mighty river which swept by them, with a volume of waters capable of sustaining the navies of the world, had been destined by Providence as a natural channel through which the productions of their imperial valley should be made to swell the commerce of the globe. But the Spaniard was seated at the outlet of this noble stream, sullenly refusing to them all access to the ocean. To him they must pay tribute. To enrich him, they must till those luxuriant lands, which gave, by an almost spontaneous production, the largest return which American labor had yet reaped under the industry of its own free hands. Their proud spirits, unaccustomed to restraint, and expanding in a liberty unknown in the older sections of the country, could not brook this vassalage. Into the comprehensive schemes of statesmen, who sought to unite them with the East by a great chain of internal improvements, and thus to blend the interests of the West with the commercial prosperity of the whole country, they were too impatient, and too intent upon the engrossing object of their own immediate advantage, to be able to enter.

What, they exclaimed, could have induced the legislature of the United States, which had been applauded for their assertion and defence of the rights and privileges of the country, so soon to endeavor to subject a large part of their dominion to a slavery worse than that to which Great Britain had presumed to subject any part of hers? To give up to the Spaniards the greatest share of the fruits of their toils,—to surrender to them, on their own terms, the produce of that large, rich, and fertile country, and thus to enable them to command the benefits of every foreign market,—was an intolerable thought. What advantage, too, would it be to the Atlantic States, when Spain, from the amazing resources of the Mississippi, could undersell them in every part of the world? Did they think by this course of policy to prevent emigration from a barren country, loaded with taxes and impoverished by debts, to the most luxurious and fertile soil within the limits of the Union? The idea was vain and presumptuous. As well might the fishes of the sea be prevented from gathering on a bank that afforded them ample nourishment. The best and largest part of the United States was not thus to be left uncultivated; a home for savages and wild beasts. Providence had destined it for nobler purposes. It was to be the abode of a great, prosperous, and cultivated people,—of Americans in feeling, in rights, in spirit, incapable of becoming the bondmen of Spain, while the rest of their country remained free. Their own strength could achieve for them what the national power refused or was unable to obtain. Twenty thousand effective men, west of the Alleghanies, were ready to rush to the mouth of the Mississippi, and drive the Spaniards into the sea. Great Britain stood with open arms to receive them. If not countenanced and succored by the federal government, their allegiance would be thrown off, and the United States would find too late that they were as ignorant of the great valley of the Mississippi, as England was of the Atlantic States when the contest for independence began.[1]

[1] See the documents laid before Congress, April 13, 1787. Secret Journals, IV. 315–328. On the 30th of January, 1787, Mr. Jefferson thus writes to Mr. Madison, from Paris: "If these transactions give me no uneasiness, I feel very differently at another piece of intelligence, to wit, the possibility that the navigation of the Mississippi may be abandoned to Spain. I never had any interest westward of the Alleghany; and I never will have any. But I have had great opportunities of knowing the character of the people who inhabit that country; and I will venture to say, that the act which abandons the navigation of the Mississippi is an act of separation between the Eastern and Western country. It is a relinquishment of five parts out of eight of the territory of the United States; an abandonment of the fairest subject for the payment of our public debts, and the chaining those debts on our own necks, *in perpetuam*. I have the utmost confidence in the honest intentions of those who concur in this measure; but I lament their want of acquaintance with the character and physical advantages of the people, who, right or wrong, will suppose their interests sacrificed on this occasion to the contrary interests of that part of the Confederacy in possession of present power. If they declare themselves a separate people, we are incapable of a single effort to retain them. Our citizens can never be induced, either as militia or as soldiers, to go there to cut the throats of their own brothers and sons, or rather, to be themselves the subjects instead of the perpetrators of the parricide. Nor would that country quit the cost of being retained against the will of its inhabitants, could it be done. But it cannot be done. They are able already to rescue the naviga-

Such was the feeling that prevailed in the Western country, as soon as it became known that a treaty was actually pending, by which the right to navigate the Mississippi might be suspended for a quarter of a century. That it should have been accompanied by acts of retaliation and outrage against the property of Spanish subjects, was naturally to have been expected. A certain General Clarke, pretending to authority from the State of Virginia, undertook to enlist men and establish a garrison at Port St. Vincennes, ostensibly for the protection of the district of Kentucky, then under the jurisdiction of Virginia. He made a seizure there of some Spanish property for the purpose of clothing and subsisting his men, and sent an officer to the Illinois, to advise the settlers there of the seizures of American property made at Natchez, and to recommend them to retaliate for any outrages the Spaniards might commit upon their property.[1]

The executive of Virginia disavowed these acts, as soon as officially informed of them; ordered the parties to be brought to punishment; and sent a formal

tion of the Mississippi out of the hands of Spain, and to add New Orleans to their own territory. They will be joined by the inhabitants of Louisiana. This will bring on a war between them and Spain; and that will produce the question with us, whether it will not be worth our while to become parties with them in the war, in order to reunite them with us, and thus correct our error. And were I to permit my forebodings to go one step further, I should predict that the inhabitants of the United States would force their rulers to take the affirmative of that question. I wish I may be mistaken in all these opinions." (Jefferson, II. 87.)

[1] Secret Journals, IV. 311-313.

disclaimer, through their delegates in Congress, to the Spanish Minister.[1] Guardoqui was not disturbed. He expected these occurrences, and maintained his ground, refusing to yield the right of navigating the river; and having assented to Mr. Jay's proposal of an article which suspended the use for a period of twenty-five years, he was quite ready to go on and conclude the treaty.

The people of the Western country, however, began to form committees of correspondence, in order to unite their counsels and interests.[2] The inhabitants of Kentucky sent a memorial to the General Assembly of Virginia, which induced them to instruct their delegates in Congress to oppose any attempt to surrender the right of the United States to the free use of the Mississippi, as a dishonorable departure from the comprehensive and benevolent feeling that constituted the vital principle of the Confederation, and as provoking the just resentment and reproaches of the Western people, whose essential rights and interests would be thereby sacrificed. They also instructed their delegates to urge such negotiations with Spain as would obtain her consent to regulations for the mutual and common use of the river.[3] The members from Virginia, with one exception, concurred in the policy of these instructions,[4]

1 February 28, 1787.

2 Madison. Elliot's Debates, V. 97.

3 These instructions were adopted in November, 1786. Pitkin, II. 207. They were laid before Congress, April 19, 1787. Madison. Elliot's Debates, V. 103.

4 Henry Lee did not approve of this policy. See Washington's Works, IX. 205, note.

and at first addressed themselves to some conciliatory expedient for obviating the effect of the vote of seven States.

They first represented to Guardoqui that it would be extremely impolitic, both for the United States and Spain, to make any treaty which should have the effect of shutting up the Mississippi. They stated to him, that such a treaty could not be enforced; that it would be the means of peopling the Western country with increased rapidity, and would tend to a separation of that country from the rest of the Union; that Great Britain would be able to turn the force that would spring up there against Spanish America; and that the result would be the creation of a power in the valley of the Mississippi hostile both to Spain and the United States. These representations produced no impression. The Spanish Minister remained firm in the position which he had held from the first, that Spain never would concede the claim of the United States to navigate the river. He answered, that the result of what had been urged was, that Congress could make no treaty at all, and consequently that the trade of the United States must remain liable to be excluded from the ports of Spain.[1]

Foiled in this quarter, the next expedient, for those who felt the necessity of preventing such a

[1] See Madison's account of two interviews with Guardoqui, March 13 and 19, 1787. Elliot, V. 98, 100. At the first of these interviews, Guardoqui stated that he had had no conference with Mr. Jay since the previous October, and never expected to confer with him again.

treaty as had been contemplated, was to gain time, by transferring the negotiation to Madrid; and Mr. Madison introduced a resolution into Congress for this purpose, which was referred to the Secretary for Foreign Affairs.[1] In a few days, the Secretary reported against the proposal, and nothing remained for the opponents of the treaty, but to attack directly the vote of seven States, under which the Secretary had acted in proceeding to adjust with the Spanish Minister an article for suspending the right of the United States to the common use of the river below their southern boundary.

The Articles of Confederation expressly declared, that the United States should not enter into any treaty or alliance, unless nine States in Congress assented to the same.[2] It was very justly contended, therefore, that, to proceed to negotiate a treaty authorized by a vote of only seven States, would expose the United States to great embarrassment with the other contracting party, since the vote made it certain that the treaty could not be constitutionally ratified; and that the vote itself, having passed in a case requiring the assent of nine States, was not valid for the purpose intended by it. This was not

[1] April 18, 1787. Madison. Elliot, V. 102. On the next day (April 19) the instructions of Virginia were laid before Congress, but a motion to refer them also to the Secretary was lost, Massachusetts and New York voting against it, and Connecticut being divided. Ibid. When Mr. Jay's report came under consideration, Mr. Gorham of Massachusetts, according to Mr. Madison, avowed his opinion, that the shutting of the Mississippi would be advantageous to the Atlantic States, and wished to see it shut. Ibid. 103.

[2] Article IX.

denied; but the advocates of the treaty, by means of a parliamentary rule, resisted the introduction of a resolution to rescind the vote of seven States.[1]

But while this dangerous subject was pending, the affairs of the country had taken a new turn. The Convention at Annapolis had been held, in the autumn of 1786, and the Convention called to revise the system of the federal government was to meet in May, 1787. It had become sure and plain, that a large increase of the powers of the national government was absolutely essential to the continuance of the Union and the prosperity of the States. Every day the situation of the country was becoming more and more critical. No money came into the federal treasury; no respect was paid to the federal authority; and all men saw and admitted that the Confederation was tottering to its fall. Some prominent persons in the Eastern States were suspected of leaning towards monarchy; others openly predicted a partition of the States into two or more confederacies; and the distrust which had been created by the project for closing the Mississippi rendered it extremely probable, that the Western country at least would be severed from the Union.

The advocates of that project recoiled, therefore, from the dangers which they had unwittingly created. They saw, that the crisis required that harmony and confidence should be studiously cherished, now that the great enterprise of remodelling the government

[1] Madison. Elliot, V. 104, 105.

upon a firmer basis was to be attempted. They saw that no new powers could be obtained for the Federal Constitution, if the government then existing were to burden itself with an act so certain to be the source of dissension, and so likely to cause a dismemberment of the Confederacy, as the closing of the Mississippi. Like wise and prudent men, therefore, they availed themselves of the expected and probable formation of a new government, as a fit occasion for disposing of this question; and after an effort to quiet the apprehensions that had been aroused, the whole matter was postponed, by general consent, to await the action of the great Convention of May, 1787.[1] After the Constitution had been formed and adopted, the negotiation was formally referred to the new federal government which was about to be organized, in March, 1789, with a declaration of the opinion of Congress that the free navigation of the river Mississippi was a clear and essential right of the United States, and ought to be so considered and supported.[2]

1 Ibid.

2 September 16, 1788. Secret Journals, IV. 449-454.

CHAPTER VI.

1783-1787.

DECAY AND FAILURE OF THE CONFEDERATION. — PROGRESS OF OPINION. — STEPS WHICH LED TO THE CONVENTION OF 1787. — INFLUENCE AND EXERTIONS OF HAMILTON. — MEETING OF THE CONVENTION.

THE prominent defects in the Confederation, which have been described in the previous chapters, and which were so rapidly developed after the treaty of 1783, made it manifest, that a mere league between independent States, with no power of direct legislation, was not a government for a country like this, in a time of peace. They showed, that this compact between the States, without any central arbiter to declare or power to enforce the duties which it involved, could not long continue. It had, indeed, answered the great purpose of forming the Union, by bringing the States into relations with each other, the continuance of which was essential to liberty; since nothing could follow the rupture of those relations but the reëstablishment of European power, or the native despotism which too often succeeds to civil commotion. By creating a corporate body of confederate States, and by enabling them to go into the money-markets of Europe for the means of carrying on and concluding the war, the Confederation had made the idea and the necessity of a Union familiar to the popular mind. But the purposes and objects of the war were far less complex and intricate than the concerns of peace. It was comparatively easy to borrow money. It was another thing to pay it. The federal power, under the Confederation, had little else to do, before the peace, than to administer the concerns of an army in the field, and to attend to the foreign relations of the country, as yet not complicated with questions of commerce. But the vast duties, capable of being discharged by no other power, which came rapidly into existence before the creation of the machinery essential to their performance, exhibited the Confederation in an alarming attitude.

It was found to be destitute of the essence of political sovereignty, — the power to compel the individual inhabitants of the country to obey its decrees. It was a system of legislation for States in their corporate and collective capacities, and not for the individuals of whom those States were composed. It could not levy a dollar by way of impost or assessment upon the property of a citizen. It had no means of annulling the action of a State legislature, which conflicted with the lawful and constitutional requirements of Congress. It made treaties, and was forced to stand still and see them violated by its own members, for whose benefit they had been made. It owed an enormous debt, and saw itself, year by year, growing more and more unable to liquidate even the annually increasing interest. It stood in the relation of a protector to the principles of republican liberty on which the institutions of the States were founded, and on the first occurrence of danger, it stretched forward only a palsied arm, to which no man could look for succor. It undertook to rescue commerce from the blighting effects of foreign policy, and failed to achieve a single conspicuous and important advantage. Every day it lost something of respect abroad and of confidence at home, until all men saw, with Washington, that it had become a great shadow without the substance of a government; while few could even conjecture what was to rise up and supplant it.

Few men could see, amidst the decay of empire and the absolute negation of all the vital and essential functions of government, what was to infuse new life into a system so nearly effete. Yet the elements of strength existed in the character of the people; in the assimilation, which might be produced, in the lapse of years, by a common language, a common origin, and a common destiny;—in the almost boundless resources of the country;—and, above all, in the principles of its ancient local institutions, that were capable, to an extent not then conceived, of expansion and application to objects of far greater magnitude than any which they had yet embraced. Through what progress of opinion the people of this country were enabled to grasp and combine these elements into a new system, which could satisfy their wants, we must now inquire.

In this inquiry, the student of political history should never fail to observe, that the great difficulty of the case, which made it so complex and embarrassing, arose from the separate, sovereign, and independent existence of the States. The formation of new constitutions, in countries not thus divided, involves only the adaptation of new institutions and forms to the genius, the laws, and the habits of the people. The monarchy of France has, in our day, been first remodelled, and afterwards swept from the face of Europe, to be followed by a republican constitution, which has in its turn been crushed and superseded. But France is a country that has long been subjected to as complete and powerful a system of centralization as has existed anywhere since the most energetic period of the Roman empire; and whether its institutions of government have or have not needed to be changed, as they have been from time to time, those changes have been made in a country in which an entire political unity has greatly facilitated the operation.

In the United States, on the contrary, a federal government was to be created; and it was to be created for thirteen distinct communities; — a government that should not destroy the political sovereignties of the States, and should yet introduce a new sovereignty, formed by means of powers, whose surrender by the States, instead of weakening their present strength, would rather develop and increase it.

This peculiar difficulty may be constantly traced, amidst all the embarrassments of the period in which the fundamental idea of the Constitution was at length evolved.

The progress of opinion and feeling in this country, on the subject of its government, from the peace of 1783 to the year 1787, may properly be introduced by a brief statement of the political tendencies of two principal classes of men. All contemporary evidence assures us that this was a period of great pecuniary distress, arising from the depreciation of the vast quantities of paper money issued by the Federal and State governments; from rash speculations; from the uncertain and fluctuating condition of trade; and from the great amount of foreign goods forced into the country as soon as its ports were opened. Naturally, in such a state of things, the debtors were disposed to lean in favor of those systems of government and legislation which would tend to relieve or postpone the payment of their debts; and as such relief could come only from their State governments, they were naturally the friends of State rights and State authority, and were consequently not friendly to any enlargement of the powers of the Federal Constitution. The same causes which led individuals to look to legislation for irregular relief from the burden of their private contracts, led them also to regard public obligations with similar impatience. Opposed to this numerous class of persons were all those who felt the high necessity of preserving inviolate every public and private obligation; who saw that the separate power of the States could not accomplish what was absolutely necessary to sustain both public and private credit; and they were as naturally disposed to look to the resources of the Union for these benefits, as the other class were to look in an opposite direction. These tendencies produced, in nearly every State, a struggle, not as between two organized parties, but one that was all along a contest for supremacy between opposite opinions, in which it was at one time doubtful to which side the scale would turn.[1]

[1] "The war, as you have very justly observed," General Washington wrote to James Warren of Massachusetts, in October, 1785, "has terminated most advantageously for America, and a fair field is presented to our view; but I confess to you, my dear Sir, that I do not think we possess wisdom or justice enough to cultivate it properly. Illiberality, jealousy, and local policy mix too much in all our public counsels for the good government of the Union. In a word, the Confederation appears to me to be little more than a shadow without the substance, and Congress a nugatory body, their ordinances being little attended to. To me it is a solecism in politics; indeed, it is one of the most extraordinary things in nature, that we should confederate as a nation, and yet be afraid to give the rulers of that nation (who are the creatures of our own making, appointed for a limited and short duration, and who are amenable for every action and may be recalled at any moment, and are subject to all the evils which they may be instrumental in producing) sufficient powers to order and direct the affairs of the same. By such policy as this, the wheels of government are clogged, and our brightest prospects, and that high expectation which was entertained of us by the wondering world, are turned into astonishment; and, from the high ground on which we stood, we are descending into the vale of confusion and darkness.

"That we have it in our power to become one of the most respectable nations upon earth, admits, in my humble opinion, of no doubt, if we would but pursue a wise, just, and liberal policy towards one another, and keep good faith with the rest of the world. That our resources are ample and increasing, none can deny; but while they are grudgingly applied, or

The three most important centres of opinion in the Union, before the formation of the Constitution, were Massachusetts, Virginia, and New York.[1] The public proceedings of each of them, in the order of time, on the subject of enlarging the federal powers, are, therefore, important to a just understanding of the course of events which ended in the calling of the Convention.

The legislature of Massachusetts was assembled in the summer of 1785. The proposal of Congress, made to the States in 1784, to grant the power of regulating trade, had been responded to by only four of the States, and the negotiations in Europe were failing from the want of it. Great uneasiness and distress pervaded all the commercial classes, and extended to every other class capable of being affected by a state of things in which a large balance, occasioned by the extravagant importation and use of

not applied at all, we give a vital stab to public faith, and shall sink, in the eyes of Europe, into contempt.

"It has long been a speculative question among philosophers and wise men, whether foreign commerce is of real advantage to any country; that is, whether the luxury, effeminacy, and corruptions which are introduced along with it are counterbalanced by the convenience and wealth which it brings. But the decision of this question is of very little importance to us. We have abundant reason to be convinced that the spirit of trade which pervades these States is not to be repressed. It behooves us, then, to establish just principles; and this cannot, any more than other matters of national concern, be done by thirteen heads differently constructed and organized. The necessity, therefore, of a controlling power, is obvious; and why it should be withheld is beyond my comprehension." Writings, IX. 139-141.

[1] They are named in this order, because it represents the order in which they respectively acted upon the enlargement of the federal powers.

foreign manufactures, was thrown against the country. The money of the State was rapidly drawn off to meet this balance, which its other exhausted means of remittance could not satisfy. It was impossible for the State to recover its former prosperity, while Great Britain and other nations continued the commercial systems which they had adopted. It had become plain to the comprehension of all intelligent persons concerned in trade, that nothing could break up those systems so long as the United States were destitute of the same power to regulate their foreign trade, by admitting or excluding foreign vessels and cargoes according to their interests; and it needed only the popular expression of this palpable truth, enforced by a clear and decided executive message, to induce the legislature to act upon it.[1] Governor

[1] One of the necessary and immediate effects of the Revolution of course was, the loss of the exclusive commercial advantages which this country had enjoyed with Great Britain and her dependencies; and the prohibitory acts and impositions, which fell with their full weight on the American trade, after the peace, were particularly disastrous to the trade of Massachusetts. The whale fishery, a business of great importance, had brought into the Province, before the war, 172,000 guineas per annum, giving employment to American seamen, and not requiring the use of any foreign materials, except a small quantity of cordage. A duty was now laid on whale oil in England of £18 per tun. In addition to the loss thus sustained, the exportation of lumber and provisions in American bottoms to the West Indies was entirely prohibited. Another great inconvenience, which came in fact to be intolerable, was the vast influx of British goods, consigned to English factors for sale, depriving the native merchants, manufacturers, and artisans of the market. At the same time, the revenue of the State, derived from impost and excise duties and a tax on auctions of one per cent., fell short of the annual interest on the private debt of the State, 30,000 pounds (currency) per annum, and a tax of 20,000 pounds (currency) was computed

Bowdoin gave the necessary impulse, and suggested the appointment of special delegates from the States to settle and define the powers with which Congress ought to be invested.[1]

This message caused the adoption of the first resolution, passed by the legislature of any State, declaring the Articles of Confederation to be inadequate to the great purposes which they were originally designed to effect, and recommending a convention of delegates from all the States, for the purpose of revising them, and reporting to Congress how far it might be necessary to alter or enlarge the powers of

to be necessary to cancel the debt, principal and interest, in fifteen years, and pay the ordinary charges of the government. Besides this, the State's proportion of the federal debt was to be provided for. It was in this state of things that two remarkable popular meetings were held in Boston, in the spring of 1785, to act upon the subject of trade and navigation, and to call the attention of Congress to the necessity for a national regulation of commerce. The first was a meeting of the merchants and tradesmen, convened at Faneuil Hall on the 18th of April. They appointed a committee to draft a petition to Congress, representing the embarrassments under which the trade was laboring, and took measures to cause the legislature to call the attention of the delegation in Congress to the importance of immediate action upon the subject. They also established a committee of correspondence with the merchants in the other seaports of the United States, to induce a similar action; and they entered into a pledge not to purchase any goods of the British merchants and factors residing in Boston, who had made very heavy importations, which tended to drain the specie of the State. The other meeting was an assembly of the artisans and mechanics, held at the Green Dragon Tavern, on the 28th of April, at which similar resolutions were adopted. It is quite apparent, from these proceedings, that all branches of industry were threatened with ruin; and in the efforts to counteract the effects of the great influx of foreign commodities, we trace the first movements of a popular nature towards a national control over commerce.

[1] Governor Bowdoin's first Message to the Legislature, May 31, 1785.

the Federal Union, in order to secure and perpetuate its primary objects. Congress was requested by these resolves to recommend such a convention. A letter, urging the importance of the subject, was addressed by the Governor of Massachusetts to the President of Congress, and another to the executive of each of the other States. The resolves were also inclosed to the delegates of the State in Congress, with instructions to lay them before that body at the earliest opportunity, and to make every exertion to carry them into effect.[1]

They were, however, never presented to Congress. That body was wholly unprepared for such a step, and the delegation of Massachusetts were entirely opposed to it, as premature. It had been all along the policy of Congress to obtain only a grant of temporary power over commerce, and to this policy they were committed by their proposition, now pending with the legislatures of the States, and by the instructions of the commissioners whom they had sent to Europe to negotiate commercial treaties. The prevalent idea in Congress was, that at the expiration of fifteen years, — the period for which they had asked the States to grant them power over commerce, — a new commercial epoch would commence, when the States would have a more clear and comprehensive view of their interests, and of the best means for promoting them, whether by treaties abroad, or by the delegation and exercise of greater power at home. It was argued,

[1] July 1, 1785.

also, that the most safe and practicable course was, to grant temporary power in the first instance, and to leave the question of its permanent adoption as a part of the Confederation to depend on its beneficial effects. Another objection, which afterwards caused serious difficulty, was, that the Articles of Confederation contained no provision for their amendment by a convention, but that changes should originate in Congress and be confirmed by the State legislatures, and that, if the report of a convention should not be adopted by Congress, great mischiefs would follow.

But a deep-seated jealousy in Congress of the radical changes likely to be made in the system of government lay at the foundation of these objections. There was an apprehension that the Convention might be composed of persons favorable to an aristocratic system; or that, even if the members were altogether republican in their views, there would be great danger of a report which would propose an entire remodelling of the government. The delegation from Massachusetts, influenced by these fears, retained the resolutions of the State for two months, and then replied to the Governor's letter, assigning these as their reasons for not complying with the directions given to them.[1] The legislature of Mas-

[1] The delegation at that time consisted of Elbridge Gerry, Samuel Holten, and Rufus King. Their "Reasons assigned for suspending the delivery to Congress of the Governor's letter for revising and altering the Confederation" may be found in the Life of Hamilton, II. 353. See also Boston Magazine for 1785, p. 475.

sachusetts thereupon annulled their resolutions recommending a Convention.[1]

It is manifest from this occurrence, that Congress in 1785 were no more in a condition to take the lead and conduct the country to a revision of the Federal Constitution, than they were in 1783, when Hamilton wished to have a declaration made of its defects, and found it impracticable. There were seldom present more than five-and-twenty members; and, at the time when Massachusetts proposed to call upon them to act upon this momentous subject, the whole assembly embraced as little eminent talent as had ever appeared in it. They were not well placed to observe that something more than "the declamation of designing men" was at work, loosening the foundations of the system which they were administering.[2] They saw some of its present inconveniences; but they did not see how rapidly it was los-

[1] November 25, 1785.

[2] Letter of Messrs. Gerry, Holten, and King, delegates in Congress, to the Governor of Massachusetts, assigning reasons for suspending the delivery of his letter to Congress, dated September 3, 1785. Life of Hamilton, II. 353, 357. "We are apprehensive," said they, "and it is our duty to declare it, that such a measure would produce throughout the Union an exertion of the friends of an aristocracy to send members who would promote a change of government; and we can form some judgment of the plan which such members would report to Congress. But should the members be altogether republican, *such have been the declamations of designing men* against the Confederation generally, against the rotation of members, which, perhaps, is the best check to corruption, and against the mode of altering the Confederation by the unanimous consent of the legislatures, which effectually prevents innovations in the articles by intrigue or surprise, that we think there is great danger of a report which would invest Congress with powers that the honorable legislature have not the most distant intention to delegate."

ing the confidence of the country, of which the following year was destined to deprive it altogether.

Before the year 1785 had closed, however, Virginia was preparing to give the weight of her influence to the advancing cause of reform.

A proposition was introduced into the House of Delegates of Virginia, to instruct the delegates of the State in Congress to move a recommendation to all the States to authorize Congress to collect a revenue by means of duties uniform throughout the United States, for a period of thirteen years.[1] The absolute necessity for such a system was generally admitted; but, as in Massachusetts, the opinions of the members were divided between a permanent grant of power and a grant for a limited term. The advocates of the limitation, arguing that the utility of the measure ought to be tested by experiment, contended, that a temporary grant of commercial powers might be and would be renewed from time to time, if experience should prove its efficacy. They forgot that the other powers granted to the Union, on which its whole fabric rested, were perpetual and irrevocable; and that the first sacrifices of sovereignty made by the States had been the result of circumstances which imperatively demanded the surrender, just as the situation of the country now demanded a similar surrender of an irrevocable power over commerce. The proposal to make this grant temporary only, was a proposal to engraft an anomaly upon the other powers of the

[1] November 30th, 1785.

Confederacy, with very little prospect of its future renewal; for the caprice, the jealousy, and the diversity of interests of the different States, were obstacles which the scheme of a temporary grant could only evade for the present, leaving them still in existence when the period of the grant should expire. But the arguments in favor of this scheme prevailed, and the friends of the more enlarged and liberal system, believing that a temporary measure would stand afterwards in the way of a permanent one, and would confirm the policy of other countries founded on the jealousies of the States, were glad to allow the subject to subside, until a new event opened the prospect for a more efficient plan.[1]

The citizens of Virginia and Maryland, directly interested in the navigation of the rivers Potomac and Pocomoke, and of the Bay of Chesapeake, had long been embarrassed by the conflicting rights and regulations of their respective States; and, in the spring of 1785, an effort at accommodation was made, by the appointment of commissioners on the part of each State to form a compact between them for the regulation of the trade upon those waters. These commissioners assembled at Alexandria in March, and while there made a visit at Mount Vernon, where a further scheme was concerted for the establishment of harmonious commercial regulations between the two

[1] The resolution introduced on the 30th of November was agreed to in the Delegates, but before it was carried up to the Senate, it was reconsidered and laid upon the table. Elliot's Debates, I. 114, 115. Letter of Mr. Madison to General Washington, of December 9, 1785, Washington's Works, IX. 508.

States.[1] This plan contemplated the appointment of other commissioners, having power to make arrangements, with the assent of Congress, for maintaining a naval force in the Chesapeake, and also for establishing a tariff of duties on imports, to be enacted by the legislatures of both the States. A report, embracing this recommendation, was accordingly made by the Alexandria commissioners to their respective governments. In the legislature of Virginia this report was received while the proposition for granting temporary commercial powers to Congress was under consideration; and it was immediately followed by a resolution directing that part of the plan which respected duties on imports to be communicated to all the States, with an invitation to send deputies to the meeting. In a few days afterwards, the cele-

[1] What direct agency General Washington had in suggesting or promoting this scheme, does not appear; although it seems to have originated, or to have been agreed upon, at his house. His published correspondence contains no mention of the visit of the commissioners; but Chief Justice Marshall states that such a visit was made, and in this statement he is followed by Mr. Sparks. (Marshall, V. 90; Sparks, I. 428.) Mr. Madison, writing to General Washington in December, 1785, refers to "the proposed appointment of commissioners for Virginia and Maryland, *concerted at Mount Vernon*, for keeping up harmony in the commercial regulations of the two States," and says that the meeting of commissioners from all the States, which had then been proposed, "seems naturally to grow out of it." (Washington's Writings, IX. 509.)

That Washington foresaw that the plan agreed upon at his house in March would lead to a general assembly of representatives of all the States, seems altogether probable, from the opinions which he entertained and expressed to his correspondents, during that summer, upon the subject of conferring adequate commercial powers upon Congress. (See his Letters to Mr. McHenry and Mr. Madison of August 22d and November 30th, Writings, IX. 121, 145.)

brated resolution of Virginia, which led the way to the Convention at Annapolis, was adopted by the legislature, directing the appointment of commissioners to meet with the deputies of all the other States who might be appointed for the same purpose, to consider the whole subject of the commerce of the United States.[1] The circular letter which transmitted this resolution to the several States proposed that Annapolis in the State of Maryland should be the place, and that the following September should be the time of meeting.

The fate of this measure now turned principally upon the action of the State of New York. The power of levying a national impost, proposed in the revenue system of 1783, had been steadily withheld from Congress by the legislature of that State. Ever since the peace, the State had been divided between two parties, the friends of adequate powers in Con-

[1] This resolution, passed January 21, 1786, was in these words: "*Resolved*, That Edmund Randolph, James Madison, Jr., Walter Jones, St. George Tucker, Meriweather Smith, David Ross, William Ronald, and George Mason, Esquires, be appointed commissioners, who, or any five of whom, shall meet such commissioners as may be appointed by the other States in the Union, at a time and place to be agreed on, to take into consideration the trade of the United States; to examine the relative situation and trade of the said States; to consider how far a uniform system in their commercial regulations may be necessary to their common interest and their permanent harmony; and to report to the several States such an act relative to this great object, as, when unanimously ratified by them, will enable the United States in Congress assembled effectually to provide for the same; that the said commissioners shall immediately transmit to the several States copies of the preceding resolution, with a circular letter respecting their concurrence therein, and proposing a time and place for the meeting aforesaid."

gress, and the adherents of State sovereignty; and the belief that the commercial advantage of the State depended upon retaining the power to collect their own revenues, had all along given to the latter an ascendency in the legislature. In 1784, they established a custom-house and a revenue system of their own. In 1785, a proposition to grant the required powers to Congress was lost in the Senate; and in 1786, it became necessary for Congress to bring this question to a final issue. Three other States, as we have seen, stood in the same category with New York, having decided in favor of no part of the plan which Congress had so long and so repeatedly urged upon their adoption.[1] Declaring, therefore, that the crisis had arrived when the people of the United States, by whose will and for whose benefit the federal government was instituted, must decide whether they would support their work as a nation, by maintaining the public faith at home and abroad, or whether, for want of a timely exertion in establishing a general revenue system, and thereby giving strength to the Confederacy, they would hazard the existence of the Union and the privileges for which they had contended, — Congress left the responsibility of the decision with the legislatures of the States.[2]

[1] Rhode Island, Maryland, and Georgia.

[2] "The committee," said the Report, "have thought it their duty candidly to examine the principles of this system, and to discover, if possible, the reasons which have prevented its adoption; they cannot learn that any member of the Confederacy has stated or brought forward any objections against it, and the result of their

It was now that the influence of Hamilton upon the destinies of this country began to be favored by the events which had brought its affairs to the present juncture. To his sagacious and watchful forecast, the proposal of a commercial convention, emanating from Virginia, presented the opportunity which he had long desired, to effect an entire change in the system of the federal government; while, at the same time, the final appeal made by Congress for the establishment of the revenue system gave him an occasion to bring the State of New York into the movement which had been originated by Virginia. He determined that this system should be again presented to the legislature, for distinct approval or rejection, and that, if it should be rejected, the State should still

impartial inquiries into the nature and operation of the plan has been a clear and decided opinion, that the system itself is more free from well-founded exceptions, and is better calculated to receive the approbation of the several States, than any other that the wisdom of Congress can devise. In the course of this inquiry, it most clearly appeared that the requisitions of Congress for eight years past have been so irregular in their operation, so uncertain in their collection, and so evidently unproductive, that a reliance on them in future, as a source from whence moneys are to be drawn to discharge the engagements of the Confederacy, definite as they are in time and amount, would be not less dishonorable to the understandings of those who entertain such confidence, than it would be dangerous to the welfare and peace of the Union. The committee are therefore seriously impressed with the indispensable obligation that Congress are under of representing to the immediate and impartial consideration of the several States, the utter impossibility of maintaining and preserving the faith of the federal government by temporary requisitions on the States, and the consequent necessity of an early and complete accession of all the States to the revenue system of the 18th of April, 1783." (Journals of Congress, XI. 35, 36. February 15, 1786.)

send a representation to the Convention at Annapolis. He therefore caused the revenue system, as proposed by Congress, to be again brought before the legislature, where it was again rejected; and he and his friends then threw their whole influence in favor of the appointment of commissioners to attend the commercial convention, and succeeded, — Hamilton himself being appointed one of them.[1]

This great step having been taken, the course of the State of New York upon the revenue system of 1783, which brought her at length to an open controversy with Congress, tended strongly to aid the plans of Hamilton, and finally gave him the ascendency in the State itself. The legislature, in May, 1786, passed an act for granting imposts and duties to the United States, and soon afterwards adjourned. It was immediately pronounced by Congress not to be a compliance with their recommendation, and the Governor was earnestly requested to reassemble the legislature. This he declined to do, upon the ground of a want of constitutional power. Congress again urged the summoning of the legislature, for the purpose of granting the system of impost in such a manner as to enable them to carry it into effect, and the Governor again refused.[2]

[1] Life of Hamilton, II. 374, 375.

[2] The legislature of New York were willing to grant the duties to Congress, but insisted upon reserving the power of levying and collecting them; and, instead of making the collectors amenable to and removable by Congress, they made them removable by the State, on conviction for default or neglect of duty in the State courts. This was a material departure from the plan recommended by Congress, and was entirely inconsistent with

Arrived at Annapolis, Hamilton found there the representatives of five States only.[1] He had come with the determination that the Convention should lay before the country the whole subject of the condition of the States and the want of an efficient federal government. But the avowed purpose of the meeting was solely to consider the means of establishing a uniform system of commercial regulations, and not to reform the existing government of the Union. New Jersey alone, of the five States represented, had empowered her commissioners to consider of "other important matters," in addition to the subject of commercial regulations. Four other States had appointed commissioners, none of whom had attended; and the four remaining States had made no appointments at all.[2]

Under these circumstances, it was certainly a mat-

the grants already made by several of the States. See the Report and proceedings in Congress on the New York Act, July 27 – August 23, 1786. Journals, XI. 153, 184, 197, 200.

[1] New York was represented by Alexander Hamilton and Egbert Benson; New Jersey by Abraham Clark, William C. Houston, and James Schureman; Pennsylvania by Tench Coxe; Delaware by George Read, John Dickinson, and Richard Bassett; Virginia by Edmund Randolph (Governor), James Madison, Jr., and St. George Tucker.

[2] General Knox, writing to General Washington under date of January 14, 1787, says: "You ask what prevented the Eastern States from attending the September meeting at Annapolis. It is difficult to give a precise answer to this question. Perhaps torpidity in New Hampshire; faction and heats about their paper money in Rhode Island; and jealousy in Connecticut. Massachusetts had chosen delegates to attend, who did not decline until very late, and the finding of other persons to supply their places was attended with delay, so that the convention had broken up by the time the new-chosen delegates had reached Philadelphia." Writings of Washington, IX. 513.

ter of great delicacy for the commissioners of five States only to pass upon the general situation of the Union, and to pronounce its existing government defective and insufficient. Hamilton, however, felt that this opportunity, once lost, might never occur again; and although willing to waive his original purpose of a full exposition of the defects of the Confederation, he did not deem it expedient that the Convention should adjourn without proposing to the country some measure that would lead to the necessary reforms. He modified his original plan, therefore, and laid before his colleagues a report, which formally proposed to the several States the assembling of a general convention, to take into consideration the situation of the United States.

In this document, it was declared that the regulation of trade, which had been made the object of the meeting at Annapolis, could not be effected alone, for the power of regulating commerce would enter so far into the general system of the federal government, that it would require a corresponding adjustment of the other parts of the system. That the system of the general government was seriously defective; that those defects were likely to be found greater on a close inspection; that they were the cause of the embarrassments which marked the state of public affairs, foreign and domestic; and that some mode by which they could be peaceably supplied was imperatively demanded by the public necessities, — were propositions which the country was then prepared to receive. A convention of deputies from the different States, for the special and sole purpose of investigating the defects of the national government, seemed to be the course entitled to preference over all others.[1]

It was indeed the only method by which the object of the great statesman who drafted this report could have been reached. The Articles of Confederation had provided, that they should be inviolably observed by every State; that the Union should be perpetual; and that no alteration should be made in any of the Articles, unless agreed to in a Congress of the United States, and confirmed by the legislature of every State.[2] To have left the whole subject to the action of Congress would have insured, at most, only a change in some of the features of the existing government, instead of the great reform which Hamilton believed to be essential, — the substitution of a totally different system. At the same time, the co-operation and assent of Congress were necessary to the success of the plan of a convention, in order that it might not seem to be a violent departure from the provisions of the Articles of Confederation, and also for the sake of their influence with the States. The proposal of the report was therefore cautious. It did not suggest the summoning of a convention to frame a new constitution of government, but "to devise such further provisions as might appear to be necessary to render the constitution of the federal

[1] Report of the Annapolis Convention, Elliot's Debates, I. 116; Hamilton's Works, II. 336.

[2] Article XIII.

government adequate to the exigencies of the Union." It proposed also, that whatever reform should be agreed on by the convention should be reported to Congress, and, when agreed to by them, should be confirmed by the *legislatures* of all the States. In this manner, the proposal avoided any seeming violence to the Articles of Confederation, and suggested the convention as a body to prepare for the use of Congress a plan to be adopted by them for submission to the States.[1]

At the same time, Hamilton undoubtedly contemplated more than any amendment of the existing constitution. In 1780, he had analyzed the defects of the general government, sketched the outline of a Federal Constitution, and suggested the calling of a convention to frame such a system.[2] The idea of such a convention was undoubtedly entertained, by many persons, before the meeting at Annapolis. It had been recommended by the legislature of New York in 1782, and by that of Massachusetts in 1785. But Hamilton had foreseen its necessity in 1780, more than seven years before the meeting at Annapolis; and, although he may not have been the author of the first public proposal of such a measure, his private correspondence contains the first suggestion of it, and proves that he had conceived the main features of the Constitution of the United States, even before the Confederation itself was established.[3]

[1] Report, ut supra.

[2] See his letter to James Duane, written in 1780, Life, I. 284-305.

[3] Ibid. The first public proposal of a continental convention is assigned by Mr. Madison to one

The recommendation of the Annapolis commissioners was variously received. In the legislature of Virginia it met with a cordial approval, and an act was passed during the autumn to provide for the

Pelatiah Webster, whom he calls "an able, though not conspicuous citizen," and who made this suggestion in a pamphlet published in May, 1781. Recent researches have not added to our knowledge of this writer. In the summer of 1782, the legislature of New York, under the suggestion of Hamilton, passed resolutions recommending such a convention. On the 1st of April, 1783, Hamilton, in a debate in Congress, expressed his desire to see a general convention take place. In 1784, the measure was a good deal talked of among the members of Congress, and in the winter of 1784-85, Noah Webster, an eminent political writer in Connecticut, suggested "a new system of government, which should act, not on the States, but directly on individuals, and vest in Congress full power to carry its laws into effect." In 1786, the subject was again talked of among members of Congress, before the meeting at Annapolis. (Madison. Elliot, V. 117, 118.) But Hamilton's letter to James Duane, in 1780, although not published at the time, was of course earlier than any of these suggestions. In that letter, after showing that the fundamental defect of the then existing system was a want of power in Congress, he thus analyzes in advance the Articles of Confederation, which had not then taken effect: — "But the Confederation itself is defective, and requires to be altered. It is neither fit for war nor peace. The idea of an uncontrollable sovereignty, in each State, over its internal police, will defeat the other powers given to Congress, and make our Union feeble and precarious. There are instances, without number, where acts necessary for the general good, and which rise out of the powers given to Congress, must interfere with the internal police of the States; and there are as many instances in which the particular States, by arrangements of internal police, can effectually, though indirectly, counteract the arrangements of Congress. You have already had examples of this, for which I refer to your own memory. The Confederation gives the States, individually, too much influence in the affairs of the army; they should have nothing to do with it. The entire foundation and disposal of our military forces ought to belong to Congress. It is an essential element of the Union; and it ought to be the policy of Congress to destroy all ideas of State attachment in the army, and make it look up wholly to them. For this purpose, all appointments, promotions, and

appointment of delegates to the proposed convention. In Congress, it was received at first with little favor. Doubts were entertained there whether any changes in the federal government could be constitu-

provisions whatsoever ought to be made by them. It may be apprehended, that this may be dangerous to liberty. But nothing appears more evident to me, than that we run much greater risk of having a weak and disunited federal government, than one which will be able to usurp upon the rights of the people. Already some of the lines of the army would obey their States in opposition to Congress, notwithstanding the pains we have taken to preserve the unity of the army. If any thing would hinder this, it would be the personal influence of the general, — a melancholy and mortifying consideration. The forms of our State constitutions must always give them great weight in our affairs, and will make it too difficult to blind them to the pursuit of a common interest, too easy to oppose what they do not like, and to form partial combinations, subversive of the general one. There is a wide difference between our situation and that of an empire under one simple form of government, distributed into counties, provinces, or districts, which have no legislatures, but merely magistratical bodies to execute the laws of a common sovereign. There the danger is that the sovereign will have too much power, and oppress the parts of which it is composed. In our case, that of an empire composed of confederate states, each with a government completely organized within itself, having all the means to draw its subjects to a close dependence on itself, the danger is directly the reverse. It is, that the common sovereign will not have power sufficient to unite the different members together, and direct the common forces to the interest and happiness of the whole. . . . . . The Confederation, too, gives the power of the purse too entirely to the State legislatures. It should provide perpetual funds in the disposal of Congress, by a land-tax, poll-tax, or the like. All imposts upon commerce ought to be laid by Congress, and appropriated to their use; for without certain revenues, a government can have no power; that power which holds the purse-strings absolutely, must rule. This seems to be a medium which, without making Congress altogether independent, will tend to give reality to its authority. Another defect in our system is, want of method and energy in the administration. This has partly resulted from the other defect; but in a great degree from prejudice and the want of a proper executive. Congress have kept the power too much in their own hands, and have meddled too much with details of every sort.

tionally made, unless they were to originate in Congress and were then to be adopted by the legislatures of the States, pursuant to the mode provided by the Articles of Confederation. The legislatures, it

Congress is properly a deliberative corps, and it forgets itself when it attempts to play the executive. It is impossible that a body, numerous as it is, constantly fluctuating, can ever act with sufficient decision, or with system. Two thirds of the members, one half the time, cannot know what has gone before them, or what connection the subject in hand has to what has been transacted on former occasions. The members who have been more permanent will only give information that promotes the side they espouse, in the present case, and will as often mislead as enlighten. The variety of business must distract, and the proneness of every assembly to debate must at all times delay. Lastly, Congress, convinced of these inconveniences, have gone into the measure of appointing boards. But this is, in my opinion, a bad plan. A single man, in each department of the administration, would be greatly preferable. It would give us a chance of more knowledge, more activity, more responsibility, and, of course, more zeal and attention. Boards partake of the inconveniences of larger assemblies; their decisions are slower, their energy less, their responsibility more diffused. They will not have the same abilities and knowledge as an administration by single men. Men of the first pretensions will not so readily engage in them, because they will be less conspicuous, of less importance, have less opportunity of distinguishing themselves. The members of boards will take less pains to inform themselves and arrive at eminence, because they have fewer motives to do it. All these reasons conspire to give a preference to the plan of vesting the great executive departments of the state in the hands of individuals. As these men will be, of course, at all times under the direction of Congress, we shall blend the advantages of a monarchy in one constitution. . . . . . I shall now propose the remedies which appear to me applicable to our circumstances, and necessary to extricate our affairs from their present deplorable situation. The first step must be to give Congress powers competent to the public exigencies. This may happen in two ways: one, by resuming and exercising the discretionary powers I suppose to have been originally vested in them for the safety of the States, and resting their conduct on the candor of their countrymen and the necessity of the conjuncture; the other, *by calling immediately a convention of all the States*, with full authority to conclude finally upon

was argued, could not adopt any scheme that might be proposed by a convention; and if it were submitted to the people, it was not only doubtful what degree of assent on their part would make it valid, but it

a general confederation, stating to them beforehand explicitly the evils arising from a want of power in Congress, and the impossibility of supporting the contest on its present footing, that the delegates may come possessed of proper sentiments, as well as proper authority, to give efficacy to the meeting. *Their commission should include a right of vesting Congress with the whole or a proportion of the unoccupied lands, to be employed for the purpose of raising a revenue, reserving the jurisdiction to the States by whom they are granted.* The Confederation, in my opinion, should give Congress a complete sovereignty; except as to that part of internal police which relates to the rights of property and life among individuals, and to raising money by internal taxes. It is necessary that every thing belonging to this should be regulated by the State legislatures. Congress should have complete sovereignty in all that relates to war, peace, trade, finance; and to the management of foreign affairs; the right of declaring war, of raising armies, officering, paying them, directing their motions in every respect; of equipping fleets, and doing the same with them; of building fortifications, arsenals, magazines, &c.; of making peace on such conditions as they think proper; of regulating trade, determining with what countries it shall be carried on; granting indulgences; laying prohibitions on all the articles of export or import; imposing duties, granting bounties and premiums for raising, exporting, or importing; and applying to their own use the product of these duties, only giving credit to the States on whom they are raised in the general account of revenues and expense; instituting admiralty courts, &c.; of coining money, establishing banks on such terms, and with such privileges, as they think proper; appropriating funds, and doing whatever else relates to the operations of finance; transacting every thing with foreign nations; making alliances offensive and defensive, and treaties of commerce, &c. . . . . . The second step I would recommend is, that Congress should instantly appoint the following great officers of state: a Secretary for Foreign Affairs; a President of War; a President of Marine; a Financier; a President of Trade. . . . . . These officers should have nearly the same powers and functions as those in France analogous to them, and each should be chief in his department, with subordinate boards, composed of assistants, clerks, &c., to execute his orders." (Life of Hamilton, I. 284–305.)

was also doubtful whether they could change the Federal Constitution by their own direct action. To these difficulties was to be added the further hazard, that, if the report of the convention should be made to Congress, as proposed, they might not finally adopt it, and if it should be rejected, that fatal consequences would ensue.[1]

The report of the Annapolis commissioners was, however, taken into consideration; and in the course of the following winter a report upon it was made in Congress, which conceded the fact that the Confederation required amendments, and that the proposed convention was the most eligible mode of effecting them.[2] But this report had to encounter the objection, entertained by many members, that the measure proposed would tend to weaken the federal authority, by lending the sanction of Congress to an extra-constitutional proceeding. Others considered that a more summary mode of proceeding was advisable, in the form of a direct appeal to the people of every State to institute State conventions, which should choose delegates to a general convention, to revise and amend, or change, the federal system, and to publish the new constitution for general observance, without any reference to the States, for their acceptance or confirmation.[3] There were

1 Abstract of an Address made to the Legislature of Massachusetts, by the Hon. Rufus King, in October, 1786. Boston Magazine for the year 1786, p. 406.

2 Mr. Madison's Notes of Debates in the Congress of the Confederation. Elliot, V. 96.

3 This was the opinion of Mr. Jay. He thought that no alterations should be attempted, unless deduced from the only source of

still others, who preferred that Congress should take up the defects of the existing system, point them out to the legislatures of the States, and recommend certain distinct alterations to be adopted by them.[1]

It was no doubt true, that a convention originating with the State legislatures was not a mode pointed out by the Articles of Confederation for effecting amendments to that instrument. But it was equally true, that the mere amendment of that instrument was not what the critical situation of the country required. On the other hand, a convention originating with the people of the States would undoubtedly rest upon the authority of the people, in its inception; but, if the system which it might frame were to go into operation without first being adopted by the people, it would as certainly want the true basis of their consent. These difficulties were felt in and out of Congress. But it does not seem to have occurred to those who raised them, that the source from which the convention should derive its powers to frame and recommend a new system of government was of far less consequence, than that the mode in which the system recommended should be adopted, should be one that would give it the

just authority, the people. He seems to have considered that, if the people of the States, acting through their primary conventions, were to send delegates to a general convention, with authority to alter the Articles of Confederation, the new system would rest upon the authority of the people, without further sanction. See his letter to General Washington, of date January 7, 1787. Writings of Washington, IX. 510.

[1] Letter of General Knox to General Washington, January 14, 1787. Writings of Washington, IX. 513.

full sanction and authority of the people themselves. A constitution might be framed and recommended by any body of individuals, whether instituted by the legislatures or by the people of the States; but if adopted and ordained by the States in their corporate capacities, it would rest on one basis, and if adopted and ordained by the people of the States, acting upon it directly and primarily, it would obviously rest upon another, a different, and a higher authority.

The latter mode was not contemplated by Congress when they acted upon the recommendation of the Annapolis commissioners. Accustomed to no other idea of a union than that formed by the States in their corporate capacities as distinct and sovereign communities; belonging to a body constituted by the States, and therefore officially related rather to the governments than to the people of the States; and entertaining a becoming and salutary fear of departing from a constitution which they had been appointed to administer, — the members of the Congress of 1786-87 were not likely to go beyond the Annapolis recommendation, which in fact proposed that the new system should be confirmed by the legislatures of the States.

But the course of events tended to a different result, — to an actual, although a peaceable revolution, by the quiet substitution of a new government in place of the old one, and resting upon an entirely different basis. While Congress were debating the objections to a convention, the necessity for action became every day more stringent. The insurrection in Massachusetts, which had followed the meeting of the commissioners at Annapolis and had reached a dangerous crisis when their report was before Congress, had alarmed the people of the older States by the dangers of an anarchy with which the existing national government would be obviously unable to cope. The peril of losing the navigation of the Mississippi, and with it the Western settlements, through the inefficiency of Congress, was also at that moment impending; while, at the same time, the commerce of the country was nearly annihilated by a course of policy pursued by England, which Congress was utterly unable to encounter. Under these dangers and embarrassments, a state of public opinion was rapidly developed, in the winter of 1787, which drove Congress to action. The objections to the proposal before them yielded gradually to the stern requirements of necessity, and a convention was at last accepted, not merely as the best, but as the only practicable, mode of reaching the first great object by which an almost despairing country might be reassured of its future welfare.

The final change in the views of Congress in regard to a convention was produced by the action of the legislature of New York. In that body, as we have seen, the impost system had been rejected, in the session of 1786, and the Governor of the State had even refused to reassemble the legislature for the reconsideration of this subject. A new session commenced in January, 1787, in the city of New York, where Congress was also sitting. A crisis now occurred, in which the influence of Hamilton was exerted in the same manner that it had been in the former session, and with a similar result. On that occasion he had followed up the rejection of the impost system with a resolve for the appointment of commissioners to attend the meeting at Annapolis. It was now his purpose, in case the impost system should be again rejected, to obtain the sanction of Congress to the recommendation of a convention, made by the Annapolis commissioners. This, he was aware, could be effected only by inducing the legislature of New York to instruct the delegates of their State in Congress to move and vote for that decisive measure. The majority of the members of Congress were indisposed to adopt the plan of a convention; and although they might be brought to recommend it at the instance of a State, they were not inclined to do so spontaneously.[1] The crisis required, therefore, all the address of Hamilton and of the friends of the Union, to bring the influence of one of these bodies to bear upon the other.

The reiterated recommendation by Congress of the impost system, now addressed solely to the State of New York, who remained alone in her refusal, necessarily occupied the earliest attention of the new legislature.[2] A warm discussion upon a bill intro-

[1] Madison. Elliot, V. 96.

[2] It was brought before them by the speech of the Governor (Clinton), informing them of the resolutions of Congress, which had requested an immediate call of the legislature to consider the revenue system, "a subject," he observed, "which had been repeatedly submitted to them, and must be well understood."

duced for the purpose of effecting the grant as Congress had asked for it, ended, on the 15th of February, in its defeat. The subject of a general convention of the States, according to the plan of the Annapolis commissioners, was then before Congress, on the report of a grand committee;[1] and Congress were hesitating upon its expediency. At this critical juncture, Hamilton carried a resolution in the legislature of New York, instructing the delegates of that State in Congress to move for an act recommending the States to send delegates to a convention for the purpose of revising the Articles of Confederation, which, four days afterwards, was laid before Congress.[2]

Virginia and North Carolina had already chosen delegates to the Convention, in compliance with the recommendation from Annapolis; and Massachusetts was about to make such an appointment, under the influence of her patriotic Bowdoin. In this posture of affairs, although the proposition of the New York delegation failed to be adopted,[3] the fact that she had

[1] Journals, XII. 15. February 21, 1787.

[2] Ibid. The vote rejecting the impost bill was taken on the 15th of February. The resolution of instructions was passed on the 17th, and was laid before Congress on the 21st.

[3] Mr. Madison has recorded the suspicions with which this resolution of the New York legislature was received. Their previous refusal of the impost act, and their known anti-federal tendencies, gave rise, he says, to the belief that their object was to obtain a convention without having it called under the authority of Congress, or else, by dividing the plans of the States in their appointments of delegates, to frustrate them all. (Madison. Elliot, V. 96.) But whatever grounds there might have been for either of these suspicions, the latter certainly was not well founded. The New York resolution was drafted by Hamilton, and although it was passed by a body in which a majority had not exhibited a disposition to enlarge the au-

thus solicited the action of Congress was of decisive influence, when the members from Massachusetts followed it immediately by a resolve more acceptable to a majority of the assembly.[1]

thority of Congress, it was manifestly not intended to prevent the adoption of the plan of a convention. It contemplated the passage by Congress of an act, recommending the States to institute a convention of representatives of the States to revise the Articles of Confederation; and the resolution introduced by the New York delegation into Congress proposed that the alterations and amendments which the convention might consider necessary to render the Articles of Confederation "adequate to the preservation and support of the Union," should be reported to Congress and to the States respectively, but did not direct how they should be adopted. This would have left open a great question, and seemed to be a departure from the mode in which the Articles of Confederation directed that amendments should be made. Probably it was Hamilton's intention to leave the form in which the new system should be adopted for future action, without fettering the movement by prescribing the mode before the convention had assembled. But this course was practically impossible. Congress could not be prevailed upon to recommend a convention, without making the condition that the new provisions should be reported to Congress and confirmed by the States. This gave rise to great embarrassment in the convention, when it came to be admitted that the Confederation must be totally superseded, and not *amended;* and it was finally disregarded. But it was the only mode in which the convention could have been recommended by Congress, and without that recommendation, probably, it could not have been instituted.

[1] The resolution introduced by the Massachusetts delegation, when that of New York had been rejected, after being amended, was finally passed in the following terms: "Whereas, there is provision in the Articles of Confederation and Perpetual Union for making alterations therein, by the assent of a Congress of the United States, and of the legislatures of the several States; and whereas experience hath evinced that there are defects in the present Confederation, as a mean to remedy which several of the States, and particularly the State of New York, by express instructions to their delegates in Congress, have suggested a convention for the purposes expressed in the following resolution; and such a convention appearing to be the most probable means of establishing in these States a firm national government, *Resolved,* That,

The recommendation, as it went forth from Congress, was strictly limited to a revision of the Articles of Confederation, by a convention of delegates, and the alterations and new provisions were to be reported to Congress, and were to be agreed to in Congress and confirmed by the States. Thus the resolution pursued carefully the mode of amendment and alteration provided by the Articles of Confederation, except that it interposed a convention for the purpose of originating the changes to be proposed in the existing form of government; adding, however, the great general purpose of rendering the Federal Constitution adequate to the exigencies of government and the preservation of the Union.

The point thus gained was of vast and decisive importance. That Congress should forego the right of originating changes in the system of government;[1] that it should advise the States to confer that power

in the opinion of Congress, it is expedient that, on the second Monday in May next, a convention of delegates, who shall have been appointed by the several States, be held at Philadelphia, for the sole and express purpose of revising the Articles of Confederation, and reporting to Congress and the several legislatures such alterations and provisions therein as shall, when agreed to in Congress and confirmed by the States, render the Federal Constitution adequate to the exigencies of government and the preservation of the Union." Journals, XII. 17. February 21, 1787.

[1] The Articles of Confederation did not expressly require that amendments should be prepared and proposed in Congress. The thirteenth Article provided, that no alteration should be made, unless it should "be agreed to in a Congress of the United States, and be afterwards confirmed by the legislatures of every State." But it was clearly implied by this, that Congress were to have the power of recommending alterations, and this power was exercised in 1783, with regard to the rule of apportionment.

upon another assembly; and that it should sanction a general revision of the Federal Constitution, with the express declaration of its present inadequacy,— were all preliminaries essential to a successful reform. Feeble as it had become from the overgrown vitality of State power, and from the lack of numbers and talent upon its roll, it was still the government of the Union; the Congress of America; the lineal successors of that renowned assembly which had defied the power of England, and brought into existence the thirteen United States. If it stood but the poor shadow of a great name, it was still a name with which to do more than conjure; for it bore a constitutional relation to the States, still reverenced by the wise and thoughtful, and still necessary to be regarded by all who desired the security of constitutional liberty. The risk of immediate attempts to establish a monarchical form of government was not inconsiderable. The risk that civil confusion would follow a longer delay to provide for the pressing wants of the country was greater. Dejection and despondency had taken hold of many minds of the highest order; while the great body of the people were desiring a change which they could not define, and which they feared, while they invited its approach. In such a state of things, considerate men were naturally unwilling to turn entirely away from Congress, or to exclude its agency altogether from the processes of reform, and to embark upon the uncertain sea of political experiment, without chart or rule to guide their course; for no man could tell what projects, what schemes, and what influences might arise to jeopard those great principles of republican liberty on which the political fabric had rested from the Declaration of Independence to the present hour of danger and distress.

For the wise precedent, thus established, of placing the formation of a new government under the direct sanction of the old one, the people of this country are indebted chiefly to Hamilton. Nothing can be more unfortunate, in any country, than the necessity or the rashness which sweeps away an established constitution, before a substitute has been devised. Whether the interval be occupied by provisional arrangements or left to a more open anarchy, it is an unfit season for the creation of new institutions. At such a time, the crude projects of theorists are boldly intruded among the deliberations of statesmen; despotism lies in wait for the hazards by which liberty is surrounded; the multitude are unrestrained by the curb of authority; and society is exposed to the necessity of accepting whatever is offered, or of submitting to the first usurper who may seize the reins of government, because it has nothing on which to rest as an alternative. True liberty has gained nothing, in any age or country, from revolutions, which have excluded the possibility of seeking or obtaining the assent of existing power to the reforms which the progress of society demands.

In the days when the Confederation was tottering to its fall; when its revenues had been long exhausted; and when its Congress embraced, in actual attendance, less than thirty delegates from only eleven of the States, it would have been the easy part of a demagogue to overthrow it by a sudden appeal to the passions and interests of the hour, as the first step to a radical change.[1] But the great man, whose mature and energetic youth, trained in the school of Washington, had been devoted to the formation and establishment of the Union, knew too well, that, if its golden cord were once broken, no human agency could restore it to life. He knew the value of habit, the respect for an established, however enfeebled authority; and while he felt and insisted on the necessity for a new constitution, and did all in his power to make the country perceive the defects of the old one, he wisely and honestly admitted that the assent of Congress must be gained to any movement which proposed to remedy the evil.

But the reason for not moving the revision of the system of government by Congress itself was one that could not be publicly stated. It was, that the highest civil talent of the country was not there. The men

1 Governor Randolph of Virginia, writing to General Washington, on the 11th of March, 1787, and urging him to attend the Convention, said: "I must call upon your friendship to excuse me for again mentioning the Convention at Philadelphia. Your determination having been fixed on a thorough review of your situation, I feel like an intruder when I again hint a wish that you would join the delegation. But every day brings forth some new crisis, and the Confederation is, I fear, the last anchor of our hope. Congress have taken up the subject, and appointed the second Monday in May next as the day of meeting. *Indeed, from my private correspondence, I doubt whether the existence of that body, even through this year, may not be questionable under our present circumstances.*" Sparks's Washington, IX. 243, note.

to whom the American people had been accustomed to look in great emergencies, — the men who were called into the Convention, and whose power and wisdom were signally displayed in its deliberations, — were then engaged in other spheres of public life, or had retired to the repose which they had earned in the great struggle with England. Had the attempt been made by Congress itself to form a constitution for the acceptance of the States, the controlling influence and wisdom of Washington, Franklin's wide experience and deep sagacity, the unrivalled capacities of Hamilton, the brilliant powers of Gouverneur Morris, Pinckney's fertility, and Randolph's eloquence, with all the power of their eminent colleagues and all the strength of principle and of character which they brought to the Convention, would have been withheld from the effort. One great man, it is true, was still there. Madison was in Congress; and Madison's part in the framing of the Constitution was eminently conspicuous and useful. But without the concentration of talent which the Convention drew together, representing every interest and every part of the Union, nothing could have been presented to the States, by the Congress of 1787, which would have commanded their assent. The Constitution owed as much, for its acceptance, to the weight of character of its framers, as it did to their wisdom and ability, for the intrinsic merits which that weight of character enforced.

It was fortunate, also, that Congress did nothing more than to recommend the Convention, without undertaking to define its powers. The doubts concerning its legality, which led many persons of great influence to hesitate in sanctioning it, were thus removed, and the States were left free to join in the movement, as an expedient to discover and remedy the defects of the federal government, without fettering their delegates with explicit instructions.[1] In

[1] The States of Virginia, New Jersey, Pennsylvania, North Carolina, and Delaware had appointed their delegates to the Convention before it was sanctioned by Congress. Virginia led the way; and the following preamble to her act shows with what motives and objects she did so. "Whereas, the commissioners who assembled at Annapolis, on the 14th day of September last, for the purpose of devising and reporting the means of enabling Congress to provide effectually for the commercial interests of the United States, have represented the necessity of extending the revision of the federal system to all its defects, and have recommended that deputies for that purpose be appointed by the several legislatures, to meet in convention in the city of Philadelphia, on the 2d day of May next, — a provision which was preferable to a discussion of the subject in Congress, where it might be too much interrupted by the ordinary business before them, and where it would, besides, be deprived of the valuable counsels of sundry individuals who are disqualified by the constitution or laws of particular States, or restrained by peculiar circumstances from a seat in that assembly: And whereas the General Assembly of this Commonwealth, taking into view the actual situation of the Confederacy, as well as reflecting on the alarming representations made from time to time by the United States in Congress, particularly in their act of the 15th day of February last, can no longer doubt that the crisis is arrived at which the good people of America are to decide the solemn question, whether they will, by wise and magnanimous efforts, reap the just fruits of that independence which they have so gloriously acquired, and of that Union which they have cemented with so much of their common blood, — or whether, by giving way to unmanly jealousies and prejudices, or to partial and transitory interests, they will renounce the auspicious blessings prepared for them by the Revolution, and furnish to its enemies an eventful triumph over those by whose virtue and valor it has been accomplished: And whereas the same noble and extended policy, and the same fraternal and affectionate sentiments, which originally

this way the Convention, although experimental and anomalous, derived its influence from the sources in which it originated, and was enabled, though not without difficulty, to meet the crisis in which the country was placed. That crisis was one of a singular character; for the continued existence of the Union, and the fate of republican governments, were both involved. It was felt and admitted by the wisest men of that day, that if the Convention should fail in devising and agreeing upon some system of government, at once capable of pervading the coun-

determined the citizens of this Commonwealth to unite with their brethren of the other States in establishing a federal government, cannot but be felt with equal force now as motives to lay aside every inferior consideration, and to concur in such further concessions and provisions as may be necessary to secure the great objects for which that government was instituted, and to render the United States as happy in peace as they have been glorious in war: *Be it therefore enacted*, &c., That seven commissioners be appointed, by joint ballot of both houses of Assembly, who, or any three of them, are hereby authorized as deputies from this Commonwealth to meet such deputies as may be appointed and authorized by other States, to assemble in convention at Philadelphia, as above recommended, and to join with them in devising and discussing all such alterations and further provisions as may be necessary to render the Federal Constitution adequate to the exigencies of the Union; and in reporting such an act, for that purpose, to the United States in Congress, as, when agreed to by them, and duly confirmed by the several States, will effectually provide for the same." (Elliot, I. 132.) The instructions of New Jersey to her delegates were, "to take into consideration the state of the Union as to trade and other important objects, and of devising such other provisions as shall appear to be necessary to render the constitution of the federal government adequate to the exigencies thereof." (Ibid. 128.) The act of Pennsylvania provided for the appointment of deputies to join with the deputies of other States "in devising, deliberating on, and discussing all such alterations and further provisions as may be necessary to render the Federal Constitution fully adequate to the exigencies of the

try with an efficient control, and essentially republican in its form, the Federal Union would be at an end. But its dissolution, in the state in which the country then was, must have been followed by an attempt to establish monarchical government; because the State institutions were destitute of the strength necessary to encounter the agitation which would have followed the downfall of the federal power, and yet some substitute for that power must have been found. But without civil war, and the most frightful social convulsions, nothing in the nature of

Union, and in reporting such act or acts, for that purpose, to the United States in Congress assembled, as, when agreed to by them, and duly confirmed by the several States, will effectually provide for the same." (Ibid. 130.) The instructions of Delaware were of the same tenor. (Ibid. 131.) The act of North Carolina directed her deputies "to discuss and decide upon the most effectual means to remove the defects of our Federal Union, and to procure the enlarged purposes which it was intended to effect; and that they report such an act to the General Assembly of this State, as, when agreed to by them, will effectually provide for the same." (Ibid. 135.) The instructions to the delegates of New Hampshire were of the same tenor. (Ibid. 126.) The appointment of the delegates of Massachusetts was made with reference to the terms of the resolve of Congress recommending the Convention, and for the purposes declared therein. (Ibid. 126, 127.) The appointment of Connecticut was made with the same reference, and with the further direction "to discuss upon such alterations and provisions, agreeably to the general principles of republican government, as they shall think proper to render the Federal Constitution adequate to the exigencies of government and the preservation of the Union; and they are further directed, pursuant to the said act of Congress, to report such alterations and provisions as may be agreed to by a majority of the United States represented in convention, to the Congress of the United States, and to the General Assembly of this State." (Ibid. 127.) The resolutions of New York, Maryland, South Carolina, and Georgia pursued nearly the same terms with the resolve of Congress. (Ibid. 127, 131, 136, 137.)

monarchy could ever have been established in this country after the Revolution. "Those who lean to a monarchical government," said Washington, "have either not consulted the public mind, or they live in a region which (the levelling principles in which they were bred being entirely eradicated) is much more productive of monarchical ideas than is the case in the Southern States, where, from the habitual distinctions which have always existed among the people, one would have expected the first generation and the most rapid growth of them. I am also clear, that, even admitting the utility, nay, necessity, of the form, the period is not arrived for adopting the change without shaking the peace of this country to its foundation. That a thorough reform of the present system is indispensable, no one, who has a capacity to judge, will deny; and with hand and heart I hope the business will be essayed in a full convention. After which, if more powers and more decision are not found in the existing form, if it still wants energy and that secrecy and despatch (either from the non-attendance or the local views of its members) which are characteristic of good government, and if it shall be found (the contrary of which, however, I have always been more afraid of than the abuse of them) that Congress will, upon all proper occasions, exert the powers which are given with a firm and steady hand, instead of frittering them back to the States, where the members, in place of viewing themselves in their national character, are too apt to be looking, — I say, after this essay is made, if the system proves inefficient, conviction of the necessity of a change will be disseminated among all classes of the people. Then, and not till then, in my opinion, can it be attempted without involving all the evils of civil discord."[1]

There were other difficulties besides those which may be called legal, or technical, attending this effort to revise the system of the federal government. The failure of that system, as it had been put in operation in 1781, had, to a great extent, chilled the hopes of many of the best statesmen of America. It had been established under auspices which seemed to promise far different fruits from those it had actually produced. Its foundations were laid in the patriotism and national feeling of the States. The concessions which had been made to secure a union of republics, having various, and, in some respects, conflicting interests, seemed at first to guarantee the prompt and faithful performance of its obligations. But this fair promise had melted into most unsubstantial performance. The Confederation was framed upon a principle which never has enabled, and probably never will enable, a government to become effective and permanent, — the principle of a league.

Another and a very serious cause for discouragement was the sectional jealousy and State pride which had been constantly growing, from the Declaration of Independence to the time when the States were called upon to meet each other upon broader

[1] Sparks's Washington, IX. 223, 225, 230, 236. 508 – 520.

grounds, and to make even larger sacrifices than at any former period. It is difficult to trace to all its causes the feeling which has at times arrayed the different extremities of this Union against each other. It was very early developed, after the different provinces were obliged to act together for their great mutual objects of political independence; but, even in its highest paroxysms, it has always at last found an antidote in the deeper feelings and more sober calculations of a consistent patriotism. Perhaps its prevalence and activity may with more truth be ascribed, in every generation, to the ambition of men who find in it a convenient instrument of local influence, rather than to any other cause. It is certain, that, when it has raged most violently, this has been its chief aggravating element. The differences of neither manners, institutions, climate, nor pursuits would at any time have been sufficient to create the perils to which the Union of the States has occasionally been exposed, without the mischievous agency of men whose personal objects are, for the time, subserved by the existence of such peculiarities. The proof of this is to be found in the fact, that the seasonable sagacity of the people has always detected the motives of those who have sought to employ their passions, and has compelled them at last to give way to that better order of men who have appealed to their reason.

The difficulty of getting the assent of all the States to radical changes in the federal system, and the uncertainty as to the mode in which such changes could be effectively adopted, were also among the reasons which led many persons to regard the Convention as an experiment of doubtful expediency. The States had hitherto acted only in their corporate capacities, in all that concerned the formation and modification of the Union. The idea of a Union founded on the direct action of the people of the States, in a primary sense, and proceeding to establish a federal government, of limited powers, in the same manner in which the people of each State had established their local constitutions, had not been publicly broached, and was not generally entertained. Indeed, there was no expectation on the part of any State, when the delegates to the Convention were appointed, that any other principle would be adopted as the basis of action, than that by which the Articles of Confederation contemplated that all changes should be effected by the action of the States assembled in Congress, confirmed by the unanimous assent of the different State legislatures.

The prevailing feeling, among the higher statesmen of the country, was, that the Convention was an experiment of doubtful tendency, but one that must nevertheless be tried. Washington, Madison, Jay, Knox, Edmund Randolph, have all left upon record the evidence of their doubts and their fears, as well as of their convictions of the necessity for this last effort in favor of the preservation of a republican form of government.[1] Hamilton advanced to meet

[1] Sparks's Washington, IX. 223, 225, 230, 236, 508 – 520.

the crisis, with perhaps less hesitation than any of the Revolutionary statesmen. His great genius for political construction; his large knowledge of the means by which a regulated liberty may be secured; and the long study with which he had contemplated the condition of the country, led him to enter the Convention with more of eagerness and hope than most of its members. He saw, with great clearness, that the difficulty which embarrassed nearly all his contemporaries — the question of the mode of enacting a new constitution — was capable of solution. He did not propound that solution in advance of the assembling of the Convention; for it was eminently necessary that the States should not be alarmed by the suggestion of a principle so novel and so unlike the existing theory of the Union. But he was fully prepared to announce it, so soon as it could be received and acted upon.

It was under such auspices and with such views that the Convention assembled at Philadelphia, on the fourteenth day of May in the year seventeen hundred and eighty-seven.

At that time, the world had witnessed no such spectacle as that of the deputies of a nation, chosen by the free action of great communities, and assembled for the purpose of thoroughly reforming its constitution, by the exercise, and with the authority, of the national will. All that had been done, both in ancient and in modern times, in forming, moulding, or modifying constitutions of government, bore little resemblance to the present undertaking of the States of America. Neither among the Greeks nor the Romans was there a precedent, and scarcely an analogy. The ancient leagues of some of the cities or republics of Greece did not amount to constitutions, in the sense of modern political science; and the Roman republic was but the domination of a single race of the inhabitants of a single city.

In modern Europe, we find no trace of political science until after the nations were divided, and partial limits set to the different orders and powers of the state. The feudal system, which acknowledged no relations in society but those of lord and serf, necessarily forbade all consideration of any forms of government which were not essentially founded on that relation; and it was not until that relation had been in some degree broken in upon, that there began to be any thing like theoretical inquiries into natural rights. When this took place, — at the end, or towards the end, of the Middle Ages, — the peculiar forms of the European governments gave rise to inquiries into the relation of sovereign and subject. From the beginning of the fifteenth down to the end of the seventeenth century, there were occasional discussions on the Continent, growing out of particular events, of such questions as the right of the people to depose bad princes, and how far it was lawful to resist oppression. But questions of constitutional form, or of the right of the people to arrange and distribute the different powers of government, or the best mode of doing it, did not arise at all.

In England, from the time of the Conquest, until Magna Charta had gone far towards destroying the system, a feudal monarchy had precluded all questions touching the form or the spirit of government. The chief traits of the present constitution, which arose in a great measure from the circumstance that the lower orders of the nobility became gradually so much amalgamated with the people as to give rise to the distinct power of the commons, have all along been inconsistent with the enactment of new forms of civil polity; although from the time of the Reformation to the Revolution of 1688, the active principles of English freedom have, at different junctures, made advances of the utmost importance. The foundations on which the Stuarts sought to establish their throne were directly at variance with the spirit and principles of the Reformation, which totally denied the doctrine of passive and unlimited obedience, and which led to the struggles that gave birth to the Puritans. Those severe reformers, whose church constitution was purely republican, naturally sought to carry its principles into the state. The result was the Parliamentary troubles of James the First, the execution of Charles the First under the forms of judicial proceeding, and the despotism of Cromwell under the forms of a commonwealth. Charles the Second returned, untaught by all that had happened, to attempt the reëstablishment of the Stuart principles of unlimited obedience; and James the Second, who naturally united to them the Catholic religion, being driven from his kingdom, the question arose of a vacant throne, and how it should be filled. In all these events, however, from the death of Elizabeth to the great discussions which followed the abdication of James the Second, the idea of calling upon the people of England to frame a government of their own choice, and to define the limits and powers of its various departments, never arose. The Convention Parliament discussed, and were summoned to discuss, but a single fundamental question, — that involving the disposal of the crown.

Still, the political troubles of England gave rise to many theoretical discussions of natural right, and of the origin and structure of society. As soon as Charles the First was executed, this discussion arose abroad, from his friends, who wrote, or influenced others to write, in defence of the divine right of kings. Hobbes and Filmer followed, in England, on the same side, and Milton, Locke, and Algernon Sidney vindicated the natural and inalienable rights of the subject and the citizen. In the works of these great writers, the foundations of society are examined with an acuteness which has left little to be done in the merely speculative part of political inquiry. But the practical effect of their theories never went farther than the promotion, to a greater or less extent, of the particular views which they desired to inculcate concerning the existing constitution, or the particular events out of which the discussions arose.

Nor should we forget what had been done in France, by the wise and cautious Montesquieu, or by the vehement and passionate Rousseau, and the writers of his school. The former, drawing all his views from history and experience, undertook to show, from the antecedents of each state, the character of its constitution, to explain and develop its peculiar properties, and thence to determine the principles on which its legislation should proceed. The latter, starting from an entirely opposite point, and designing to write a treatise on Politics in the widest sense of the term, became a mere theorist, and produced only certain brilliant speculations upon the social compact, of a purely democratic character, as fragments of a work which he never finished. The crowd of writers, too, who preceded, and in part created the French Revolution, which was just commencing its destructive activity as our Constitution was formed, really contributed nothing of practical value to the solution of such great questions as the mode of forming, vesting, and distributing the various branches of sovereign power.

Thus there was little for American statesmen of that day to look to, in the way of theories which had been practically proved to be sound and useful. The constitution of England, it is true, presented to them certain great maxims, the application of which was not unsuited to the circumstances and habits of a people whose laws and institutions had been derived from their English ancestors and their English blood. But the constitution of England, embracing the three estates of King, Lords, and Commons, had become what it was, only by the extortion from the crown of the rights and privileges of the two orders of the people. The American Revolution, on the other hand, had settled, as the fundamental principle of American society, that all sovereignty resides originally in the people; that they derive no rights by way of grant from any other source; and consequently, that no powers or privileges can exist in any portion of the people as distinct from the whole. The English constitution could, therefore, furnish only occasional analogies for particular details in the structure of departments, which might after all really require to be founded on different fundamental principles. But the great problem to be solved—for which English experience was of no value—was, so to parcel out those portions of original sovereignty, which the people of the States might be willing to withdraw from their State institutions, as to constitute an efficient federal republic, which yet would not control and absorb the powers that might be reserved. But to comprehend the results that were accomplished, and to understand the true nature of the system bequeathed to us, it is indispensable to examine in detail the means and processes by which it was formed. Before we turn, however, to this great subject, the characters of the principal framers of the Constitution demand our attention.

CHAPTER VII.

THE FRAMERS OF THE CONSTITUTION.—WASHINGTON, PRESIDENT OF THE CONVENTION.

THE narrative to which the reader has thus far attended must now be interrupted for a while, that he may pause upon the threshold of an assembly which had been summoned to the grave task of remodelling the constitution of this country, and here consider the names and characters of the men to whom its responsible labors had been intrusted. The civil deeds of statesmen and lawgivers, in establishing and forming institutions, incorporating principles into the forms of public administration, and setting up the defences of public security and prosperity, are far less apt to attract and hold the attention of mankind, than the achievements of military life. The name, indeed, may be for ever associated with the work of the hand; but the mass of mankind do not study, admire, or repeat the deeds of the lawgiver, as they do those of the hero. Yet he who has framed a law, or fashioned an institution in which some great idea is made practical to the conditions of human existence, has exercised the highest attributes of human reason, and is to be counted among the benefactors of his race.

The framers of the Constitution of the United States assembled for their work amidst difficulties and embarrassments of an extraordinary nature. No general concert of opinion had taken place as to what was best, or even as to what was possible to be done. Whether it were wise to hold a convention, whether it were even legal to hold it, and whether, if held, it would be likely to result in any thing useful to the country, were points upon which the most opposite opinions prevailed in every State of the Union. But it was among the really fortunate, although apparently unhappy, circumstances under which they were assembled, that the country had experienced much trial, suffering, distress, and failure. It has been a disagreeable duty to describe the disasters and errors of a period during which the national character was subjected to the discipline of adversity. We now come to the period of compensation which such discipline inevitably brings.

There is a law of the moral government of the universe, which ordains that all that is great and valuable and permanent in character must be the result, not of theoretical teaching, or natural aspiration, — of spontaneous resolve, or uninterrupted success, — but of trial, of suffering, of the fiery furnace of temptation, of the dark hours of disappointment and defeat. The character of the man is distinguishable from the character of the child that he once was, chiefly by the effects of this universal law. There are the same natural impulses, the same mental, moral, and physical constitution, with which he was born into the world. What is it that has given him the strength, the fortitude, the unchanging principle, and the moral and intellectual power, which he exhibits in after years? It has not been constant pleasure and success, nor unmingled joy. It has been the hard discipline of pain and sorrow, the stern teachings of experience, the struggle against the consequences of his own errors, and the chastisement inflicted by his own faults.

This law pertains to all human things. It is as clearly traceable in its application to the character of a people, as to that of an individual; and as the institutions of a people, when voluntarily formed by them out of the circumstances of their condition, are necessarily the result of the previous discipline and the past teachings of their career, we can trace this law also in the creation and growth of what is most valuable in their institutions. When we have so traced it, the unalterable relations of the moral universe entitle us to look for the elements of greatness and strength in whatever has been the product of such teachings, such discipline, and such trials.

The Constitution of the United States was eminently the creature of circumstances; — not of circumstances blindly leading the blind to an unconscious submission to an accident, but of circumstances which offered an intelligent choice of the means of happiness, and opened, from the experience of the past, the plain path of duty and success, stretching onward to the future. All that has been said in the previous chapters tends to illustrate this fact. We have seen the American people, — divided into separate and isolated communities, without nationality, except such as resulted from a general community of origin, — undertaking together the work of throwing off the domination of their parent state. We have seen them enter upon this undertaking without forming any political bond of a national character, and without instituting any proper national agency. We have seen, that the first government which they created was, practically, a mere general council for the recommendation of measures to be adopted and executed by the several constituencies represented. We have seen no machinery instituted for the accomplishment, by the combined authority of these separate communities, of the great objects at which they were aiming; and although in theory the Revolutionary Congress would have been entitled to assume and exercise the powers necessary to accomplish the objects for which it was assembled, we have seen that the people of the country, from a jealous and unreasonable fear of all power, would not permit this to be done.

The consequences of this want of power were inevitable. An army could not be kept in the field, on a permanent footing, capable of holding the enemy in check. The city of New York fell into the hands of that enemy, the intermediate country between that city and the city of Philadelphia was overrun, and from the latter capital, the seat of the general government, the Congress was obliged to fly before the invading foe.

Taught by these events that a more effective union was necessary to the deliverance of the country from a foreign yoke, the States at length united in the establishment of a government, the leading purpose of which was mutual defence against external attacks, and called it a Confederation. But its powers were so restricted, and its operations so clogged and impeded by State jealousies and State reservations of power, that it lacked entirely the means of providing the sinews of war out of the resources of the country, and was driven to foreign loans and foreign arms for the means of bringing that war to a close. A vast load of debt was thus accumulated upon the country; and, as soon as peace was established, it became apparent, that, while the Confederation was a government with the power of contracting debts, it was without the power of paying them. This incapacity revealed the existence of great objects of government, without which the people of the several States could never prosper, and which, in their separate capacities, the States themselves could never accomplish.

Now it is as certain as history can make any thing, that the whole period, from the commencement of the war to the end of the Confederation, was a period of great suffering to the people of the United States. The trials and hardships of war were succeeded by the greater trials and hardships of a time of peace, in which the whole nation experienced that greatest of all social evils, the want of an efficient and competent government. There was a gloom upon the minds of men, — a sense of insecurity, — a consciousness that American society was not fulfilling the ends of its being by the development of its resources and the discharge of its obligations, — which constituted altogether a discipline and a chastisement of the whole nation, and which we are not at liberty to regard as the mere accidents of a world ungoverned by an overruling Power.

It was from the midst of that discipline that the American people came to the high undertaking of forming for themselves a constitution, by which to work out the destiny of social life in this Western World. Had they essayed their task after years of prosperity, and after old institutions and old forms of government had, upon the whole, yielded a fair amount of success and happiness, they would have wanted that power which comes only from failure and disappointment, — the power to adapt the best remedy to the deepest social defects, and to lay hold on the future with the strength given by the hard teachings of the past.

Civil liberty, — American liberty, — that liberty which resides in law, which is protected by great institutions and upheld by the machinery of a popular government, — is not simply the product of a desire, or a determination, to be free. Such liberty comes, if it comes at all, only after serious mistakes, — after frightful deficiencies have taught men that power must be lodged somewhere. It comes when a people have learned, by adversity and disappointment, that a total negation of all authority, and a jealousy of all restraint, can end only in leaving society without the defences and securities which nothing but law can raise for it. It comes when the passions are exhausted, and the rivalries of opposing interests have worn themselves out, in the vain endeavor to reach what reason and justice and self-sacrifice alone can procure. Then, and then only, is the intellect of a nation sure to operate with the fidelity and energy of its native power. Then only does it grasp the principles of freedom with the ability to incorporate them into the practical forms of a public administration whose strength and energy shall give them vitality, and prevent their diffusion into the vagueness of mere abstractions, which return to society the cold and mocking gift of a stone for its craving demand of bread.

The Convention was a body of great and disinterested men, competent, both morally and intellectually to the work assigned them. High qualities of character are requisite to the formation of a system of government for a wide country with different interests. Mere talent will not do it. Intellectual power and ingenuity alone cannot compass it.

There must be a moral completeness in the characters of those who are to achieve such a work; for it does not consist solely in devising schemes, or creating offices, or parcelling out jurisdictions and powers. There must be adaptation, adjustment of conflicting interests, reconciliation of conflicting claims. There must be the recognition and admission of great expedients, and the sacrifice, often, of darling objects of ambition, or of local policy, to the vast central purpose of the greatest happiness of the greatest number. Hence it is, that, wherever this mighty work is to be successfully accomplished, there must be a high sense of justice; a power of concession; the qualities of magnanimity and patriotism; and that broad moral sanity of the intellect, which is farthest removed from fanaticism, intolerance, or selfish adhesion either to interest or to opinion.

These qualities were preëminently displayed by many of the framers of the Constitution. There was certainly a remarkable amount of talent and intellectual power in that body. There were men in that assembly, whom, for genius in statesmanship, and for profound speculation in all that relates to the science of government, the world has never seen overmatched.

But the same men, who were most conspicuous for these brilliant gifts and acquirements, for their profound theories and their acute perception of principles, were happily the most marked, in that assembly, for their comprehensive patriotism, their justice, their unselfishness and magnanimity. Take, for instance, Hamilton. Where, among all the speculative philosophers in political science whom the world has seen, shall we find a man of greater acuteness of intellect, or more capable of devising a scheme of government which should appear theoretically perfect? Yet Hamilton's unquestionable genius for political disquisition and construction was directed and restrained by a noble generosity, and an unerring perception of the practicable and the expedient, which enabled him to serve mankind without attempting to force them to his own plans, and without compelling them into his own views. Take Washington, whose peculiar greatness was a moral elevation, which secured the wisest and best use of all his powers in either civil or military life. Take Madison, who certainly lacked neither ability nor inclination for speculative inquiries, and who had a mind capable of enforcing the application of whatever principles he espoused. Yet his calm good sense, and the tact with which he could adapt theory to practice, were no less among his prominent characteristics. Take Franklin, who sometimes held extreme opinions, and occasionally pushed his peculiar fancies, springing from an excess of worldly wisdom, to the utmost verge of truth, but whose intellect was tempered, and whose whole character was softened, by the wide and varied experience of a life that had been commenced in obscurity, and was now closing with the honors of a reputation that filled the Eastern as well as the Western hemisphere. Take Gouverneur Morris, who was ardent, impulsive, and not disinclined to tenacity of opinion; but he rose above all local and narrow objects, and embraced, in the scope of his clear and penetrating vision, the happiness and welfare of this whole continent.

It was a most fortunate thing for America, that the Revolutionary age, with its hardships, its trials, and its mistakes, had formed a body of statesmen capable of framing for it a durable constitution. The leading persons in the Convention which formed the Constitution had been actors, either in civil or military life, in the scenes of the Revolution. In those scenes their characters as American statesmen had been formed. When the condition of the country had fully revealed the incapacity of its government to provide for its wants, these men were naturally looked to, to construct a system which should save it from anarchy. And their great capacities, their high, disinterested purposes, their freedom from all fanaticism and illiberality, and their earnest, unconquerable faith in the destiny of their country, enabled them to found that government, which now upholds and protects the whole fabric of liberty in the States of this Union.

Of course no such assembly, in that or in any other age, in this or in any other country, could be called together for such a purpose, without exhibiting a great diversity of opinions, wishes, and views. The very object for which they were assembled was of a nature to develop, to the fullest extent, the most conflicting opinions and the most opposite theories. That object was to devise a system which should best secure the permanent liberty and happiness of a vast country. What subject, in the whole range of human thought and human endeavor, could be more complex than this? What occasion, among all the diversities of human affairs, could present a wider field for honest differences of opinion, and for severe conflicts of mind with mind? Yet it should never be forgotten, as the merit of this assembly, that, collectively and individually, they were animated by the most pure and exclusive devotion to the object for which they were called together. It was this high patriotism, this deep and never-ceasing consciousness that the great experiment of republican liberty turned on the result of their labors, as on the hazard of a die, that brought at last all conflicts of interest, all diversities of opinion and feeling, into a focus of conciliation and unanimity. More than once the reader will find them on the point of separating without having accomplished any thing; and more than once he will see them recalled to their mighty task by the eloquence of some master-spirit, who knew how to touch the key-note of that patriotic feeling, which was never wholly lost in the jarring discords of debate and intellectual strife. For four months the laborious effort went on. The serene and unchanging presence of Washington presided over all. The chivalrous sincerity and disinterestedness of Hamilton pervaded the assembly with all the power of his fascinating manners. The flashing eloquence of Gouverneur Morris recalled the dangers of anarchy, which must be accepted as the alternative of an abortive experiment. The calm, clear, statesmanlike views of Madison, the searching and profound expositions of King, the prudent influence of Franklin, at length ruled the hour.

In examining their work, and in reading all that is left to us of their discussions, we are to consider the materials out of which they had to frame a system of republican liberty, and the point of view, in reference to the whole subject, at which they stood. We are to remember how little the world had then seen of real liberty united with personal safety and public security; and how entirely novel the undertaking was, to form a complete system of government, wholly independent on tradition, exactly defined in a written constitution, to be created at once, and at once set in motion, for the accomplishment of the great objects of human liberty and social progress. The examples of Greece and Rome, the modern republics of Italy, the federal relations of the Swiss Cantons, and the distant approach to republicanism that had been seen in Holland, might be resorted to for occasional and meagre illustrations of a few general principles. But, unquestionably, the country which, up to that moment, had exhibited, by the working of its government, the greatest amount of liberty combined with the greatest public security, was England. England, however, was a monarchy; and monarchy was the system which they both desired, and were obliged, to avoid. If it was within the range of human possibility to establish a system of republican government, which would fulfil its appropriate duties, over this vast and rapidly extending country, *that* they felt, one and all, to be their great task. On the other hand, they knew that, if to that form they could not succeed in giving due stability and wisdom, it would be, in the words of Hamilton, "disgraced and lost among ourselves, disgraced and lost to mankind for ever."[1]

[1] Madison's Debates in the Federal Convention. Elliot, V. 244.

Here was their trial, — the difficulty of all their difficulties; and it was here that they exhibited a wisdom, a courage, and a capacity, which have been surpassed by no other body of lawgivers ever assembled in the world.

Their country had, a few years before, passed through a long and distressing war with its parent state. The yoke of her domination had been thrown off, and its removal was naturally followed by a loosening of the bands of all authority, and an indisposition to all new restraints. The American Colonies had become independent States; and as the spirit of liberty which pervaded them made individuals impatient of control in their political relations, so the States reflected the same spirit in their corporate conduct, and looked with jealousy and distrust upon all powers which were not to be exercised by themselves. Yet it was clear that there were powers and functions of government, which, for the absolute safety of the country, must be withdrawn from the States, and vested in some national head, which should hold and exercise them in the name of the whole, for the good of the whole. The great question was, what that national head was to be; and the great service performed by the framers of the Constitution consisted in devising a system by which a national sovereignty might be endowed with energy, dignity, and power, and the forms and substance of popular liberty still be preserved; a system by which a supreme authority in all the matters which it touched might be created, resting directly on the popular will, and to be exercised, in all coming time, through forms and institutions under which that will should have a direct and perpetual and perpetually renewed expression. This they accomplished. They accomplished it, too, without abolishing the State governments, and without impairing a single personal right which existed before they began their work. They accomplished it without violence; without the disruption of a single fibre in that whole delicate tissue of which society is made up. No drop of blood was shed to establish this government, the work of their hands; and no moment of interruption occurred to the calm, even tenor of the pursuits of men, — the daily on-goings of society, in which the stream of human life and happiness and progress flows on in beneficence and peace.

First upon the list of those who had been called together for this great purpose, we are to mention him, without whose presence and countenance all men felt that no attempt to meliorate the political condition of the country could succeed.

I have already given an account of the proceedings which led directly to the calling of the Convention; and have mentioned the interesting fact, that the impulse to those proceedings was given at Mount Vernon. Thither General Washington had retired, at the close of the war, with no thought of ever engaging again in public affairs. He supposed that for him the scene was closed. "The noontide of life," said he, in a letter to the Marchioness de Lafayette, "is now past, with Mrs. Washington and myself; and all we have to do is to glide gently down a stream which no human effort can ascend."[1]

But wise and far-seeing as he was, he did not foresee how soon he was to be called from that grave and sweet tranquillity. He was busy with the concerns of his farm; he was tasting the happiness of home, from which he had been absent nine long years; he was "cultivating the affections of good men, and practising the domestic virtues." But it was not in his nature to be inattentive to the concerns of that country for whose welfare he had labored and suffered so much. He maintained an active correspondence with several of the most eminent and virtuous of his compatriots in different parts of the Union; and in that correspondence, running through the years 1784, 1785, and 1786, there exists the most ample evidence of the downward tendency of things, and of the fears it excited.

It had become evident to him that we never should establish a national character, nor be justly considered and respected by the nations of Europe, without enlarging the powers of the federal government for the regulation of commerce. The objection which had been hitherto urged, that some States might be more benefited than others by a commercial regulation, seemed to him to apply to every mat-

[1] Washington's Writings, IX. 166.

ter of general utility. "We are," said he, writing in the summer of 1785, "either a united people under one head, and for federal purposes, or we are thirteen independent sovereignties eternally counteracting each other. If the former, whatever such a majority of the States as the constitution points out conceives to be for the benefit of the whole, should, in my humble opinion, be submitted to by the minority. Let the Southern States always be represented; let them act more in union; let them declare freely and boldly what is for the interest of, and what is prejudicial to, their constituents; and there will, there must be, an accommodating spirit. In the establishment of a navigation act, this, in a particular manner, ought and will doubtless be attended to. If the assent of nine States, or, as some propose, of eleven, is necessary to give validity to a commercial system, it insures this measure, or it cannot be obtained.

"Wherein, then, lies the danger? But if your fears are in danger of being realized, cannot certain provisos in the ordinance guard against the evil? I see no difficulty in this, if the Southern delegates would give their attendance in Congress, and follow the example, if it should be set them, of adhering together to counteract combination. I confess to you candidly, that I can foresee no evil greater than disunion; than those unreasonable jealousies (I say *unreasonable*, because I would have a *proper* jealousy always awake, and the United States on the watch to prevent individual States from infracting the constitution with impunity) which are continually poisoning our minds and filling them with imaginary evils for the prevention of real ones."[1]

But, while he desired to see the ninth article of the Confederation so amended and extended as to give adequate commercial powers, he feared that it would be of little avail to give them to the existing Congress. The members of that body seemed to him to be so much afraid of exerting the powers which they already possessed, that they lost no opportunity of surrendering them, or of referring their exercise to the individual States. The speculative question, whether foreign commerce is of any real advantage to a country, he regarded as of no importance, convinced that the spirit of trade which pervaded these States was not to be restrained. It behooved us, therefore, to establish just principles of commercial regulation, and this could not, any more than other matters of national concern, be done by thirteen heads differently constructed and organized. The necessity, in fact, of a controlling power was obvious, and why it should be withheld was, he declared, beyond his comprehension. With these views, he looked to the Convention at Annapolis as likely to result in a plan which would give to the federal government efficient powers for all commercial purposes, although he regretted that more objects had not been embraced in the project for the meeting.

The failure of this attempt to enlarge the commercial powers of Congress, and the recommenda-

[1] Washington's Writings, IX. 121.

tion of a general convention made by the Annapolis commissioners, placed the country in an extremely delicate situation. Washington thought, when this recommendation was announced, that the people were not then sufficiently misled to retract their error, and entertained some doubt as to the consequences of an attempt to revise and amend the Articles of Confederation. Something, however, must be done, he said, or the fabric which was certainly tottering, would inevitably fall. "I think," said he, "often of our situation, and view it with concern. From the high ground we stood upon, from the plain path which invited our footsteps, to be so fallen, so lost, is really mortifying; but virtue, I fear, has in a great degree taken its departure from our land, and the want of a disposition to do justice is the source of the national embarrassments; for, whatever guise or color is given to them, this I apprehend is the origin of the evils we now feel, and probably shall labor under for some time yet."[1]

At this time the legislature of Virginia were acting upon the subject of a delegation to the Federal Convention, and a general wish was felt to place Washington at the head of it. No opposition had been made in that body to the bill introduced for the purpose of organizing and instructing such a delegation, and it was thought advisable to give the proceeding all the weight which could be derived from a single State. To a private intimation of this

[1] Washington's Writings, IX. 167.

desire of the legislature he returned a decided refusal. Several obstacles appeared to him to put his attendance out of the question. The principal reason that he assigned was, that he had already declined a re-election as President of the Society of the Cincinnati, and had signified that he should not attend their triennial general meeting, to be held in Philadelphia in the same month with the Convention.[1] He felt a great reluctance to do any thing which might give offence to those patriotic men, the officers of the army who had shared with him the labors and dangers of the war. He had declined to act longer with that Society, because the motives and objects of its founders had been misconceived and misrepresented. Originally a charitable institution, it had come to be regarded as anti-republican in its spirit and tendencies. Desiring, on the one hand, to avoid the charge of deserting the officers who had nobly supported him, and had always treated him with the greatest attention and attachment; and wishing, on the other hand, not to be thought willing to give his support to an institution generally believed incompatible with republican principles, — he had excused his attendance upon the ground of the necessity of attending to his private concerns. He had, in truth, a great reluctance to appear again upon any public theatre. His health was far from being firm; he felt the need and coveted the blessing of retirement for the remainder of

[1] Washington's Writings, IX. 212.

his days; and although some modifications of the Society whose first President he had been, were then allaying the jealousies it had excited, he withdrew from this, the last relation which had kept him in a conspicuous public position.

But Washington at Mount Vernon, cultivating his estate, and rarely leaving his own farms, was as conspicuous to the country as if he were still placed in the most active and important public stations. All eyes were turned to him in this emergency; all thoughts were employed in considering whether his countenance and his influence would be given to this attempt to create a national government for the States whose liberties he had won. And his friends represented to him, that the posture of public affairs would prevent any criticism on the situation in which the contemporary meeting of the Cincinnati would place him, if he were to accept a seat in the Convention. Still, when the official notice of his appointment came, in December, he formally declined, but was requested by the Governor of the State to reserve his decision.[1] At this moment, the insurrection in Massachusetts broke upon him like a thunderbolt. "What, gracious God!" he exclaimed, "is man, that there should be such inconsistency and perfidiousness in his conduct! It was but the other day that we were shedding our blood to obtain the constitutions under which we now live, — constitutions of our own choice and

[1] Washington's Writings, IX. 219.

making, — and now we are unsheathing the sword to overturn them! The thing is so unaccountable, that I hardly know how to realize it, or to persuade myself that I am not under the illusion of a dream."[1]

It was clear that, in case of civil discord and open confusion extending through any considerable part of the country, he would be obliged to take part on one side or the other, or to withdraw from the continent; and he, as well as other reflecting men, were not without fears that the disturbances in the Eastern States might extend throughout the Union. He consulted with his friends in distant parts of the country, and requested their advice, but still, as late as February, hesitated whether he should attend the Convention. In that month, he heard of the suppression of the rebellion in Massachusetts; but the developments which it had made of the state of society, the necessity which it had revealed for more coercive power in the institutions of the country, and the fear which it had excited that this want might lead men's minds to entertain the idea of monarchical government, finally decided him to accept the appointment. The possibility that his absence at such a juncture might be construed into what he called "a dereliction of republicanism," seems to have influenced his decision more than all other reasons. Congress, it is true, had now sanctioned the Convention, and this had removed one obstacle which had weighed

[1] Washington's Writings, IX. 221.

with him and with others. He entertained great doubts as to the result of the experiment, but was entirely satisfied that it ought to be tried.[1]

He left Mount Vernon in the latter part of April. Public honors attended him everywhere on his route. At Chester, fifteen miles from the city of Philadelphia, he was met by the Speaker of the Assembly of Pennsylvania and several officers and gentlemen of distinction, who accompanied him to Gray's Ferry, where a military escort was in waiting to receive him and conduct him into the city. On his arrival, he immediately paid a visit to Dr. Franklin, at that time President of the State of Pennsylvania.[2]

On the assembling of the Convention, Robert Morris, by the instruction and in behalf of the deputation of Pennsylvania, proposed that General Washington should be elected President. John Rutledge of South Carolina seconded this suggestion, observing that the presence of General Washington forbade any observations on the occasion which might otherwise be proper.[3] His opinions, at the time when he took the chair of the Convention, as to what was proper to be done, and what was practicable, can only be gathered from his correspondence. He had formed some general views of the principles on which a national government should be framed, but he had not proceeded at all

[1] Washington's Writings, IX. 236.

[2] Sparks's Life of Washington, p. 435.

[3] Madison's Debates, Elliot, V. 123.

to the consideration of details. The first and most important object he held to be, to establish such a constitution as would secure and perpetuate the republican form of government, by satisfying the wants of the country and the time, and thus checking all tendency to monarchical ideas. He had come to the Convention, as we have seen, in order that the great experiment of self-government, on which this country had entered at the Revolution, might have a further trial beyond the hazards of the hour. He knew — he had had occasion to know — that the thought of a monarchy, as being necessary to the safety of the country, had been to some extent entertained. There had been those in a former day, in the darkest period of the war, who had proposed to him to assume a crown, — men who could possibly have bestowed it upon him, or have assisted him to acquire it, — but who met a rebuke which the nature of their proposition and his character should have taught them to expect. There were those in that day who sincerely despaired of republican liberty, and who had allowed themselves to think that some of the royal families of Europe might possibly furnish a sovereign fitted to govern and control the turbulent elements of our political condition. Washington understood the genius and character of the people of this country so well, that he held it to be impossible ever to establish that form of government over them without the deepest social convulsions. It was the form of the government against which they had waged a seven years' war; and it was certain that, apart from all questions of theoretical fitness or value, nothing but the most frightful civil disorders, menacing the very existence of society itself, could ever bring them again under its sway.

He was also satisfied, that, whatever particular system was to be adopted, it must be one that would create a national sovereignty and give it the means of coercion. What the nature of that coercion ought to be, he had not considered; but that obedience to the ordinances of a general government could not be expected, unless it was clothed with the power of enforcing them, all his experience during the war, and all his observation since, had fully satisfied him. He was convinced, also, that powers of a more extensive nature, and which would comprehend other objects, ought to be given to the general government; that Congress should be so placed as to enable and compel them to exert their constitutional authority with a firm and steady hand, instead of referring it back to the States. He proposed to adopt no temporizing expedients, but to have the defects of the Confederation thoroughly examined and displayed, and a radical cure provided, whether it were accepted or not. A course of this kind, he said, would stamp wisdom and dignity on their proceedings, and hold up a light which sooner or later would have its influence.[1]

Persuaded that the primary cause of all the public

[1] Washington's Writings, IX. 250.

disorders lay in the different State governments, and in the tenacity with which they adhered to their State powers, he saw that incompatibility in the laws of different States and disrespect to the authority of the Union must continue to render the situation of the country weak, inefficient, and disgraceful. The principle with which he entered the Convention, and on which he acted throughout to the end, was, "with a due consideration of circumstances and habits, to form such a government as will bear the scrutinizing eye of criticism, and trust it to the good sense and patriotism of the people to carry it into effect."[1]

The character of Washington as a statesman has, perhaps, been somewhat undervalued, from two causes; one of them being his military greatness, and the other, the extraordinary balance of his mind, which presented no brilliant and few salient qualities. Undoubtedly, as a statesman he was not constructive, like Hamilton, nor did he possess the same abundant and ever-ready resources. He was eminently cautious, but he was also eminently sagacious. He had had a wide field of observation during the war, the theatre of which, commencing in New England, had extended through the Middle and into the Southern States. He had, of course, been brought in contact with the men and the institutions of all the States, and had been concerned in their conflicts with the federal authority, to a greater extent than any other

[1] Washington's Writings, IX. 258.

public man of the time. This experience had not prepared him — as the character of his mind had not prepared him — to suggest plans or frame institutions fitted to remedy the evils he had observed, and to apply the principles which he had discovered. But it had revealed to him the dangers and difficulties of our situation, and had made him a national statesman, as incapable of confining his politics to the narrow scale of local interests and attachments, as he had been of confining his exertions to the object of achieving the liberties of a single state.

He would have been fitly placed in the chair of any deliberative assembly into which he might have been called at any period of his life; but it was preeminently suitable that he should occupy that of the Convention for forming the Constitution. He had no talent for debate, and upon the floor of this body he would have exerted less influence, and have been far less the central object towards which the opinions and views of the members were directed, than he was in the high and becoming position to which he was now called.

CHAPTER VIII.

Hamilton.

Next to the august name of the President should be mentioned that great man who, as a statesman, towered above all his compeers, even in that assembly of great men, — Alexander Hamilton.

This eminent person is probably less well known to the nation at the present day, than most of the leading statesmen of the Revolution. There are causes for this in his history. He never attained to that high office which has conferred celebrity on inferior men. The political party of which he was one of the founders and one of the chief leaders became unpopular with the great body of his countrymen before it was extinct. His death, too, at the early age of forty-seven, while it did not leave an unfinished character, left an unfinished career, for the contemplation of posterity. In this respect, his fate was unlike that of nearly all his most distinguished contemporaries. Washington, Adams, Jefferson, Madison, Jay, and in fact almost all the prominent statesmen of the Revolution, died in old age or in advanced life, and after the circle of their public honors and usefulness had been completed.

Hamilton was cut off at a period of life when he may be said to have had above a third of its best activity yet before him: and this is doubtless one cause why so little is popularly known, by the present generation, of him who was by far the greatest statesman of the Revolutionary age.

It is known, indeed, traditionally, what a thrill of horror — what a sharp, terrible pang — ran through the nation, proving the comprehension by the entire people of what was lost, when Aaron Burr took from his country and the world that important life. In the most distant extremities of the Union, men felt that one of the first intellects of the age had been extinguished. From the utmost activity and public consideration, in the fulness of his strength and usefulness, the bullet of a duellist had taken the first statesman in America; — a man who, while he had not been without errors, and while his life had not been without mistakes, had served his country, from his boyhood to that hour of her bitter bereavement, with an elevation of purpose and a force of intellect never exceeded in her history, and which had caused Washington to lean upon him and to trust him, as he trusted and leaned upon no other man, from first to last. The death of such a man, under such circumstances, cast a deep gloom over the face of society; and Hamilton was mourned by his contemporaries with a sorrow founded on a just appreciation of his greatness, and of what they owed to his intellect and character. But by the generations that have succeeded he has been less intimately known than many of his compatriots, who lived longer, and reached stations which he never occupied.

He was born in the island of St. Christopher's, in the year 1757; his mother being a native of that island, and his father being a Scotchman. At the age of fifteen, after having been for three years in the counting-house of a merchant at Santa Cruz, he was sent to New York to complete his education, and was entered as a private student in King's (now Columbia) College. At the age of seventeen, his political life was already begun; for at that age, and while still at college, he wrote and published a series of essays on the Rights of the Colonies, which attracted the attention of the whole country. These essays appeared in 1774, in answer to certain pamphlets on the Tory side of the controversy; and in them Hamilton reviewed and vindicated the whole of the proceedings of the first Continental Congress. There are displayed in these papers a power of reasoning and sarcasm, a knowledge of the principles of government and of the English Constitution, and a grasp of the merits of the whole controversy, that would have done honor to any man at any age, and in a youth of seventeen are wonderful. To say that they evince precocity of intellect, gives no idea of their main characteristics. They show great maturity; — a more remarkable maturity than has ever been exhibited by any other person, at so early an age, in the same department of thought. They produced, too, a great effect. Their influence in bringing the public mind to the point of resistance to the mother country, was important and extensive.

Before he was nineteen years old, Hamilton entered the army as a captain of artillery; and when only twenty, in 1777, he was selected by Washington to be one of his aides-de-camp, with the rank of lieutenant-colonel. In this capacity he served until 1782, when he was elected a member of Congress from the State of New York, and took his seat. In 1786, he was chosen a member of the legislature of New York. In 1787, he was appointed as a delegate to the Convention which framed the Constitution. In the following year, when only thirty years old, he published, with Madison and Jay, the celebrated essays called "The Federalist," in favor of the form of government proposed by the Convention. In 1788, he became a member of the State Convention of New York, called to ratify the Constitution, and it was chiefly through his influence that it was adopted in that State. In 1789, he took office in Washington's administration, as Secretary of the Treasury. In 1795, he retired to the practice of the law in the city of New York. In 1798, at Washington's absolute demand, he was appointed second in command of the provisional army, raised under the elder Adams's administration, to repel an apprehended invasion of the French. On the death of Washington, in 1799, he succeeded to the chief command. When the army was disbanded, he again returned to the bar, and practised with great reputation until the year 1804, when his life was terminated in a duel with Colonel Burr, concerning which the sole blame that has ever been imputed to Hamilton is, that he felt constrained to accept the challenge.

His great characteristic was his profound insight into the principles of government. The sagacity with which he comprehended all systems, and the thorough knowledge he possessed of the working of all the freer institutions of ancient and modern times, united with a singular capacity to make the experience of the past bear on the actual state of society, rendered him one of the most useful statesmen that America has known. Whatever in the science of government had already been ascertained; whatever the civil condition of mankind in any age had made practicable or proved abortive; whatever experience had demonstrated; whatever the passions, the interests, or the wants of men had made inevitable, — he seemed to know intuitively. But he was no theorist. His powers were all eminently practical. He detected the vice of a theory instantly, and shattered it with a single blow.

His knowledge, too, of the existing state of his own and of other countries was not less remarkable than his knowledge of the past. He understood America as thoroughly as the wisest of his contemporaries, and he comprehended Europe more completely than any other man of that age upon this continent.[1]

[1] While these sheets are passing through the press, Mr. Ticknor writes to me as follows: "One day in January, 1819, talking with

To these characteristics he added a clear logical power in statement, a vigorous reasoning, a perfect frankness and moral courage, and a lofty disdain of all the arts of a demagogue. His eloquence was distinguished for correctness of language and distinctness of utterance, as well as for grace and dignity.

In theory, he leaned decidedly to the constitution of England, as the best form of civil polity for the attainment of the great objects of government. But he was not, on that account, less a lover of liberty than those who favored more popular and democratic institutions. His writings will be searched in vain for any disregard of the natural rights of mankind, or any insensibility to the blessings of freedom. It was because he believed that those blessings can be best secured by governments in which a change of rulers is not of frequent occurrence, that he had so high an estimate of the English Constitution. At the period of the Convention, he held that the chief want of this country was a government into which the element of a permanent tenure of office could be largely infused; and he read in the Convention — as

Prince Talleyrand, in Paris, about his visit to America, he expressed the highest admiration of Mr. Hamilton, saying, among other things, that he had known nearly all the marked men of his time, but that he had never known one, on the whole, equal to him. I was much surprised and gratified with the remark; but still, feeling that, as an American, I was in some sort a party concerned by patriotism in the compliment, I answered with a little reserve, that the great military commanders and the great statesmen of Europe had dealt with larger masses and wider interests than he had. 'Mais, Monsieur,' the Prince instantly replied, 'Hamilton avoit *deviné* l'Europe.' "

an illustration of his views, but without pressing it — a plan by which the Executive and the Senate could hold their offices during good behavior. But the idea, which has sometimes been promulgated, that he desired the establishment of a monarchical government in this country, is without foundation. At no period of his life did he regard that experiment as either practicable or desirable.

Hamilton's relation to the Constitution is peculiar. He had less direct agency in framing its chief provisions than many of the other principal persons who sat in the Convention; and some of its provisions were not wholly acceptable to him when framed. But the history, which has been detailed in the previous chapters of this work, of the progress of federal ideas, and of the efforts to introduce and establish principles tending to consolidate the Union, has been largely occupied with the recital of his opinions, exertions, and prevalent influence. Beginning with the year 1780, when he was only three-and-twenty years of age, and when he sketched the outline of a national government strongly resembling the one which the Constitution long afterwards established; passing through the term of his service in Congress, when his admirable expositions of the revenue system, the commercial power, and the ratio of contribution, may justly be said to have saved the Union from dissolution; and coming down to the time when he did so much to bring about, first, the meeting at Annapolis, and then the general and final Convention of all the States; — the whole period is marked by his wisdom and filled with his power. He did more than any other public man of the time to lessen the force of State attachments, to create a national feeling, and to lead the public mind to a comprehension of the necessity for an efficient national sovereignty.

Indeed, he was the first to perceive and to develop the idea of a real union of the people of the United States. To him, more than to any one else, is to be attributed the conviction that the people of the different States were competent to establish a general government by their own direct action; and that this mode of proceeding ought to be considered within the contemplation of the State legislatures, when they appointed delegates to a convention for the revision and amendment of the existing system.[1]

The age in which he lived, and the very extraordinary early maturity of his character, naturally remind us of that remarkable person who was two years his junior, and who became prime-minister of England at the age of twenty-four. The younger Pitt entered public life with almost every possible advantage. Inheriting "a great and celebrated name,"[2] educated expressly for the career of a statesman, and introduced into the House of Commons at a moment when power was just ready to drop into the hands of any man capable of wielding it, he had only to prove himself a brilliant and powerful debater, in order to become the ruler of an empire,

[1] See his first speech in the Convention, as reported by Mr. Madison.

[2] Burke, speaking of Lord Chatham.

whose constitution had been settled for ages, and was necessarily administered by the successful leaders of regular parties in its legislative body. That he was a most eminent parliamentary orator, a consummate tactician and leader of party, a minister of singular energy, and a statesman of a very high order of mind and character, at an age when most men are scarcely beginning to give proofs of what they may become, — all this History has deliberately and finally recorded. What place it may assign to him among the statesmen by whose lives and actions England and the world have been materially and permanently benefited is not yet settled, and it is not to the present purpose to consider.

The theatre in which Hamilton appeared, lived, and acted, was one of a character so totally different, that the comparison necessarily ends with the contrast which it immediately suggests. Like Pitt, indeed, he seems to have been born a statesman, and to have had no such youth as ordinarily precedes the manhood of the mind. But, in the American colonies, no political system of things existed that was fitted to train him for a career of usefulness and honor; and yet, when the years of his boyhood were hardly ended, he sprang forth into the troubled affairs of the time, with the full stature of a matured and well-furnished statesman. He, in truth, showed himself to be already the man that was wanted. Every thing was in an unsettled and anxious state; — a state of change and transition. There was no regular, efficient government. It was all but a state of civil war, and the more clear-sighted saw that this great disaster was coming. He was compelled, therefore, to mark out for himself, step by step, beginning in 1774, a system of political principles which should serve, not to administer existing institutions with wisdom and beneficence, but to create institutions able to unite a people divided into thirteen independent sovereignties; to give them the attitude and capacity of an independent nation; and then to carry them on, with constantly increasing prosperity and power, to their just place in the affairs of the world. It was a great work, but Mr. Hamilton was equal to it. He was by nature, by careful study, and by still more careful, anxious, and earnest thought, eminently fitted to detect and develop those resources of power and progress, which, in the dark condition of society that attends and follows an exhausting period of revolution, lie hidden, like generous seeds, until some strong hand disencumbers them of the soil with which they had been oppressed, and gives them opportunity to germinate and bear golden fruit. At the age of three-and-twenty he had already formed well-defined, profound, and comprehensive opinions on the situation and wants of these States. He had clearly discerned the practicability of forming a confederated government, and adapting it to their peculiar condition, resources, and exigencies. He had wrought out for himself a political system, far in advance of the conceptions of his contemporaries, and one which, in the hands of those who most opposed him in life, became, when he was laid in a premature grave, the basis on which this government was consolidated; on which, to the present day, it has been administered; and on which alone it can safely rest in that future, which seems so to stretch out its unending glories before us.

Mr. Hamilton, therefore, I conceive, proved himself early to be a statesman of greater talent and power than the celebrated English minister whose youthful success was in the eyes of the world so much more brilliant, and whose early death was no less disheartening; for none can doubt, that to build up a free and firm state out of a condition of political chaos, and to give it a government capable of developing the resources of its soil and people, and of insuring to it prosperity, power, and permanence, is a greater work than to administer with energy and success — even in periods of severe trial — the constitution of an empire whose principles and modes of action have been settled for centuries.

Hamilton was one of those statesmen who trust to the efficacy of the press for the advancement and inculcation of correct principles of public policy, and who desire to accomplish important results mainly through the action of an enlightened public opinion. That he had faith in the intelligence and honesty of his countrymen, is proved by the numerous writings which he constantly addressed to their reason and good sense, in the shape of essays or letters, from the beginning to the end of his career, upon subjects on which it was important that they should act with wisdom and principle.

His own opinions, although held with great firmness, were also held in subordination to what was practicable. It was the rare felicity of his temperament, to be able to accept a less good than his principles might have led him to insist upon, and to labor for it, when nothing better could be obtained, with as much patriotic energy and zeal as if it had been the best result of his own views. The Constitution itself remains, in this particular, a monument of the disinterestedness of his character. He thought it had great defects. But he accepted it, as the best government that the wisdom of the Convention could frame, and the best that the nation would adopt. In this spirit, as soon as it was promulgated for the acceptance of the country, he came forward and placed himself in the foremost rank of its advocates, making himself, for all future time, one of the chief of its authoritative expounders. He was very ably assisted in the Federalist by Madison and Jay; but it was from him that the Federalist derived the weight and the power which commanded the careful attention of the country, and carried conviction to the great body of intelligent men in all parts of the Union. The extraordinary forecast with which its luminous discussions anticipated the operation of the new institutions, and its profound elucidation of their principles, gave birth to American constitutional law, which was thus placed at once above the field of arbitrary constructions and in the domain of legal truth. They made it a science; and so long as the Constitution shall exist, they will continue to be resorted to as the most important source of contemporaneous interpretation which the annals of the country afford.[1]

In the two paramount characters of statesman and

[1] The current editions of the Federalist are taken from an edition published at Washington in 1818, by Jacob Gideon, in which the numbers written by Mr. Madison purport to have been corrected by himself. There had been three editions previous to this. The first edition was published in 1788, in two small volumes, by J. & A. M'Lean, 41 Hanover Square, New York, under the following title: "The Federalist: a Collection of Essays written in Favor of the New Constitution, as agreed upon by the Federal Convention, September 17, 1787." The first volume was issued before the last of the essays were written, and the second followed it, as soon as the series was completed. The authentic text of the work is to be found in this edition; two of the authors were in the city of New York at the time it was printed, and probably superintended it. It was reissued from the same type, in 1789, by John Tiebout, 358 Pearl Street, New York. A second edition was published in 1802, at New York, in two volumes, containing also "Pacificus on the Proclamation of Neutrality, and the Constitution, with its Amendments." A third edition was published in 1810, by Williams & Whiting, New York. I have seen copies of the first and second editions only, in the library of Peter Force, Esq., of Washington, editor of the "American Archives." There are some discrepancies between the text of the first edition and that of 1818, from which the current editions are taken. By whom or on what authority the alterations were made, I have not been able to ascertain, nor have I learned when, or why, or how far Mr. Madison may have corrected or altered the papers which he wrote. Such of the changes as I have examined do not materially affect the sense; but it is very desirable that the true text of the Federalist should be reproduced. That text exists in the first edition, which was issued while the Constitution was before the people of the United States for their ratification; and as the Federalist was an argument addressed to the people in favor of the adoption of the Constitution, the exact text of that argument, as it was read and acted upon, ought to be restored, without regard to the reasons which may have led any of the writers, or any one else, to alter it. I know of no evidence that Colonel Hamilton ever made or sanctioned the alteration of a word. After the text of the Constitution itself, there is scarcely any thing the preservation of which is more important than the text of the Federalist as it was first published.

jurist, in the comprehensive nature of his patriotism, in his freedom from sectional prejudices, in his services to the Union, and in the kind and magnitude of his intellect, posterity will recognize a resemblance to him whom America still mourns with the freshness of a recent grief, and who has been to the Constitution, in the age that has succeeded, what Hamilton was in the age that witnessed its formation and establishment. Without the one of these illustrious men, the Constitution probably would never have existed; without the other, it might have become a mere record of past institutions, whose history had been glorious until faction and civil discord had turned it into a record of mournful recollections.

The following sentences, written by Hamilton soon after the adjournment of the Convention, contain a clew to all his conduct in support of the plan of government which that body recommended: — "It may be in me a defect of political fortitude, but I acknowledge that I cannot feel an equal tranquillity with those who affect to treat the dangers of a longer continuance in our present situation as imaginary. A nation without a national government is an awful spectacle. The establishment of a constitution, in a time of profound peace, by the voluntary consent of a whole people, is a prodigy, to the completion of which I look forward with trembling anxiety."

CHAPTER IX.

Madison.

From Hamilton we naturally turn to his associate in the Federalist, — James Madison, afterwards fourth President of the United States, — whose faithful and laborious record has preserved to us the debates of the Convention.

Mr. Madison was thirty-six years old when he entered that assembly. His previous life had fitted him to play a conspicuous and important part in its proceedings. He was born in 1751, of a good family, in Orange County, Virginia, and was educated at Princeton College in New Jersey, where he took the degree of Bachelor of Arts in 1772. He returned to Virginia in the spring of 1773, and commenced the usual studies preparatory to an admission to the bar; but the disputes between the Colonies and the mother country soon drew him into public life. In 1776, he became a member of the State Convention which formed the first Constitution of Virginia. He was afterwards a member of the legislature and of the Council of the State, until he was appointed one of its delegates in Congress, where he took his seat in March, 1780.[1]

From this time to the assembling of the Federal Convention in 1787, his services to the Union were of the most important character. He entered Congress without a national reputation, but with national views. Indeed, it may be said of him, that he came from his native Commonwealth, — "mother of great men," — grown to the full proportions of a continental statesman. At the moment when he appeared upon the larger theatre of the national interests, the Articles of Confederation had not been finally ratified by all the States. Maryland had insisted, as a necessary condition of her accession to the new Confederacy, that the great States should surrender to the Union their immense claims to the unoccupied territories of the West; Virginia had remonstrated against this demand; and the whole scheme of the Confederation had thus been long encountered by an apparently insurmountable obstacle.[2] The generous example of New York, whose Western claims were ceded to the United States in the month preceding Mr. Madison's entry into Congress, had furnished to the advocates of the Union the means for a powerful appeal to both sides of this critical and delicate controversy; but it required great tact, discretion, and address to make that appeal effectual, by inducing Maryland to trust to the

[1] Article "Madison" in the Penny Encylopædia, written for that work by Professor George Tucker of the University of Virginia.

[2] Ante, pp. 131 – 141.

influence of this example upon Virginia, and by inducing Virginia to make a cession that would be satisfactory to Maryland. In this high effort of statesmanship — a domestic diplomacy full of difficulties — Mr. Madison took part. He did not prepare the very skilful report which, while it aimed to produce cessions of their territorial claims by the larger States, appealed to Maryland to anticipate the result;[1] but the vast concession by which Virginia yielded the Northwestern Territory to the Union was afterwards brought about mainly by his exertions.

In 1782, he united with Hamilton in the celebrated report prepared by the latter upon the refusal of the State of Rhode Island to comply with the recommendations of Congress for a duty on imports.[2]

In 1783, he was named first upon a committee with Ellsworth and Hamilton, to prepare an Address to the States, urging the adoption of the revenue system which has been described in a previous chapter, and the Address was written by him.[3] The great ability and high tone of this paper gave it a striking effect. The object of this plan of revenue was, as we have seen, to fund the national debts, and to make a sufficient provision for their discharge. I have already assigned to it the merit of having preserved the Union from the premature decay that had begun to destroy its vitality;[4] and it may here be added, that the statesman whose pen could produce

[1] It was drawn by James Duane of New York.

[2] Ante, pp. 174, 206 – 208.

[3] Ante, pp. 177 – 179.

[4] Ante, pp. 176, 186, 188.

the comprehensive and powerful appeal by which it was pressed upon the States, was certain to become one of the chief founders of the Constitution of which the plan itself was the forerunner. It settled the fact, that a national unity in dealing with the debts of the Revolution was "necessary to render its fruits a full reward for the blood, the toils, the cares, and the calamities which had purchased them."

Such were Mr. Madison's most important services in the Congress of the Confederation; but they are of course not the whole. A member so able and of such broad and national views must have had a large agency in every important transaction; and accordingly the Journals, during the whole period of his service, bear ample testimony to his activity, his influence, and his zeal.

At the close of the war, he retired to Virginia, and during the three following years was a member of the legislature, still occupied, however, with the interests of the Union. His attention was specially directed to the subject of enlarging the powers of Congress over the foreign trade of the country. It is a striking fact, and a proof of the comprehensive character of Mr. Madison's statesmanship, that Virginia, a State not largely commercial, should have taken so prominent a part in the efforts to give the control of commerce to the general government; — an object which has justly been regarded as the corner-stone of the Constitution. It arose partly from the accident of her geographical position, which made it necessary for her to aim at something like uniformity of regulation with the other States which bordered upon her contiguous waters; but it is also to be attributed to the enlightened liberality and forecast of her great men, who saw in the immediate necessities of their own State the occasion for a measure of general advantage to the country.

Mr. Madison's first effort was, to procure a declaration by the legislature of Virginia of the necessity for a uniform regulation of the commerce of the States by the federal authority. For this purpose, he introduced into the legislature a series of propositions, intended to instruct the delegates of the State in Congress to propose a recommendation to the States to confer upon Congress power to regulate their trade and to collect a revenue from such regulation. This measure, as we have seen, encountered the opposition of those who preferred a temporary to a perpetual and irrevocable grant of such power; and the propositions were so much changed in the Committee of the Whole, that they were no longer acceptable to their original friends. The steps which finally led the legislature of Virginia to recommend a general convention of all the States have been detailed in a previous chapter of this work; but it is due to Mr. Madison's connection with this movement, that they should here be recapitulated with reference to his personal agency in the various transactions.

A conflict of jurisdiction between the two States of Virginia and Maryland over the waters which separated them had, in the spring of 1785, led to the appointment of commissioners on the part of each State, who met at Alexandria in March. These commissioners, of whom Mr. Madison was one, made a visit to General Washington at Mount Vernon, and it was there proposed that the two States, whose conflicting regulations, ever since the peace, had produced great inconvenience to their merchants, and had been a constant source of irritation, should be recommended by the commissioners to make a compact for the regulation of their impost and foreign trade. Mr. Madison has left no written claim, that I am aware of, to the authorship of this suggestion, but there exists evidence of his having claimed it in conversation.[1] The recommendation was made by the commissioners, and their report was adopted by both States; — by Virginia unconditionally, and by Mary-

[1] In preparing the note to page 342 (ante), I refrained from attributing to General Washington the suggestion of the enlarged plan recommended by the Alexandria commissioners, although it was concerted at his house, because there is no evidence, beyond that fact, of his having proposed this enlargement of the plan. Since that note was printed, I have learned in a direct manner, that Mr. Madison had stated to the Hon. Edward Coles, formerly his private secretary and afterwards Governor of Illinois, that he (Mr. Madison) first suggested it. In assigning, therefore, to the different individuals who took a prominent part in the measures which led to the formation of the Constitution, the various suggestions which had an important influence upon the course of events, — a curious and interesting inquiry, — I consider that to Mr. Madison belongs the credit of having originated that series of Virginia measures which brought about the meeting of commissioners of all the States at Annapolis, for the purpose of enlarging the powers of Congress over commerce; while Hamilton is to be considered the author of the plan in which the Convention at Annapolis was merged, for an entire revision of the federal system and the formation of a new constitution.

land with the qualification that the States of Delaware and Pennsylvania should be invited to unite in the plan.

After the commercial propositions introduced by Mr. Madison had lain on the table for some time as a report from the Committee of the Whole, the report of the Alexandria commissioners was received and ratified by the legislature of Virginia. Although the friends of those propositions were gradually increasing, Mr. Madison had no expectation that a majority could be obtained in favor of a grant of commercial powers to Congress for a longer term than twenty-five years. The idea of a general convention of delegates from all the States, which had been for some time familiar to Mr. Madison's mind, then suggested itself to him, and he prepared and caused to be introduced the resolution which led to the meeting that afterwards took place at Annapolis, for the purpose of digesting and reporting the requisite augmentation of the powers of Congress over trade.[1] His resolution, he says, being, on the last day of the session, "the alternative of adjourning without any effort for the crisis in the affairs of the Union, obtained a general vote; less, however, with some of its friends, from a confidence in the success of the experiment, than from a hope that it might

[1] The resolve was introduced by Mr. Tyler, father of the Ex-President, a person of much influence in the legislature, and who had never been in Congress. Although prepared by Mr. Madison, it was not offered by him, for the reason that a great jealousy was felt against those who had been in the federal councils, and because he was known to wish for an enlargement of the powers of Congress. See Madison's Introduction to the Debates in the Convention, Elliot, V. 113.

prove a step to a more comprehensive and adequate provision for the wants of the Confederacy."[1]

Mr. Madison was appointed one of the commissioners of Virginia to the meeting at Annapolis. There he met Hamilton, who came meditating nothing less than the general revision of the whole system of the Federal Union, and the formation of a new government. Mr. Madison, although less confident than the great statesman of New York as to the measures that ought to be taken, had yet for several years been equally convinced that the perpetuity and efficacy of the existing system could not be confided in. He therefore concurred readily in the report recommending a general convention of all the States; and when that report was received in the legislature of Virginia, he became the author of the celebrated act which passed that body on the 4th of December, 1786, and under which the first appointment of delegates to the Convention was made. It was also chiefly through his exertions, combined with the influence of Governor Randolph, that General Washington's name was placed at the head of the delegation, and that he was induced to accept the appointment. Mr. Madison himself was the fourth member of the delegation.

In the Convention, his labors must have been far more arduous than those of any other member of the body. He took a leading part in the debates, speaking upon every important question; and in addition to

[1] Ibid., p. 114.

all the usual duties devolving upon a person of so much ability and influence, he preserved a full and careful record of the discussions with his own hand. Impressed, as he says, with the magnitude of the trust confided to the Convention, and foreseeing the interest that must attach to an authentic exhibition of the objects, the opinions, and the reasonings from which the new system of government was to receive its peculiar structure and organization, he devoted the hours of the night succeeding the session of each day to the preparation of the record with which his name is imperishably associated. "Nor was I," he adds, "unaware of the value of such a contribution to the fund of materials for the history of a Constitution on which would be staked the happiness of a people, great even in its infancy, and possibly the cause of liberty throughout the world."[1]

As a statesman, he is to be ranked, by a long interval, after Hamilton; but he was a man of eminent talent, always free from local prejudices, and sincerely studious of the welfare of the whole country. His perception of the principles essential to the continuance of the Union and to the safety and prosperity of the States, was accurate and clear. His studies had made him familiar with the examples of ancient and modern liberty, and he had carefully reflected upon the nature of the government necessary to be established. He was one of the few persons who carried into the Convention a conviction

[1] Introduction to the Debates, Elliot, V. 121.

that an amendment of the Articles of Confederation would not answer the exigencies of the time. He regarded an individual independence of the States as irreconcilable with an aggregate sovereignty of the whole, but admitted that a consolidation of the States into a simple republic was both impracticable and inexpedient. He sought, therefore, for some middle ground, which would at once support a due supremacy of the national authority, and leave the local authorities in force for their subordinate objects.

For this purpose, he conceived that a system of representation which would operate without the intervention of the States was indispensable; that the national government should be armed with a positive and complete authority in all cases where a uniformity of measures was necessary, as in matters of trade, and that it should have a negative upon the legislative acts of the States, as the crown of England had before the Revolution. He thought, also, that the national supremacy should be extended to the judiciary, and foresaw the necessity for national tribunals, in cases in which foreigners and citizens of different States might be concerned, and also for the exercise of the admiralty jurisdiction. He considered two branches of the legislature, with distinct origins, as indispensable; recognized the necessity for a national executive, and favored a council of revision of the laws, in which should be included the great ministerial officers of the government. He saw also, that, to give the new system its proper energy, it would be necessary to have it ratified by the authority of the people, and not merely by that of the legislatures.[1]

Such was the outline of the project which he had formed before the assembling of the Convention. How far his views were modified by the discussions in which he took part will be seen hereafter. As a speaker in a deliberative assembly, the successive schools in which he had been trained had given him a habit of self-possession which placed all his resources at his command. "Never wandering from his subject," says Mr. Jefferson, "into vain declamation, but pursuing it closely, in language pure, classical, and copious, soothing always the feelings of his adversaries by civilities and softness of expression, he rose to the eminent station which he held in the great national Convention of 1787; and in that of Virginia which followed, he sustained the new Constitution in all its parts, bearing off the palm against the logic of George Mason and the fervid declamation of Mr. Henry. With these consummate powers were united a pure and spotless virtue, which no calumny has ever attempted to sully."[2]

Mr. Madison's greatest service in the national Convention consisted in the answers which he made to the objections of a want of power in that assembly to frame and propose a new constitution, and his paper on this subject in the Federalist is one of the ablest in the series.

As this work is confined to the period which ter-

[1] Letter to Edmund Randolph, dated New York, April 8th, 1787.

[2] Jefferson's Autobiography. Works, I. 41, edition of 1853.

minated with the adoption of the Constitution, it is not necessary to examine those points on which the two principal writers of the Federalist became separated from each other, when the administration of the government led to the formation of the first parties known in our political history. These topics it may become my duty to discuss hereafter, should I pursue the constitutional history of the country through the administration of Washington. At present, it may be recorded of both, that, upon almost all the great questions that arose before the Constitution was finally adopted, the single purpose of establishing a system as efficient as the theory of a purely republican government would admit, was the object of their efforts; and that, although they may have differed with regard to the details and methods through which this object was to be reached, the purpose at which they both aimed places them in the same rank at the head of those founders of our government, towards whom the gratitude of the succeeding generations of America must be for ever directed.

1 The following extract from an autograph letter of Mr. Madison, hitherto unpublished, which lies before me, written after the adoption of the Constitution, shows very clearly that he concurred with Hamilton in the opinion that the strongest government consistent with the republican form was necessary in the situation of this country. The letter is dated at Philadelphia, December 10th, 1788, and is addressed to Philip Mazzei, at Paris.

"Your book, as I prophesied, sells nowhere but in Virginia; a very few copies only have been called for, either in New York or in this city. The language in which it is written will account for it. In order to attract notice, I translated the panegyric in the French Mercure, and had it made part of the advertisement. I did not translate the comment on the Federal Constitution, as you wished, because I could not spare the time.

as well as because I did not approve the tendency of it. Some of your remarks prove that Horace's '*Cœlum non animum mutant qui trans mare currunt*' does not hold without exception. In Europe, the abuses of power continually before your eyes have given a bias to your political reflections, which you did not feel in equal degree when you left America, and which you would feel less of, if you had remained in America. Philosophers on the old continent, in their zeal against tyranny would rush into anarchy; as the horrors of superstition drive them into atheism. Here, perhaps, the inconveniences of relaxed government have reconciled too many to the opposite extreme. If your plan of a single legislature, as in Pennsylvania, &c., were adopted, I sincerely believe that it would prove the most deadly blow ever given to republicanism. Were I an enemy to that form, I would preach the very doctrines which are preached by the enemies to the government proposed for the United States. Many of our best citizens are disgusted with the injustice, instability, and folly which characterize the American administrations. The number has for some time been rapidly increasing. Were the evils to be much longer protracted, the disgust would seize citizens of every description.

"It is of infinite importance to the cause of liberty to ascertain the degree of it which will consist with the purposes of society. An error on one side may be as fatal as on the other. Hitherto, the error in the United States has lain in the excess.

"All the States, except North Carolina and Rhode Island, have ratified the proposed Constitution. Seven of them have appointed their Senators, of whom those of Virginia, R. H. Lee and Colonel Grayson, alone are among the opponents of the system. The appointments of Maryland, South Carolina, and Georgia will pretty certainly be of the same stamp with the majority. The House of Representatives is yet to be chosen, everywhere except in Pennsylvania. From the partial returns received, the election will wear a federal aspect unless the event in one or two particular counties should contradict every calculation. If the eight members from this State be on the side of the Constitution, it will in a manner secure the majority in that branch of the Congress also. The object of the anti-Federalists is, to bring about another general convention, which would either agree on nothing, as would be agreeable to some, and throw every thing into confusion, or expunge from the Constitution parts which are held by its friends to be essential to it. The latter party are willing to gratify their opponents with every supplemental provision for general rights, but insist that this can be better done in the mode provided for amendments.

"I remain, with great sincerity, your friend and servant,

"Jas. Madison, Jr."

CHAPTER X.

FRANKLIN.

THE Convention was graced and honored by the venerable presence of Dr. Franklin, then President of the State of Pennsylvania, and in his eighty-second year. He had returned from Europe only two years before, followed by the admiration and homage of the social, literary, and scientific circles of France; laden with honors, which he wore with a plain and shrewd simplicity; and in the full possession of that predominating common-sense, which had given him, through a long life, a widely extended reputation of a peculiar character. The oldest of the public men of America, his political life had embraced a period of more than half a century, extending back to a time when independence had not entered into the dreams of the boldest among the inhabitants of the English Colonies. For more than twenty years before the Revolution commenced, he had held a high and responsible office under the crown, the administration of which affected the intercourse and connection of all the Colonies;[1] and more than twenty years

[1] In 1753, he was appointed Deputy Postmaster-General for the British Colonies, from which place he was dismissed in 1774, while in

before the first Continental Congress was assembled, he had projected a plan of union for the thirteen Provinces which then embraced the whole of the British dominions in North America.[1] Nearly as long, also, before the Declaration of Independence, he had become the resident agent in England of several of the Colonies, in which post he continued, with a short interval, through all the controversies that preceded the Revolution, and until reconciliation with the mother country had become impossible.[2]

Returning in 1775, he was immediately appointed by the people of Pennsylvania one of their delegates in the second Continental Congress. In the following year, he was sent as commissioner to France, where he remained until he was recalled, and was succeeded by Mr. Jefferson, in 1785.

With the fame of his two residences abroad — the one before and the other after the country had severed its connection with England — the whole land was filled. The first of them, commencing with an employment for settling the miserable disputes between the people and the Proprietaries of Pennsyl-

England, on account of the part he had taken in American affairs.

[1] In 1754. See an account of this plan, ante, p. 8.

[2] He first went to England in 1757, as agent of the Pennsylvania Assembly to settle their difficulties with the Proprietaries, where he remained until 1762. In 1764, he was reappointed provincial agent in England for Pennsylvania; in 1768, he received a similar appointment from Georgia; in 1769, he was chosen agent for New Jersey; and in 1770, he became agent for Massachusetts. His whole residence in England, from 1757 to 1775, embraced a period of sixteen years, two years having been passed at home. He resided in France about nine years, from 1776 to 1785.

vania, was extended to an agency for the three other Colonies of Georgia, New Jersey, and Massachusetts, which finally led him to take part in the affairs of all British America, and made him virtually the representative of American interests. His brief service in Congress, during which he signed the Declaration of Independence, was followed by his appointment as Commissioner at the Court of Versailles, which he made the most important sphere that has ever been filled by any American in Europe, and in which that treaty of alliance with France was negotiated which enabled the United States to become in fact an independent nation.

His long career of public service; his eminence as a philosopher, a philanthropist, and a thinker; the general reverence of the people for his character; his peculiar power of illustrating and enforcing his opinions by a method at once original, simple, and attractive, — made his presence of the first importance in an assembly which was to embrace the highest wisdom and virtue of America.

It is chiefly, however, by the countenance he gave to the effort to frame a Constitution, that his services as a member of this body are to be estimated. His mind was at all times ingenious, rather than large and constructive; and his great age, while it had scarcely at all impaired his natural powers, had confirmed him in some opinions which must certainly be regarded as mistaken. His desire, for example, to have the legislature of the United States consist of a single body, for the sake of simplicity, and his idea that the chief executive magistrate ought to receive no salary for his official services, for the sake of purity, were both singular and unsound.

But there were points upon which he displayed extraordinary wisdom, penetration, and forecast. When an objection to a proportionate representation in Congress was started, upon the ground that it would enable the larger States to swallow up the smaller, he declared that, as the great States could propose to themselves no advantage by absorbing their inferior neighbors, he did not believe they would attempt it. His recollection carried him back to the early part of the century, when the union between England and Scotland was proposed, and when the Scotch patriots were alarmed by the idea that they should be ruined by the superiority of England, unless they had an equal number of members in Parliament; and yet, notwithstanding the great inferiority in their representation as established by the act of union, he declared, that, down to that day, he did not recollect that any thing had been done in the Parliament of Great Britain to the prejudice of Scotland.[1]

Although he spoke but seldom in the Convention, his influence was very great, and it was always exerted to cool the ardor of debate, and to check the tendency of such discussions to result in

[1] He added, with his usual quiet humor, that "whoever looks over the lists of public officers, civil and military, of that nation, will find, I believe, that the North Britons enjoy their full proportion of emolument." Madison, Elliot, V. 179

irreconcilable differences. His great age, his venerable and benignant aspect, his wide reputation, his acute and sagacious philosophy,—which was always the embodiment of good sense,—would have given him a controlling weight in a much more turbulent and a far less intelligent assembly. When—after debates in which the powerful intellects around him had exhausted the subject, and both sides remained firm in opinions diametrically opposed—he rose and reminded them that they were sent to consult and not to contend, and that declarations of a fixed opinion and a determination never to change it neither enlightened nor convinced those who listened to them, his authority was felt by men who could have annihilated any mere logical argument that might have proceeded from him in his best days.

Dr. Franklin was one of those who entertained serious objections to the Constitution, but he sacrificed them before the Convention was dissolved. Believing a general government to be necessary for the American States; holding that every form of government might be made a blessing to the people by a good administration; and foreseeing that the Constitution would be well administered for a long course of years, and could only end in despotism when the people should have become so corrupted as to be incapable of any other than a despotic government, he gladly embraced a system which he was astonished to find approaching so near to perfection.

"The opinions I have had of its errors," said he, "I sacrifice to the public good. Within these walls they were born, and here they shall die. If every one of us, in returning to our constituents, were to report the objections he has had to it, and endeavor to gain partisans in support of them, we might prevent its being generally received, and thereby lose all the salutary effects and great advantages, resulting naturally in our favor, among foreign nations as well as among ourselves, from our real or apparent unanimity. Much of the strength and efficiency of any government in procuring and securing happiness to the people depends on opinion, — on the general opinion of the goodness of the government, as well as of the wisdom and integrity of its governors. I hope, therefore, that for our own sakes as a part of the people, and for the sake of posterity, we shall act heartily and unanimously in recommending this Constitution (approved by Congress and confirmed by the conventions) wherever our influence may extend, and turn our future thoughts and endeavors to the means of having it well administered."[1]

And thus, with a cheerful confidence in the future, sustaining the hopes of all about him, and hailing every omen that foretold the rising glories of his country,[2] this wise old man passed out from the assembly, when its anxious labors had been brought

[1] Madison, Elliot, V. 554.

[2] Mr. Madison has recorded the following anecdote at the end of the Debates, as an incident worthy of being known to posterity. "Whilst the last members were signing, Dr. Franklin, looking towards the President's chair, at the back of which a rising sun happened to be painted, observed to a few members near him, that painters had often found it difficult, in their art, to distinguish a rising from a setting sun. 'I have,' said he,

to a close with a nearer approach to unanimity than had ever been expected. He lived, borne down by infirmities,

"To draw his breath in pain"

for nearly three years after the Convention was dissolved; but it was to see the Constitution established, to witness the growing strength of the new government, and to contemplate the opening successes and the beneficent promise of Washington's administration. Writing to the first President in 1789, he said: "For my own personal ease, I should have died two years ago; but though those years have been spent in excruciating pain, I am pleased that I have lived them, since they have brought me to see our present situation."[1]

'often and often, in the course of the session, and the vicissitude of my hopes and fears as to its issue, looked at that behind the President, without being able to tell whether it was rising or setting; but now, at length, I have the happiness to know that it is a rising, and not a setting sun.'"

[1] Sparks's Life of Franklin, 528

CHAPTER XI.

Gouverneur Morris.

This brilliant, energetic, and patriotic statesman was born in the Province of New York, at Morrisania, — the seat of his family for several generations, — in the year 1752. He was educated for the bar; but in 1775, at the age of three-and-twenty, he was elected a member of the Provincial Congress of New York, in which he became at once distinguished. When the recommendation of the Continental Congress to the Colonies, to organize new forms of government, was received, he took a leading place in the debates on the formation of a new constitution for the State; and when the subject of independence was brought forward, in order that the delegates of New York in the Continental Congress might be clothed with sufficient authority, he delivered a speech of great power, of which fragments only are preserved, but which evidently embraced the most comprehensive and statesmanlike views of the situation and future prospects of this country. Speaking of the capacity of America to sustain herself without a connection with Great Britain, he said: —

"Thus, Sir, by means of that great gulf which rolls its waves between Europe and America; by the situation of these Colonies, always adapted to hinder or interrupt all communication between the two; by the productions of our soil, which the Almighty has filled with every necessary to make us a great maritime people; by the extent of our coasts and those immense rivers, which serve at once to open a communication with our interior country, and to teach us the arts of navigation; by those vast fisheries, which, affording an inexhaustible mine of wealth and a cradle of industry, breed hardy mariners, inured to danger and fatigue; finally, by the unconquerable spirit of freemen, deeply interested in the preservation of a government which secures to them the blessings of liberty and exalts the dignity of mankind; — by all these, I expect a full and lasting defence against any and every part of the earth; while the great advantages to be derived from a friendly intercourse with this country almost render the means of defence unnecessary, from the great improbability of being attacked. So far, peace seems to smile upon our future independence. But that this fair goddess will equally crown our union with Great Britain, my fondest hopes cannot lead me to suppose. Every war in which she is engaged must necessarily involve us in its detestable consequences; whilst, weak and unarmed, we have no shield of defence, unless such as she may please (for her own sake) to afford, or else the pity of her enemies and the insignificance of slaves beneath the attention of a generous foe."[1]

In 1778, Mr. Morris was chosen a delegate to the Continental Congress from the State of New York. His reputation for talent, zeal, activity, and singular capacity for business, had preceded him. On the very day when he presented his credentials, he was placed upon a committee to proceed to Valley Forge, to confer with General Washington on the measures necessary for a reorganization of the army. He remained in Congress for two years, discharging, with great ability and high patriotism, the most important functions, and subjected all the while to the most unjust popular suspicions of his fidelity to the cause of the country. Few of all the prominent men of the Revolution sacrificed or suffered more than Gouverneur Morris. The fact that all the other members of his family adhered to the royalist side, and an ineffectual effort which he once made to visit his mother, at his ancestral home, then within the British lines, gave his enemies the means of inflicting upon him a deep injury in the popular estimation. He was not re-elected to Congress; but short as his career in that body was, it was filled with services inferior to those of none of his associates.

[1] Sparks's Life of G. Morris, I. 103. The florid and declamatory style of this speech belongs to the period and to the youth of the speaker. The breadth of its views and its vigor of thought display the characteristics which belonged to him through life. He had a prophetic insight of the future resources of this country, and made many remarkable predictions of its greatness. His biographer has claimed for him the suggestion of the plan for uniting the waters of Lake Erie with those of the Hudson, and upon very strong evidence.

Before he left Congress, in February, 1779, he made — as chairman of a committee to whom certain communications from the French minister in the United States were referred — a report which became the basis of the peace that afterwards followed; and when the principles on which the peace was to be negotiated had been settled, he drew the instructions to the commissioners, and they were unanimously adopted without change.[1]

On leaving Congress, Mr. Morris took up his residence in Philadelphia, and resumed the practice of the law. His remarkable talent for business, however, and his intimate knowledge of financial subjects, led to his appointment as Assistant Financier with Robert Morris. In this capacity, he suggested the idea of the decimal notation, which was afterwards made the basis of the coinage of the United States.[2]

[1] See the Report and the debates thereon, Secret Journals, II. 132 et seq.

[2] In January, 1782, the Financier made a report, which was officially signed by him, but which Mr. Jefferson says was prepared by his Assistant, Gouverneur Morris. It embraced an elaborate statement of the denominations and comparative value of the foreign coins in circulation in the different States, and proposed the adoption of a money unit and a system of decimal notation for a new coinage. The unit suggested was such a portion of pure silver as would be a common measure of the penny of every State, without leaving a fraction. This common divisor Mr. Morris found to be one 1440th of a dollar, or one 1600th of the crown sterling. The value of a dollar was therefore to be expressed by 1,440 units, and that of a crown by 1,600, each unit containing a quarter of a grain of fine silver. Nothing, however, was done, until 1784, when Mr. Jefferson, being in Congress, took up the subject. He approved of Mr. Morris's general views, and his method of decimal notation, but objected to his unit as too minute for ordinary use. Mr. Jefferson proposed the dollar as the unit of account and payment, and that its

Having been appointed one of the delegates from the State of Pennsylvania to the Convention for forming the Constitution of the United States, Mr. Morris attended the whole session, with the exception of a few days in June, and entered into its business with his accustomed ardor. To remove impediments, obviate objections, and conciliate jarring opinions, he exerted all his fine faculties, and employed his remarkable eloquence. But he is chiefly to be remembered, in connection with the Constitution, as the author of its text. To his pen belongs the merit of that clear and finished style, — that *lucidus ordo,* — that admirable perspicuity, which have so much diminished the labors and hazards of interpretation for all future ages.[1]

The character of Gouverneur Morris was balanced by many admirable qualities. His self-possession was so complete in all circumstances, that he is said to have declared, that he never knew the sensation

divisions and subdivisions should be in the decimal ratio. This plan was adopted in August, 1785, and in 1786 the names and characters of the coins were determined. The ordinance establishing the coinage was passed August 8, 1786, and that establishing the mint, on the 16th of October, in the same year. (Jefferson's Autobiography, Works, I. 52-54. Life of Gouverneur Morris, I. 273. Journals of Congress, XI. 179, 254.)

[1] The materials for the final preparation of the instrument, consisting of a reported draft in detail and the various resolutions which had been adopted, were placed in the hands of a committee of revision, of which Dr. William Samuel Johnson, of Connecticut, was the chairman; the other members being Messrs. Hamilton, Gouverneur Morris, Madison, and King. The chairman committed the work to Mr. Morris, and the Constitution, as adopted, was prepared by him. (See Mr. Madison's letter to Mr. Sparks, Life of Gouverneur Morris, I. 284. Madison's Debates, Elliot, V. 530.)

of fear, inferiority, or embarrassment, in his intercourse with men. Undoubtedly, his self-confidence amounted sometimes to boldness and presumption; but we have it on no less an authority than Mr. Madison's, that he added to it a candid surrender of his opinions, when the lights of discussion satisfied him that they had been too hastily formed.[1] He was a man of genius, fond of society and pleasure, but capable of prodigious exertion and industry, and possessed of great powers of eloquence.

He loved to indulge in speculations on the future condition of the country, and often foresaw results which gave him patience under the existing state of things. In 1784, writing to Mr. Jay, at a time when the clashing commercial regulations of the States seemed about to put an end to the Union, he said: "True it is, that the general government wants energy, and equally true it is, that this want will eventually be supplied. A national spirit is the natural result of national existence, and although some of the present generation may feel colonial oppositions of opinion, yet this generation will die away and give place to a race of Americans."[2]

He was himself, at all times, an American, and never more so than during the discussions of the Convention. Appealing to his colleagues to extend their views beyond the narrow limits of place whence they derived their political origin, he declared, with his characteristic energy and point, that

[1] Life of Morris, I. 284-286. [2] Ibid. 266.

State attachments and State importance had been the bane of this country. "We cannot annihilate," said he, "but we may perhaps take out the teeth of the serpents."[1]

In truth, the circumstances of his life had prevented him from feeling those strong local attachments which he considered the great impediments to the national prosperity. Born in one State, he had then resided for seven years in another, from whose inhabitants he had received at least equal marks of confidence with those that had been bestowed upon him by the people among whom he first entered public life.

In his political opinions, he probably went farther in opposition to democratic tendencies than any other person in the Convention. He was in favor of an executive during good behavior, of a Senate for life, and of a freehold qualification for electors of representatives. In several other respects, the Constitution, as actually framed, was distasteful to him; but, like many of the other eminent men who doubted its theoretical or practical wisdom, he determined at once to abide by the voice of the majority. He saw that, as soon as the plan should go forth, all other considerations ought to be laid aside, and the great question ought to be, Shall there be a national government or not? He acknowledged that the alternatives were, the adoption of the system proposed, or a general anarchy; — and before this single and fear-

[1] Madison, Elliot, V. 276, 277.

ful issue all questions of individual opinion or preference sank into insignificance.[1] It is a proof both of his sincerity and of the estimate in which his abilities were held, that, when this great issue was presented to the people, he was invited by Hamilton to become one of the writers of the Federalist.[2] It is not known why he did not embrace the opportunity of connecting himself with that celebrated publication; but his correspondence shows that it was from no want of interest in the result. He took pains to give to Washington his decided testimony, from personal observation, that the idea of his refusing the Presidency would, if it prevailed, be fatal to the Constitution in many parts of the country.[3]

Mr. Morris filled two important public stations, after the adoption of the Constitution. He was the first Minister to France appointed by General Washington, and filled that office from May, 1792, until August, 1794. In February, 1800, he was chosen by the legislature of New York to supply a vacancy in the Senate of the United States, which he filled until the 4th of March, 1803. He died at Morrisania on the 6th of November, 1818. "Let us forget party," said he, "and think of our country, which embraces all parties."[4]

1 Madison, Elliot, V. 556.
2 Life, I. 287.
3 Ibid. 288-290.
4 Ibid. 517.

CHAPTER XII.

KING.

RUFUS KING, celebrated as a jurist, a statesman, an orator, and a diplomatist, was sent to the Convention by the Commonwealth of Massachusetts. Born in her District of Maine, in 1755, and graduated at Harvard College in 1777, he came very early into public life, and was rarely out of it until his death, which occurred in 1827, in the seventy-third year of his age.

His first public service was in the year 1778, as a volunteer in the expedition against the British in Rhode Island, in which he acted as aide-de-camp to General Sullivan. In 1780, he commenced the practice of the law in the town of Newburyport, and was soon after elected from that town to the legislature of the State. There he distinguished himself by a very powerful speech in favor of granting to the general government the five per cent. impost recommended by Congress as part of the revenue system of 1783.

He was soon after elected a member of Congress from Massachusetts, in which body he took his seat on the 6th of December, 1784, and served until the close of the year 1787. He was thus a member both of the Convention for forming the Constitution and of the Congress which sanctioned and referred it to the people. He was also a member of the Convention of Massachusetts, in which the Constitution was ratified by that State.

Mr. King did not favor the plan of a convention for the revision of the federal system, until after the meeting at Annapolis had been held; and, indeed, he did not concur in its expediency, until after the troubles in Massachusetts had made its necessity apparent. In 1785, as we have seen, he joined with the other members of the Massachusetts delegation in opposing it.[1] In the autumn of 1786, when the report of the Annapolis Convention was before Congress, he expressed the opinion, in person, to the legislature of Massachusetts, that the Articles of Confederation could not be altered, except by the consent of Congress and the confirmation of the several legislatures; that Congress ought, in the first instance, to make the examination of the federal system, since, if it was done by a convention, no legislature would have a right to confirm it; and further, that, if Congress should reject the report of a convention, the most fatal consequences might follow. For these reasons, he at that time held Congress to be the proper body to propose alterations.[2]

1 Ante, p. 339, note.

2 Mr. King being in Boston in October, 1786, was desired by the legislature to attend and give an account of the state of national affairs. For an abstract of his address, see Boston Magazine for the year 1786, p. 406.

At the moment when he was making this address to the legislature, the disturbances in Massachusetts were fast gathering into that formidable insurrection, which two months afterwards burst forth in the interior of the State.[1] Mr. King spoke of these commotions in grave and pointed terms. He told the legislature that Congress viewed them with deep anxiety; that every member of the national councils felt his life, liberty, and property to be involved in the issue of their decisions; that the United States would not be inactive on such an occasion, for, if the lawful authority of the State were to be prostrated, every other government would eventually be swept away. He entreated them to remember, that, if the government were in a minority in the State, they had a majority of every State in the Union to join them.[2]

He returned to Congress immediately. But there he found that the reliance which he had placed upon the ability of the Confederation to interfere and suppress such a rebellion was not well founded. The power was even doubted, or denied, by some of the best statesmen in that body; and although the insurrection was happily put down by the government of the State itself, the fearful exposure of a want of external power adequate to such emergencies produced in Mr. King, as in many others, a great change of views, both as to the necessity for a radical change of the national government and as to the mode of

[1] Ante, p. 266 et seq. [2] Ibid

effecting it. His vote, in February, was given to the proposition introduced by the delegation of New York for a national convention; and when that failed, he united with his colleague, Mr. Dane, in bringing forward the resolution by which the Convention was finally sanctioned in Congress.[1]

The Convention having been sanctioned by Congress, no man was more ready than Mr. King to maintain its power to deliberate on and propose any alterations that Congress could have suggested in the Federal Articles. He held that the proposing of an entire change in the mode of suffrage in the national legislature, from a representation of the States alone to a representation of the people, was within the scope of their powers, and consistent with the Union; for if that Union, on the one hand, involved the idea of a confederation, on the other hand it contained also the idea of consolidation, from which a national character resulted to the individuals of whom the States were composed. He doubted the practicability of annihilating the State governments, but thought that much of their power ought to be taken from them.[2] He declared, that, when every *man* in America might be secured in his rights, by a government founded on equality of representation, he could not sacrifice such a substantial good to the phantom of *State* sovereignty. If this illusion were to continue to prevail, he should be prepared for any event, rather than sit down under a government founded on a vicious prin-

1 Journals, XII. 15-17. 2 Madison, Elliot, V. 212, 213.

ciple of representation, and one that must be as short-lived as it would be unjust.[1]

There is one feature of the Constitution with which the name of Mr. King should always be connected, and of which he may be said, indeed, to have been the author. Towards the close of the session, he introduced the prohibition on the States to pass laws affecting the obligation of contracts. It appears that the Ordinance for the government of the Northwestern Territory, which had been passed by Congress about a month previous, contained a similar prohibition on the States to be formed out of that territory. That any of the jurists who were concerned in the framing of either instrument foresaw at the moment all the great future importance and extensive operation of this wise and effective provision, we are not authorized to affirm. But a clause which has enabled the supreme national judicature to exercise a vast, direct, and uniform influence on the security of property throughout all the States of this Confederacy, should be permanently connected with the names of its authors.[2]

[1] Madison, Elliot, V. 266.

[2] The Ordinance for the government of the Northwestern Territory was drawn by Nathan Dane of Massachusetts. It was reported in Congress July 11th, 1787, and was passed July 13th. The committee by whom it was reported were Messrs. Carrington and R. H. Lee of Virginia, Kearney of Delaware, Smith of New York, and Mr. Dane. The clause relating to contracts was in these words: "And in the just preservation of rights and property, it is understood and declared, that no law ought ever to be made or have force in the said territory, that shall in any manner whatever interfere with or affect private contracts or engagements, *bonâ fide* and without fraud previously formed." On the 28th of August, Mr. King moved in the Conven-

Mr. King was but little past the age of thirty when the Constitution was adopted. After that event, he went to reside in the city of New York, and entered upon the career of distinction which filled up the residue of his life, as a Senator in Congress, and as Minister to England. No formal biography of him has yet appeared; but when that duty shall have been discharged by those to whom it appropriately belongs, there will be added to our literature an account of a man of the most eminent abilities and the purest patriotism, whose influence and agency in the great transactions which attended the origin and first operations of the government were of the utmost importance.

tion to insert the same clause in the Constitution; but it was opposed, and was not finally adopted until September 14, when it was incorporated in the phraseology in which it now stands in the Constitution. (Madison, Elliot, V. 485; Journal of the Convention, Elliot, I. 311.)

CHAPTER XIII.

Charles Cotesworth Pinckney.

Charles Cotesworth Pinckney of South Carolina, the eldest son of a chief justice of that Colony, distinguished both as a soldier and a civilian, was educated in England, and read law at the Temple. He returned to his native province in 1769, and commenced the practice of his profession; which, like many of the young American barristers of that day, he was obliged to abandon for the duties of the camp, when the troubles of the Revolution began. He became colonel of the first regiment of the Carolina infantry, and served under General Moultrie in the defence of the fort on Sullivan's Island. This gallant resistance having freed the South, for a time, from invasion, Pinckney repaired to the Northern army, and was made aide-de-camp to General Washington; in which capacity he served at the battles of the Brandywine and Germantown. He afterwards acquired great distinction in the defence of South Carolina against the British under Sir Henry Clinton.

On the return of peace, he devoted himself to the law, in which he became eminent. He belonged to that school of public men, who had been trained in the service of the country under the eye of Washington, and who had experienced with him the fatal defects of the successive governments which followed the Declaration of Independence. Of his abilities, patriotism, and purity of character we have the strongest evidence, in the repeated efforts made by Washington, after the establishment of the Constitution, to induce him to accept some of the most important posts in the government.

He was, indeed, one of that order of men to whom Washington gave his entire confidence from the first. A ripe scholar, a profound lawyer, with Revolutionary laurels of the most honorable kind, — wise, energetic, and disinterested, — it is not singular that the people of South Carolina should have selected him as one of their delegates to an assembly, which was to frame a new constitution of government for the country to whose service his earlier years had been devoted.

General Pinckney entered the Convention with a desire to adhere, if possible, to the characteristic principles of the Confederation; but also with the wish to make that government more effective, by giving to it distinct departments and enlarged powers.[1] But in the progress of the discussions, he surrendered these views, and became a party to those arrangements by which mutual concessions between the opposing sections of the Union made a different form of government a practicable result.

[1] Madison, Elliot, V. 133.

He was a strenuous supporter of the interests of the slaveholding States, in all that related to their right to hold and increase their slave population. He contended earnestly against a grant of authority to the general government to prohibit the importation of slaves; for he supposed that his constituents would not surrender that right. But he finally entered into the arrangement, by which the postponement of the power to prohibit the slave-trade to the year 1808 was made a ground of consent on the part of the Southern States to give the regulation of commerce to the Union. He considered it, he said, the true interest of the Southern States to have no regulation of commerce; but he yielded it, in consideration of the losses brought upon the commerce of the Eastern States by the Revolution, and of their liberality towards the interests of the Southern portion of the Confederacy.

The framers of the Constitution of the United States have often been bitterly reproached for permitting the slave-trade to be carried on for twenty years after the period of its formation; and the Eastern States have been especially accused of a sordid spirit of trade in purchasing for themselves the advantage of a national regulation of commerce by this concession. It is the duty of History, however, to record the facts in their true relations.

At the time when the Convention for framing our Constitution was assembled, no nation had prohibited the African slave-trade. The English Quakers, following the example of their American brethren, had begun to move upon the subject, but it was not brought formally before Parliament until 1788; the trade was not abolished by act of Parliament until 1807, nor made a felony until 1810. Napoleon's decree of 1815 was the first French enactment against the traffic.

But in 1787, many of the members of the American Convention insisted that the power to put an end to this trade ought to be vested in the new government which they were endeavoring to form. But they found certain of the Southern States unwilling to deprive themselves of the supply of this species of labor for their new and yet unoccupied lands. Those States would not consent to a power of immediate prohibition, and they were extremely reluctant to yield even a power that might be used at a future period. They preferred to keep the whole subject in their own hands, and to determine for themselves when the importation should cease. The members of the Convention, therefore, who desired the abolition of this trade, found that, if they attempted to force these States to a concession that it ought to be immediately prohibited, either the regulation of commerce — the chief object for which the Convention had been called — could not be obtained for the new Constitution, or, if it were obtained, several of the Southern States would be excluded from the Union. The question, then, that presented itself to them was a great question of humanity and public policy, to be judged and decided upon all the circumstances that surrounded it.

Were they to form a Union that should include only those States willing to consent to an immediate prohibition of the slave-trade, and thus leave the rest of the States out of that Union, and independent of its power to restrain the importation of slaves? Were they to abandon the hope of forming a new Constitution for the thirteen States that had gone together through all the conflicts and trials and sacrifices of the Revolution, or were they to form such a government, and secure to it the power at some early period of putting an end to this traffic? If they were to do the latter, — if the cause of humanity demanded action upon this and all the other great objects dependent upon their decisions, — how could the commercial interests of the country be better used, than in the acquisition of a power to free its commerce from the stain and reproach of this inhuman traffic? By the arrangement which was to form one of the principal "compromises" of the Constitution, American commerce might achieve for itself the opportunity to do what no nation had yet done. By this arrangement, it might be implied in the fundamental law of the new government about to be created for the American people, that the abolition of the slave-trade was an object that ought to engage the attention of Christian states. Without it, the abolition of this trade could not be secured within any time or by any means capable of being foreseen or even conjectured.

That the framers of the Constitution judged wisely: that they acted upon motives which will enable

History to shield them from all reasonable reproach; and that they brought about a result alike honorable to themselves and to their country, — will not be denied by those who remember and duly appreciate the fact, that the Congress of the United States, under the Constitution, was the first legislative body in the world to prohibit the carrying of slaves to the territories of foreign countries.[1]

It is no inconsiderable honor to the statesmen situated as General Pinckney and other representatives of the Southern States were, that they should have frankly yielded the prejudices, and what they supposed to be the interests, of their constituents, to the great object of forming a more perfect union. Certainly they could urge, with equal if not greater force and truth, the same arguments for the continuance of the slave-trade, which for nearly twenty years afterwards were continually heard in the British Parliament, and which postponed its abolition until long after the people of England had become satisfied both of its inhumanity and its impolicy. Whether General Pinckney was right or wrong in the opinion that his constituents needed no national regulation of commerce, there can be no doubt of his sincerity when he expressed it. Nor can there be any doubt that he was fully convinced of the fact, when he asserted that they would not adopt a

[1] Denmark, it is said, abolished the foreign slave-trade and the importation into her colonies in 1792, but the prohibitions were not to take effect until 1804. 1 Kent's Commentaries, 198, note (citing Mr. Wheaton).

constitution that should vest in the national government an immediate power to prohibit the importation of slaves. He made, therefore, a real concession, when he consented to the prohibition at the end of twenty years, and he made it in order that the union of the thirteen States might be preserved under a Constitution adequate to its wants.

For this, as well as for other services, he is entitled to a place of honor among the great men who framed the charter of our national liberties; and when we recollect that by his action he armed the national government with a power to free the American name from the disgrace of tolerating the slave-trade, before it was effectually put down by any other people in Christendom, we need not hesitate to rank him high among those who made great sacrifices for the general welfare of the country and the general good of mankind.[1]

[1] In the first draft of the Constitution reported by the Committee of Detail, it was provided that the importation of such persons as the States might think proper to admit should not be prohibited. When the committee to arrange, if possible, certain compromises between the Northern and Southern States was raised, this provision, with other matters, was referred, and it was finally agreed that the importation should not be prohibited before the year 1808. After the adoption of the Constitution, Congress, by the acts of March 22d, 1794, and May 10, 1800, prohibited the citizens and residents of the United States from carrying slaves to any foreign territory for the purpose of traffic. By the act of March 2, 1807, the importation of slaves into the United States after January 1, 1808, was prohibited under severe penalties. In 1818 and 1819 these penalties were further increased, and in 1820, the offence was made piracy. Although the discussion of the subject commenced in England at about the same time (1788), it was nearly twenty years before a bill could be carried through Parliament for the abolition of

the traffic. Through the whole of that period, and down to the very last, counsel were repeatedly heard at the bar, in behalf of interested parties, to oppose the reform. The trade was finally abolished by act of Parliament in March, 1807; it was made a felony in 1810, and declared to be piracy in 1824. While, therefore, the representatives of a few of the Southern States of this Union refused to consent to an immediate prohibition, they did consent to engraft upon the Constitution what was in effect a declaration that the trade should be prohibited at a fixed period of time; and the trade was thus abolished by the United States, under a government of limited powers, with respect to their own territories, as soon as it was abolished by the "omnipotent" Parliament of Great Britain. Moreover, by consenting to give to the Union the power to regulate commerce, the Southern States enabled Congress to abolish the slave-trade with foreign countries thirteen years before the same trade was made unlawful to British vessels.

CHAPTER XIV.

WILSON.

JAMES WILSON, a signer of the Declaration of Independence, and one of the early Judges of the Supreme Court of the United States, was one of the first jurists in America during the latter part of the last century.

He was born in Scotland about the year 1742. After studying at Glasgow, St. Andrews, and Edinburgh, he emigrated to Pennsylvania in 1766. He became, soon after his arrival, a tutor in the Philadelphia College, in which place he acquired great distinction as a classical scholar. He subsequently studied the law, and was admitted to the bar; and, after practising at different places, took up his residence at Philadelphia, where he continued to reside during the rest of his life.[1]

For six years out of the twelve that elapsed from 1775 to the summoning of the Convention of 1787, he was a member of Congress. Concerned in all the great measures of independence, the establishment of the Confederation, the peace, and the reve-

[1] Encyclopædia Americana, Art. "Wilson, James."

nue system of 1783, he had acquired a fund of political experience, which became of great value to the country and to himself. Although a foreigner by birth, he was thoroughly American in all his sentiments and feelings, and, at the time he entered the Convention, there were few public men in the country who perceived more clearly the causes of the inherent weakness of the existing government. During the war, he had always considered the States, with respect to that war, as forming one community;[1] and he did not admit the idea, that, when the Colonies became independent of Great Britain, they became independent of each other.[2] From the Declaration of Independence he deduced the doctrine that the States by which that measure was adopted were independent in their confederated character, and not as individual communities. This rather subtile distinction may seem now to have been of no great practical moment, since the Confederation had actually united the States as such, rather than the inhabitants of the States. But it was one of the positions assumed by those who desired to combat the idea that the States, when assembled in Convention, were restrained, by their position as equal and independent sovereignties, from adopting a plan of government founded on a representation of the people. To this objection Mr. Wilson repeatedly addressed himself, and his efforts had great influence in causing the adoption of the principle by which

[1] Madison, Elliot, V. 78.
[2] Ibid. 213.

the people of the States became directly represented in the government in the ratio of their numbers. He showed that this principle had been improperly violated in the Confederation, in consequence of the urgent necessity of forming a union, and the impossibility at that time of forming any other than a union of the States. As a new partition of the States was now impracticable, it became necessary for them to surrender a portion of their sovereignties, and to permit their inhabitants to enter into direct relations with a new federal union. He pointed out the twofold relation in which the people must henceforth stand; — in the one, they would be citizens of the general government; in the other, they would be citizens of their particular State. As both governments were derived from the people, and both were designed for them, both ought to be regulated on the same principles. In no other way could the larger States consent to a new union; and if the smaller States could not admit the justice of a proportionate representation, it was in vain to expect to form a constitution that would embrace and satisfy the whole country.

This great idea of a representative government was in fact the aim of all Mr. Wilson's exertions; and when the Constitution was formed, he enforced this idea in the Convention of Pennsylvania with singular power. His speech in that body is one of the most comprehensive and luminous commentaries on the Constitution that have come down to us from that period. It drew from Washington a high encomium, and it gained the vote of Pennsylvania for the new government, against the ingenious and captivating objections of its opponents.

The life of this wise, able, and excellent man was comparatively short. In 1789, he was appointed by Washington a Judge of the Supreme Court of the United States. While on a circuit in North Carolina, in the year 1798, he died at Edenton, at about the age of fifty-six. The character of his mind and the sources of his influence will be best appreciated, by examining some of the more striking passages of his great speech on the Constitution.[1]

[1] The following extracts from the speech referred to will well repay a careful perusal.

"*Tacitus*, — the profound politician Tacitus, — who lived towards the latter end of those ages which are now denominated *ancient*, who undoubtedly had studied the constitutions of all the states and kingdoms known before and in his time, and who certainly was qualified, in an uncommon degree, for understanding the full force and operation of each of them, considers, after all he had known and read, a mixed government, composed of the three simple forms, as a thing rather to be wished than expected. And he thinks that, if such a government could even be instituted, its duration could not be long. One thing is very certain, — that the doctrine of representation in government was altogether unknown to the ancients. Now, the knowledge and practice of this doctrine is, in my opinion, essential to every system that can possess the qualities of freedom, wisdom, and energy.

"It is worthy of remark, and the remark may, perhaps, excite some surprise, that representation of the people is not, even at this day, the sole principle of any government in Europe. Great Britain boasts — and she may well boast — of the improvement she has made in politics by the admission of representation; for the improvement is important as far as it goes; but it by no means goes far enough. Is the executive power of Great Britain founded on representation? This is not pretended. Before the Revolution, many of the kings claimed to reign by divine right, and others by hereditary right; and even at the Revolution, nothing further was effected or attempted than the recognition of certain parts of an original contract (*Blackstone*, 233), supposed, at some former remote period, to have been made between the king and the people. A contract seems to exclude, rather than to imply, delegated power. The judges of Great Britain are appointed by the crown. The judicial authority, therefore, does not depend upon representation, even in its most remote degree. Does representation prevail in the legislative department of the British government? Even here it does not predominate, though it may serve as a check. The legislature consists of three branches, — the king, the lords, and the commons. Of these, only the latter are supposed by the constitution to represent the authority of the people. This short analysis clearly shows to what a narrow corner of the British constitution the principle of representation is confined. I believe it does not extend farther, if so far, in any other government in Europe. For the American States were reserved the glory and the happiness of diffusing this vital principle throughout the constituent parts of government. Representation is the chain of communication between the people and those to whom they have committed the exercise of the powers of government. This chain may consist of one or more links, but in all cases it should be sufficiently strong and discernible.

"To be left without guide or precedent was not the only difficulty in which the Convention were involved, by proposing to their constituents a plan of a confederate republic. They found themselves embarrassed with another, of peculiar delicacy and importance. I mean that of drawing a proper line between the national government and the governments of the several States. It was easy to discover a proper and satisfactory principle on the subject. Whatever object of government is confined, in its operation and effects, within the bounds of a particular State, should be considered as belonging to the government of that State; whatever object of government extends, in its operation or effects, beyond the bounds of a particular State, should be considered as belonging to the government of the United States. But though this principle be sound and satisfactory, its application to particular cases would be accompanied with much difficulty, because, in its application, room must be allowed for great discretionary latitude of construction of the principle. In order to lessen or remove the difficulty arising from discretionary construction on this subject, an enumeration of particular instances, in which the application of the principle ought to take place, has been attempted with much industry and care. It is only in mathematical science that a line can be described with mathematical precision. But I flatter myself that, upon the strictest investigation, the enumeration will be found to be safe and unexceptionable, and accurate, too, in as great a degree as accuracy can be expected in a subject of this nature. Particulars under this head will be more properly explained, when we descend to the minute view of the enumeration which is made in the proposed Constitution.

"After all, it will be necessary that, on a subject so peculiarly delicate as this, much prudence, much candor, much moderation, and much liberality should be exercised and displayed both by the federal government and by the governments of the several States. It is to be hoped that those virtues in government will be exercised and displayed, when we consider that the powers of the federal government and those of the State governments are drawn from sources equally pure. If a difference can be discovered between them, it is in favor of the federal government, because that government is founded on a representation of the *whole* Union; whereas the government of any particular State is founded only on the representation of a part, inconsiderable when compared with the whole. Is it not more reasonable to suppose that the counsels of the whole will embrace the interest of every part, than that the counsels of any part will embrace the interests of the whole?

"I intend not, Sir, by this description of the difficulties with which the Convention were surrounded, to magnify their skill or their merit in surmounting them, or to insinuate that any predicament in which the Convention stood should prevent the closest and most cautious scrutiny into the performance which they have exhibited to their constituents and to the world. My intention is of far other and higher aim, — to evince, by the conflicts and difficulties which must arise from the many and powerful causes which I have enumerated, that it is hopeless and impracticable to form a constitution which, in every part, will be acceptable to every citizen, or even to every government, in the United States; and that all which can be expected is, to form such a constitution as, upon the whole, is the best that can possibly be obtained. Man and perfection! — a state and perfection! — an assemblage of states and perfection! Can we reasonably expect, however ardently we may wish, to behold the glorious union?

"I can well recollect, though I believe I cannot convey to others, the impression which, on many occasions, was made by the difficulties which surrounded and pressed the Convention. The great undertaking sometimes seemed to be at a stand; at other times, its motion seemed to be retrograde. At the conclusion, however, of our work, many of the members expressed their astonishment at the success with which it terminated.

"Having enumerated some of the difficulties which the Convention were obliged to encounter in the course of their proceedings, I shall next point out the end which they proposed to accomplish. Our wants, our talents, our affections, our passions, all tell us that we were made for a state of society. But a state of society could not be supported long or happily without some civil restraint. It is true, that, in a state of nature, any one individual may act uncontrolled by others; but it is equally true, that, in such a state, every other individual may act uncontrolled by him. Amidst this universal independence, the dissensions and animosities between interfering members of the society would be numerous and ungovernable. The consequence would be, that each member, in such a natural state, would enjoy less liberty, and suffer more interruption, than he would in a regulated society. Hence the universal introduction of governments of some kind or other into the social state. The liberty of every member is increased by this introduction; for each gains more by the limitation of the freedom of every other member, than he loses by the limitation of his own. The result is, that civil government is necessary to the perfection and happiness of man. In forming this government, and carrying it into execution, it is *essential* that the *interest* and *authority* of the whole community should be binding in every part of it.

"The foregoing principles and conclusions are generally admitted to be just and sound with regard to the nature and formation of single governments, and the duty of submission to them. In some cases, they will apply, with much propriety and force, to states already formed. The advantages and necessity of civil government among individuals in society are not greater or stronger than, in some situations and circumstances, are the advantages and necessity of a federal government among states. A natural and very important question now presents itself, — Is such the situation, are such the circumstances, of the United States? A proper answer to this question will unfold some very interesting truths.

"The United States may adopt any one of four different systems. They may become consolidated into one government, in which the separate existence of the States shall be entirely absolved. They may reject any plan of union or association, and act as separate and unconnected States. They may form two or more confederacies. They may unite in one federal republic. Which of these systems ought to have been formed by the Convention? To support, with vigor, a single government over the whole extent of the United States, would demand a system of the most unqualified and the most unremitted despotism. Such a number of separate States, contiguous in situation, unconnected and disunited in government, would be, at one time, the prey of foreign force, foreign influence, and foreign intrigue; at another, the victims of mutual rage, rancor, and revenge. Neither of these systems found advocates in the late Convention. I presume they will not find advocates in this. Would it be proper to divide the United States into two or more confederacies? It will not be unadvisable to take a more minute survey of this subject. Some aspects under which it may be viewed are far from being, at first sight, uninviting. Two or more confederacies would be each more compact and more manageable than a single one extending over the same territory. By dividing the United States into two or more confederacies, the great collision of interests apparently or really different and contrary, in the *whole extent* of their dominion, would be broken, and, in a great measure, disappear, in the several parts. But these advantages, which are discovered from certain points of view, are greatly overbalanced by inconveniences that will appear on a more accurate examination. Animosities, and perhaps wars, would arise from assigning the extent, the limits, and the rights of the different confederacies. The expenses of governing would be multiplied by the number of federal governments. The danger resulting from foreign influence and mutual dissensions would not, perhaps, be less great and alarming in the instance of different confederacies, than in the instance of different, though more numerous, unassociated States.

"These observations, and many others that might be made on the subject, will be sufficient to evince that a division of the United States into a number of separate confederacies would probably be an unsatisfactory and an unsuccessful experiment. The remaining system which the American States may adopt, is a union of them under one confederate republic. It will not be necessary to employ much time, or many arguments, to show that this is the most eligible system that can be proposed. By adopting this system, the vigor and decision of a wide-spreading monarchy may be joined to the freedom and beneficence of a contracted republic. The extent of territory, the diversity of climate and soil, the number and greatness and connection of lakes and rivers with which the United States are intersected and almost surrounded, — all indicate an enlarged government to be fit and advantageous for them. The principles and dispositions of their citizens indicate that, in this government, liberty shall reign triumphant. Such, indeed, have been the general opinions and wishes entertained since the era of independence. If those opinions and wishes are as well founded as they have been general, the late Convention were justified in proposing to their constituents *one* confederate republic, as the best system of a national government for the United States.

"In forming this system, it was proper to give minute attention to the interest of all the parts; but there was a duty of still higher import, — to feel and to show a predominating regard to the superior interests of the whole. If this great principle had not prevailed, the plan before us would never have made its appearance. The same principle that was so necessary in forming it is equally necessary in our deliberations, whether we should reject or ratify it.

"I make these observations with a design to prove and illustrate this great and important truth, — that, in our decisions on the work of the late Convention, we should not limit our views and regards to the State of Pennsylvania. The aim of the Convention was to form a system of good and efficient government, on the more extensive scale of the United States. In this, and in every other instance, the work should be judged with the same spirit with which it was performed. A principle of duty, as well as candor, demands this.

"We have remarked, that civil government is necessary to the perfection of society; we now remark, that civil liberty is necessary to the perfection of civil government. Civil liberty is natural liberty itself, divested of only that part which, placed in the government, produces more good and happiness to the community than if it had remained in the individual. Hence it follows that civil liberty, while it resigns a part of natural liberty, retains the free and generous exercise of all the human faculties, so far as it is compatible with the public welfare.

"In considering and developing the nature and end of the system before us, it is necessary to mention another kind of liberty, which has not yet, as far as I know, received a name. I shall distinguish it by the appellation of *federal liberty*. When a single government is instituted, the individuals of which it is composed surrender to it a part of their natural independence, which they before enjoyed as men. When a confederate republic is instituted, the communities of which it is composed surrender to it a part of their political independence, which they before enjoyed as States. The principles which directed, in the former case, what part of the natural liberty of the man ought to be given up, and what part ought to be retained, will give similar directions in the latter case. The States should resign to the national government that part, and that part only, of their political liberty, which, placed in that government, will produce more good to the whole than if it had remained in the several States. While they resign this part of their political liberty, they retain the free and generous exercise of all their other faculties, as States, so far as it is compatible with the welfare of the general and superintending confederacy.

"Since *States*, as well as *citizens*, are represented in the Constitution before us, and form the objects on which that Constitution is proposed to operate, it was necessary to notice and define *federal* as well as *civil* liberty.

"These general reflections have been made in order to introduce, with more propriety and advantage, a practical illustration of the end proposed to be accomplished by the late Convention.

"It has been too well known, it has been too severely felt, that the present Confederation is inadequate to the government, and to the exigencies, of the United States. The great struggle for Liberty in this country, should it be unsuccessful, will probably be the last one which she will have for her existence and prosperity in any part of the globe. And it must be confessed that this struggle has, in some of the stages of its progress, been attended with symptoms that foreboded no fortunate issue. To the iron hand of Tyranny, which was lifted up against her, she manifested, indeed, an intrepid superiority. She broke in pieces the fetters which were forged for her, and showed that she was unassailable by force. But she was environed with dangers of another kind, and springing from a very different source. While she kept her eye steadily fixed on the efforts of oppression, licentiousness was secretly undermining the rock on which she stood.

"Need I call to your remembrance the *contrasted* scenes of which we have been witnesses? On the glorious conclusion of our conflict with Britain, what high expectations were formed concerning us by others! What high expectations did we form concerning ourselves! Have those expectations been realized? No. What has been the cause? Did our citizens lose their perseverance and magnanimity? No. Did they become insensible of resentment and indignation at any high-handed attempt that might have been made to injure or enslave them? No. What, then, has been the cause? The truth is, we dreaded danger only on one side: this we manfully repelled. But, on another side, danger, not less formidable, but more insidious, stole in upon us; and our unsuspicious tempers were not sufficiently attentive either to its approach or to its operations. Those whom foreign strength could not overpower have wellnigh become the victims of internal anarchy.

"If we become a little more particular, we shall find that the foregoing representation is by no means exaggerated. When we had baffled all the menaces of foreign power, we neglected to establish among ourselves a government that would insure domestic vigor and stability. What was the consequence? The commencement of peace was the commencement of every disgrace and distress that could befall a people in a peaceful state. Devoid of *national power*, we could not prohibit the extravagance of our importations, nor could we derive a revenue from their excess. Devoid of national *importance*, we could not procure for our exports a tolerable sale at foreign markets. Devoid of national *credit*, we saw our public securities melt in the hands of the holders, like snow before the sun. Devoid of national *dignity*, we could not, in some instances, perform our treaties on our part; and, in other instances, we could neither obtain nor compel the performance of them on the part of others. Devoid of national *energy*, we could not carry into execution our own resolutions, decisions, or laws.

"Shall I become more particular still? The tedious detail would disgust me. The years of languor are now over. We have felt the dishonor with which we have been covered; we have seen the destruction with which we have been threatened. We have penetrated to the causes of both, and when we have once discovered them, we have begun to search for the means of removing them. For the confirmation of these remarks, I need not appeal to an enumeration of facts. The proceedings of Congress, and of the several States, are replete with them. They all point out the weakness and insufficiency as the cause, and an *efficient* general government as the only cure, of our political distempers.

"Under these impressions, and with these views, was the late Convention appointed; and under these impressions, and with these views, the late Convention met.

"We now see the great end which they proposed to accomplish. It was to frame, for the consideration of their constituents, one federal and national constitution, — a constitution that would produce the advantages of good, and prevent the inconveniences of bad government; — a constitution whose beneficence and energy would pervade the whole Union, and bind and embrace the interests of every part; — a constitution that would insure peace, freedom, and happiness to the States and people of America.

"We are now naturally led to examine the means by which they proposed to accomplish this end. This opens more particularly to our view the discussion before us. But, previously to our entering upon it, it will not be improper to state some general and leading principles of government, which will receive particular application in the course of our investigations.

"There necessarily exists, in every government, a power from which there is no appeal, and which, for that reason, may be termed supreme, absolute, and uncontrollable. Where does this power reside? To this question writers on different governments will give different answers.

Sir William Blackstone will tell you, that in Britain the power is lodged in the British Parliament; that the Parliament may alter the form of the government; and that its power is absolute, without control. The idea of a constitution, limiting and superintending the operations of legislative authority, seems not to have been accurately understood in Britain. There are, at least, no traces of practice conformable to such a principle. The British Constitution is just what the British Parliament pleases. When the Parliament transferred legislative authority to Henry VIII., the act transferring could not, in the strict acceptation of the term, be called unconstitutional.

"To control the power and conduct of the legislature by an overruling constitution, was an improvement in the science and practice of government reserved to the American States.

"Perhaps some politician, who has not considered with sufficient accuracy our political systems, would answer that, in our governments, the supreme power was vested in the constitutions. This opinion approaches a step nearer to the truth, but does not reach it. The truth is, that, in our governments, the supreme, absolute, and uncontrollable power *remains* in the people. As our constitutions are superior to our legislatures, so the people are superior to our constitutions. Indeed, the superiority, in this last instance, is much greater; for the people possess over our constitutions control in *act*, as well as right.

"The consequence is, that the people may change the constitutions whenever and however they please. This is a right of which no positive institution can ever deprive them.

"These important truths, Sir, are far from being merely speculative. We, at this moment, speak and deliberate under their immediate and benign influence. To the operation of these truths we are to ascribe the scene, hitherto unparalleled, which America now exhibits to the world, — a gentle, a peaceful, a voluntary, and a deliberate transition from one constitution of government to another. In other parts of the world, the idea of revolutions in government is, by a mournful and an indissoluble association, connected with the idea of wars, and all the calamities attendant on wars. But happy experience teaches us to view such revolutions in a very different light, — to consider them only as progressive steps in improving the knowledge of government, and increasing the happiness of society and mankind.

"Oft have I marked, with silent pleasure and admiration, the force and prevalence, through the United States, of the principle that the supreme power resides in the people, and that they never part with it. It may be called the *panacea* in politics. There can be no disorder in the community but may here receive a radical cure. If the error be in the legislature, it may be corrected by the constitution; if in the constitution, it may be corrected by the people. There is a remedy, therefore, for every distemper in government, if the people are not wanting to themselves; if they are wanting to themselves, there is no remedy. From their power, as we have seen, there is no appeal; of their error, there is no superior principle of correction.

"There are three simple species of government; — monarchy, where the supreme power is in a single person; aristocracy, where the supreme power is in a select assembly, the members of which either fill up, by election, the vacancies in their own body, or succeed to their places in it by inheritance, property, or in respect of some *personal* right or qualification; a republic or democracy, where the people at large *retain* the supreme power, and act either collectively or by representation.

"Each of these species of government has its advantages and disadvantages.

"The advantages of a *monarchy* are strength, despatch, secrecy, unity of counsel. Its disadvantages are tyranny, expense, ignorance of the situation and wants of the people, insecurity, unnecessary wars, evils attending elections or successions.

"The advantages of *aristocracy* are wisdom, arising from experience and education. Its disadvantages are dissensions among themselves, oppression to the lower orders.

"The advantages of *democracy* are liberty, equality, cautious and salutary laws, public spirit, frugality, peace, opportunities of exciting and producing abilities of the best citizens. Its disadvantages are dissensions, the delay and disclosure of public counsels, the imbecility of public measures, retarded by the necessity of a numerous consent.

"A government may be composed of two or more of the simple forms above mentioned. Such is the British government. It would be an improper government for the United States, because it is inadequate to such an extent of territory, and because it is suited to an establishment of different orders of men. A more minute comparison between some parts of the British Constitution, and some parts of the plan before us, may perhaps find a proper place in a subsequent period of our business.

"What is the nature and kind of that government which has been proposed for the United States by the late Convention? In its principle, it is purely democratical. But that principle is applied in different forms, in order to obtain the advantages, and exclude the inconveniences, of the simple modes of government.

"If we take an extended and accurate view of it, we shall find the streams of power running in different directions, in different dimensions, and at different heights, — watering, adorning, and fertilizing the fields and meadows through which their courses are led; but if we trace them, we shall discover that they all originally flow from one abundant fountain.

"In this Constitution, *all authority is derived from the people.*

"Fit occasions will hereafter offer for particular remarks on the different parts of the plan."

After an elaborate examination of the Constitution, he thus concludes: —

"A free government has often been compared to a pyramid. This allusion is made with peculiar propriety in the system before you; it is laid on the broad basis of the people; its powers gradually rise, while they are confined in proportion as they ascend, until they end in that most permanent of all forms. When you examine all its parts, they will invariably be found to preserve that essential mark of free governments, — a chain of connection with the people.

"Such, Sir, is the nature of this system of government; and the important question at length presents itself to our view, — Shall it be ratified, or shall it be rejected, by this Convention? In order to enable us still further to form a judgment on this truly momentous and interesting point, on which all we have, or can have, dear to us on earth is materially depending, let us for a moment consider the consequences that will result from one or the other measure. Suppose we reject this system of government; what will be the consequence? Let the farmer say, — he whose produce remains unasked for; nor can he find a single market for its consumption, though his fields are blessed with luxuriant abundance. Let the manufacturer, and let the mechanic, say; they can feel, and tell their feelings. Go along the wharves of Philadelphia, and observe the melancholy silence that reigns. I appeal not to those who enjoy places and abundance under the present government; they may well dilate upon the easy and happy situation of our country. Let the merchants tell you what is our commerce; let them say what has been their situation since the return of peace, — an era which they might have expected would furnish additional sources to our trade, and a continuance, and even an increase, to their fortunes. Have these ideas been realized? or do they not lose some of their capital in every adventure, and continue the unprofitable trade from year to year, subsisting under the hopes of happier times under an efficient general government? The ungainful trade carried on by our merchants has a baneful influence on the interests of the manufacturer, the mechanic, and the farmer; and these, I believe, are the chief interests of the people of the United States.

"I will go further. Is there now a government among us that can do a single act that a national government ought to do? Is there any power of the United States that can *command* a single shilling? This is a plain and a home question.

"Congress may recommend; they can do no more: they may require; but they must not proceed one step further. If things are bad now, — and that they are not worse is only owing to hopes of improvement or change in the system, — will they become better when those hopes are disappointed? We have been told, by honorable gentlemen on this floor, that it is improper to urge this kind of argument in favor of a new system of government, or against the old one: unfortunately, Sir, these things are too severely felt to be omitted; the people feel them; they pervade all classes of citizens, and every situation from New Hampshire to Georgia: the argument of necessity is the patriot's defence, as well as the tyrant's plea.

"Is it likely, Sir, that, if this system of government is rejected, a better will be framed and adopted? I will not expatiate on this subject; but I believe many reasons will suggest themselves to prove that such expectation would be illusory. If a better could be obtained at a future time, is there any thing wrong in this? I go further. Is there any thing wrong that cannot be amended more easily by the mode pointed out in the system itself, than could be done by calling convention after convention, before the organization of the government? Let us now turn to the consequences that will result if we assent to and ratify the instrument before you. I shall trace them as concisely as I can, because I have trespassed already too long on the patience and indulgence of the house.

"I stated, on a former occasion, one important advantage; by adopting this system, we become a *nation;* at present, we are not one. Can we perform a single national act? Can we do any thing to procure us dignity, or to preserve peace and tranquillity? Can we relieve the distress of our citizens? Can we provide for their welfare or happiness? The powers of our government are mere sound. If we offer to treat with a nation, we receive this humiliating answer: 'You cannot, in propriety of language, make a treaty, because you have no power to execute it.' Can we borrow money? There are too many examples of unfortunate creditors existing, both on this and the other side of the Atlantic, to expect success from this expedient. But could we borrow money, we cannot command a fund, to enable us to pay either the principal or interest; for, in instances where our friends have advanced the principal, they have been obliged to advance the interest also, in order to prevent the principal from being annihilated in their hands by depreciation. Can we raise an army? The prospect of a war is highly probable. The accounts we receive, by every vessel from Europe, mention that the highest exertions are making in the ports and arsenals of the greatest maritime powers. But whatever the consequence may be, are we to lie supine? We know we are unable, under the Articles of Confederation, to exert ourselves; and shall we continue so, until a stroke be made on our commerce, or we see the debarkation of a hostile army on our unprotected shores? Who will guarantee that our property will not be laid waste, that our towns will not be put under contribution, by a small naval force, and subjected to all the horror and devastation of war? May not this be done without opposition, at least effectual opposition, in the present situation of our country? There may be safety over the Appalachian Mountains, but there can be none on our sea-coast. With what propriety can we hope our flag will be respected, while we have not a single gun to fire in its defence?

"Can we expect to make internal improvement, or accomplish any of those great national objects which I formerly alluded to, when we cannot find money to remove a single rock out of a river?

"This system, Sir, will at least make us a nation, and put it in the power of the Union to act as such. We shall be considered as such by every nation in the world. We shall regain the confidence of our citizens, and command the respect of others.

"As we shall become a nation, I trust that we shall also form a national character, and that this character will be adapted to the principles and genius of our system of government: as yet we possess none; our language, manners, customs, habits, and dress depend too much upon those of other countries. Every nation, in these respects, should possess originality; there are not, on any part of the globe, finer qualities for forming a national character, than those possessed by the children of America. Activity, perseverance, industry, laudable emulation, docility in acquiring information, firmness in adversity, and patience and magnanimity under the greatest hardships; — from these materials, what a respectable national character may be raised! In addition to this character, I think there is strong reason to believe that America may take the lead in literary improvements and national importance. This is a subject which, I confess, I have spent much pleasing time in considering. That language, Sir, which shall become most generally known in the civilized world will impart great importance over the nation that shall use it. The language of the United States will, in future times, be diffused over a greater extent of country than any other that we know.

The French, indeed, have made laudable attempts towards establishing a universal language; but, beyond the boundaries of France, even the French language is not spoken by one in a thousand. Besides the freedom of our country, the great improvements she has made, and will make, in the science of government, will induce the patriots and *literati* of every nation to read and understand our writings on that subject; and hence it is not improbable that she will take the lead in political knowledge.

"If we adopt this system of government, I think we may promise security, stability, and tranquillity to the governments of the different States. They would not be exposed to the danger of competition on questions of territory, or any other that have heretofore disturbed them. A tribunal is here found to decide, justly and quietly, any interfering claim; and now is accomplished what the great mind of Henry IV. of France had in contemplation, — a system of government for large and respectable dominions, united and bound together, in peace, under a superintending head, by which all their differences may be accommodated, without the destruction of the human race. We are told by Sully that this was the favorite pursuit of that good king during the last years of his life; and he would probably have carried it into execution, had not the dagger of an assassin deprived the world of his valuable life. I have, with pleasing emotion, seen the wisdom and beneficence of a less efficient power under the Articles of Confederation, in the determination of the controversy between the States of Pennsylvania and Connecticut; but I have lamented that the authority of Congress did not extend to extinguish, entirely, the spark which has kindled a dangerous flame in the district of Wyoming.

"Let gentlemen turn their attention to the amazing consequences which this principle will have in this extended country. The several States cannot war with each other; the general government is the great arbiter in contentions between them; the whole force of the Union can be called forth to reduce an aggressor to reason. What a happy exchange for the disjointed, contentious State sovereignties!

"The adoption of this system will also secure us from danger, and procure us advantages from foreign nations. This, in our situation, is of great consequence. We are still an inviting object to one European power at least; and, if we cannot defend ourselves, the temptation may become too alluring to be resisted. I do not mean that, with an efficient government, we should mix with the commotions of Europe. No, Sir; we are happily removed from them, and are not obliged to throw ourselves into the scale with any. This system will not hurry us into war;

it is calculated to guard against it. It will not be in the power of a single man, or a single body of men, to involve us in such distress; for the important power of declaring war is vested in the legislature at large: this declaration must be made with the concurrence of the House of Representatives: from this circumstance we may draw a certain conclusion, that nothing but our national interest can draw us into a war. I cannot forbear, on this occasion, the pleasure of mentioning to you the sentiments of the great and benevolent man, whose works I have already quoted on another subject. M. Necker has addressed this country in language important and applicable in the strictest degree to its situation and to the present subject. Speaking of war, and the greatest caution that all nations ought to use in order to avoid its calamities,—'And you, rising nation,' says he, 'whom generous efforts have freed from the yoke of Europe! let the universe be struck with still greater reverence at the sight of the privileges you have acquired, by seeing you continually employed for the public felicity: do not offer it as a sacrifice at the unsettled shrine of political ideas, and of the deceitful combinations of warlike ambition; avoid, or at least delay, participating in the passions of our hemisphere; make your own advantage of the knowledge which experience alone has given to our old age, and preserve, for a long time, the simplicity of childhood; in short, honor human nature, by showing that, when left to its own feelings, it is still capable of those virtues that maintain public order, and of that prudence which insures public tranquillity.'

"Permit me to offer one consideration more, that ought to induce our acceptance of this system. I feel myself lost in the contemplation of its magnitude. By adopting this system, we shall probably lay a foundation for erecting temples of liberty in every part of the earth. It has been thought by many, that on the success of the struggle America has made for freedom will depend the exertions of the brave and enlightened of other nations. The advantages resulting from this system will not be confined to the United States, but will draw from Europe many worthy characters, who pant for the enjoyment of freedom. It will induce princes, in order to preserve their subjects, to restore to them a portion of that liberty of which they have for many ages been deprived. It will be subservient to the great designs of Providence with regard to this globe,—the multiplication of mankind, their improvement in knowledge, and their advancement in happiness." (Elliot's Debates, II. 423-434, 524-529.)

CHAPTER XV.

Randolph.

Edmund Randolph, a "child of the Revolution,"[1] was Governor of Virginia at the time of the Federal Convention. Probably it was on account of his position as the chief magistrate of the State that he was, by the general consent of his colleagues, selected to bring forward the Virginia plan of government, which was submitted at an early period of the deliberations, and which became, after great modifications, the nucleus of the Constitution.

At an early age, in August, 1775, this gentleman joined the army at Cambridge, and was immediately taken into Washington's military family as an aide-de-camp.[2] He served in this capacity, however, no longer than until the following November, when he was suddenly recalled to Virginia by the death of his relative, Peyton Randolph, the President of the First Continental Congress.

In 1779, he became a member of Congress from Virginia, and served until March, 1782.

[1] His own description of himself in a speech made in the Virginia Convention which ratified the Constitution. Elliot, III. 65.

[2] Washington's Writings, IX. 66.

In 1786, he was elected Governor of Virginia, succeeding in that office Patrick Henry. In this capacity, it became his duty to secure the attendance of Washington upon the Federal Convention. This matter he managed with great tact and delicacy; and, by the aid of other friends, he succeeded in overcoming the scruples of the illustrious patriot then reposing in the retirement of Mount Vernon.

Governor Randolph's conduct with regard to the Constitution might seem to be marked by inconsistency, if we were not able to explain it by the motive of disinterested patriotism from which he evidently acted. He brought to the Convention the most serious apprehensions for the fate of the Union. But he thought that the dangers with which it was surrounded might be averted, by correcting and enlarging the Articles of Confederation. When, at length, the government which was actually framed was found to be a system containing far greater restraints upon the powers of the States than he believed to be either expedient or safe, he endeavored to procure a vote authorizing amendments to be submitted by the State conventions and to be finally decided on by another general convention. This proposition having been rejected, he declined to sign the Constitution, desiring to be free to oppose or advocate its adoption, when it should come before his own State, as his judgment might dictate.

When the time for such action came, he saw that the rejection of the Constitution must be followed by disunion. He had wearied himself in endeavoring to find a possibility of preserving the Union without an unconditional ratification by Virginia. To the people of Virginia, therefore, he painted with great force and eloquence the consequences of their becoming severed from the rest of the country. Virginia was not, he said, invulnerable. She was accessible to a foreign enemy by sea, and through the waters of the Chesapeake. Her situation by land was not less exposed. Her frontiers adjoined the States of Pennsylvania, Maryland, and North Carolina. With the first she had long had a disputed boundary, concerning which there had been imminent danger of a war, that had been averted with the greatest difficulty. With Maryland, there was an ancient controversy upon the navigation of the Potomac, and that controversy, if decided on grounds of strict right, would be determined by the charter of Maryland in favor of that State. With North Carolina, too, the boundary was still unsettled. Let them call to mind, then, the history of every part of the world, where independent nations bordered in the same way on one another. Such countries had ever been a perpetual scene of bloodshed; the inhabitants of one escaping from punishment into the other, — protection given to them, — consequent pursuit, violence, robbery, and murder. A numerous standing army, that dangerous expedient, could alone defend such borders.

On her Western frontier, Virginia was peculiarly exposed to the savages, the natural enemies of the white race, whom foreign gold could always incite to commit the most horrible ravages upon her people. Her slave population, bearing a very large proportion to the whites,[1] necessarily weakened her capacity to defend herself against such an enemy.

Virginia, then, must be defended. Could they rely on the militia? Their militia did not, at the utmost, exceed sixty thousand men. They had performed exploits of great gallantry during the late war, but no militia could be relied on as the sole protectors of any country. Besides, a part of them would be wanted for the purposes of agriculture, for manufactures, and for the mechanic arts necessary for the aid of the farmer and the planter. They must have an army; and they must also have a navy. But how were these to be maintained without money? The enormous debt of Virginia, including her proportion of the Continental debts, was already beyond her ability to pay from any revenue that could be derived from her present commerce.

In this state of things, looking forward to the consequences of a dissolution of the Union, he could not but remind the people of Virginia of what took place in 1781, when the power of a dictator was given to the commander-in-chief, to save the country from destruction. At some period, not very remote, might not their future distress impel them to do what the Dutch had done, — throw all power into the hands of a Stadtholder? How infinitely more wise and eligible than this desperate alternative would be a

[1] He stated the number of blacks to be 236,000, and that of the whites only 352,000.

union with their American brethren. "I have labored," said he, "for the continuance of the Union, — the rock of our salvation. I believe, as surely as that there is a God, that our safety, our political happiness and existence, depend on the union of the States; and that, without this union, the people of this and the other States will undergo the unspeakable calamities which discord, faction, turbulence, war, and bloodshed have produced in other countries. The American spirit ought to be mixed with American pride, to see the Union magnificently triumphant. Let that glorious pride, which once defied the British thunder, reanimate you again. Let it not be recorded of Americans, that, after having performed the most gallant exploits, after having overcome the most astonishing difficulties, and after having gained the admiration of the world by their incomparable valor and policy, they lost their acquired reputation, their national consequence and happiness, by their own indiscretion. Let no future historian inform posterity that they wanted wisdom and virtue to concur in any regular, efficient government. Should any writer, doomed to so disagreeable a task, feel the indignation of an honest historian, he would reprehend our folly with equal severity and justice. Catch the present moment, — seize it with avidity, — for it may be lost, never to be regained! If the Union be now lost, I fear it will remain so for ever. I believe gentlemen are sincere in their opposition, and actuated by pure motives; but when I maturely weigh the advantages of the

Union, and the dreadful consequences of its dissolution; when I see safety on my right, and destruction on my left; when I behold respectability and happiness acquired by one course, but annihilated by the other, — I cannot hesitate in my decision." [1]

Note. — The following account of the genealogy of Governor Randolph, for which I am indebted to one of his female descendants, was not received in season to be incorporated in the text.

Edmund Randolph was the son of John Randolph and grandson of Sir John Randolph, each of whom was Attorney-General of the Colony under the royal government. He was educated at William and Mary's College. Peyton Randolph, President of the First Continental Congress, was also a son of Sir John Randolph, and of course was uncle of Edmund Randolph, to whom he devised his estate. Sir John Randolph was one of five or six sons of William Randolph of Turkey Island in Virginia, from whom all the Randolphs in Virginia are descended. Of this William Randolph little is known, beyond the fact that he was a large landholder, and a nephew of Thomas Randolph, the poet, who flourished in the reigns of James I. and Charles I., 1605 - 1634.

[1] Debates in the Virginia Convention, Elliot, III. 65 - 84, 85, 86.

CHAPTER XVI.

Conclusion of the Present Volume.

The limits of this volume do not admit of a farther description of the Framers of the Constitution. The nine persons of whom some account has been given were the most important members of the Convention, and those who exercised the largest influence upon its decisions. But the entire list embraced other men of great distinction and ability, celebrated, before and since the Convention, in that period of the political history of America which commenced with the Revolution and closed with the eighteenth century. Such were Roger Sherman of Connecticut, Robert Morris of Pennsylvania, John Dickinson of Delaware, John Rutledge and Charles Pinckney of South Carolina, and George Mason of Virginia. Of the rest, all were men of note and influence in their respective States, possessing the full confidence of the people whom they represented.

The whole assembly consisted of only fifty-five members, representing twelve sovereign and distinct communities.[1] That so small a body should have

[1] For a full list of the Delegates, see the Appendix to this volume.

contained so large a number of statesmen of preeminent ability is a striking proof of the nature of the crisis which called it into existence. The age which had witnessed the Revolution, and the wants and failures that succeeded it, produced and trained these great men, made them capable of the highest magnanimity, and gave them the intellectual power necessary to surmount the difficulties that obstructed the progress of their country to prosperity and renown. These, with a few of their contemporaries at that moment engaged in other spheres of public duty, are the men who illustrate and adorn it, and the knowledge of their lives and actions is of unspeakable importance to the people of the United States.

To that people is committed a trust, which imposes upon them a greater responsibility than now rests upon any other people on the globe. They possess a written and exact constitution of government, framed with great wisdom by their own deputed agents, and deliberately adopted and enacted by themselves. That Constitution rules over a country of vast extent, inhabited by more than twenty millions of prosperous and intelligent freemen, who constitute one of the first nations of the world. Nowhere on the face of the globe has the experiment of self-government — that experiment so rarely tried, so rarely successful, and so important to the welfare of mankind — been conducted on a scale so grand and imposing. To prevent a failure so disastrous to the best interests of the human race as the failure of that experiment here must inevitably become; to guard this Constitution, the work of their own hands, from every kind of attack; to administer it in the wise spirit in which it was framed; to draw from it the blessings which it was designed to confer; to unfold, to cherish, and to defend its great principles for the benefit of a countless posterity; — this is the high duty imposed by a noble ancestry and an overruling Providence upon the people of this Union of each succeeding generation.

It calls upon them, with a remonstrance in whose tones there is both a warning and a cheering voice, to remember that they have a country; to appreciate and fearlessly to survey the truth, that national honor and success, internal tranquillity and peace, reputation abroad and safety at home, can exist, for them, only under the Union which the Divine government, for its own all-wise purposes, has made a necessity of their condition; and to see that the ruin of self-government in America must involve its ruin for the whole world.[1]

[1] In this connection, I cannot avoid a reference to Dr. Francis Lieber's profound and admirable work "On Civil Liberty and Self-government." Whoever will follow that very able writer in his masterly exposition of the principles of Anglican liberty, will become satisfied that the American branch of it is more strictly a system of "self-government" than any other, speaking with reference to the application of the principle to every department. The destruction of such a system, therefore, would be the destruction of self-government in its most complete form. No one can suppose that the popular principles in the English Constitution would continue to expand, as they have done for the last fifty years, if the corresponding principles in America were to be overthrown, or even if they were to receive a sensible check.

APPENDIX.

APPENDIX.

IN CONGRESS.

Circular Letter of Congress recommending the Adoption of the Articles of Confederation.

In Congress, Yorktown, November 17th, 1777.

Congress having agreed upon a plan of confederacy for securing the freedom, sovereignty, and independence of the United States, authentic copies are now transmitted for the consideration of the respective legislatures.

This business, equally intricate and important, has in its progress been attended with uncommon embarrassments and delay, which the most anxious solicitude and persevering diligence could not prevent. To form a permanent union, accommodated to the opinion and wishes of the delegates of so many States differing in habits, produce, commerce, and internal police, was found to be a work which nothing but time and reflection, conspiring with a disposition to conciliate, could mature and accomplish.

Hardly is it to be expected that any plan, in the variety of provisions essential to our union, should exactly correspond with the maxims and political views of every particular State. Let it be remarked, that, after the most careful inquiry and the fullest information, this is proposed as the best which could be adapted to the circumstances of all, and as that alone which affords any tolerable prospect of general satisfaction.

Permit us, then, earnestly to recommend these articles to the immediate and dispassionate attention of the legislatures of the respective States. Let them be candidly reviewed, under a sense of the difficulty of combining in one general system the various sentiments and interests of a continent divided into so many sovereign and independent communities, under a conviction of the absolute necessity of uniting all our counsels and all our strength to maintain and defend our common liberties; let them be examined with a liberality becoming brethren and fellow-citizens surrounded by the same imminent dangers, contending for the same illustrious prize, and deeply interested in being for ever bound and connected together by ties the most intimate and indissoluble; and, finally, let them be adjusted with the temper and magnanimity of wise and patriotic legislators, who, while they are concerned for the prosperity of their own more immediate circle, are capable of rising superior to local attachments, when they may be incompatible with the safety, happiness, and glory of the general confederacy.

We have reason to regret the time which has elapsed in preparing this plan for consideration; with additional solicitude we look forward to that which must be necessarily spent before it can be ratified. Every motive loudly calls upon us to hasten its conclusion.

More than any other consideration, it will confound our foreign enemies, defeat the flagitious practices of the disaffected, strengthen and confirm our friends, support our public credit, restore the value of our money, enable us to maintain our fleets and armies, and add weight and respect to our counsels at home and to our treaties abroad.

In short, this salutary measure can no longer be deferred. It seems essential to our very existence as a free people, and without it we may feel constrained to bid adieu to independence, to liberty and safety, — blessings which, from the justice of our cause and the favor of our Almighty Creator visibly manifested in our protection, we have reason to expect, if, in an humble dependence on his divine providence, we strenuously exert the means which are placed in our power.

To conclude, if the legislature of any State shall not be assembled, Congress recommend to the executive authority to convene it without delay; and to each respective legislature it is recommended to invest its delegates with competent powers ultimately, in the name and behalf of the State, to subscribe Articles of Confederation and Perpetual Union of the United States; and to attend Congress for that purpose on or before the tenth day of March next.

NEW JERSEY.

Representation of the State of New Jersey on the Articles of Confederation, read in Congress, June 25, 1778.

To the United States in Congress assembled: The Representation of the Legislative Council and General Assembly of the State of New Jersey showeth: —

That the Articles of Confederation and Perpetual Union between the States of New Hampshire, Massachusetts Bay, Rhode Island and Providence Plantations, Connecticut, New York, New Jersey, Pennsylvania, Delaware, Maryland, Virginia, North Carolina, South Carolina, and Georgia, proposed by the honorable the Congress of the said States, severally for their consideration, have been by us fully and attentively considered; on which we beg leave to remark as follows: —

1. In the fifth article, where, among other things, the qualifications of the delegates from the several States are described, there is no mention of any oath, test, or declaration, to be taken or made by them previous to their admission to seats in Congress. It is, indeed, to be presumed the respective States will be careful that the delegates they send to assist in managing the general interest of the Union take the oaths to the government from which they derive their authority; but as the United States, collectively considered, have interests, as well as each particular State, we are of opinion that some test or obligation binding upon each delegate while he continues in the trust, to consult and pursue the former as well as the latter, and particularly to assent to no vote or proceeding which may violate the general confederation, is necessary. The laws and usages of all civilized nations evince the propriety of an oath on such occasions; and the more solemn and important the deposit, the more strong and explicit ought the obligation to be.

2. By the sixth and ninth articles, the regulation of trade seems to be committed to the several States within their separate jurisdictions, in such a degree as may involve many difficulties and embarrassments, and be attended with injustice to some States in the Union. We are of opinion, that the sole and exclusive power of regulating the trade of the United States with foreign nations ought to be clearly vested in the Congress; and that the revenue arising from all duties and customs

imposed thereon ought to be appropriated to the building, equipping, and manning a navy for the protection of the trade and defence of the coasts, and to such other public and general purposes as to the Congress shall seem proper, and for the common benefit of the States. This principle appears to us to be just, and it may be added, that a great security will by this means be derived to the Union from the establishment of a common and mutual interest.

3. It is wisely provided, in the sixth article, that no body of forces shall be kept up by any State in time of peace, except such number only as, in the judgment of the United States in Congress assembled, shall be deemed requisite to garrison the forts necessary for the defence of such States. We think it ought also to be provided and clearly expressed, that no body of troops be kept up by the United States in time of peace, except such number only as shall be allowed by the assent of the nine States. A standing army, a military establishment, and every appendage thereof, in time of peace, is totally abhorrent from the ideas and principles of this State. In the memorable act of Congress declaring the United Colonies free and independent States, it is emphatically mentioned, as one of the causes of separation from Great Britain, that the sovereign thereof had kept up among us, in time of peace, standing armies without the consent of the legislatures. It is to be wished the liberties and happiness of the people may by the Confederation be carefully and explicitly guarded in this respect.

4. On the eighth article we observe, that, as frequent settlements of the quotas for supplies and aids to be furnished by the several States in support of the general treasury will be requisite, so they ought to be secured. It cannot be thought improper, or unnecessary, to have them struck once at least in every five years, and oftener if circumstances will allow. The quantity or value of real property in some States may increase much more rapidly than in others; and therefore the quota which is at one time just will at another be disproportionate.

5. The boundaries and limits of each State ought to be fully and finally fixed and made known. This we apprehend would be attended with very salutary effects, by preventing jealousies, as well as controversies, and promoting harmony and confidence among the States. If the circumstances of the times would not admit of this, previous to the proposal of the Confederation to the several States, the establishment of the principles upon which and the rule and mode by which the determination might be conducted at a time more convenient and favorable for despatching the same at an early period, not exceeding five years from the final ratification of the Confederation, would be satisfactory.

6. The ninth article provides, that no State shall be deprived of territory for the benefit of the United States. Whether we are to understand, that by territory is intended any land, the property of which was heretofore vested in the crown of Great Britain, or that no mention of such land is made in the Confederation, we are constrained to observe, that the present war, as we always apprehended, was undertaken for the general defence and interest of the confederating Colonies, now the United States. It was ever the confident expectation of this State, that the benefits derived from a successful contest were to be general and proportionate; and that the property of the common enemy, falling in consequence of a prosperous issue of the war, would belong to the United States, and be appropriated to their use. We are therefore greatly disappointed in finding no provision made in the Confederation for empowering the Congress to dispose of such property, but especially the vacant and impatented lands, commonly called the crown lands, for defraying the expenses of the war, and for such other public and general purposes. The jurisdiction ought in every instance to belong to the respective States within the charter or determined limits of which such lands may be seated; but reason and justice must decide that the property which existed in the crown of Great Britain, previous to the present Revolution, ought now to belong to the Congress, in trust for the use and benefit of the United States. They have fought and bled for it in proportion to their respective abilities; and therefore the reward ought not to be predilectionally distributed. Shall such States as are shut out by situation from availing themselves of the least advantage from this quarter be left to sink under an enormous debt, whilst others are enabled, in a short period, to replace all their expenditures from the hard earnings of the whole confederacy?

7. The ninth article also provides, that requisitions for the land forces to be furnished by the several States shall be proportioned to the number of *white* inhabitants in each. In the act of Independence we find the following declaration: "We hold these truths to be self-evident, that all men are created equal; that they are endued by their Creator with certain unalienable rights, among which are life, liberty, and the pursuit of happiness." Of this doctrine it is not a very remote consequence, that all the inhabitants of every society, be the color of their complexion what it may, are bound to promote the interest thereof, according to their respective abilities. They ought, therefore, to be brought into the account on this occasion. But admitting necessity or expediency to justify the refusal of liberty in certain circumstances to persons of a peculiar color, we think it unequal to reckon upon such in this case. Should it

be improper, for special local reasons, to admit them in arms for the defence of the nation, yet we conceive the proportion of forces to be embodied ought to be fixed according to the whole number of inhabitants in the State, from whatever class they may be raised. If the whole number of inhabitants in a State, whose inhabitants are all whites, both those who are called into the field, and those who remain to till the ground and labor in the mechanical arts and otherwise, are reckoned in the estimate for striking the proportion of forces to be furnished by that State, ought even a part of the latter description to be left out in another? As it is of indispensable necessity in every war, that a part of the inhabitants be employed or the uses of husbandry and otherwise at home, while others are called into the field, there must be the same propriety that the owners of a different color who are employed for this purpose in one State, while whites are employed for the same purpose in another, be reckoned in the account of the inhabitants in the present instance.

8. In order that the quota of troops to be furnished in each State on occasion of a war may be equitably ascertained, we are of opinion that the inhabitants of the several States ought to be numbered as frequently as the nature of the case will admit, once at least every five years. The disproportioned increase in the population of different States may render such provisions absolutely necessary.

9. It is provided in the ninth article, that the assent of nine States out of the thirteen shall be necessary to determine in sundry cases of the highest concern. If this proportion be proper and just, it ought to be kept up, should the States increase in number, and a declaration thereof be made for the satisfaction of the Union.

That we think it our indispensable duty to solicit the attention of Congress to these considerations and remarks, and to request that the purport and meaning of them be adopted as part of the general confederation; by which means we apprehend the mutual interest of all the States will be better secured and promoted, and that the legislature of this State will then be justified in ratifying the same.

Act of New Jersey accepting the Confederation, passed November 19, 1778.

An Act to authorize and empower the Delegates of the State of New Jersey in Congress to subscribe and ratify the Articles of Confederation and Perpetual Union between the several States.

Whereas, Articles of Confederation and Perpetual Union between the States of New Hampshire, Massachusetts Bay, Rhode Island and Providence Plantations, Connecticut, New York, New Jersey, Pennsylvania, Delaware, Maryland, Virginia, North Carolina, South Carolina, and Georgia, signed in the Congress of the said States by the Honorable Henry Laurens, Esquire, their President, have been laid before the legislature of this State, to be ratified by the same, if approved: And whereas, notwithstanding the terms of the said Articles of Confederation and Perpetual Union are considered as in divers respects unequal and disadvantageous to this State, and the objections to several of the said articles, lately stated and sent to the general Congress aforesaid on the part of this State, are still viewed as just and reasonable, and sundry of them as of the most essential moment to the welfare and happiness of the good people thereof: Yet, under the full conviction of the present necessity of acceding to the confederacy proposed, and that every separate and detached State interest ought to be postponed to the general good of the Union: And moreover, in firm reliance that the candor and justice of the several States will, in due time, remove as far as possible the inequality which now subsists: —

Sect. 1. Be it enacted by the Council and General Assembly of this State, and it is hereby enacted by the authority of the same, That the Honorable John Witherspoon, Abraham Clark, Nathaniel Scudder, and Elias Boudinot, Esquires, delegates representing this State in the Congress of the United States, or any one or more of them, be and they are hereby authorized, empowered, and directed, on behalf of this State, to subscribe and ratify the said Articles of Confederation and Perpetual Union between the States aforesaid.

Sect. 2. And be it further enacted by the authority aforesaid, That the said Articles of Confederation and Perpetual Union, so as aforesaid subscribed and ratified, shall thenceforth become conclusive as to this State, and obligatory thereon.

DELAWARE.

Resolutions passed by the Council of the State of Delaware, January 23, 1779, respecting the Articles of Confederation and Perpetual Union, and concurred in by the House of Assembly, January 28, 1779, previous to their passing a Law to empower their Delegates to sign and ratify the said Articles of Confederation and Perpetual Union.

Resolved, That the paper laid before Congress by the delegate from Delaware, and read, be filed; provided, that it shall never be considered as admitting any claim by the same set up or intended to be set up.

The paper is as follows, viz.: —

In the Council, Saturday, January 23, 1779, P. M.

The Council, having resumed the consideration of the committee's report on the Articles of Confederation and Perpetual Union, &c., came to the following resolutions therein: —

Resolved, That this State think it necessary for the peace and safety of the States to be included in the Union, that a moderate extent of limits should be assigned for such of those States as claim to the Mississippi or South Sea; and that the United States in Congress assembled should and ought to have the power of fixing their western limits.

Resolved also, That this State consider themselves justly entitled to a right, in common with the members of the Union, to that extensive tract of country which lies to the westward of the frontiers of the United States, the property of which was not vested in, or granted to, individuals at the commencement of the present war: That the same hath been, or may be, gained from the king of Great Britain, or the native Indians, by the blood and treasure of all, and ought therefore to be a common estate, to be granted out on terms beneficial to the United States.

Resolved also, That the courts of law established within this State are competent for the purpose of determining all controversies concerning the private right of soil claimed within the same; and they now, and at all times hereafter, ought to have cognizance of all such controversies: That the indeterminate provision, in the ninth article of the Confederation, for deciding upon controversies that may arise about some of those private rights of soil, tends to take away such cognizance, and is contrary to the declaration of rights of this State; and therefore ought to receive an alteration.

The Council, then, taking into consideration the strong and earnest recommendations of Congress forthwith to accede to the present plan of confederacy, and the probable disadvantages that may attend the further delaying a ratification thereof, —

Resolved, That, notwithstanding the terms of the Articles of Confederation aforesaid are considered as in divers respects unequal and disadvantageous to this State, and the objections in the report of the committee of this house, and the resolves made thereon, are viewed as just and reasonable, and of great moment to the welfare and happiness of the good people thereof; yet, under the full conviction of the present necessity of acceding to the confederacy proposed, and in firm reliance that the candor and justice of the several States will in due time remove as far as possible the objectionable parts thereof, the delegates appointed to represent this State in Congress, or any one or more of them, be authorized, empowered, and directed, on behalf of this State, to subscribe and ratify the said Articles of Confederation and Perpetual Union between the several States of New Hampshire, Massachusetts Bay, Rhode Island and Providence Plantations, Connecticut, New York, New Jersey, Pennsylvania, Delaware, Maryland, Virginia, North Carolina, South Carolina, and Georgia; and that the said articles, when so subscribed and ratified, shall be obligatory on this State.

Extract from the Minutes.

BENJAMIN VINING, *Clerk of the Council.*

Sent for concurrence.

IN HOUSE OF ASSEMBLY, Thursday, January 28, 1779.

The foregoing resolutions being read three times, and considered, are concurred in.

NICHOLAS VAN DYKE, *Speaker.*

THURSDAY, FEBRUARY 16, 1779.

MR. M'KEAN, a delegate for Delaware, laid before Congress the following instrument, empowering the delegates of that State, or any of them, to ratify and sign the Articles of Confederation.

His Excellency Cesar Rodney, Esquire, President, Captain-General, and Commander-in-Chief of the Delaware State, to all to whom these Presents shall come, — Greeting.

Know ye, That, among the records remaining in the rolls office in the Delaware State, there is a certain instrument of writing, purporting to be an act of the General Assembly of the said State, which said act is contained in the words and tenor here following, to wit:

IN THE YEAR 1779.

An Act to authorize and empower the Delegates of the Delaware State to subscribe and ratify the Articles of Confederation and Perpetual Union between the several States.

Whereas Articles of Confederation and Perpetual Union between the States of New Hampshire, Massachusetts Bay, Rhode Island and Providence Plantations, Connecticut, New York, New Jersey, Pennsylvania, Delaware, Maryland, Virginia, North Carolina, South Carolina, and Georgia, signed in the general Congress of the said States by the Honorable Henry Laurens, Esquire, their then President, have been laid before the legislature of this State, to be ratified by the same, if approved: And whereas, notwithstanding the terms of the Articles of Confederation and Perpetual Union are considered as in divers respects unequal and disadvantageous to this State; and the objections stated on the part of this State are viewed as just and reasonable, and of great moment to the welfare and happiness of the good people thereof; yet, under the full conviction of the present necessity of acceding to the present confederacy proposed, and that the interest of particular States ought to be postponed to the general good of the Union; and moreover, in firm reliance that the candor and justice of the several States will in due time remove as far as possible the objectionable parts thereof:

Be it enacted by the General Assembly of Delaware, and it is hereby enacted by the authority of the same, That the Honorable John Dickinson, Nicholas Van Dyke, and Thomas M'Kean, Esquires, delegates appointed to represent this State in Congress, or any one or more of them, be, and they hereby are, authorized, empowered, and directed, on behalf of this State, to subscribe and ratify the said Articles of Confederation and Perpetual Union between the several States aforesaid.

And be it further enacted by the authority aforesaid, That the said Articles of Confederation and Perpetual Union, so as aforesaid subscribed and ratified, shall thenceforth become obligatory on this State.

Signed by order of the House of Assembly.

NICHOLAS VAN DYKE, *Speaker.*

Signed by order of the Council.

THOMAS COLLINS, *Speaker.*

Passed at Dover, February 1, 1779.

All which, by the tenor of these presents, I have caused to be exemplified.

In testimony whereof, the great seal of the Delaware State is hereunto affixed, at Dover, the sixth day of February, in the year of our Lord one thousand seven hundred and seventy-nine, and in the third year of the Independence of the United States of America.

CESAR RODNEY.

By his Excellency's command.

JAMES BOOTH, *Secretary.*

MARYLAND.

FRIDAY, MAY 21, 1779.

THE delegates of Maryland informed Congress that they have received instructions respecting the Articles of Confederation, which they are directed to lay before Congress, and have entered on their Journals. The instructions, being read, are as follows: —

Instructions of the General Assembly of Maryland, to George Plater, William Paca, William Carmichael, John Henry, James Forbes, and Daniel of St. Thomas Jenifer, Esquires.

GENTLEMEN, —

Having conferred upon you a trust of the highest nature, it is evident we place great confidence in your integrity, abilities, and zeal to promote the general welfare of the United States, and the particular interest of this State, where the latter is not incompatible with the former; but to add greater weight to your proceedings in Congress, and take away all suspicion that the opinions you there deliver and the votes you give may be the mere opinions of individuals, and not resulting from your knowledge of the sense and deliberate judgment of the State you represent, we think it our duty to instruct as followeth on the subject of the Confederation, — a subject in which, unfortunately, a supposed difference of interest has produced an almost equal division of sentiments among the several States composing the Union. We say a supposed difference of interests; for if local attachments and prejudices, and the avarice and ambition of individuals, would give way to the dictates of a sound policy, founded on the principles of justice, (and no other policy but what is founded on those immutable principles deserves to be called sound,) we flatter ourselves this apparent diversity of interests would soon vanish, and all the States would confederate on terms mutually advantageous to all; for they would then perceive that no other confederation than one so formed can be lasting. Although the pressure of immediate calamities, the dread of their continuance from the appearance of disunion, and some other peculiar circumstances, may have induced some States to accede to the present Confederation, contrary to their own interests and judgments, it requires no great share of foresight to predict, that, when those causes cease to operate, the States which have thus acceded to the Confederation will consider it as no longer binding, and will eagerly embrace the first occasion of asserting their just rights, and securing their independence. Is it possible that those States who are ambitiously grasping at territories to which, in our judgment, they have not the least shadow of exclusive right, will use with greater moderation the increase of wealth and power derived from those territories, when acquired, than what they have displayed in their endeavors to acquire them? We think not. We are convinced the same spirit which hath prompted them to insist on a claim so extravagant, so repugnant to every principle of justice, so incompatible with the general welfare of all the States, will urge them on to add oppression to injustice. If they should not be incited by a superiority of wealth and strength to oppress by open force their less wealthy and less powerful neighbors, yet depopulation, and consequently the impoverishment, of those States will necessarily follow, which, by an unfair construction of the Confederation, may be stripped of a common interest, and the common benefits derivable from the Western country. Suppose, for instance, Virginia indisputably possessed of the extensive and fertile country to which she has set up a claim, what would be the probable consequences to Maryland of such an undisturbed and undisputed possession? They cannot escape the least discerning.

Virginia, by selling on the most moderate terms a small proportion of the lands in question, would draw into her treasury vast sums of money; and in proportion to the sums arising from such sales would be enabled to lessen her taxes. Lands comparatively cheap, and taxes comparatively low, with the lands and taxes of an adjacent State, would quickly drain the State thus disadvantageously circumstanced of its most useful inhabitants; its wealth and its consequence in the scale of the confederated States would sink of course. A claim so injurious to more than one half, if not to the whole, of the United States, ought to be supported by the clearest evidence of the right. Yet what evidences of that right have been produced? What arguments alleged in support either of the evidences or the right? None that we have heard of deserving a serious refutation.

It has been said, that some of the delegates of a neighboring State have declared their opinion of the practicability of governing the extensive dominion claimed by that State. Hence also the necessity was admitted of dividing its territory, and erecting a new State under the auspices and direction of the elder, from whom no doubt it would receive its form of government, to whom it would be bound by some alliance or confederacy, and by whose councils it would be influenced. Such a measure, if ever attempted, would certainly be opposed by the other States as inconsistent with the letter and spirit of the proposed Confederation. Should it take place by establishing a sub-confederacy, *imperium in imperio*, the State possessed of this extensive dominion must then either submit to all the inconveniences of an overgrown and unwieldy government, or suffer the authority of Congress to interpose at a future time, and to lop off a part of its territory, to be erected into a new and free State, and admitted into a confederation on such conditions as shall be settled by nine States. If it is necessary for the happiness and tranquillity of a State thus overgrown, that Congress should hereafter interfere and divide its territory, why is the claim to that territory now made, and so pertinaciously insisted on? We can suggest to ourselves but two motives; either the declaration of relinquishing at some future period a proportion of the country now contended for was made to lull suspicion asleep, and to cover the designs of a secret ambition, or, if the thought was seriously entertained, the lands are now claimed to reap an immediate profit from the sale. We are convinced, policy and justice require, that a country unsettled at the commencement of this war, claimed by the British crown, and ceded to it by the treaty of Paris, if wrested from the common enemy by the blood and treasure of the thirteen States, should be considered as a common property, subject to be parcelled out by Congress into free, convenient, and independent governments, in such manner and at such times as the wisdom of that assembly shall hereafter direct.

Thus convinced, we should betray the trust reposed in us by our constituents, were we to authorize you to ratify, on their behalf, the Confederation, unless it be further explained. We have coolly and dispassionately considered the subject; we have weighed probable inconveniences and hardships against the sacrifice of just and essential rights; and do instruct you not to agree to the Confederation, unless an article or articles be added thereto in conformity with our declaration. Should we succeed in obtaining such article or articles, then you are hereby fully empowered to accede to the Confederation.

That these our sentiments respecting our Confederation may be more publicly known, and more explicitly and concisely declared, we have drawn up the annexed declaration, which we instruct you to lay before Congress, to have it printed, and to deliver to each of the delegates of the other States in Congress assembled copies thereof, signed by yourselves, or by such of you as may be present at the time of delivery; to the intent and purpose that the copies aforesaid may be communicated to our brethren of the United States, and the contents of the said declaration taken into their serious and candid consideration.

Also we desire and instruct you to move, at a proper time, that these instructions be read to Congress by their Secretary, and entered on the Journals of Congress.

We have spoken with freedom, as became freemen; and we sincerely wish that these our representations may make such an impression on that assembly as to induce them to make such addition to the Articles of Confederation as may bring about a permanent union.

A true copy from the proceeding of December 15, 1778.

Test, T. Duckett, *C. H. D.*

IN CONGRESS.

Saturday, April 1, 1780.

The committee to whom was referred the act of the legislature of the State of New York, entitled, "An Act to facilitate the completion of the Articles of Confederation and Perpetual Union among the United States of America," report, —

That, having met on the business, but not being able to agree to any resolution thereon, desire to be discharged; which act is in the words following, viz.: —

An Act to facilitate the Completion of the Articles of Confederation and Perpetual Union among the United States of America.

Whereas nothing under Divine Providence can more effectually contribute to the tranquillity and safety of the United States of America than a federal alliance, on such liberal principles as will give satisfaction to its respective members: And whereas the Articles of Confederation and Perpetual Union recommended by the honorable the Congress of the United States of America have not proved acceptable to all the States, it having been conceived that a portion of the waste and uncultivated territory, within the limits or claim of certain States, ought to be appropriated as a common fund for the expenses of the war: And the people of the State of New York being on all occasions disposed to manifest their regard for their sister States, and their earnest desire to promote the general interest and security; and more especially to accelerate the federal alliance, by removing, as far as it depends upon them, the beforementioned impediment to its final accomplishment:

Be it therefore enacted, by the people of the State of New York, represented in Senate and Assembly, and it is hereby enacted by the authority of the same, That it shall and may be lawful to and for the delegates of this State, in the honorable Congress of the United States of America, or the major part of such of them as shall be assembled in Congress, and they the said delegates, or a major part of them, so assembled, are hereby fully authorized and empowered, for and on behalf of this State, and by proper and authentic acts or instruments, to limit and restrict the boundaries of this State, in the western parts thereof, by such line or lines, and in such manner and form, as they shall judge to be expedient, either with respect to the jurisdiction as well as the right or preëmption of soil, or reserving the jurisdiction in part, or in the whole, over the lands which may be ceded, or relinquished, with respect only to the right or preëmption of the soil.

And be it further enacted by the authority aforesaid, That the territory which may be ceded or relinquished by virtue of this act, either with respect to the jurisdiction as well as the right or preëmption of soil, or the right or preëmption of soil only, shall be and enure for the use and benefit of such of the United States as shall become members of the federal alliance of the said States, and for no other use or purpose whatever.

And be it further enacted by the authority aforesaid, That all the lands to be ceded and relinquished by virtue of this act, for the benefit of the United States, with respect to property, but which shall nevertheless remain under the jurisdiction of this State, shall be disposed of and appropriated in such manner only as the Congress of the said States shall direct; and that a warrant under the authority of Congress for surveying and laying out any part thereof shall entitle the party in whose favor it shall issue to cause the same to be surveyed and laid out and returned according to the directions of such warrant; and thereupon letters patent under the great seal of this State shall pass to the grantee for the estate specified in the said warrant; for which no other fee or reward shall be demanded or received than such as shall be allowed by Congress.

Provided always, and be it further enacted by the authority aforesaid, That the trust reposed by virtue of this act shall not be executed by the delegates of this State, unless at least three of the said delegates shall be present in Congress.

State of New York, ss.

I do hereby certify that the aforegoing is a true copy of the original act, passed the 19th of February, 1780, and lodged in the Secretary's office.

ROBERT HARPUR, *D'y Sec'y State.*

WEDNESDAY, SEPTEMBER 6, 1780.

CONGRESS took into consideration the report of the committee to whom were referred the instructions of the General Assembly of Maryland to their delegates in Congress respecting the Articles of Confederation, and the declaration therein referred to; the act of the legislature of New York on the same subject; and the remonstrance of the General Assembly of Virginia, which report was agreed to, and is in the words following: —

That, having duly considered the several matters to them submitted, they conceive it unnecessary to examine into the merits or policy of the instructions or declaration of the General Assembly of Maryland, or of the remonstrances of the General Assembly of Virginia, as they involve questions a discussion of which was declined, on mature consideration, when the Articles of Confederation were debated; nor, in the opinion of the committee, can such questions be now revived with any prospect of conciliation: That it appears more advisable to press upon these States which can remove the embarrassments respecting the Western country a liberal surrender of a portion of their territorial claims, since they cannot be preserved entire without endangering the stability of the general confederacy; to remind them how indispensably necessary it is to establish the Federal Union on a fixed and permanent basis, and on principles acceptable to all its respective members; how essential to public credit and confidence, to the support of our army, to the vigor of our councils, and success of our measures, to our tranquillity at home, our reputation abroad, to our very existence as a free, sovereign, and independent people; that we are fully persuaded the wisdom of the respective legislatures will lead them to a full and impartial consideration of a subject so interesting to the United States, and so necessary to the happy establishment of the Federal Union; that they are confirmed in these expectations by a view of the before-mentioned act of the legislature of New York, submitted to their consideration; that this act is expressly calculated to accelerate the federal alliance, by removing, as far as depends on that State, the impediment arising from the Western country, and for that purpose to yield up a portion of territorial claim for the general benefit.

Whereupon,

Resolved, That copies of the several papers referred to the committee be transmitted, with a copy of the report, to the legislatures of the several States; and that it be earnestly recommended to these States who have claims to the Western country to pass such laws, and give their delegates in Congress such powers, as may effectually remove the only obstacle to a final ratification of the Articles of Confederation: and that the legislature of Maryland be earnestly requested to authorize their delegates in Congress to subscribe the said articles.

MARYLAND.

Monday, February 12, 1781.

The delegates of Maryland laid before Congress a certified copy of an act of the legislature of that State, which was read as follows: —

An Act to empower the Delegates of this State in Congress to subscribe and ratify the Articles of Confederation.

Whereas it hath been said that the common enemy is encouraged, by this State not acceding to the Confederation, to hope that the union of the sister States may be dissolved; and therefore prosecute the war in expectation of an event so disgraceful to America; and our friends and illustrious ally are impressed with an idea, that the common cause would be promoted by our formally acceding to the Confederation: This General Assembly, conscious that this State hath from the commencement of the war strenuously exerted herself in the common cause, and fully satisfied that, if no formal confederation was to take place, it is the fixed determination of this State to continue her exertions to the utmost, agreeable to the faith pledged in the union, — from an earnest desire to conciliate the affections of the sister States, to convince all the world of our unalterable resolution to support the independence of the United States, and the alliance with his most Christian Majesty; and to destroy for ever any apprehension of our friends, or hope in our enemies, of this State being again united to Great Britain:

Be it enacted by the General Assembly of Maryland, That the delegates of this State in Congress, or any two or three of them, shall be, and are hereby, empowered and required, on behalf of this State, to subscribe the Articles of Confederation and Perpetual Union between the States of New Hampshire, Massachusetts Bay, Rhode Island and Providence Plantations, Connecticut, New York, New Jersey, Pennsylvania, Delaware, Maryland, Virginia, North Carolina, South Carolina, and Georgia, signed in the general Congress of the said States by the Honorable Henry Laurens, Esquire, their then President, and laid before the legislature of this State to be ratified, if approved; and that the said Articles of Confederation and Perpetual Union, so as aforesaid subscribed, shall thenceforth be ratified and become conclusive as to this State, and obligatory thereon.

And it is hereby declared, that, by acceding to the said Confederation, this State doth not relinquish, or intend to relinquish, any right or interest she hath with the other united or confederated States to the back country; but claims the same as fully as was done by the legislature of this State in their declaration which stands entered on the journals of Congress: this State relying on the justice of the several States hereafter, as to the said claim made by this State.

And it is further declared, That no article in the said Confederation can or ought to bind this or any other State to guarantee any exclusive claim of any particular State to the soil of the said back lands, or any such claim of jurisdiction over the said lands, or the inhabitants thereof.

By the House of Delegates, January 30, 1781.

Read and assented to.

By order,

F. GREEN, *Clerk.*

By the Senate, February 2, 1781.

Read and assented to.

By order,

JAS. MACCUBBIN, *Clerk.*

THOMAS LEE. [L. S.]

ARTICLES OF CONFEDERATION AND PERPETUAL UNION

BETWEEN THE STATES OF NEW HAMPSHIRE, MASSACHUSETTS BAY, RHODE ISLAND AND PROVIDENCE PLANTATIONS, CONNECTICUT, NEW YORK, NEW JERSEY, PENNSYLVANIA, DELAWARE, MARYLAND, VIRGINIA, NORTH CAROLINA, SOUTH CAROLINA, AND GEORGIA.

ART. 1. The style of this Confederacy shall be "The United States of America."

ART. 2. Each State retains its sovereignty, freedom, and independence, and every power, jurisdiction, and right which is not by this Confederation expressly delegated to the United States in Congress assembled.

ART. 3. The said States hereby severally enter into a firm league of friendship with each other for their common defence, the security of their liberties, and their mutual and general welfare; binding themselves to assist each other against all force offered to or attacks made upon them on account of religion, sovereignty, trade, or any other pretence whatever.

ART. 4. The better to secure and perpetuate mutual friendship and intercourse among the people of the different States in this union, the free inhabitants of each of these States (paupers, vagabonds, and fugitives from justice excepted) shall be entitled to all privileges and immunities of free citizens in the several States; and the people of each State shall have free ingress and regress to and from any other State, and shall enjoy therein all the privileges of trade and commerce, subject to the same duties, impositions, and restrictions as the inhabitants thereof respectively, provided that such restriction shall not extend so far as to prevent the removal of property imported into any State to any other State, of which the owner is an inhabitant; provided also, that no imposition, duties, or restriction shall be laid by any State on the property of the United States, or either of them.

If any person guilty of or charged with treason, felony, or other high misdemeanor in any State, shall flee from justice and be found in any of the United States, he shall, upon demand of the Governor or executive power of the State from which he fled, be delivered up and removed to the State having jurisdiction of his offence.

Full faith and credit shall be given in each of these States to the records, acts, and judicial proceedings of the courts and magistrates of every other State.

ART. 5. For the more convenient management of the general interests of the United States, delegates shall be annually appointed, in such manner as the legislature of each State shall direct, to meet in Congress on the first Monday in November, in every year, with a power reserved to each State to recall its delegates, or any of them, at any time within the year, and to send others in their stead, for the remainder of the year.

No State shall be represented in Congress by less than two nor by more than seven members; and no person shall be capable of being a delegate for more than three years in any term of six years; nor shall any person, being a delegate, be capable of holding any office under the United States, for which he, or any other for his benefit, receives any salary, fees, or emolument of any kind.

Each State shall maintain its own delegates in any meeting of the States, and while they act as members of the committee of the States.

In determining questions in the United States in Congress assembled, each State shall have one vote.

Freedom of speech and debate in Congress shall not be impeached or questioned in any court or place out of Congress; and the members of Congress shall be protected in their persons from arrests and imprisonments, during the time of their going to and from and attendance on Congress, except for treason, felony, or breach of the peace.

ART. 6. No State, without the consent of the United States in Congress assembled, shall send any embassy to, or receive any embassy from, or enter into any conference, agreement, alliance, or treaty with any king, prince, or state; nor shall any person holding any office of profit or trust under the United States, or any of them, accept of any present, emolument, office, or title of any kind whatever from any king, prince, or foreign state; nor shall the United States in Congress assembled, or any of them, grant any title of nobility.

No two or more States shall enter into any treaty, confederation, or alliance whatever between them, without the consent of the United States in Congress assembled, specifying accurately the purposes for which the same is to be entered into, and how long it shall continue.

No State shall lay any imposts or duties, which may interfere with any stipulations in treaties entered into by the United States in Congress assembled, with any king, prince, or state, in pursuance of any treaties already proposed by Congress to the courts of France and Spain.

No vessels of war shall be kept up in time of peace by any State, except such number only as shall be deemed necessary by the United States in Congress assembled for the defence of such State or its trade; nor shall any body of forces be kept up by any State, in time of peace, except such number only as, in the judgment of the United States in Congress assembled, shall be deemed requisite to garrison the forts necessary for the defence of such State; but every State shall always keep up a well-regulated and disciplined militia, sufficiently armed and accoutred, and shall provide and have constantly ready for use, in public stores, a due number of field-pieces and tents, and a proper quantity of arms, ammunition, and camp equipage.

No State shall engage in any war without the consent of the United States in Congress assembled, unless such State be actually invaded by enemies or shall have certain advice of a resolution being formed by some nation of Indians to invade such State, and the danger is so imminent as not to admit of a delay till the United States in Congress assembled can be consulted; nor shall any State grant commission to any ships or vessels of war, nor letters of marque or reprisal, except it be after a declaration of war by the United States in Congress assembled, and then only against the kingdom or state and the subjects thereof against which war has been so declared, and under such regulations as shall be established by the United States in Congress assembled, unless such State be infested by pirates, in which case vessels of war may be fitted out for that occasion and kept so long as the danger shall continue, or until the United States in Congress assembled shall determine otherwise.

Art. 7. When land forces are raised by any State for the common defence, all officers of or under the rank of colonel shall be appointed by the legislatures of each State respectively by whom such forces shall be raised, or in such manner as such State shall direct; and all vacancies shall be filled up by the State which first made the appointment.

Art. 8. All charges of war and all other expenses that shall be incurred for the common defence or general welfare, and allowed by the United States in Congress assembled, shall be defrayed out of a common treasury, which shall be supplied by the several States in proportion to the value of all land within each State granted to or surveyed for any person, as such land and the buildings and improvements thereon shall be estimated, according to such mode as the United States in Congress assembled shall from time to time direct and appoint.

The taxes for paying that proportion shall be laid and levied by the authority and direction of the legislatures of the several States, within the time agreed upon by the United States in Congress assembled.

Art. 9. The United States in Congress assembled shall have the sole and exclusive right and power of determining on peace and war, except in the cases mentioned in the sixth article; of sending and receiving ambassadors; entering into treaties and alliances, provided that no treaty of commerce shall be made, whereby the legislative power of the respective States shall be restrained from imposing such imposts and duties on foreigners as their own people are subjected to, or from prohibiting the exportation or importation of any species of goods or commodities whatsoever; of establishing rules for deciding in all cases what captures on land or water shall be legal, and in what manner prizes taken by land or naval forces in the service of the United States shall be divided or appropriated; of granting letters of marque and reprisal in time of peace; appointing courts for the trial of piracies and felonies committed on the high seas, and establishing courts for receiving and determining finally appeals in all cases of captures, provided that no member of Congress shall be appointed judge of any of the said courts.

The United States in Congress assembled shall also be the last resort on appeal in all disputes and differences now subsisting or that hereafter may arise between two or more States concerning boundary, jurisdiction, or any other cause whatever, which authority shall always be exercised in the manner following: whenever the legislative or executive authority or lawful agent of any State in controversy with another shall present a petition to Congress, stating the matter in question and praying for a hearing, notice thereof shall be given by order of Congress to the legislative or executive authority of the other State in controversy, and a day assigned for the appearance of the parties by their lawful agents, who shall then be directed to appoint by joint consent commissioners or judges to constitute a court for hearing and determining the matter in question;

but if they cannot agree, Congress shall name three persons out of each of the United States, and from the list of such persons each party shall alternately strike out one, the petitioners beginning, until the number shall be reduced to thirteen; and from that number not less than seven nor more than nine names, as Congress shall direct, shall, in the presence of Congress, be drawn out by lot; and the persons whose names shall be so drawn, or any five of them, shall be commissioners or judges to hear and finally determine the controversy, so always as a major part of the judges who shall hear the cause shall agree in the determination: and if either party shall neglect to attend at the day appointed, without showing reasons which Congress shall judge sufficient, or, being present, shall refuse to strike, the Congress shall proceed to nominate three persons out of each State, and the Secretary of Congress shall strike in behalf of such party absent or refusing; and the judgment and sentence of the court to be appointed, in the manner before prescribed, shall be final and conclusive; and if any of the parties shall refuse to submit to the authority of such court, or to appear or defend their claim or cause, the court shall nevertheless proceed to pronounce sentence or judgment, which shall in like manner be final and decisive, the judgment or sentence and other proceedings being in either case transmitted to Congress, and lodged among the acts of Congress, for the security of the parties concerned: provided, that every commissioner, before he sits in judgment, shall take an oath, to be administered by one of the judges of the Supreme or Superior Court of the State where the cause shall be tried, "well and truly to hear and determine the matter in question, according to the best of his judgment, without favor, affection, or hope of reward"; provided, also, that no State shall be deprived of territory for the benefit of the United States.

All controversies concerning the private right of soil, claimed under different grants of two or more States, whose jurisdictions as they may respect such lands and the States which passed such grants are adjusted, the said grants or either of them being at the same time claimed to have originated antecedent to such settlement of jurisdiction, shall, on the petition of either party to the Congress of the United States, be finally determined, as near as may be in the same manner as is before prescribed for deciding disputes respecting territorial jurisdiction between different States.

The United States in Congress assembled shall also have the sole and exclusive right and power of regulating the alloy and value of coin struck by their own authority, or by that of the respective States; fixing the standard of weights and measures throughout the United States; regulating the trade and managing all affairs with the Indians not members of any of the States, provided that the legislative right of any State within its own limits be not infringed or violated; establishing and regulating post-offices from one State to another throughout all the United States, and exacting such postage on the papers passing through the same as may be requisite to defray the expenses of the said office; appointing all officers of the naval forces, and commissioning all officers whatever in the service of the United States; making rules for the government and regulation of the said land and naval forces, and directing their operations.

The United States in Congress assembled shall have authority to appoint a committee to sit in the recess of Congress, to be denominated "a Committee of the States," and to consist of one delegate from each State, and to appoint such other committees and civil officers as may be necessary for managing the general affairs of the United States, under their direction; to appoint one of their number to preside, provided that no person be allowed to serve in the office of President more than one year in any term of three years; to ascertain the necessary sums of money to be raised for the service of the United States, and to appropriate and apply the same for defraying the public expenses; to borrow money or emit bills on the credit of the United States, transmitting every half-year to the respective States an account of the sums of money so borrowed or emitted; to build and equip a navy; to agree upon the number of land forces, and to make requisitions from each State for its quota, in proportion to the number of white inhabitants in such State; which requisition shall be binding, and thereupon the legislature of each State shall appoint the regimental officers, raise the men, and clothe, arm, and equip them in a soldierlike manner, at the expense of the United States; and the officers and men to be clothed, armed, and equipped shall march to the place appointed, and within the time agreed on, by the United States in Congress assembled: but if the United States in Congress assembled shall, on consideration of circumstances, judge proper that any State should not raise men or should raise a smaller number than its quota, and that any other State should raise a greater number of men than the quota thereof, such extra number shall be raised, officered, clothed, armed, and equipped in the same manner as the quota of such State, unless the legislature of such State shall judge that such extra number cannot be safely spared out of the same, in which case they shall raise, officer, clothe, arm, and equip as many of such extra number as they judge can be safely spared. And the officers and men so clothed, armed, and equipped shall march to the place appointed, and within the time agreed on, by the United States in Congress assembled.

The United States in Congress assembled shall never engage in a war nor grant letters of marque and reprisal in time of peace, nor enter into any treaties or alliances, nor coin money nor regulate the value thereof, nor ascertain the sums and expenses necessary for the defence and welfare of the United States, or any of them; nor emit bills, nor borrow money on the credit of the United States, nor appropriate money, nor agree upon the number of vessels of war to be built or purchased, or the number of land or sea forces to be raised, nor appoint a commander-in-chief of the army or navy, unless nine States assent to the same; nor shall a question on any other point, except for adjourning from day to day, be determined, unless by the votes of a majority of the United States in Congress assembled.

The Congress of the United States shall have power to adjourn to any time within the year, and to any place within the United States, so that no period of adjournment be for a longer duration than the space of six months, and shall publish the journal of their proceedings monthly, except such parts thereof relating to treaties, alliances, or military operations, as in their judgment require secrecy; and the yeas and nays of the delegates of each State on any question shall be entered on the journal, when it is desired by any delegate; and the delegates of a State, or any of them, at his or their request, shall be furnished with a transcript of the said journal, except such parts as are above excepted, to lay before the legislatures of the several States.

Art. 10. The Committee of the States, or any nine of them, shall be authorized to execute, in the recess of Congress, such of the powers of Congress as the United States in Congress assembled, by the consent of nine States, shall, from time to time, think expedient to vest them with; provided that no power be delegated to the said Committee, for the exercise of which, by the Articles of Confederation, the voice of nine States in the Congress of the United States assembled is requisite.

Art. 11. Canada, acceding to this Confederation, and joining in the measures of the United States, shall be admitted into and entitled to all the advantages of this Union; but no other Colony shall be admitted into the same unless such admission be agreed to by nine States.

Art. 12. All bills of credit emitted, moneys borrowed, and debts contracted by or under the authority of Congress, before the assembling of the United States, in pursuance of the present Confederation, shall be deemed and considered as a charge against the United States, for payment and satisfaction whereof the said United States and the public faith are hereby solemnly pledged.

Art. 13. Every State shall abide by the determinations of the United

States in Congress assembled on all questions which by this Confederation are submitted to them. And the Articles of this Confederation shall be inviolably observed by every State, and the Union shall be perpetual; nor shall any alteration at any time hereafter be made in any of them; unless such alteration be agreed to in a Congress of the United States, and be afterwards confirmed by the legislatures of every State.

These Articles shall be proposed to the legislatures of all the United States, to be considered, and if approved of by them, they are advised to authorize their delegates to ratify the same in the Congress of the United States; which being done, the same shall become conclusive.

MEMBERS OF THE CONVENTION WHICH FORMED THE CONSTITUTION.*

Those with numbers before their names signed the Constitution. Those without numbers attended, but did not sign. The dates denote the first day of their attendance. Those in italics never attended.

New Hampshire.

1.	John Langdon,	23 July.	2.	Nicholas Gilman,	23 July.
	John Pickering.			*Benjamin West.*	

Massachusetts.

	Francis Dana.		4.	Rufus King,	25 May.
	Elbridge Gerry,	29 May.		Caleb Strong,	28 May.
3.	Nathaniel Gorham,	28 May.			

Rhode Island. [No appointment.]

Connecticut.

5.	William S. Johnson,	2 June.		Oliver Ellsworth,	29 May.
6.	Roger Sherman,	30 May.			

* This Table is taken from the 12th volume of Mr. Sparks's edition ot Washington's Writings, p. 426.

New York.

Robert Yates, 25 May.
7. Alexander Hamilton, 25 May.
John Lansing, 2 June.

New Jersey.

8. William Livingston, 5 June.
9. David Brearley, 25 May.
William C. Houston, 25 May.
10. William Patterson, 25 May.
John Neilson.
Abraham Clark.
11. Jonathan Dayton, 21 June.

Pennsylvania.

12. Benjamin Franklin, 28 May.
13. Thomas Mifflin, 28 May.
14. Robert Morris, 25 May.
15. George Clymer, 28 May.
16. Thomas Fitzsimons, 25 May.
17. Jared Ingersoll, 28 May.
18. James Wilson, 25 May.
19. Gouverneur Morris, 25 May.

Delaware.

20. George Read, 25 May.
21. Gunning Bedford, Jr. 28 May.
22. John Dickinson, 28 May.
23. Richard Bassett, 25 May
24. Jacob Broom, 25 May.

Maryland.

25. James McHenry, 29 May.
26. Daniel of St. Thomas Jenifer, 2 June.
27. Daniel Carroll, 9 July.
John Francis Mercer, 6 Aug.
Luther Martin, 9 June.

Virginia.

28. George Washington, 25 May.
Patrick Henry (declined).
Edmund Randolph, 25 May.
29. John Blair, 25 May.
30 James Madison, Jr. 25 May.
George Mason, 25 May.
George Wythe, 25 May.
James McClurg (in the room of P. Henry) 25 May.

North Carolina.

Richard Caswell (resigned).
Alexander Martin, 25 May.
William R. Davie, 25 May.
31. William Blount (in the room of R. Caswell) 20 June.
Willie Jones (declined).
32. Richard D. Spaight, 25 May.
33. Hugh Williamson (in the room of W. Jones), 25 May.

South Carolina.

34. John Rutledge, 25 May.
35. Charles C. Pinckney, 25 May.
36. Charles Pinckney, 25 May.
37. Pierce Butler, 25 May

GEORGIA.

38.	William Few,	25 May.	*George Walton.*	
39.	Abraham Baldwin,	11 June.	William Houstoun,	1 June
	William Pierce,	31 May.	*Nathaniel Pendleton.*	

END OF VOL. I.